"Questions about sexuality represent the most confusing landscape for today's Christian leaders. I am tremendously thankful for the effort and wisdom that went into creating this biblically based and practical resource! It contains a wonderful variety of voices that together will equip Christian leaders to address sexuality with integrity and compassion for years to come."

—Juli Slattery, PsyD,
Co-founder of Authentic Intimacy
and author of *Rethinking Sexuality*

"When the topic of sexuality comes up among Christians, those who engage are often throwing Bible verses like knives at a circus show, hoping to pin anyone who disagrees with them to a wall. Instead of arming their audience with more weapons, Dr. Glahn and Dr. Barnes have curated a book that turns the words of the Bible from weapons into tools that guide thoughtful readers into a life of wisdom. Beginning with creation and a theology of the body, and working through more specific issues of sexuality, each contributor adds to a framework of sexual ethics that helps readers make order out of the chaos surrounding the topic of sexuality. If you are looking for rigorous academics and humble, gracious engagement on a seminal topic of our day, you'll find it in these pages."

—Kelsey Hency,
Editor in chief of Fathom

"*Sanctified Sexuality* is a treasure! It will be a go-to resource for my research and message preparation."

—Kat Armstrong,
Author of *No More Holding Back*,
Bible teacher and co-founder of Polished Ministries

"Just a few years ago a book of this scope and depth might be critiqued as superfluous or unnecessarily ambitious, but today pastors and ministry leaders will find themselves grateful Glahn and Barnes labored to produce this relevant and exceedingly necessary resource. *Sanctified Sexuality* meets the onslaught of nuanced sexual issues emerging in the church today with clarity, kindness, and depth of expertise. The plurality of voices serve as a trustworthy guide for those hoping to avoid breaking bruised reeds. I expect to return to this deep well again and again and suspect other readers will as well."

—Nika Spaulding,
Resident theologian at St. Jude Oak Cliff

"Christian leaders have longed for a book like *Sanctified Sexuality* for many years. This book should be on the shelf of every pastor and consulted often. It will be both for me."

—Todd Hunter
Bishop, Anglican Church of North America

"What does the Bible really teach about sexuality? This book will help answer the question fairly and honestly. It is based on an online course (optional "at DTS") in biblical sexual ethics. Sixteen scholars with biblical/theological, psychological, and medical training have joined to produce a comprehensive, biblical, and well documented resource book. I highly recommend it for pastors, teachers, and other interested persons."

—Edwin A. Blum,
general editor of the Holman Christian Standard Bible

"*Sanctified Sexuality* embraces a complex and multi-faceted subject with a beautiful balance of cultural intelligence and biblical relevance. Anyone interested in countering popular perspectives about marriage, sex, and human sexuality will certainly find wisdom and direction—anchored in God's Word—through this array of topics Glahn and Barnes have arranged. Equally critical is the tone of charity this book exemplifies—a tone the editors lay forth as essential for all relationships."

—Mark Yarbrough,
President, Dallas Theological Seminary

"Courageous and grounded: These are the words that best describe *Sanctified Sexuality*. Drs. Glahn and Barnes have brought to bear a most outstanding array of authors in the fields of theology, psychology, sociology, and sexuality to address not only the easier topics in a biblically-grounded and research-based manner, but to ply the same tools to courageously take on the toughest and most salient issues concerning sexuality in our time. Whether you agree or disagree with some of the positions, you will find this book informative and challenging for the very topics and issues that matter most in our society. The reader will especially appreciate the poignant and helpful discussion questions at the end of each chapter to bring home and continue the important discussion. Where we have milled around for years in confusion about sex and sexuality, this book moves us forward with clarity and conviction."

—Terry D. Hargrave,
Evelyn and Frank Freed Professor of Marriage and Family Therapy,
Fuller Theological Seminary

"A book with an oxymoron for a title is usually a book that breaks new ground. *Sanctified Sexuality* is exactly such a book because it shows that no aspect of human sexuality is beyond the reach of God's purpose, wisdom, and passionate desire for our highest good as persons made in God's image. With all the noisy, confused, and confusing conversations now taking place around sexuality, this collaboration offers a breath of fresh air, from experts who actually know what they are talking about and have humbly pooled their expertise to assemble a compelling vision for sex as God intends for us to steward it."

—Bill Hendricks,
Executive Director for Christian Leadership,
The Hendricks / Dallas Theological Seminary

Sanctified Sexuality

VALUING SEX IN AN OVERSEXED WORLD

SANDRA L. GLAHN & C. GARY BARNES

EDITORS

KREGEL ACADEMIC

Sanctified Sexuality: Valuing Sex in an Oversexed World

For our students
May your shepherding be filled
with grace and truth

CONTENTS

CONTRIBUTORS

C. Gary Barnes (ThM, PhD) is professor of biblical counseling at Dallas Theological Seminary. He is a licensed clinical psychologist, board certified by the American Board of Christian Sex Therapists, a clinical member of Sexual Wholeness, and an ordained Anglican priest.

Darrell L. Bock (ThM, PhD) is executive director of cultural engagement and senior research professor of New Testament studies at Dallas Theological Seminary. He is the author or coauthor of more than forty books, including well-regarded commentaries on Luke and Acts and studies of the historical Jesus.

James K. Childerston (PhD) is a licensed clinical psychologist, board certified by the American Board of Christian Sex Therapists, a clinical member of Sexual Wholeness, and an author who maintains a full-time private practice.

Robert B. Chisholm (ThM, ThD) is chairman of the Old Testament Studies Department at Dallas Theological Seminary and the author or coauthor of numerous works including Old Testament commentaries.

Chelsi A. Creech (MA) is a doctoral candidate in clinical psychology. She has worked with teens to help them better understand their sexuality in light of God's Word and has a heart to serve those with type 2 diabetes.

Joseph D. Fantin (ThM, PhD) is professor of New Testament Studies at Dallas Theological Seminary and is the author of *Lord of the Entire World: Lord Jesus, a Challenge to Lord Caesar?*

Sandra L. Glahn (ThM, PhD) is professor of Media Arts and Worship at Dallas Theological Seminary. She is the author or coauthor of more than twenty-five books, including *Sexual Intimacy in Marriage*, now in its fourth edition; two books on infertility; and one book on contraception.

W. Hall Harris (ThM, PhD) is senior professor of New Testament Studies at Dallas Theological Seminary and is the author of numerous works. He is also the project director and managing editor of the NET Bible.

Wesley Hill (MA, PhD) is associate professor of biblical studies at Trinity School for Ministry in Ambridge, Pennsylvania. He is the author of numerous works including *Paul and the Trinity: Persons, Relations, and the Pauline Letters* and *Spiritual Friendship: Finding Love in the Church as a Celibate Gay Christian.*

J. Scott Horrell (ThM, ThD) is professor of Theological Studies at Dallas Theological Seminary and is the author of numerous theological works in English and Portuguese.

Glenn R. Kreider (ThM, PhD) is professor of Theological Studies at Dallas Theological Seminary and is the author of *God with Us: Exploring God's Interaction with God's People throughout the Bible.* He is also a contributing author to numerous academic works.

Abraham Kuruvilla (MD, ThM, PhD) is senior research professor of preaching and pastoral ministries at Dallas Theological Seminary and is the author of numerous works including *Text to Praxis: Hermeneutics and Homiletics in Dialogue.*

Jessica N. McCleese (PsyD) is a licensed clinical psychologist, board certified by the American Board of Christian Sex Therapists, a clinical member of Sexual Wholeness, and maintains a full-time private practice.

Douglas E. Rosenau (ThM, EdD) is adjunct professor at Dallas Theological Seminary. He is cofounder of Sexual Wholeness, a licensed psychologist, board certified by the American Board of Christian Sex Therapists, a clinical member of Sexual Wholeness, and an author of numerous works, including *Celebration of Sex.*

Julia A. Sadusky (PsyD) is a graduate of Regent University, where she served as research assistant in the Institute for the Study of Sexual Identity and completed an advanced clinical rotation through the Sexual and Gender Identity Clinic.

Joy Pedrow Skarka (MACE) is a graduate teaching assistant at Dallas Theological Seminary and director of discipleship at Authentic Intimacy while she is completing a Doctor of Educational Ministry degree studying sexual shame. She founded Joy Pedrow Ministries to create spaces to set women free from sexual shame and addiction.

Jay E. Smith (ThM, PhD) is chair and professor of New Testament Studies at Dallas Theological Seminary. He regularly contributes to leading academic journals.

Scott M. Stanley (PhD) is research professor of psychology at the University of Denver. He is one of the leading researchers on prevention of marital distress and divorce, and on commitment and cohabitation. He has authored numerous books and is published extensively in scholarly journals.

Michael R. Sytsma (PhD) is cofounder of Sexual Wholeness, a licensed clinical psychologist, and board certified by the American Board of Christian Sex Therapists. He is also a clinical member of Sexual Wholeness, an author, and maintains a full-time private practice.

Richard L. Voet (MD, MABS, MA) is adjunct professor in pastoral ministries at Dallas Theological Seminary. He has degrees from Dallas Theological Seminary and Trinity Graduate School with advanced studies in medical bioethics. He is chairman of the Bioethics Committee at Texas Health Presbyterian Hospital Dallas, and is a member of the Ethics Committee of the Christian Medical Association.

Debby Wade (MA) is a licensed professional counselor and a licensed marriage and family therapist. She is board certified by the American Board of Christian Sex Therapists, a certified sex addictions therapist, a clinical member of Sexual Wholeness, and founder of ACTSoulutions.

Christopher West (MTS) is a world-renowned teacher, author, and speaker on the theology of the body. He is founder and president of The Cor Project, a global outreach ministry, and senior lecturer at the Theology of the Body Institute in Pennsylvania.

Mark A. Yarhouse (PsyD) is the Dr. Arthur P. Rech and Mrs. Jean May Rech Chair in Psychology at Wheaton College. He served for eleven years as the Hughes Endowed Chair at Regent University, where he directed the Institute for the Study of Sexual Identity.

INTRODUCTION

SANDRA L. GLAHN & C. GARY BARNES

Most people don't readily recognize the names Obergefell and Hodges, but they probably remember the landmark civil rights case that bears their names—and the finding of the Supreme Court of the United States that the fundamental right to marry is guaranteed to same-sex couples. The five-four decision requires all fifty states, the District of Columbia, and the insular areas to perform and recognize same-sex couples' marriages on the same terms and conditions as the marriages of opposite-sex couples, with all the accompanying rights and responsibilities.

The case began in 2012, and it continued in headlines, on talk shows, in political campaigns, and certainly in churches and on social media. So by the time the Supreme Court handed down the decision on June 26, 2015, a lot of good people had said and continued to say a lot of unfortunate things. As professors at a theological seminary, we cringed as we watched people use Genesis out of context, say horrible things about people with same-sex attraction, and alienate people—and then describe some of the justified criticism they evoked as persecution. In the midst of all this, we had a conversation one afternoon in which we said to each other, basically, "We need to do a better job of training ministry workers in these areas of sexual ethics."

So we created a course we titled Sexual Ethics. But we did not serve as the sole lecturers, because indeed we were not experts in all the ways the church needs input on this subject. Rather, we curated a course filmed for online use in which top Christian experts on theology of the body, same-sex attraction, addiction, Hebrew, New Testament Greek, and much more would speak in their areas of expertise and then hold a question-and-answer time with students. The lecturers were scholars—men and women from differing specialties, educational institutions, and religious traditions who addressed these issues from the perspective of theologians, exegetes, and practitioners. We chose as our textbook the late Stanley Grenz's *Sexual Ethics*, but because much of it is now outdated, we asked each lecturer to offer a chapter on the topic addressed for this work. Laura Bartlett, director of Academic and Ministry Books at Kregel Publications, provided encouragement and support for the project, and we were aided in our task by the expert editorial direction of Shawn Vander Lugt and Robert Hand.

The work you hold in your hands is the result of this collaboration. Some contributors, like Christopher West and Wesley Hill, provided transcripts of talks they had given. Others provided deeply technical exegesis. And still others wrote in a more casual, first-person style. Some chapters came in longer than others. Some authors reached conclusions that differed from those of other authors. And we decided to keep the differences, letting each contributor speak in his or her voice, rather than making all the chapters match an imposed template. So you will find variety in tone, style, and even the number of footnotes and transliterations from chapter to chapter. Part of our goal is to help people develop a hermeneutic of charity—seeing each presentation through a grid acknowledging that good people may differ yet still engage in civil discourse. In including varying views, we hope to challenge our readers' thinking and drive them back to the text. We've been guided in this by Rupertus Meldenius (ca. 1627), who wrote, "In essentials unity, in non-essentials liberty, in all things charity."

While we contributors may have our differences, we are most certainly united on some key points: We all desire to be faithful to the biblical text and help the body of Christ live out her calling in the world in a Christ-honoring way, full of both grace and truth. Additionally, it is our view that there is only one effective alternative to the slippery slope of demonizing sexuality or deifying sexuality, and that is an approach to sexuality and ethics that is not simply promoting a moral code of dos and don'ts. Rather, we have the much higher calling of elevating God's sacred sexuality to a place that transforms hearts and motivations as well as behaviors.

To help the church flourish in our thinking, teaching, and interaction about sexual ethics, the authors have agreed that all royalties will benefit the Institute for Sexual Wholeness. A nonprofit organization, the Institute for Sexual Wholeness is dedicated to training Christian therapists and ministry leaders to unveil God's truth about sexuality and bring healing. They believe that God has a sexual plan that promotes integrity, maturity, and passionate intimacy, and desire to partner in cultivating a sexually healthy church.

God created humans in his image as sexual beings before pronouncing his creation very good. And while we continue to witness many cultural changes relating to sex and gender, one thing that remains unchanged and timeless is the foundation for sexual intimacy—God's beautiful design for the flourishing of those created in his image. And it is our hope that the expertise in various disciplines offered here by those committed to this foundation will benefit you and those for whom you provide spiritual care—that we might all model what it looks like to imitate Jesus, who was and is full of grace and truth.

Dallas, Texas
2019

CHAPTER 1

OUR BODIES TELL GOD'S STORY

| CHRISTOPHER WEST |

I know some muddle-headed Christians have talked as if Christianity thought that sex, or the body, or pleasure were bad in themselves. But they were wrong.
—C. S. Lewis

In the early 1900s, a "respectable" woman wore an average of twenty-five pounds of clothing when she appeared in public. The sight of an ankle could cause scandal. Over the next one hundred years, the pendulum swung to the other extreme. Today scantily clad, hyper-eroticized images of the human body have become the cultural wallpaper, and graphic, hard-core pornography has become the main reference point for the "facts of life."

Is it any wonder in the post-sexual-revolution world that humanity's deepest, most painful wounds often center on sexuality? And by sexuality I mean not only what we do with our genitals behind closed doors but our very sense of ourselves as male and female. We live in a world of chaotic, widespread gender confusion, a world that seems intent on erasing the essential meaning of the sexual difference from the individual and collective consciousness.

A BOLD, BIBLICAL RESPONSE TO THE SEXUAL REVOLUTION

All of this has posed an enormous challenge to Christians. How have we responded? Those who began acquiescing to what might be called "the new morality" had to reinterpret the Bible in order to do so, a move that eventually led many believers and denominations to abandon the basic tenets of the Christian faith. On the other hand, Christian leaders who upheld traditional biblical faith and morality often found themselves without a convincing language to engage their own congregations, who were being increasingly influenced and formed by the ethos of the secular culture. The same held true for parents with their children. The silence was deafening. "The Bible says so" and "thou shalt not" weren't enough to prevent people from getting carried away by the tide of so-called sexual "liberation."

In the early 1950s, right at the time Hugh Hefner launched *Playboy* magazine, a young Polish priest, philosopher, and theologian named Karol Wojtyła (pronounced "voy-TEE-wa") started quietly formulating a fresh, bold, compelling, biblical response to this modern brand of liberation. This was a man steadfast in his commitment to traditional Christian values, but also open and attentive to the challenges being raised by the modern world. As a student of contemporary philosophy himself, he understood how modern men and women thought, and he believed he could explain the biblical vision of sex in a way that would ring true in their hearts and minds. From Wojtyła's perspective, the problem with the sexual revolution was not that it overvalued sex, but that it failed to see how astoundingly valuable it really is. He was convinced that if he could show the utter beauty and splendor of God's plan for the body and sexuality, it would open the way to *true freedom*—the freedom to love as Christ loves.

Over the next twenty years, he continually refined and deepened his vision via the pulpit, the university classroom, and in countless conversations and counseling sessions with dating, engaged, and married couples. (Wojtyła's open, honest approach with young people—no subject was off-limits if sought honestly—was very similar to that of Francis Schaeffer.) In December of 1974, now as archbishop of Krakow, he began putting this bold, biblical vision to paper. On page 1 of his handwritten manuscript, he gave it the title *Theology of the Body*.

This was an altogether different kind of Bible study on sex. It was not the all too common attempt to scour the Scriptures looking for proof texts on immorality. The goal was to examine key passages from Genesis to Revelation, over a thousand in all, in order to paint a "total vision" of human love in God's plan. In essence, Wojtyła was saying to the modern world, "Okay, you wanna talk about sex? No problem. But let's *really* talk about it. Let's not stop at the surface. Let's have the courage to enter together into what the Bible calls the 'great mystery' of our sexuality. If we do, we'll discover something more grand and glorious than we have ever dared to imagine."

This was a vision that had the power to change the world—*if* the world only had a chance to hear it. That chance came when, in October of 1978, this little-known Polish bishop was chosen as the first non-Italian pope in 450 years, taking the name John Paul II. Having only recently completed his theology of the body manuscript (it was originally intended as a book to be published in Poland), he decided to make it his first major teaching project as pope, delivering small portions of the text over the course of 129 weekly addresses between September of 1979 and November of 1984.

It took some time, however, for people to grasp the significance of what this in-depth Bible study had given the world. It wasn't until 1999, for example, that his biographer George Weigel described the theology of the body to a wide readership as "a kind of *theological time-bomb* set to go off with dramatic consequences . . . perhaps in the twenty-first century."[1] While John Paul's vision of the body and of sexual love had barely begun to shape the way Christians engaged their faith, Weigel predicted that when it did, it would "compel a dramatic development of thinking" about virtually every major tenet of the Christian faith.[2]

GOD, SEX, AND THE MEANING OF LIFE

What might the human body and sex have to do with the basic tenets of Christianity? There's a deep, organic connection, in fact, between the two. As we observed above, rejection of the biblical vision of sexuality has led in practice to a rejection of the basic principles of the faith. And here's why: if we are made in the image of God as male and female (see Gen. 1:27), and if joining in "one flesh" is a "great mystery" that refers to Christ and the church (see Eph. 5:31–32), then our understanding of the body, gender, and sexuality has a direct impact on our understanding of God, Christ, and the church.

To ask questions about the meaning of the body starts us on an exhilarating journey that, if we stay the course, leads us from the body to the mystery of sexual difference; from sexual difference to the mystery of communion in "one flesh"; from communion in "one flesh" to the mystery of Christ's communion with the church; and from the communion of Christ and the church to the greatest mystery of all: the eternal communion found in God among Father, Son, and Holy Spirit. This is what the tenets of the Christian faith are all about.

Hence, as we're already seeing, the body is not only biological. Since we're made in the image of God as male and female, the body, as we will see in some detail, is also *theological*. The body tells an astounding divine story. And it does so precisely through the mystery of sexual difference and the call of the two to become "one flesh." This means when we get the body and sex wrong, we get the divine story wrong as well.

Sex is not just about sex. The way we understand and express our sexuality points to our deepest-held convictions about who we are, who God is, who Jesus is, what the church is (or should be), the meaning of love, the ordering of society, and the mystery of the universe. This means John Paul II's *Theology of the Body* is much more than a biblical reflection on sex and married love. Through that, it leads us to "the rediscovery of the meaning of the whole of existence . . . the meaning of life."[3]

---

1. George Weigel, *Witness to Hope: The Biography of Pope John Paul II* (New York: Harper-Collins, 1999), 343.
2. Weigel, *Witness to Hope*, 853.
3. John Paul II, *Man and Woman He Created Them: A Theology of the Body*, trans. Michael Waldstein (Boston: Pauline Books and Media, 2006), 46:6. This work (henceforth *TOB*) is compiled from John Paul II's general-audience addresses on human love in the divine plan. Citation numbers are to address and paragraph number.

Christ teaches that his highest will for our lives is to love as he loves (see John 15:12). One of John Paul's main insights is that God inscribed this vocation to love as he loves *right in our bodies* by creating us male and female and calling us to become "one flesh" (see Gen. 2:24). Far from being a footnote in the Christian life, the way we understand the body and the sexual relationship "concerns the whole Bible."[4] It plunges us into "the perspective of the whole gospel, of the whole teaching, even more, of the whole mission of Christ."[5]

Christ's mission is to reconcile us to the Father and, through that, to restore the order of love in a world seriously distorted by sin. And the union of the sexes, as always, lies at the basis of the human "order of love." Therefore, what we learn in the *Theology of the Body* is obviously "important with regard to marriage." However it "is equally essential and *valid for the [understanding] of humanity* in general: for the fundamental problem of understanding humanity and for the self-understanding of his being in the world."[6]

Looking for the meaning of life? Looking to understand the fundamental questions of existence? Our bodies tell the story. But we must learn how to "read" that story properly, and doing so is not easy. A great many obstacles, prejudices, taboos, and fears can derail us as we seek to enter the "great mystery" of our own embodiment as male and female. Indeed, the temptation to disincarnate our humanity and, even more, to disincarnate the Christian faith is constant and fierce. But ours is an *enfleshed* faith—*everything* hinges on the incarnation! We must be very careful never to *unflesh* it. It's the enemy who wants to deny Christ's coming in the flesh (see 1 John 4:2–3).

SPIRIT AND FLESH

When it comes to present-day Christianity, people are used to an emphasis on "spiritual" things. In turn, many Christians are unfamiliar, and sometimes rather uncomfortable, with an emphasis on the physical realm, especially the human body. But this is a false and dangerous split. Spirit has priority over matter, since God in himself is pure Spirit. Yet God is the author of the physical world, and in his wisdom, he designed physical realities to convey spiritual mysteries. "There is no good trying to be more spiritual than God," as C. S. Lewis wrote. "God never meant man to be a purely spiritual creature. That is why he uses material things like bread and wine to put the new life into us. We may think this rather crude and unspiritual. God does not. . . . He likes matter. He invented it."[7]

We should like it too. For we are not angels "trapped" in physical bodies. We are *incarnate spirits*; we are a marriage of body and soul, of the physical and the spiritual. Living a "spiritual life" as a Christian *never* means fleeing from or

---

4. *TOB* 69:8.
5. *TOB* 49:3.
6. *TOB* 102:5.
7. C. S. Lewis. *Mere Christianity* (1952; repr., San Francisco: HarperOne, 2013), 64.

disparaging the physical world. Tragically, many Christians grow up thinking of the physical world (especially their own bodies and sexuality) as the main obstacle to the spiritual life, as if the physical world itself were "bad." Much of this thinking, it seems, comes from a faulty reading of the distinction the apostle Paul makes in his letters between spirit and flesh (see Rom. 8:1–17 and Gal. 5:16–26, for example).

In Paul's terminology, "the flesh" refers to the whole person (body and soul) cut off from God's "in-spiration"—cut off from God's indwelling Spirit. It refers to a person dominated by vice. And, in this sense, as Christ himself asserted, "the flesh counts for nothing" (John 6:63 NIV). But those who open themselves to life "according to the Spirit" do *not* reject the body; it's this body that becomes the very dwelling place of the Spirit: "Do you not know that your body is a temple of the Holy Spirit, who is in you, whom you have received from God? . . . Therefore honor God with your body" (1 Cor. 6:19–20, NIV 1984).

We honor God with our bodies precisely by welcoming God's Spirit into our entire body-soul personality and allowing the Spirit to guide what we do with our bodies. In this way, even our bodies "pass over" from death to life: "And if the Spirit of him who raised Jesus from the dead is living in you, he who raised Christ from the dead will also give life to your mortal bodies through his Spirit, who lives in you" (Rom. 8:11, NIV 1984).

CHRISTIANITY DOES NOT REJECT THE BODY

The "spirit-good/body-bad" dualism that often passes for Christianity is actually an ancient gnostic error called Manichaeism, and it couldn't be further from a biblical perspective. In fact, it's a direct attack on Christianity at its deepest roots. If we're to rediscover God's glorious plan for our sexuality, it will be necessary to contend with some ingrained habits in our way of thinking that stem from Manichaeism. So let's take a closer look.

Mani (or Manichaeus, AD 216–74), after whom this heresy is named, condemned the body and all things sexual because he believed the material world was evil. Scripture, however, is very clear that everything God created is "very good" (see Gen. 1:31). This is a critical point to let sink in. Unwittingly, we often give evil far more weight than it deserves, as if the devil had created his own "evil world" to battle God's "good world." But the devil is a creature, not a creator. And this means *the devil does not have his own clay*. All he can do is take *God's* clay (which is always very good) and twist it, distort it. That's what evil *is*: the twisting or distortion of good. Redemption, therefore, involves the "untwisting" of what sin and evil have twisted so we can recover the true good.

In today's world, sin and evil have twisted the meaning of the body and sexuality almost beyond recognition. But the solution is *never* to blame the body itself; it's *never* to reject or eschew or flee from our sexuality. That approach is gnostic and Manichaean in its very essence. And if that's our approach, we haven't overcome the devil's lies. We've fallen right into his trap. His fundamental goal is always to split body and soul. Why? Well, there's a fancy word for the separation of body and soul. Perhaps you've heard of it. *Death.* That's where Manichaeism, like all heresies, leads.

The true solution to all of the pornographic distortions of the body so prevalent today is not the *rejection* of the body, but the *redemption* of the body (see Rom. 8:23)—the "untwisting" of what sin has twisted so we can recover the true glory, splendor, and inestimable value of the body. John Paul II summarized the critical distinction between the Manichaean and Christian approaches to the body as follows: If the Manichaean mentality places an "antivalue" on the body and sex, Christianity teaches that the body and sex "always remain a 'value not sufficiently appreciated.'"[8] In other words, if Manichaeism says "the body is bad," Christianity says "the body is so good we have yet to fathom it."

We must say this loudly, clearly, and repeatedly until it sinks in and heals our wounds: *Christianity does not reject the body!* As C. S. Lewis insisted, "Christianity is almost the only one of the great religions which thoroughly approves of the body—which believes that matter is good, that God himself once took on a human body, that some kind of body is going to be given to us even in Heaven and is going to be an essential part of our happiness."[9]

Of course, it would be an oversight not to acknowledge that, in this life, our bodies are often a source of great unhappiness and sometimes terrible suffering. Genetic defects, disease, sickness, injury, and a great many other maladies and misfortunes, not the least of which is the inevitability of death, can cause us to loathe our bodily existence. Or, united to the bodily sufferings and death of Christ, our bodily maladies and misfortunes can become something redemptive both for us and for others. Suffering, as I once heard it said, can either *break us* or *break us open* to the mystery of Christ. Matthew Lee Anderson expresses the conundrum well: "This is the paradox of the body: The body is a temple, but the temple is in ruins. The incarnation of Jesus affirms the body's original goodness. The death of Jesus reminds us of its need for redemption. And the resurrection of Jesus gives us hope for its restoration."[10]

WORD MADE FLESH

Establishing the fundamental *goodness* of the body and the hope of bodily redemption is one thing. But what is it that makes the body a "theology," a study of God?

We cannot see God. As pure Spirit, God is totally beyond our vision. Yet the Bible teaches that the invisible God has made himself visible: "That which was from the beginning, which we have heard, which we have seen with our own eyes,

---

8. *TOB* 45:3.
9. Lewis, *Mere Christianity*, 98.
10. Matthew Lee Anderson, *Earthen Vessels: Why Our Bodies Matter to Our Faith* (Blooming-ton, MN: Bethany House, 2011), 31.

which we have gazed upon and touched with our own hands—this is the Word of life. And this is the life that was revealed; we have seen it" (1 John 1:1–2 BSB).

How did John and the other disciples *see* "that which was from the beginning"? How did they *touch* "the Word of life"? "The Word became flesh. . . . We have seen his glory" (John 1:14). Everything about our faith hinges on the incarnation of the Son of God, on the idea that Christ's flesh—and ours, for it's our flesh he took on—has the ability to reveal God's mystery, to make visible the invisible.

If the phrase "theology of the body" seems odd, perhaps it's because we haven't taken the reality of the incarnation as seriously as Scripture invites us to do. There's nothing surprising about looking to the human body as a "study of God" if we believe in Christmas. "Through the fact that the Word of God became flesh, the body entered theology . . . through the main door."[11]

"Theology of the body," therefore, is not only the title of a series of talks by John Paul II on sex and marriage. The term "theology of the body" expresses the very *logic* of Christianity. We must say it again (and again) until it sinks in: *everything* in Christianity hinges on the incarnation of the Son of God.

THE THESIS STATEMENT

This brings us to the thesis statement of the *Theology of the Body*, the brush with which John Paul paints the entire vision: "The body, in fact, and only the body, is capable of making visible what is invisible: the spiritual and divine. It has been created to transfer into the visible reality of the world the mystery hidden from eternity in God, and thus to be a sign of it."[12]

Think of your own experiences as a human being: your body is not just a "shell" in which you dwell. Your body is not just *a* body. Your body is not just *any* body. Your body is *some*body—you! Through the profound unity of your body and your soul, your body *reveals* or "makes visible" the invisible reality of your spiritual soul. The "you" you are is not just a soul "in" a body. Your body is not something you "have" or "own" alongside yourself. Your body *is* you. Which is why if someone broke your jaw in a fit of rage, you wouldn't take him to court for "property damage" but for personal assault. What we do with our bodies, and what is done to our bodies, we do or have done to *ourselves*.

Once again, our bodies make visible what is invisible, the spiritual *and the divine*. Aren't we made in the image of God as male and female (see Gen. 1:27)? This means the very design of our sexually differentiated bodies reveals something about the mystery of God. The phrase "theology of the body" is just another way of stating the bedrock biblical truth that man and woman image God.

The body is not divine, of course. Rather, it's an "image" or a "sign" of the divine. A sign points us to a reality beyond itself and, in some way, makes that

---

11. *TOB* 23:4.
12. *TOB* 19:4.

reality present to us. The divine mystery always remains infinitely "beyond"; it cannot be reduced to its sign. Yet the sign is indispensable in "making visible" the invisible mystery. Human beings need signs and symbols to communicate. There's no way around it. The same holds true in our relationship with God. God speaks to us in sign language.

Tragically, after sin, the "body loses its character as a sign"[13]—not objectively, but in our subjective perception of it. In other words, in itself, the body still speaks God's sign language, but we don't know how to read it. We've been blinded to the true meaning and beauty of the body. As a result, we tend to consider the body merely as a physical "thing," entirely separated from the spiritual and the divine realms. Tragically, we can spend our whole lives as Christians stuck in this blindness, never knowing that our bodies are a sign revealing the "mystery hidden in God."

THE DIVINE MYSTERY

Paul wrote that his mission as an apostle of Jesus Christ was "to make plain to everyone . . . this mystery, which for ages past was kept hidden in God" (Eph. 3:9, NIV 1984). What is that "mystery hidden in God," and how can it be "made plain to everyone"?

God is not a tyrant, God is not a slave driver, God is not merely a legislator or lawgiver, and he's certainly not an old man with a white beard waiting to strike us down whenever we fail. God is an eternal exchange of love and bliss. He's an infinite "Communion of Persons," to use John Paul II's preferred expression. And he created us for one reason: to share his eternal love and bliss with us. This is what makes the gospel *good news*: there is a banquet of love that corresponds to the hungry cry of our hearts, and it is God's free gift to us! He has *destined us in Christ* "before the foundation of the world" to be part of his family, to share in his love (see Eph. 1:9–14).

This is the "mystery, which for ages past was kept hidden in God" that Paul wanted to "make plain to everyone." How did he do it? In Ephesians 5, Paul reveals that this "mystery" isn't far from us. We needn't climb some high mountain to find it. We needn't cross the sea. It's already as "plain" to us as the bodies God gave us when he created us male and female and called the two to become "one flesh." We need only recover our ability to read God's sign language to see it.

THE BIBLE TELLS A MARITAL STORY

Scripture uses many images to help us understand God's love. Each has its own valuable place. But the gift of Christ's body on the cross gives "definitive prominence to the spousal meaning of God's love."[14] In fact, from beginning

---

13. *TOB* 40:4.
14. John Paul II, *On the Dignity and Vocation of Women: Mulieris Dignitatem*, Apostolic Letter (Culver City, CA: Pauline Books and Media, 1988), §26.

to end, in the mysteries of our creation, fall, and redemption, the Bible tells a covenant story of marital love.

That story begins in Genesis with the marriage of the first man and woman, and it ends in Revelation with the marriage of Christ and the church. These spousal "bookends" provide the key for understanding all that lies between. Indeed, we can summarize all of sacred Scripture with five simple, yet astounding, words: *God wants to marry us.*

> As a young man marries a maiden
> So will your Builder marry you;
> As a bridegroom rejoices over his bride,
> So will your God rejoice over you. (Isa. 62:5)

God is inviting each of us, in a unique and unrepeatable way, to an unimagined intimacy with him, akin to the intimacy of spouses in "one flesh." While we may need to work through some discomfort or fear here to reclaim the true sacredness, the true holiness of the imagery, the "scandalous" truth is that Scripture describes God's love for his people using boldly erotic images. One need only think of the Song of Songs. This unabashed celebration of erotic love is not only a biblical celebration of marital intimacy. It's also an image of how God loves his people, fulfilled in the "marriage of the Lamb" (Rev. 19:7).

But there's more. Remember that pithy rhyme we learned as children: "First comes love, then comes marriage, then comes the baby in the baby carriage"? We probably didn't realize that we were actually reciting some profound *theology*: theology *of the body*. Our bodies tell the story that God loves us, wants to marry us, and wants us (the bride) to "conceive" his eternal life within us. And this isn't merely a metaphor. Two thousand years ago, a young Jewish woman gave her *yes* to God's marriage proposal with such totality, with such fidelity, that she literally conceived eternal life in her womb. This is why Christians have always honored Mary: she is the biblical model par excellence of what it means to be a believer, of what it means to surrender to Jesus, of what it means to receive him and bear him forth to others. God was revealed through Mary's body by the fact that her body gave God a body. Astounding.

CLIMAX OF THE SPOUSAL ANALOGY

"It is obvious that the analogy of . . . human spousal love, cannot offer an adequate and complete understanding of . . . the divine mystery." God's "*mystery* remains *transcendent with respect to this analogy* as with respect to any other analogy." At the same time, however, the spousal analogy allows a certain "penetration" into the very essence of the mystery.[15] No biblical author reaches more deeply into this essence than the apostle Paul in Ephesians 5.

---

15. See *TOB* 95b:1.

Quoting directly from Genesis 2:24, Paul states, "For this reason a man will leave his father and mother and be united to his wife, and the two will become one flesh." Then, linking the original marriage with the ultimate marriage, he adds, "This is a great mystery—but I am talking about Christ and the church" (Eph. 5:31–32). Inspired by the Holy Spirit, Paul employs the intimacy of marital union to reveal not just some aspect of the Christian mystery. Rather, spousal union illuminates the reality of our union with Christ in its entirety, the reality of salvation itself.

But let's be more specific. How does Genesis 2:24 refer to Christ and the church? Christ, the new Adam, "left" his Father in heaven. He also left the home of his mother on earth. Why? To give up his body for his bride (the church) so that we might enter into holy communion with him. In the breaking of the bread, "Christ is united with his 'body' as the bridegroom with the bride. All this is contained in the Letter to the Ephesians."[16]

THE FOUNDATION OF ETHICS AND CULTURE

The stakes are incredibly high in the cultural debate about the meaning of sex and marriage. In short, as sex goes, so goes marriage; as marriage goes, so goes the family. And because the family is the fundamental cell of society, as the family goes, so goes the culture. This is why confusion about sexual morality "involves a danger perhaps greater than is generally realized: the danger of confusing the basic and fundamental human tendencies, the main paths of human existence. Such confusion must clearly affect the whole spiritual position of man."[17]

This is why it "is an illusion to think we can build a true culture of human life if we do not . . . accept and experience sexuality and love and the whole of life according to their true meaning and their close inter-connection."[18] But that will never happen unless we can demonstrate that the biblical sexual ethic is not the prudish list of prohibitions it's so often assumed to be. Rather, it's an invitation to live and embrace the love for which we most deeply yearn.

---

16. John Paul II, *On the Dignity and Vocation of Women: Mulieris Dignitatem*, §26.
17. Karol Wojtyła (John Paul II), *Love and Responsibility* (San Francisco: Ignatius, 1993), 66. This is John Paul II's philosophical work on sexuality.
18. John Paul II, *The Gospel of Life: Evangelium Vitae*, Encyclical Letter (Culver City, CA: Pauline Books and Media, 1995), §97.

FOR DISCUSSION

1. Most of us have been taught that sex is meant to be beautiful and intimate and holy. Most of us have also been taught that sex can be something dirty and perverted and sinful. How can it be both? What makes it one or the other?

2. What was the Manichaean heresy? What are some ways you see such thinking among Christians? Have you felt that your body hindered your spiritual life? Explain your answer.

3. How has the enemy's deception about sex affected everything else in our culture? How can we counter such deception and create a culture of life?

FOR FURTHER READING

John Paul II. *The Theology of the Body according to John Paul II: Human Love in the Divine Plan.* Boston: Pauline Books and Media, 1997.

West, Christopher. *Fill These Hearts: God, Sex, and the Universal Longing.* Cicero, NY: Image, 2013.

West, Christopher, and Charles J. Chaput. *Good News about Sex and Marriage.* Rev. ed. Atlanta: Charis, 2004.

CHAPTER 2

THE "TWO ADAMS" AND SPIRITUAL IDENTITY

GLENN R. KREIDER

Jeff Buchanan, a pastor who has served on the front lines in the media and in the pastor's study helping those with same-sex attraction, says this about identity: "Understanding our identity in Christ is essential for Christian living. When we were born again, we received a new identity, and we are complete in Christ (Col. 2:10). We will share in Christ's inheritance, and as we grow in the revelation of our new identity, we will increasingly be enabled to live according to God's will. If our identity is "in Christ," can we add to this identity without implying that Christ is somehow deficient?"[1] For the Christian, understanding the relationship we have with God through the Holy Spirit because of the work of Christ is essential, and is a source of hope and comfort. We have received an incredible gift, unearned, undeserved, and unmerited. Salvation and the hope of eternal life is an indescribable gift (2 Cor. 9:15).

Yet, is our identity limited to our relationship with Christ? Do other aspects and characteristics of the person disappear or shrink in importance when one places faith in Christ? Or is our identity a complex combination of a variety of characteristics and properties? This essay argues that as important as our identity "in Christ" is, our relationship to him and his body does not supersede or replace

---

1. Jeff Buchanan, "The New Sexual Identity Crisis," The Gospel Coalition, July 10, 2012, https://www.thegospelcoalition.org/article/the-new-sexual-identity-crisis-2. See also S. M. Hutchens, "Just Christians: On Homosexuality and Christian Identity," *Touchstone*, July/August 2013, 3–4. Both of these authors argue that identifying oneself by sexual orientation is inconsistent with one's identity in Christ.

the other elements of our identity. We are each an integrated complexity of multiple characteristics.

PERSONAL IDENTITY

Identity is defined in *Merriam-Webster* as "the distinguishing character or personality of an individual." Thus our identity is a combination of many things. I am a White, middle-aged (or maybe a bit older), married, heterosexual male, Christian, son of parents who are both deceased, married to my best friend for more than forty years (her parents are also both deceased); I am a father of two children, father-in-law of one son-in-law, grandfather of one adorable granddaughter, middle-class American, native of the northeastern United States but have now lived over half my life in Texas, professor of theological studies, owner of multiple rescued dogs, homeowner, lover of bold coffee and good music . . . I could go on. My identity is a combination of those things and many more. Some of those characteristics are a result of birth; I had nothing to do with being born a White male. Some of those characteristics have been chosen, such as rescuing dogs. Some of those characteristics have been graciously given to me; I am grateful to have the privilege of teaching theology courses at Dallas Theological Seminary. Some of those characteristics have evolved, and some have been consistent. I have always been White and male and a son. But I only recently became a son whose parents are both deceased. I have not always been married, or a father, or a grandfather, or a Christian.

My identity was formed at birth, evolves and changes over time, and will one day be consummated in the new creation. Some of the aspects of my identity will continue into that stage of the work of redemption; others will not. I will always be the son of Elvin and Thelma Kreider, the husband of Janice, father of Michael and Jeneec, and grandfather of Marlo. I expect to be able to *enjoy* dogs (as I doubt we will "own" animals in the kingdom), bold coffee, and good music on the new earth. I will not, however, continue to struggle with my own sinfulness, live in a world that is cursed by sin, or experience the effects of the curse in my own body and relationships with others.

Every person's identity is a composite of a variety of features, including character traits; aspects of personality; skills and talents; body traits; social relations and status; personal history, religious and political persuasions and commitments; distinctive ways of thinking and acting; and many more.[2] Individual identity is also connected to the identity of the group of which the individual is a part, and that group identity shapes and is shaped by the individuals who are part of that group.

---

2. See Rom Harré, foreword to *Analyzing Identity: Cross-Cultural, Societal and Clinical Contexts*, ed. Peter Weinreich and Wendy Saunderson (New York: Routledge, 2003), xvii.

PERSONAL IDENTITY IS NOT STATIC

Identity is not static, because people age and change in many ways. Yet, in spite of those changes, there is a sense in which the person remains the same. Avrum Stroll explains:

> Philosophical reflections about the nature of change, about the problem of identifying or reidentifying something or someone, gives rise to a set of issues which cluster under the name "the problem of identity." In its simplest form, this problem may be thought of as the problem of trying to give a true explanation of those features of the world which account for its sameness, on the one hand, and for its diversity and change, on the other.[3]

Eric Olson helpfully explains the problem of identity:

> Outside of philosophy, "personal identity" usually refers to certain properties to which a person feels a special sense of attachment or ownership. Someone's personal identity in this sense consists of those features she takes to "define her as a person" or "make her the person she is." . . . One's personal identity in this sense is contingent and changeable: different properties could have belonged to the way one defines oneself as a person, and what properties these are can change over time.[4]

Another author puts it this way:

> Personal identity is the concept you develop about yourself that evolves over the course of your life. This may include aspects of your life that you have no control over, such as where you grew up or the color of your skin, as well as choices you make in life, such as how you spend your time and what you believe. You demonstrate portions of your personal identity outwardly through what you wear and how you interact with other people. You may also keep some elements of your personal identity to yourself, even when these parts of yourself are very important.[5]

---

3. Avrum Stroll, "Identity," in *The Encyclopedia of Philosophy*, ed. Paul Edwards (New York: Macmillan and Free Press, 1967), 4:121. A variety of philosophical approaches are discussed in this essay. For a short and nontechnical discussion of the philosophical landscape see Joshua Farris, "What's So Simple about Personal Identity?," *Philosophy Now*, April/May 2015, https://philosophynow.org/issues/107/Whats_So_Simple_About_Personal_Identity.

4. Eric T. Olson, "Personal Identity," in *Stanford Encyclopedia of Philosophy*, ed. Edward N. Zalta, Summer 2017 ed., https://plato.stanford.edu/archives/sum2017/entries/identity-personal/.

5. Christine Serva, "What Is Personal Identity? Definition, Philosophy and Development," Study.com, http://study.com/academy/lesson/what-is-personal-identity-definition-philosophy-development.html.

In short, personal identity develops and changes, sometimes in clear and observable ways. Other changes are hidden and private. Yet, in the midst of the growth and development, there is continuity in personhood. I am no longer five years old, nor even fifty-five, but I am still the same person I was when I was those ages. I did not pass out of existence and then reappear as a different person. The visible, external changes are observable to all, and yet the continuity is visible as well. I recently met a classmate from high school whom I had not seen since graduation. Although both of us are considerably different than we were then, we each recognized the other immediately. On the other hand, some developments are not visible externally. Having been married to Janice for more than forty years, my love for her has been tested, challenged, nurtured, and is still maturing; those changes are not visible. Although they are not observable to others, those developments are no less real. Largely due to the relationship my wife and I have built over those four decades, there are elements of my personal identity that only she knows.

SPIRITUAL IDENTITY

Personal identity is the combination of characteristics that make up the person. But *spiritual identity* is more difficult to define. One way to de-jargonize spiritual identity and provide clarity is first to define the term *spiritual* or *spirituality*, because "spirituality" means something different to everyone. For some, it's about participating in organized religion: going to a church, synagogue, mosque, and so on. For others, it's more personal—some people get in touch with their spiritual side through private prayer, yoga, meditation, quiet reflection, or even long walks."[6] Within Christianity, usage of the term "identity" is sometimes unclear. Charles Ryrie observed, "Oddly enough, the concept of spirituality, though the subject of much preaching, writing and discussion, is seldom defined. Usually anything that approaches a definition merely describes the characteristics of spirituality, but one searches in vain for a concise definition of the concept itself."[7] A dictionary of theological terms defines *Christian spirituality* as "the believer's relationship with God and life in the Spirit as a member of the church of Jesus Christ. Today spirituality often refers to an interest in or concern for matters of the 'spirit' in contrast to the mere interest and focus on the material."[8] Theologian Alister McGrath writes, "Christian spirituality concerns the quest for a fulfilled and authentic Christian experience, involving the bringing together of the fundamental ideas of Christianity and the whole experience of living on the basis and within the scope of the Christian faith."[9]

---

6. *Psychology Today*, "Spirituality," https://www.psychologytoday.com/basics/spirituality.
7. Charles Caldwell Ryrie, *Balancing the Christian Life* (Chicago: Moody Press, 1969), 12.
8. Stanley J. Grenz, David Guretzki, and Cherith Fee Nordling, *Pocket Dictionary of Theological Terms* (Downers Grove, IL: InterVarsity Press, 1999), 109.
9. Alister E. McGrath. *Christian Spirituality* (Malden, MA: Blackwell, 1999), 2.

When people speak of one's "spiritual identity" in the context of sexuality, they often mean one's identity in Christ as described in Scripture. And in the New Testament "spiritual" can be defined simply in terms of relationship to the Spirit of God. John Murray states this point succinctly: "'Spiritual' in the New Testament refers to that which is of the Holy Spirit. The spiritual [person] is the person who is indwelt and controlled by the Holy Spirit and a spiritual state of mind is a state of mind that is produced and maintained by the Holy Spirit. Hence, when we say that union with Christ is Spiritual we mean, first of all, that the bond of this union is the Holy Spirit himself."[10] Ryrie says something similar: "The word is, of course, built on the root word for spirit and thus means 'pertaining to the spirit.' Actually, it has a rather wide range of uses, all of which are consistent with this basic idea of pertaining to spirit."[11] Ryrie continues, "However, the distinctive use in the New Testament of the word *spiritual* is in connection with the believer's growth and maturing in the Christian life. A spiritual man must first of all be one who has experienced the regenerating work of the Holy Spirit giving him new life in Christ."[12]

Spiritual identity, thus, is who the Christian is, a human being indwelt by the Spirit of God. By means of the indwelling Spirit, the believer is united to Christ, her identity is linked to his, her hope is found in him. In short, "spiritual identity" and "union with Christ" are two ways of expressing this reality. Murray notes, "Union with Christ is really the central truth of the whole doctrine of salvation not only in its application but also in its once-for-all accomplishment in the finished work of Christ. Indeed, the whole process of salvation has its origin in one phase of union with Christ and salvation has in view the realization of other phases of union with Christ."[13]

But this union with Christ is not individualistic: "Faith union with Christ means union with other believers. When people trust Christ for salvation, the Holy Spirit links them spiritually to Christ and at the same time links them to all others who are 'in him.'"[14] Union with Christ identifies the Christian as a new creation, a new person; and this union is accomplished through the indwelling of the Spirit. No longer who she was, she is not yet what she will be. This hope of new creation is the plot line of the biblical story of God's work of redemption.

---

10. John Murray, *Redemption Accomplished and Applied* (Grand Rapids: Eerdmans, 1955), 166. Since the Spirit is not material, the doctrine of indwelling does not indicate his location but his control or influence over the person. The Spirit is the means by which the believer experiences union with Christ.
11. Ryrie. *Balancing the Christian Life*, 10.
12. Ryrie, *Balancing the Christian Life*, 10–11.
13. Murray, *Redemption Accomplished and Applied*, 161.
14. Robert A. Peterson, *Salvation Applied by the Spirit: Union with Christ* (Wheaton, IL: Crossway, 2014), 415–16.

TWO ADAMS IN THE BIBLICAL NARRATIVE

Because our spiritual identity is grounded in new creation, and this new creation is, indeed, the telos of the plot line of the biblical story of redemption, it is instructive to review how the biblical story unfolds. Many of us describe it as doing so in three acts: creation, fall (and redemption), and re-creation.[15] In the first act God creates a heaven and earth; God is the source of everything that is. He creates dry ground by separating the waters, and fills the earth with plants, trees, and other vegetation. He creates creatures that live in the water and fly in the skies. He creates land animals great and small and fills the earth he has made. He calls what he has made "good." Then he creates caretakers, creatures whose responsibility will be to care for the world he has created. The creation of humanity is summarized in Genesis 1:26–28:

> Then God said, "Let us make Adam in our image, in our likeness, so that they may rule over the fish in the sea and the birds in the sky, over the livestock and all the wild animals, and over all the creatures that move along the ground."
>   So God created Adam in his own image,
>   in the image of God he created them;
>   male and female he created them.
> God blessed them and said to them, "Be fruitful and increase in number; fill the earth and subdue it. Rule over the fish in the sea and the birds in the sky and over every living creature that moves on the ground."[16]

These first humans, named "Adam" by their Creator, are the only creatures designated as divine imagers, created in the likeness of deity.[17] Since he is immaterial, God is not visible; he is invisible. Although he is everywhere present, he is not physically present in the world that he has made. But he is physically present by means of these imagers. Human beings reveal him, represent him, and rule for him in the world that God has created. In human reproduction, "be fruitful and increase in number," humans expand and increase the presence of God in creation,

---

15. See Glenn R. Kreider, *God with Us: Exploring God's Interactions with His People throughout the Bible* (Phillipsburg, NJ: P&R, 2014).

16. All Bible citations in this chapter, unless indicated otherwise, are from the New International Version. The NIV translates the Hebrew word אדם as "mankind" in this context. As will become clear later, this unfortunately obscures the Adam/Christ pattern which is established in the New Testament; thus, I have left the word transliterated (Adam) rather than interpreted (mankind).

17. "Human significance is attached to the One who has no beginning and has no end. Any consideration, then, of human identity must consider the God who created humans in his image or suffer the consequences of denying that linkage." Richard Lints, "Introduction: Theological Anthropology in Context," in *Personal Identity in Theological Perspective*, ed. Richard Lints, Michael S. Horton, and Mark R. Talbot (Grand Rapids: Eerdmans, 2006), 1. Later, Moses reiterates that "Adam" is the name given to both the male and female (Gen. 5:1–2).

covering the whole earth with his manifestation. Ruling or subduing creation and the creatures must be understood in the context of God's having blessed those creations (v. 22). Humans are to be mediators of blessing to the creatures God has blessed, in a good world that God created, as an act of worship of their Creator.[18]

Because humans are created in the image of God, they have dignity. And the Scriptures teach that humans retain this dignity even after the fall, a truth we see in both the Old (Gen. 9:5–7) and New Testaments (James 3:9). Thus every human without exception deserves honor and respect, from the preborn to the Alzheimer's sufferer. Life is sacred, a gracious gift from the Creator. Only the Creator has the power over life and death.

Tragically, God's idyllic world does not last long. In a story told with little attention to detail, a serpent comes into the garden, contradicts the command of the Creator to eat from any tree in the garden except one (2:16–17), and invites Adam—male and female—to rebel against God (3:1–6). They listen. They eat. Their eyes are opened to their nakedness.[19] God then comes into their world and pronounces judgment on the serpent, the man, and woman, and curses the ground (vv. 14–19).[20]

But, surprisingly, the judgment of God does not include the immediate death of the man and woman. God responds to their rebellion in mercy. He clothes them in animal skins (v. 21) and exiles them from the garden (vv. 23–24).[21] They do eventually die, centuries later (5:3–4), but not immediately. They live in hope, the hope of all creation, that one day all will be made new. All the descendants of this couple will also live in hope, albeit not always conscious of it.

The hope of the world to come becomes clearer and clearer as the biblical story unfolds.[22] The content of that hope is Jesus, the second or last Adam.[23] His first advent introduces the new covenant, and his return will bring the plan of

---

18. See Eugene H. Merrill. "Image of God," in *Dictionary of the Old Testament: Pentateuch*, ed T. Desmond Alexander and David W. Baker (Downers Grove: InterVarsity Press, 2003), 441–45. Merrill concludes, "Humankind is *in* the image of God but also serves *as* the image. Humans have resemblance to God, even if limited, but stand in God's place in the administration of God's creation" (444). See also J. Richard Middleton, *The Liberating Image: The* Imago Dei *in Genesis 1* (Grand Rapids: Brazos, 2005).

19. "Nakedness" is more than lack of clothes. It symbolizes exposure, helplessness, humiliation, shame, guilt, and more. See "Nakedness," in *Dictionary of Biblical Imagery*, ed. Leland Ryken, James C. Wilhoit, and Tremper Longman III (Downers Grove, IL: InterVarsity Press, 1998), 581–82.

20. The ground is cursed "because of you" (Gen. 3:17).

21. Substitutionary atonement is introduced in the beginning of the biblical story of redemption. An animal dies rather than the guilty human. Since in the Mosaic law, the sacrifice is required of the sinner, presumably, the man and woman offered the sacrifice, and God made garments from the animal skins.

22. See Kreider, *God with Us: Exploring God's Interactions with His People throughout the Bible* (Phillipsburg, NJ: P&R, 2014), for an explanation of the unfolding of the story.

23. Jesus is not merely the one who brings that hope to fulfillment; he is the hope itself (1 Peter 1:3–12).

redemption to completion. The apostle Paul draws out the contrast between the two Adams most clearly in the book of Romans. After an extended argument that demonstrates that "all have sinned and fall short of the glory of God" (Rom. 3:23), Paul celebrates the good news that we have peace with God by grace through faith in Jesus Christ (5:1). He then explains that sin and death entered the world through one man, Adam (v. 12). One man's sin brought death to all, but through one man grace comes to all (vv. 15–17). In short, "Just as one trespass resulted in condemnation for all people, so also one righteous act resulted in justification and life for all people. For just as through the disobedience of the one man the many were made sinners, so also through the obedience of the one man the many will be made righteous" (vv. 18–19).[24] Paul concludes, "Where sin increased, grace increased all the more, so that, just as sin reigned in death, so also grace might reign through righteousness to bring eternal life through Jesus Christ our Lord" (v. 21).

But the work of redemption is not yet complete. We wait for the culmination of God's plan. We live in the space between the first and second coming of Christ. Jesus Christ came to earth, was born of the virgin Mary, lived a sinless life, suffered under Pontius Pilate, died, rose from the dead, and is coming back to this earth to make all things new. That newness is the final act of the biblical story (Rev. 21–22). In the meantime, all creation groans in hope of its liberation from bondage to decay (Rom 8:19–21). Those who are united to Christ also groan as we wait (vv. 22–25).

The eternal life that is promised to those who are in Christ is both a quality of life now and a quality and quantity of life to come. Eternal life is not just life that never ends. It is abundant life here and now (John 10:10; 17:3). But the life we experience now is not the fullness of the life to come. We wait for resurrection and glorification. The apostle explains that our hope is rooted in the resurrection of the Savior: "For if we have been united with him in a death like his, we will certainly also be united with him in resurrection like his" (Rom. 6:5). And "if we died with Christ, we believe that we will also live with him" (v. 8). In 1 Corinthians 15, Paul argues that the resurrection of Christ guarantees our resurrection, and he calls this hope the gospel (vv. 1–8). Later, Paul asserts that the work of redemption will be incomplete until death has been defeated (vv. 25–28). So we wait, in hope for that day.

Salvation has a past, present, and future aspect. We are no longer who we were. Our identity is no longer rooted in Adam, but in Christ. Theologian Robert Peterson explains, "When Paul thinks of salvation, he thinks of faith union with Christ. . . . One of the most important consequences of faith union with Christ is that it defines believers. It gives them an identity in relation to

---

24. Clearly, Adam's sin brought death to all humanity, while Christ's obedience brings life only to those who are united with him.

Christ."[25] But we are also not yet who we will be. We are in the process of being transformed into the image of Christ, and that transformation occurs in community, within the body of Christ. One day, we will be new creations, and will live with Christ and his body in a new creation. We are not there yet. But we trust the God who brought the original creation into existence and who has been at work redemptively in this fallen world to complete what he started (Phil. 1:6).

Salvation is by grace alone through faith alone in Christ alone. This salvation is a process that has a beginning. Born in Adam, inheriting the guilt of original sin, we demonstrate that we are sinners from our earliest days. We sin because we are sinners, and our sin continues to demonstrate that reality. Then, through the transformative power of the gospel (Rom. 10:17), through faith in Christ we are transferred from the kingdom of darkness into the kingdom of the Son of God (Col. 1:13). Through the work of the Spirit, we are now united with Christ; we are in him (Rom. 8:1). Graham Cole puts it this way: "Union with Christ by the Spirit . . . is the *central* blessing of the gospel since all the blessings of salvation are found in Christ. Union with Christ by the Spirit relocates the believer from Adam to Christ. Significantly, our union with Christ by the Spirit not only brings us into relationship to God as Father but also to one another as Christ's body."[26]

But the beginning is not the end. For even though we have been born again by the Spirit of God, we continue to live in a fallen world, we continue to demonstrate our sinfulness to ourselves and those around us, and, eventually, we die. If the wages of sin is death (6:23), death is proof that we are sinners. But death is not the end. Because Jesus is alive, we too shall live (1 Cor. 15). If we were united with him in his death and burial, we shall also be united with him in resurrection (Rom. 6:5–8; 8:11).

WHAT ARE THE PRACTICAL IMPLICATIONS OF OUR IDENTITY "IN CHRIST"?

Numerous practical implications flow from our having been united with Christ by the Spirit. Our redemption is not yet complete. We were born in Adam "by nature deserving of wrath" (Eph. 2:3). But now, only because of God's grace, we are "raised up with Christ and seated with him in the heavenly realms in Christ Jesus" (v. 6). Clearly "seated with him in the heavenly realms" is not our present experience. As I write this, it is August in Dallas, where temperatures hover around one hundred degrees Fahrenheit and plants, pets, and people struggle to find relief from the heat. I love this city and am grateful to live here, but it is not heaven; it is not the new creation. I've recently lost two long-term colleagues and friends, watched a close friend's marriage dissolve, and prayed fervently for a sick infant—who died

---

25. Peterson, *Salvation Applied by the Spirit*, 413–14.
26. Graham A. Cole, *He Who Gives Life: The Doctrine of the Holy Spirit*, Foundations of Evangelical Theology (Wheaton, IL: Crossway, 2007), 240–41.

just days after birth. We live in a fallen world, and we see constant and graphic reminders of its brokenness, in small and big ways. We do not live in the heavenly realms or in the new creation. Yet. In this text in Ephesians, Paul is not describing our location, but our inheritance. Because we are "in Christ" we can be assured that where he is we will be also, in the age to come (John 14:1–3). We are citizens of heaven, and we are waiting for our Savior to come back to earth for us. Then he, "by the power that enables him to bring everything under his control, will transform our lowly bodies so that they will be like his glorious body" (Phil. 3:21).

To be "in Christ" does not mean that we no longer sin. As fallen creatures who struggle with the temptations and patterns of behavior and thinking that characterize life in a fallen world, we continue to sin. The fact that we are dying and one day will die is the ultimate proof that we are still sinners. The apostle Paul's testimony is ours as well: "Here is a trustworthy saying that deserves full acceptance: Christ Jesus came into the world to save sinners—of whom I am the worst. But for that very reason I was shown mercy so that in me, the worst of sinners, Christ Jesus might display his immense patience as an example for those who would believe in him and receive eternal life" (1 Tim. 1:15–16). We are all sinners, being saved by grace through faith, waiting for the day of resurrection and the new creation. The new creation has come, through the indwelling Spirit (2 Cor. 5:17), but is not yet here in its fullness.

"Union with Christ" is a comprehensive descriptor; it is not merely one of our identities. But to be a Christian also does not deny all the other aspects of our identity. I remain a White, heterosexual male who is a son, father, and grandfather. None of those identities disappeared when I became a Christian, nor does the fact that I am a Christian mean that I am no longer broken and fallen. All of my desires are corrupted. All of my inclinations are self-centered, self-protective, and self-promoting. All of my decisions are rooted in my selfishness. And all the aspects of my identity need to be redeemed.

The aspects of our identity are not hierarchical. In short, we are a complex unity of all of our attributes and characteristics. All of them are broken, tainted by sin, and in need of redemption. To admit I am a sinner is not to deny Christ's work of redemption; it is simply to confess that sinfulness is part of who I currently am, and not who I will be in the new creation. It is not negative or pessimistic to acknowledge my sinfulness. Rather, such honesty of brokenness and the need of redemption enhances hope in the resurrection, in the world to come, when all will be made new.

And God is at work in those who are in Christ, redeeming the whole person, not just the parts. When the work of redemption is complete, the whole person will be made new. Then we will love God completely (Mark 12:30; Luke 10:27). Until then, our hearts are not fully devoted to him, our desires are motivated by selfishness, and our wills tend to be bent in other directions than following Christ.

And as I mentioned earlier, our identity "in Christ" is not primarily individual. It is corporate. We are each members of the body of Christ, one body made up of many members (1 Cor. 12). Sanctification—or growth in holiness—is not ultimately about me, but focused on helping the body grow to maturity. In the biblical metaphors, each Christian is part of a body (1 Cor. 12), participating in an agricultural enterprise (3:5–9), and on the jobsite of a building project (vv. 10–14). And in each of these, the focus cannot be terminated on the individual. Rather, Paul explains, by "speaking the truth in love, we will grow to become in every respect the mature body of him who is the head, that is Christ" (Eph. 4:15). Our goal must be the edification, the building up, of the body. That said, the individual is still important. After all, the health of the body is dependent on the health of each part. But the parts of the body have a more holistic goal, the health of the whole.

Being "in Christ" does not mean we have received our inheritance—yet. That God "has blessed us in the heavenly realms with every spiritual blessing in Christ" (1:3) does not mean that we have already received those blessings. They are promised, and the promise is sure. But the blessings are in heaven. Those blessings are Christ himself. We have received the Holy Spirit who is not the blessing, Jesus is. The Spirit is a deposit or down payment on the inheritance (1:13–14; cf. 2 Cor. 1:22). The Holy Spirit is the firstfruit of the harvest, not the complete harvest (Rom. 8:22–25). Our inheritance "can never perish, spoil or fade. . . . [It] is kept in heaven" (1 Peter 1:4). Because God will complete what he has started (Phil. 1:6), we have confidence to wait in hope. And yet, as Cole explains, "The Spirit brings something of the future that God has in store for his people into our lives in the here and now."[27] The present experience of the Spirit intensifies our longing for what is to come and is a foretaste of that inheritance.[28]

CONCLUSION

Through faith in Jesus we have hope. In fact, he himself is the content of our hope. We are "in him" now, but our present experience is not the end; we look forward to the completion of the work of redemption. Our Savior has been here, and he is coming back. When we see him, we will be like him (1 John 3:2). The dead will be resurrected, and the living, glorified (1 Thess. 4:14–17). We have received the Spirit as a foretaste of that living hope; the Spirit is not the hope.

Our identity is in Christ. Our hope is in Christ. Our destiny is in Christ. Our past, present, and future is in Christ. One day, all will be made new, in Christ. Until that day, we walk by faith in hope empowered by the love of our Savior because "we know that the whole creation has been groaning as in the pains of childbirth right up to the present time. Not only so, but we ourselves, who have the firstfruits of the Spirit, groan inwardly as we wait eagerly for our adoption to sonship, the redemption of our bodies. For in this hope we were saved" (Rom. 8:22–24).

---

27. Cole, *He Who Gives Life*, 238–39.
28. I believe this is the way to understand 2 Cor. 5:17. We have not yet been made new creations, but the future has invaded the present in the work of the Spirit.

FOR DISCUSSION

1. What are some implications of seeing identity as holistic rather than hierarchical? How could one choose to grow in areas of weakness and flourish in areas of strength while retaining a holistic understanding of the aspects of identity?

2. The promise of a new creation, in which all the effects of sin are removed, is the basis of the Christian hope. One day, our hope of union with Christ will be realized on this earth. How does the recognition of this hope have an impact on the way you live your life in a fallen world?

3. Paul uses various corporate metaphors to describe our spiritual identity; for example, body (1 Cor. 12), household (1 Tim. 3:14–15), family (Eph. 1:5), building (2:21–22), temple (vv. 21–22), and nation (v. 19). Such pictures are at odds with the overwhelmingly individualistic thinking of the culture in North America. How does this corporate emphasis affect the practice of spiritual growth? How can Christians change the church culture, especially the tendency of the church in North America to adopt the individualism of the subcultures in which we live?

FOR FURTHER READING

Cole, Graham A. *He Who Gives Life: The Doctrine of the Holy Spirit.* Foundations of Evangelical Theology. Wheaton, IL: Crossway, 2007.

Lints, Richard, Michael S. Horton, and Mark R. Talbot, eds. *Personal Identity in Theological Perspective.* Grand Rapids: Eerdmans, 2006.

Peterson, Robert A. *Salvation Applied by the Spirit: Union with Christ.* Wheaton, IL: Crossway, 2014.

C H A P T E R   3

SEXUALITIES IN THE FIRST-CENTURY WORLD: A SURVEY OF RELEVANT TOPICS

JOSEPH D. FANTIN

INTRODUCTION

The Bible was written during different times and, for most of us, in a different geographical space from the world we inhabit today. Whether due to lack of conveniences such as cell phones, televisions, and automobiles or the presence of puzzling customs such as polygamy (Gen. 16:3; 29:27–28; Judg. 8:30; 1 Kings 11:3), head coverings (1 Cor. 11:2–16), or kiss greetings (1 Cor. 16:20; 2 Cor. 13:12; 1 Thess. 5:26; 1 Peter 5:14), the modern reader soon realizes that he or she is at a disadvantage when trying to understand aspects of the biblical text. When encountering such "foreign" concepts and practices, the Bible student will often consult commentaries or other authoritative sources, including teachers, for explanation.

Although the ancient customs and ideas are often initially incomprehensible to the modern reader, their foreignness makes them easily recognizable. As a result, understanding is usually sought quickly. More difficult and problematic for a correct understanding of the Bible are practices that we share with the ancient world but that somewhat or significantly differ from those practiced by the ancients. Thus we unknowingly import our ideas into the ancient practice.

For example, modern readers assume adoption is a practice whereby a couple adopts a baby or young child (and in some cases an older child) in order to nurture that individual and raise him or her as their own. But the childless (probably mainly wealthy) Romans adopted adults who could care for them in their old age and inherit their property.[1] There is certainly overlap between the two approaches to adoption, but Roman adoption significantly differed from what is practiced today. A more accurate understanding of Roman adoption will help today's reader better understand the adoption passages in the Pauline corpus (Rom. 8:15, 23; 9:4; Gal. 4:5; Eph. 1:5).[2]

Familiar practices and concepts such as marriage, family, and sexuality are also ripe for misunderstanding. Every culture has its own traditions and practices. One need only look at the modern world, where in some cultures brides and grooms generally choose one another, in contrast with other cultures that practice arranged marriages. It is natural for modern biblical interpreters to consider their own customs when they read about practices in the ancient world.

The purpose of this essay is to make the reader aware of the significant differences in the area of sexuality between our culture and that of the Bible's. This article will proceed as follows. First, I will briefly cover select aspects of ancient marriage and family life,[3] both to illustrate differences between "then" and "now" and to provide some overall general context. Second, in light of the cultural context, the article will examine sexuality in the first century.

PRELIMINARY CONSIDERATIONS

Five preliminary remarks are necessary before proceeding. First, my comments are primarily directed at those whose experiences are shaped by modern Western ideas. In the area of marriage and family, some non-Western cultures

---

1. Hugh Lindsay, *Adoption in the Roman World* (Cambridge: Cambridge University Press, 2009), 21–22, 25, 28, 41, 97–122; Christiane Kunst, *Römische Adoption: Zur Strategie einer Familienorganisation*, Frankfurter althistorische Beiträge (Hennef, Germany: Marthe Clauss, 2005), 15. The adopted person took on all the legal rights and responsibilities of a natural child (Jane F. Gardner, *Family and* Familia *in Roman Law and Life* [Oxford: Clarendon, 1998], 114–26). I wish to thank Jay Smith for carefully reading a draft of this article and providing me with helpful feedback.

2. See for example Erin M. Heim, *Adoption in Galatians and Romans: Contemporary Metaphor Theories and the Pauline* Huiothesia *Metaphors*, Biblical Interpretation Series (Leiden: Brill, 2017); Robert Brian Lewis, *Paul's "Spirit of Adoption" in Its Roman Imperial Context*, Library of New Testament Studies (London: T&T Clark, 2016); Bradley R. Trick, *Abrahamic Descent, Testamentary Adoption, and the Law in Galatians: Differentiating Abraham's Sons, Seed, and Children of Promise*, Supplements to Novum Testamentum (Leiden: Brill, 2016); S. M. Baugh, *Ephesians*, Evangelical Exegetical Commentary (Bellingham, WA: Lexham, 2016), 84–88.

3. My research on this topic has led me to the conclusion that sexuality and sexual activity in the ancient world were not necessarily the domain of the topic of family. Sex and sexual activity were, of course, necessary for establishing and continuing families, but if we restrict ourselves to thinking of them only in this way, our understanding will be insufficient. Although an absolute statement on the classification of sexuality cannot be sustained (pleasure and relational aspects cannot be excluded), in general, the purpose of sexual activity in the family was procreation. Especially with reference to males, sexual activity could involve socially acceptable expressions outside of marriage. Such activity will be discussed further below.

have more in common with the ancient world. However, such readers are also in danger of reading their own culture back into the ancient world. No modern culture is exactly like that of the ancient biblical cultures. There will be similarities with the ancient world, but these points of connection will be different for each modern culture. This is true for marriage and the family.[4] As we will see, however, ancient sexual practices significantly differed from those of any modern culture of which I am aware.

Second, my comments must be selective. Concerning marriage, I will highlight areas I consider most significant for biblical interpretation, but my comments will not be exhaustive. I hope to demonstrate that differences exist, and that one may need to do further research on specific areas as necessary. My treatment of sexuality will be more comprehensive but will, nevertheless, provide only an introduction to the topic.[5]

---

4. For further information on marriage and the family see David L. Balch and Carolyn Osiek, eds., *Early Christian Families in Context: An Interdisciplinary Dialogue*, Religion, Marriage, and Family (Grand Rapids: Eerdmans, 2003); Gardner, *Family and* Familia; Carolyn Osiek and David L. Balch, eds., *Families in the New Testament World: Households and House Churches*, The Family, Religion, and Culture (Louisville: Westminster John Knox, 1997); Beryl Rawson, ed., *A Companion to Families in the Greek and Roman Worlds*, Blackwell Companions to the Ancient World (Chichester, UK: Wiley-Blackwell, 2011); Rawson, ed., *Marriage, Divorce, and Children in Ancient Rome* (Oxford: Oxford University Press, 1991); Susan Treggiari, *Roman Marriage: Iusti Coniuges from the Time of Cicero to the Time of Ulpian* (Oxford: Oxford University Press, 1991).

5. For an excellent in-depth overview of Greek and Roman sexuality, see Marilyn B. Skinner, *Sexuality in Greek and Roman Culture*, 2nd ed. (London: Wiley-Blackwell, 2014). For a helpful and up-to-date introduction to various topics on sexuality, see Thomas K. Hubbard, ed., *A Companion to Greek and Roman Sexualities*, Blackwell Companions to the Ancient World (Chichester, UK: Wiley-Blackwell, 2014). For articles furthering discussion, see Mark Masterson, Nancy Sorkin Rabinowitz, and James Robson, eds., *Sex in Antiquity: Exploring Gender and Sexuality in the Ancient World*, Rewriting Antiquity (New York: Routledge, 2015). A number of ancient primary sources are collected in Jennifer Larson, ed., *Greek and Roman Sexualities: A Sourcebook*, Bloomsbury Sources in Ancient History (London: Bloomsbury, 2012). Concerning Jewish (with overlap in Greek and Roman and including New Testament) sexuality, unsurpassed for depth and thoroughness is the five-volume series by William Loader called, Attitudes towards Sexuality in Judaism and Christianity in the Hellenistic and Greco-Roman Era (*Enoch, Levi, and Jubilees on Sexuality: Attitudes towards Sexuality in the Early Enoch Literature, the Aramaic Levi Document, and the Book of Jubilees* [Grand Rapids: Eerdmans, 2007]; *The Dead Sea Scrolls on Sexuality: Attitudes towards Sexuality in Sectarian and Related Literature at Qumran* [Grand Rapids: Eerdmans, 2009]; *The Pseudepigrapha on Sexuality: Attitudes towards Sexuality in Apocalypses, Testaments, Legends, Wisdom, and Related Literature* [Grand Rapids: Eerdmans, 2011]; *Philo, Josephus, and the Testaments on Sexuality: Attitudes towards Sexuality in the Writings of Philo and Josephus and in the Testaments of the Twelve Patriarchs* [Grand Rapids: Eerdmans, 2011]; *The New Testament on Sexuality* [Grand Rapids: Eerdmans, 2012]). Loader's work is comprehensive. It surveys the ancient Jewish literature and comments on many passages. Its content is much broader than a narrow discussion of sexuality. Much more manageable is Loader's *Making Sense of Sex: Attitudes towards*

Third, my main focus is on the first-century world in which the New Testament was written. Although the Old Testament has much of value to say on the topic of sexuality, customs are less accessible, and Old Testament teaching and application are assumed in the first-century context. In other words, the New Testament is using the Old Testament as a primary source on such issues. Further, the modern church is building off of the New Testament.

When approaching the New Testament, it is common to think of three ethnic groups: Jews, Greeks, and Romans. There are some differences between these groups. When one considers Greeks, he or she is usually assuming classical Greeks represented by the vast amount of literature from Athens in the fifth to fourth centuries BC. Such peoples and practices are not those that interest us, however. Our Jewish focus is on the first-century Jews living in Israel and throughout the Roman world. Thus the Greeks, Jews, and Romans under consideration here are those under Roman rule in the first century AD. Although differences exist, there are considerable similarities in the general areas I am discussing here. Jews certainly were more restrictive in their sexual practices than many of their neighbors, but these Jews still would have been aware of much of what was happening around them. They were Jews, but they were Roman Jews. A sharp distinction between Jews and their Roman neighbors that fails to recognize how Hellenized or Romanized the Jews were cannot be sustained.[6] The classical Greeks were more sexually permissive from our perspective than their Roman and Jewish counterparts. It is likely, however, that they shared many of the values of the wider Roman world during the first century. Thus it is this wider Roman perspective (with specific adjustments made as necessary for Jews and Greeks) that will be my area of inquiry.

Fourth, although there is a wealth of primary material for this period, there is much we do not know. Certainly, there were differences in time and

---

Sexuality in Early Jewish and Christian Literature (Grand Rapids: Eerdmans, 2013), which also surveys this material. Loader also includes an excellent overview of Jewish and Greco-Roman sexualities in separate chapters in *The New Testament on Sexuality*, 3–108. Of interest for Old Testament and ancient Mesopotamian sexuality is Gwendolyn Leick, *Sex and Eroticism in Mesopotamian Literature* (London: Routledge, 1994); and Martii Nissinen, *Homoeroticism in the Biblical World: A Historical Perspective*, trans. Kirsi Stjerna (Minneapolis: Fortress, 1998), 1–56. For a broad collection of texts on marriage and sexuality from the early church, see David G. Hunter, ed., *Marriage and Sexuality in Early Christianity*, Ad Fontes: Early Christian Texts (Minneapolis: Fortress, 2018). K. J. Dover's 1978 work on Greek homosexuality was groundbreaking for the study of ancient sexuality in general (*Greek Homosexuality* [Cambridge, MA: Harvard University Press, 1978; updated with a new postscript, 1989]). Further, influential to this discussion is Michel Foucault's three-volume *The History of Sexuality* (repr., New York: Vintage, 1978–1990). However, this is not the place to interact directly with his contribution.

6. See the introduction and articles in Troels Engberg-Pedersen, ed., *Paul beyond the Judaism/Hellenism Divide* (Louisville: Westminster John Knox, 2001). However, differences still existed. See Margaret Williams, "The Jewish Family in Judaea From Pompey to Hadrian—The Limits of Romanization," in *The Roman Family in the Empire: Rome, Italy, and Beyond*, ed. Michele George (Oxford: Oxford University Press, 2005), 159–82.

place on these issues. There is no single "sexuality" for the period under consideration. Although sensitivity to such factors will be assumed, the nature of our sources does not always allow for pinpoint specificity. Further, our sources mainly come from the elite segment of society. Nevertheless, with the cautious use of our sources, and sensitivity to source purpose, bias, time, and provenance, we can carefully create a picture of sexuality within the world of the New Testament.[7] Additionally, based on our sources, my reconstruction is attempting to portray a common description of sexuality. As with any societal practice, there are almost always dissenting voices. I will note these on occasion. Nevertheless, it is the overall picture that is important. Differing voices add color, but a lengthy, nuanced study cannot be presented here. One cannot fit all sexual expressions into a single model. The descriptions in this article are intended to be general, and I make no claim that they represent all first-century sexual activity.[8]

Finally, my purpose is descriptive. My desire is to provide a glimpse into the ancient context. And this glimpse does not demand that such practices be viewed in any sense as correct or incorrect. Thus I will attempt to be rather objective and, in almost all cases, avoid judgment. There may be a place for judgment; it is not here. It is only by describing these practices on their own terms that we can we hope to understand them.

SELECT ASPECTS OF ANCIENT MARRIAGE

Although the topic is quite familiar to modern readers, marriage looked quite different in the first century than it does today. It will be helpful to briefly explore select differences in Roman marriage that will help reveal this reality to the modern reader. Such an exploration is intended to provide context for discussion below and does not imply (as noted above) that sexuality and sexual activity were restricted to marriage in the ancient world.

Arranged Marriages

As is still true in many traditional modern cultures, Roman marriages were often the result of an agreement between the bride's father and either the

---

7. For the value of different types of sources, see F. Gerald Downing, "*A bas les aristo*: The Relevance of Higher Literature for the Understanding of the Earliest Christian Writing," *Novum Testamentum* 30 (1988): 212–30; Joseph D. Fantin, "Background Studies: Grounding the Text in Reality," in *Interpreting the New Testament Text: Introduction to the Art and Science of Exegesis*, ed. Darrell L. Bock and Buist M. Fanning (Wheaton, IL: Crossway, 2006), 167–96; and Justin J. Meggitt, "Sources: Use, Abuse, Neglect; The Importance of Ancient Popular Culture," in *Christianity at Corinth: The Quest for the Pauline Churches*, ed. Edward Adams and David G. Horrell (Louisville: Westminster John Knox, 2004), 241–53.
8. See the helpful caution in Rebecca Langlands, *Sexual Morality in Ancient Rome* (Cambridge: Cambridge University Press, 2006), 13–17.

groom's father or the groom himself.[9] However, the fathers' wives were often the ones who actually arranged everything (without legal authority),[10] and the consent of all parties was expected and legally essential. (What constitutes "consent" is unclear; also, to what extent that such "consent" gave any power or choice in the matter to brides is uncertain.)[11] Marriages allied families together.[12] These marriages often were intended to benefit the larger families involved.[13] The well-being and compatibility of the marriage partners were not the main concern. Of course, a happy marriage would have been desired, but it was not the deciding factor.

Marriage Age

In first-century marriages, it was common for the husband to be much older than the bride. Girls could marry at twelve.[14] Nevertheless, women usually married after fifteen, and men after twenty-five.[15] There are many reasons for this,

9.   Suzanne Dixon, *The Roman Family*, Ancient Society and History (Baltimore: Johns Hopkins University Press, 1992), 47; Judith Evans Grubbs, "Parent-Child Conflict in the Roman Family: The Evidence of the Code of Justinian," in *The Roman Family in the Empire: Rome, Italy, and Beyond*, ed. Michele George (Oxford: Oxford University Press, 2005), 99–100. Concerning the significance of the wedding ceremony, see Karen K. Hersch, *The Roman Wedding: Ritual and Meaning in Antiquity* (Cambridge: Cambridge University Press, 2010).

10. Dixon, *The Roman Family*, 36, 47.

11. Treggiari, *Roman Marriage*, 16, 54, 83, 147, 170–80; Grubbs, "Parent-Child Conflict," 100. In the Roman context, because continual mutual consent was necessary, divorce was always an option and could be initiated by either party (Susan Treggiari, "Divorce Roman Style: How Easy and How Frequent Was It?," in Rawson, *Marriage, Divorce, and Children*, 31–46).

12. Concerning the Roman aristocracy, Mireille Corbier states, "marriage was not for sex but for alliance" ("Divorce and Adoption as Roman Familial Strategies (*Le divorce et l'adoption 'en plus*)," in Rawson, *Marriage, Divorce, and Children*, 51). As will be discussed below, for the vast majority of Romans, there was another more important purpose for marriage. Corbier's statement is also likely hyperbolic. She is summarizing her view of the aristocratic reaction to a passage in Tacitus (early second century AD). Also, I note the marriage of Caesar's daughter and Pompey below. Marriage can also ally nations. See Solomon's marriage to Pharaoh's daughter (1 Kings 3:1). It is likely many of his marriages served this purpose (1 Kings 11:1–3).

13. Loader, *Making Sense of Sex*, 40.

14. Treggiari, *Roman Marriage*, 39; Allison Glazebrook and Kelly Olson, "Greek and Roman Marriage," in Hubbard, *Companion*, 75.

15. Treggiari, *Roman Marriage*, 400. Of course, local customs could affect the size of this age gap. Further, the age gap between marriage partners is more significant when one considers that many Romans did not survive to reach marriageable age. Also, marriage age would be closer when a women married for the second time (Treggiari, *Roman Marriage*, 401). The Jewish situation in Israel was similar. Michael L. Satlow, after discussing the ideal that Jews were supposed to marry early, concludes that in reality the evidence suggests otherwise (*Jewish Marriage in Antiquity* [Princeton, NJ: Princeton University Press, 2001], 106–11). It is likely that Jews in Babylon married earlier than their counterparts

including maximizing the fertility of the bride and the economic establishment of the groom.[16] In rare cases, the age gap could be considerably more. For example, for political reasons Julia, the daughter of Julius Caesar married Pompey, who was six years older than her father.[17]

Authority and the Marriage

Usually the bride entered into the household of the groom, who was often under the authority of his father or the eldest male of the family (the *paterfamilias*).[18] In the first century, the main type of Roman marriage was called "marriage *sine manu*," in which the bride's father maintained the authority over his now married daughter.[19] The authoritative focus of this type of marriage was on the wife's property, but it probably had broader implications. The wife's property was still part of her original family under the authority of her father. If her father was dead, "the wife continued to own, inherit, and bequeath her own property"

---

living in Israel (104–6). Considering sources reflecting life in Israel, Satlow concludes that Jewish men in Israel married around age thirty, and their spouses were ten to fifteen years younger (108–9; followed by Loader in *The New Testament on Sexuality*, 448, and *Making Sense of Sex*, 33). It must be remembered that our sources are limited; there was significant variety in practice; and we are unsure to what extent our evidence reflects the non-elite. Satlow's marital age of thirty is challenged by Catherine Hezser, Review of *Jewish Marriage in Antiquity* by Michael L. Satlow, *Journal of Jewish Studies* 55, no. 1 (Spring 2004): 179. We may be unable to know the actual average age of Jewish couples at the time of marriage (the same can be said of all ancient marriage statistics); however, it is almost certain that the male was older, and the age gap could be significant. Étan Levine notes that, based on the order of creation in Gen. 2 and Greek influence, many Hellenistic Jews considered a man marrying an older woman as "against nature" (*Marital Relations in Ancient Judaism*, Beihefte zur Zeitschrift für Altorientalische und Biblische Rechtsgeschichte [Wiesbaden: Harrassowitz, 2009], 248; see also Philo, *Questions and Answers on Genesis 1* 27 [mid first century AD]).

16. Treggiari, *Roman Marriage*, 400.
17. Adrian Goldsworthy, *Caesar: The Life of a Colossus* (2006; repr., London: Phoenix, 2007), 212.
18. Gardner, *Family and* Familia, 1–2, 6. For the strict earlier Roman period that continued in some form, see Treggiari, *Roman Marriage*, 15–16.
19. Glazebrook and Olson, "Greek and Roman Marriage," 78; Treggiari, *Roman Marriage*, 32–33. There were two types of marriage in ancient Rome: "marriage *sine manu*" and "marriage *cum manu*." The latter was probably older, and is the type of marriage most familiar to our modern world. In marriage *cum manu*, the authority or power (*potestas*) over the bride is transferred to the husband, and she becomes part of his household. In marriage *sine manu*, the authority or power (*potestas*) over the bride remained with her father, and she remained part of her birth family. The husband had no rights to the wife's property, and she could still inherit from her birth family (Glazebrook and Olson, "Greek and Roman Marriage," 78; for a detailed discussion of these two types of marriage, see Treggiari, *Roman Marriage*, 16–36). It is possible that marriage *cum manu* stopped being practiced by the end of the period of the republic (31 BC) or earlier (Glazebrook and Olson, "Greek and Roman Marriage," 78). Thus, for the New Testament period, marriage *sine manu* is most relevant.

through a "financial guardian."[20] Marriage *sine manu* did not mean that the wife was not subject to the household rules of her new family. She was not some type of independent individual freelancing in the new household. However, one wonders what this type of external authority did to the dynamics in the wife's new household. It is difficult to assume it had no effect. For example, the reality that a wife's father could force a divorce and have his daughter marry another must have had some relational consequences.[21] Essentially, from the Roman legal perspective, "she was related by lineage neither to her husband nor her children, but 'remained' in her natal family."[22]

It is difficult to know whether Jews practiced *sine manu* marriage, and if so, how prominent it was. The marriage example in Genesis 2:24[23] was quite influential in Jewish thinking, which would suggest that *sine manu* marriage was not practiced.[24] However, it may have been attractive to Jews interested in their social status. Whether they practiced *sine manu* marriage, it is likely that they were aware of it. Further, it is difficult to know how such a marriage arrangement, despite being the "main form" of marriage in the first century, was practiced among the lower classes in the empire. In any case, it would have been an option for all or most of the original intended audience (Jew and gentile) of the New Testament.[25]

Purpose of Marriage and Use of Sex

Although other purposes existed, the main purpose of marriage was procreation.[26] In fact, debates within Judaism and the wider world questioned whether one

---

20. Glazebrook and Olson, "Greek and Roman Marriage," 78.
21. For further practical implications of marriage *sine manu*, see Lynn H. Cohick, *Women in the World of the Earliest Christians: Illuminating Ancient Ways of Life* (Grand Rapids: Baker Academic, 2009), 100–101.
22. Glazebrook and Olson, "Greek and Roman Marriage," 78.
23. "Therefore a man leaves his father and his mother and clings to his wife, and they become one flesh" (NRSV).
24. See Loader, *Making Sense of Sex*, 10–11, 33.
25. It is uncertain just how practical it would have been for a father from a family of little means to remove his daughter from her new household. Nevertheless, the option was probably there. One wonders if Paul's instruction in Eph. 5:21–33 is in part an argument intended for gentiles to reject the *sine manu* marriage in favor of the Gen. 2 model.
26. Treggiari, *Roman Marriage*, 11; Treggiari, "Marriage and Family in Roman Society," in *Marriage and Family in the Biblical World*, ed. Ken M. Campbell (Downers Grove, IL: InterVarsity Press, 2003), 132–33; Beryl Rawson, "The Roman Family," in *The Family in Ancient Rome*, ed. Beryl Rawson (Ithaca, NY: Cornell University Press, 1986), 15. For Jews, see Josephus, *Against Apion* 2.199 (written early second century AD). The Stoic first-century Roman writer Musonius Rufus argues against this common assumption and believes that the relational aspect is more important (*What Is the Chief End of Marriage?* 13a, 13b). Further, the second-century Plutarch's *Advice to the Bride and Groom* contains much in the way of relational encouragement (e.g., 3, 15, 29). See also, Dixon, *The Roman Family*, 83–85.

should have sex for enjoyment.[27] The mid first-century-AD Jewish author Philo maintained that it was wrong to marry a woman who was unable to have children, because this would suggest the purpose of the marriage was pleasure.[28]

Adultery

Adultery was a much more limited concept in the ancient Roman world than it is today. For a man, it generally meant having relations with a married woman.[29] However, if a married man chose to have sex with his slaves or use a prostitute, such actions were not considered adultery.[30] In contrast, married women did not have any options to fulfill their sexual desires outside of marriage. Nevertheless, some Romans advocated for men restricting sexual activity to their spouses as the ideal.[31] Such a definition of adultery stems from an ancient mind-set in which women belonged to men (father or husband).[32] In both Jewish and the wider culture, an adulterous wife must be divorced.[33] Of course, Jews and Christians had other instruction that prohibited sexual activity outside of marriage.[34] The ancient notion of adultery may be why Paul uses a theological argument against prostitution with the Corinthians (1 Cor. 6:15–20) and does not simply quote the seventh commandment.

The Double Standard

Men could "use" prostitutes and slaves; women could have sex only with their husbands. This certainly is a double standard.[35] However, given Roman society's

---

27. See Philo, *On the Creation* 151–52; *On Special Laws* 3.34 (mid first century AD); implied in Josephus, *Against Apion* 2.199 (written very early second century AD). It may not be pleasure itself that is the problem, but the focus and the potential for excess (Loader, *Making Sense of Sex*, 56–58, 111, 128–31).
28. Philo, *On Special Laws* 3.34.
29. Treggiari, *Roman Marriage*, 264; Glazebrook and Olson, "Greek and Roman Marriage," 79.
30. See Plutarch, *Advice to the Bride and Groom* 16 (early second century AD). Here Plutarch goes so far as to suggest that a bride should not be angry if her husband participates in tasteless sexual acts with another woman. This is because her husband is showing respect for her by not subjecting her to such activity.
31. Musonius Rufus, *On Sexual Indulgence* 5–8 (mid-first century AD).
32. Loader, *Making Sense of Sex*, 63–64.
33. Loader, *Making Sense of Sex*, 64–65. This can be a complex situation (Treggiari, *Roman Marriage*, 285–90).
34. Concerning Second Temple Judaism, see David W. Chapman, "Marriage and Family in Second Temple Judaism," in Campbell, *Marriage and Family*, 220.
35. Treggiari, *Roman Marriage*, 264, 299–309. The "he may but she may not" is certainly a double standard by modern standards. Treggiari seems to consider this to be the case for the ancient world as well. I would agree but must acknowledge that given the values of ancient Rome (in part as described below) and the means by which women attained honor, we do not know whether or to what extent women in that day would have been as offended by it. It certainly varied. In one example, a husband's fidelity was explicitly written into a marriage contract (Tebtunis Papyri 104 [92 BC]; Bernard P. Grenfell, Arthur S. Hunt, and J. Gilbart Smyly, eds., *The Tebtunis Papyri*, part 1 [London: Henry Frowde, 1902], 451–52). However, such an agreement is probably the exception to the

values, although this double standard is unacceptable, it is understandable. The purpose of sex was to have legitimate children. If a woman had sex outside of her marriage, the legitimacy of any children can be put into doubt.[36] No such consequences would result if the husband had relations with a prostitute or slave. Also, as honor was an important aspect of Roman society (this will be briefly addressed below as well),[37] one of the chief virtues a matron could possess was chastity (*pudicitia*).[38] Again, this reality does not make the double standard acceptable. It is the result of rules essentially being made by men for men.[39]

Implications

It is worth pausing and reflecting on the implications of what has been suggested above. The husband-and-wife relationship could be one in which the couple knew very little about one another, shared few or no interests, and had no real relationship. Even sex was not necessarily the exclusive domain of marriage, nor was it necessarily intended to be fulfilling.

It is difficult to know exactly how much of this reality reflects Jewish customs in the first century. Jews were under Roman law, and all of the above practices could reflect what they would have experienced, or at least of which

---

standard. My description is only a cultural observation and not intended to condone the practice. Of course, the reality of the ancient double standard is affirmed when we acknowledge that the values and customs were primarily created and established by men. Thus the statement about there being a double standard is true (this is why it appears so in the text above) but needs some measure of qualification and perspective (which is not intended to diminish the reality of a double standard). Interestingly, Treggiari tentatively suggests that Roman society cannot be blamed for the double standard, but rather evolution and biology are the culprits (*Roman Marriage*, 319). I think she lets the Romans (and other societies) off the hook too easily.

36. Catharine Edwards, *The Politics of Immorality in Ancient Rome* (Cambridge: Cambridge University Press, 1993), 49; Loader, *Making Sense of Sex*, 63.

37. Langlands, *Sexual Morality*, 18.

38. Concerning Seneca's view (mid first century AD), see Liz Gloyn, *The Ethics of the Family in Seneca* (Cambridge: Cambridge University Press, 2017), 91. The translation "chastity" does not satisfactorily translate the Latin term *pudicitia*. It also includes "modesty" and other nuances (Gloyn, *Ethics of the Family*, 89–94). However, see Kirk Ormand, *Controlling Desires: Sexuality in Ancient Greece and Rome*, Praeger Series on the Ancient World (Westport, CN: Praeger, 2009), 137. *Pudicitia* was a significant concept in the Roman world and went beyond personal virtue. It was manifested as a goddess and was an object of worship (Langlands, *Sexual Morality*, 37–77).

39. The sixth-century-BC example of Lucretia as written about by the first-century-BC historian Livy (and others) is revealing. It sheds light on the male-focused values of the Romans. Lucretia was raped by an Etruscan leader's son. Rather than live in shame, Lucretia committed suicide (Livy, *History of Rome* 1.58). This sparked the Roman revolution that led to the republic. Lucretia was viewed as a model, and was highly praised by the Romans throughout their history. In reality, however, she was a victim twice: once through rape, and second through a society (but not her father or husband) that demanded an innocent woman take her life to maintain her honor.

they were aware. A more appropriate question may be, Do these practices reflect the vast majority of poorer people in the empire whose voices are virtually silent? As with all contextual information, caution relative to the confidence we have in the thoroughness of our sources is appropriate. The general principle that men were older than their brides at the time of marriage is probably accurate; however, poorer people probably did not have the opportunities in which a change of a marriage partner would have been beneficial. It then seems likely that although there were no cultural or legal restrictions to multiple marriages in one's lifetime,[40] the average person married, and that marriage probably lasted until one of the parties died.

ORIENTATION AND SEXUALITY

One of the most surprising differences between modern and first-century concepts of sexuality is the way in which sexual orientation was perceived. The term *orientation* is anachronistic. The ancients were not thinking about the psychology behind desire and/or attraction. Today we assign labels to individuals as heterosexual, homosexual, and bisexual. These words reflect modern notions of desire and/or attraction but often involve lifestyle and other aspects of one's life not reflective of first-century society. Also, as already introduced, for the general population in the Roman world, sex was not the exclusive domain of marriage. Since marriage essentially was for procreation, sexual orientation and preference by modern standards was not as important in marriage as it is in much of the Western world today. Further, even desire and attraction were secondary.

Sex and Culture

Before getting into specifics, it is important to realize that within a culture, sex is not an isolated phenomenon. Rather, sex is linked to and influenced by various social features of a culture. Sex is part of the fabric of a society. Initially, many of these cultural factors seem unrelated to sex. Cultures differ on specifics, but recognizing these features and their relationship to sex will help the student of any specific expression of sexuality to understand it more accurately. Although not exhaustive, a number of cultural features can be described here.

Social Structure

Roman society was strictly structured.[41] A strong hierarchy was in place that

---

40. Romans could marry multiple times in their lifetimes but never have more than one wife at a time (Treggiari, "Marriage and Family," 169). Among Jews in the Second Temple period, polygamy, or more accurately, polygyny, the practice in which a man could have multiple wives (as Old Testament figures such as Abraham, Jacob, David, and Solomon did), was permitted, but was probably practiced only by the wealthy (Loader, *Making Sense of Sex*, 51).

41. On the social structure of Rome during the empire (including the New Testament period), see Géza Alföldy, *The Social History of Rome*, trans. David Braund and Frank Pollock (Totowa, NJ: Barnes and Noble, 1985), 106–56. More generally, see Peter Garnsey and

dictated everything from clothing to whom one could marry or even with whom one could have sex.[42] For example, it was acceptable for higher-class males to have sex with those of lower classes; however, women were restricted in their sexual expression (including but not limited to social hierarchy).[43]

Gender Roles

Gender roles were intended to be strictly adhered to. It was improper for those of one sex to act or function like those of the other sex.[44] Men and women were compelled to do what was socially defined for their roles;[45] crossing gender boundaries was considered improper, and could even be dangerous.[46]

Honor and Shame

The principal value for the relevant cultures of the biblical periods was honor.[47] Honor was to be sought and shame to be avoided.[48]

Richard P. Saller, *The Roman Empire: Economy, Society and Culture* (Berkeley: University of California Press, 1987), 107–25.

42. Skinner, *Sexuality in Greek and Roman Culture*, 256–58

43. Skinner, *Sexuality in Greek and Roman Culture*, 256–58. Ormand, *Controlling Desires*, 164–82.

44. Skinner, *Sexuality in Greek and Roman Culture*, 280–81. Skinner notes two sexes: "man" and "not man." Nevertheless, more generally, there were two sexes based on biology: male and female. The intersex person, one with both male and female genitalia, was uncommon, but demanded specific consideration by the ancients (see Luc Brisson, *Sexual Ambivalence: Androgyny and Hermaphroditism in Graeco-Roman Antiquity*, trans. Janet Lloyd [Berkeley: University of California Press, 2002]). For a particularly Jewish perspective that seems to consider intersex persons as males, see Mishnah Yebamot (m. Yebam.) 8.6.d–e (early second century AD), Tosefta Yebamot (t. Yebam.) 10.2.n–p (early second century AD, a generation after the Mishnah), and commentary in the Jerusalem Talmud Yebamot (y. Yebam.) 8.6.ii.2–iii.2 (completed early fifth century AD) and the Babylonian Talmud Yebamot (b. Yebam.) 83b (8.6.iii.1–iv.1) (completed early sixth century AD). I do not think that this affected the general perception of gender.

45. Due to our sources and the Roman culture, most of this discussion focuses on men. See, e.g., Craig A. Williams, *Roman Homosexuality*, 2nd ed. (Oxford: Oxford University Press, 2010), 137–245.

46. With reference to sex, if a woman penetrated a man, it was feared she could dominate him (Jonathan Walters, "Invading the Roman Body: Manliness and Impenetrability in Roman Thought," in *Roman Sexualities*, ed. Judith P. Hallett and Marilyn B. Skinner [Princeton, NJ: Princeton University Press, 1997], 29–33).

47. Honor and shame are often discussed within a social-scientific approach to the Bible. This method can help one understand the culture of a society. For a brief overview of this method for Old Testament studies, see Philip F. Esler, "Social-Scientific Models in Biblical Interpretation," in *Ancient Israel: The Old Testament in Its Social Context*, ed. Philip F. Esler (London: SCM, 2005), 3–14; and Philip F. Esler and Anselm C. Hagedorn, "Social-Scientific Analysis of the Old Testament," in Esler, *Ancient Israel*, 15–32. On the New Testament period, see Bruce J. Malina, *The New Testament World: Insights from Cultural Anthropology*, 3rd ed. (Louisville: Westminster John Knox, 2001). Specifically on honor and shame, see 27–57.

48. For applications of honor-and-shame insights to the New Testament, see Malina, *New*

Self-Control and Moderation

Self-control and moderation in all things (such as food, drink, sex, and emblems of class) were virtues.[49] If one wanted to shame an opponent, it was common to accuse him or her of some lack of self-control.[50] In fact, it may have even been considered improper to be too attracted to or affectionate toward one's spouse.[51]

Sexual Modesty

Although some Romans wore minimal clothing, people generally were very modest. In contrast to Greeks, who seemed to accept male public nudity,[52] Romans wore clothing that fully covered them.[53] Christopher Hallett notes that the Greek and Latin terms for *nudity* were different. The Greek term γυμνός usually meant fully naked, while the Latin *nudus* often meant "lightly clad."[54] Although in general such an observation appears accurate, conclusions

---

Testament World, 27–57, and David A. deSilva, *Honor, Patronage, Kinship and Purity: Unlocking New Testament Culture* (Downers Grove, IL: InterVarsity Press, 2000), 23–93.

49. Langlands, *Sexual Morality*, 134–37; Skinner, *Sexuality in Greek and Roman Culture*, 258–60. See also Jewish concerns for excess in Sir. 18:30–19:3 (Apocrypha; second century BC).

50. Propaganda suggesting that a rival was excessive in areas such as drink and sex was common. Examples of this tactic include Suetonius, *Augustus* 69, and Plutarch, *Pompey* 2 (both early second century AD). See Edwards, *Politics of Immorality*, 47. Suetonius uses such a tactic in describing emperors before his time. He catalogues Tiberius's sexual deviance (*Tiberius* 41–45) and describes various types of excesses associated with Nero (*Nero* 26–31). Such statements fuel the modern notion that the Romans were drunkards and sexually debauched. Whether these statements are accurate is uncertain; however, given their purposes, it is wise to be cautious when using them to understand individuals specifically and Roman society generally.

51. See the OT pseudepigraphal book Pseudo-Phocylides 193 (first century BC to first century AD). Plutarch (early second century BC) records Cato's example of expelling a man from the senate for kissing his wife in front of his daughter (*Advice to the Bride and Groom* 13). Although extreme, this reveals the value of modesty. Another extreme example is when the author of the OT apocryphal book Sirach (second century BC) accuses Solomon of being controlled by his wives (Sir. 47:19–21). The principle is clear. People must not allow their passion for anything to control them. Given the value of self-control and moderation, it is even considered possible that one may have too much sex with one's own spouse.

52. Christopher H. Hallett, *The Roman Nude: Heroic Portrait Statuary 200 BC–AD 300*, Oxford Studies in Ancient Culture and Representation (Oxford: Oxford University Press, 2005), 6–8, 61. This was primarily a male phenomenon; women were expected to be fully clothed (6–8).

53. Hallett, *The Roman Nude*, 61.

54. While the first definition of γυμνός in Henry George Liddell et al., eds., *A Greek-English Lexicon*, 9th ed. (Oxford: Clarendon, 1940), 362–63; supplement, 80, is "naked" or "unclad," it can also mean "lightly clad" or "in the undergarment only." Hallett suggests that the later use is rare (*The Roman Nude*, 61) with support (61n1). The first definition of *nudus*, in P. G. W. Glare, ed., *Oxford Latin Dictionary* (Oxford: Clarendon, 1982), 1200, is also "naked," "nude," or "unclothed," and it lists second, "having one's main

about habits of sexual modesty cannot be based on the Greek and Latin words alone.[55] Artistic representations of nudity tended to be heroic, or, as Hallett suggests, nudity was a "heroic costume."[56] In the late first to early second centuries funerary examples of Roman matrons with young nude bodies (with their older faces) existed. It is likely that the nudity depicted in these statues was intended to represent Venus and her matronly characteristics.[57] Again, like the "heroic costume," nudity was intended to be seen as a garment. Although this description is probably accurate, to modern sensitivities it seems rather ironic to have someone clothed with nudity. When public nudity did occur, it seemed to have a purpose, such as humiliation, punishment, or displaying of slaves for purchase. And nudity was accepted practice in the baths.[58] Also, the subject of many nude statues were deities. It is unlikely that this statuary art was intended to be erotic.[59] There are examples of more explicit art;[60] however, it is

---

garment removed, stripped." Based on these definitions alone, one cannot make much of a distinction. Determining precise meaning is dependent on the context of the occurrences. See the discussion in Hallett, *The Roman Nude*, 61–62. Hallett rightly focuses on the adjectives, which are often translated by the English "naked" or "nude"; however, the verb forms may make Hallett's distinction more obvious (compare γυμνόω [Liddell et al., *Greek-English Lexicon*, 363] with *nudo* [Glare, *Oxford Latin Dictionary*, 1199]).

55. Such distinctions based on the Greek and Latin words are little more than curious areas of interest. These observations carry some, but very little, weight on their own. The words can mean both completely and partially naked. Contextual factors such as the society's view of nudity and the contexts of the various usages are determinative of understanding the precise nuances of the words. The observation is valid because of contextual factors. It is not valid because of something inherent in the words.

56. Hallett, *The Roman Nude*, 102.

57. Eve D'Ambra, "The Calculus of Venus: Nude Portraits of Roman Matrons," in *Sexuality in Ancient Art: Near East, Egypt, Greece, and Italy*, ed. Natalie Boymel Kampen (Cambridge: Cambridge University Press, 1996), 219–32.

58. Hallett, *The Roman Nude*, 61, 64–5, 94–95, 78–87. It appears bathers may have had coverings at times, and that mixed nude bathing occurred (e.g., Martial, *Epigrams* 3.3, 87 [late first to very early second century AD]). Nudity in the baths had its critics (Pliny the Elder, *Natural History* 33.153 [mid first century AD]. Pliny appears to be the first to complain [see also Fikret Yegül, *Bathing in the Roman World* (Cambridge: Cambridge University Press, 2010), 22–34]), and it is uncertain how common it was (Garrett G. Fagan, *Bathing in Public in the Roman World* [Ann Arbor: University of Michigan Press, 1999], 24–29). The first baths built in Rome had separate baths for men and women (Varro, *On the Latin Language* 9.68 [mid first century BC]; Hallett, *The Roman Nude*, 84–85; Yegül, *Bathing in the Roman World*, 32). Essentially, mixed bathing occurred, but as to specifics such as its frequency or locations, little is known.

59. Hallett, *The Roman Nude*, 87–101. Hallett notes nudity can suggest "divine status" (223).

60. See, e.g., some of the art discovered at Pompeii in Michael Grant and Antonia Mulas, *Eros in Pompeii: The Secret Rooms of the National Museum of Naples* (Milan: Arnoldo Mondadori, 1975; repr., n.p.: Bonanza Books, 1982). For an analysis and suggestion that such art's meaning was different from today, see John R. Clarke, *Looking at Lovemaking: Constructions of Sexuality in Roman Art: 100 B.C.–A.D. 250* (Berkeley: University of California Press, 1998). Be aware that these books contain sexually explicit images

questionable whether such explicit displays were considered comparable to our notion of pornography (though they still may have been considered obscene or objectionable to many).[61]

Roman Cultural Beliefs and the Jews

It is likely that the above values would have applied to the first-century Roman Jews as well. They certainly would not have endorsed a less restrictive lifestyle than that of their Roman neighbors.

ORIENTATION PARADIGM

Concept Confusion and Terminological Clarification

For the Romans, society ultimately dictated what was permissible during the sex act. They conceptualized desire and behavior in a very different manner from how we do today.[62] Biological sex was an essential component of how all this was perceived.

It is best to abandon labels such as "homosexual" and "heterosexual" as we consider this period. Such labels are anachronistic and can lead to a misunderstanding

---

from the Roman world. Clarke helpfully demonstrates that the Romans viewed sexuality quite differently from how we typically do today (*Looking at Lovemaking*, 8). I believe that this art was accessible, but not necessarily as prevalent as sometimes assumed. First, the Romans as a people were rather modest. Second, the wealthy seemed to be fascinated with Greece and its culture, which was more sexually open than that of the Romans (at least this is what the Romans thought) (Skinner, *Sexuality in Greek and Roman Culture*, 256–58). Third, Pompeii was a wealthy area with strong Greek influence (see Hallett, *The Roman Nude*, 93–94).

61. I am reluctant to call this "pornography" in a modern sense. Greeks and Romans classified genres by form, not function (Holt N. Parker, "Love's Body Anatomized: The Ancient Erotic Handbooks and the Rhetoric of Sexuality," in *Pornography and Representation in Greece and Rome*, ed. Amy Richlin [New York: Oxford University Press, 1992], 91). Therefore, there was no specific genre for obscene material. This does not mean some material within other genres was not offensive or considered obscene in some way (Amy Richlin, *The Garden of Priapus: Sexuality and Aggression in Roman Humor*, rev. ed. [New York: Oxford University Press, 1992], 1–26). The meaning of explicit art is a complex phenomenon. See the articles in Richlin, *Pornography and Representation*, which examines some of this material from a feminist perspective. However, not everything we consider offensive may have been so to the Romans (the opposite is also possible). See for example the use of phallic jewelry as a means to avoid evil (Skinner, *Sexuality in Greek and Roman Culture*, 256; Alissa M. Whitmore, "Fascinating *Fascina*: Apotropaic Magic and How to Wear a Penis," in *What Shall I Say of Clothes? Theoretical and Methodological Approaches to the Study of Dress in Antiquity*, ed. Megan Cifarelli and Laura Gawlinski [Boston: Archaeological Institute of America, 2017], 47–65).

62. Jennifer Ingleheart, "Introduction: Romosexuality: Rome, Homosexuality, and Reception," in *Ancient Rome and the Construction of Modern Homosexual Identities*, ed. Jennifer Ingleheart, Classical Presences (Oxford: Oxford University Press, 2015), 1.

of Roman sexuality.[63] Rather, terminology focused on the act itself is preferred (same sex, opposite sex). Using such terminology will permit a new paradigm to be considered. Abandoning modern terminology avoids the various modern implications associated with the words and permits us to describe the ancient perspective accurately. Thus, instead of "homosexuality," which today includes much more than the sex act itself, people in the first century were involved in "same-sex sexual acts/activity." For example, modern homosexuality can be considered in a discussion of marriage. However, in part due to the role of procreation in marriage, it is unlikely "same-sex" sexual activity would have been associated with marriage in any serious manner in the ancient Roman world.[64] Further, as noted above, the term *orientation* may include some measure of anachronism. If we wish to consider ancient orientation, we might speak of "same-sex sexual desire" and "attraction toward the same sex."[65] These terms are sufficient to label same-sex sexual desire; however, if specifically intended to communicate an ancient form of orientation, these labels are limiting. Nevertheless, with the clarification of terms above and the abandonment of modern labels such as "homosexuality," the word *orientation* can still be useful. Thus I will proceed from the assumption that ancient Romans conceptualized sexual orientation differently from the way those in modern societies do.[66]

Sex and Marriage
In our thinking it is worth reiterating and further developing the gap between sex and marriage. Theoretically, the primary purpose of marriage was to build

---

63. Ingleheart, "Introduction," 1.
64. The traditional labels are still used in the literature (see, e.g., Williams, *Roman Homosexuality*). Also, Ingleheart organizes her edited volume using the term "Romosexuality" (*Ancient Rome*, ix–x). However, the traditional terminology and Ingleheart's can be confusing and will be avoided here.
65. I wish to thank Gregory Coles for a helpful email exchange concerning terminology. He suggested these phrases.
66. See Richard Hays's criticism of John Boswell (published form: *Christianity, Social Tolerance, and Homosexuality: Gay People in Western Europe From the Beginning of the Christian Era to the Fourteenth Century* [Chicago: University of Chicago Press, 1980], 107–14) in "Relations Natural and Unnatural: A Response to John Boswell's Exegesis of Romans 1," *Journal of Religious Ethics* 14, no. 1 (1986): 204. Also, concerning Jews, there is no evidence that ancient Jews "believed that there were people with a natural sexual orientation towards people of their own sex" (Loader, *Making Sense of Sex*, 146). This does not mean there was no concept of orientation in the first century. Such concepts were simply different from our own understanding. Bernadette J. Brooten suggests a complex paradigm that likely included much more than simple attraction (*Love between Women: Early Christian Responses to Female Homoeroticism*, Chicago Series on Sexuality, History, and Society [Chicago: University of Chicago Press, 1996], 242). Brooten does not suggest that this is the same as modern sexual orientation. Her point helps illuminate the fact that things are not as simple as is sometimes assumed. However, Brooten's paradigm seems to simply further nuance the importance of societal roles and the paradigm being suggested here. Loader also, in his more detailed work, endorses Brooten's nuanced approach to "orientation" (*The New Testament on Sexuality*, 322–23).

one's family. And such family building could happen only in a context of male and female marriage partners. These husband-wife relationships could blossom into the kinds of close relationships we view today as important for marriages. However, closeness and even love were unnecessary for a marriage to be successful. In theory, a marriage in which the couple despised one another but had children was more successful than the barren couple who loved one another. This is an extreme example and certainly not ideal.[67] Nevertheless, the example illustrates the point. As mentioned above, for men, this separation between sex and marriage did not hinder their sexual experiences, since they had access to other options; women did not have other options.

The Penetration Paradigm: The Ancient Perspective on Sexual Desire and Behavior

As noted above, in order to understand ancient sexuality, we must dispose of the binary paradigm that classifies individuals as homosexual or heterosexual.[68] This is our inherited assumption, and we generally do not consider other ways of viewing sexual desire and behavior. So unless purpose demands, I will not use these labels, because they may bring unwanted modern notions into the discussion and they do not reflect ancient reality.[69]

Again, gender roles were important to the Romans. One's biological sex dictated how one was supposed to act in sexual activity.[70] Essentially, "in the realm of sexual matters, the Romans were particularly concerned with the issue of who penetrated whom."[71] Citizen adult males could only properly be *penetrators*, and females could only be *penetrated*.[72] The status of male slaves and male noncitizens

67. For example, Plutarch (early second century AD) discusses the importance of compatibility (*Advice to the Bride and Groom* 3, 4, 11,15, 19).
68. Ingleheart, "Introduction," 1. Although there are other labels, such as "bisexual," the fundamental distinction goes back to the binary homosexual/heterosexual paradigm.
69. Eva Cantarella, *Bisexuality in the Ancient World*, trans. Cormac Ó. Cuilleanáin, 2nd ed. (New Haven, CT: Yale University Press, 2002), viii.
70. The following basic paradigm of participatory roles in ancient Greek and Roman sexual activity has been widely accepted (see, e.g., Cantarella, *Bisexuality*, viii, xviii; John J. Winkler, *The Constraints of Desire: The Anthropology of Sex and Gender in Ancient Greece* [New York: Routledge, 1990], 36; and many of the works cited below). This paradigm will be described below. I am indebted to the work of Deborah Kamen and Sarah Levin-Richardson, whose two coauthored articles on the topic have refined terminology and made the paradigm more precise and accurate. The articles focus on males and females respectively: "Revisiting Roman Sexuality: Agency and Conceptualization of Penetrated Males," in Masterson, Sorkin Rabinowitz, and Robson eds, *Sex in Antiquity*, 449–60, and "Lusty Ladies in the Roman Imaginary," in *Ancient Sex: New Essays*, ed. Ruby Blondell and Kirk Ormand (Columbus: Ohio State University Press, 2015), 231–52.
71. Kamen and Levin-Richardson, "Revisiting Roman Sexuality," 449.
72. Holt N. Parker, "The Teratogenic Grid," in Hallett and Skinner, *Roman Sexualities*, 48–50, 53; Skinner, *Sexuality in Greek and Roman Culture*, 7–8. Penetration can be vaginally,

was more ambiguous. As males, they could be *penetrators*; their social status (or lack of status), however, made it acceptable to be *penetrated*.[73] To be clear, a male being penetrated was not seen positively.[74] However, the social stain was either minimal or nonexistent, because of slaves' lesser status.[75] It seems likely that in the Roman context, penetrated males were prostitutes, slaves, and/or adolescent males (children).[76] Adult males having sexual relations with boys was called "pederasty" and will be discussed further below. Although not fully acceptable, in general, classical Greece seemed more open to adult males being penetrated.[77]

Thus, to reiterate, an adult male Roman citizen must be a penetrator.[78] He should never be penetrated.[79] This standard has social connotations as well as sexual.[80] However, whom he penetrated (within the law), male or female, was unimportant.[81] The male penetrator experienced no specific shame or negative stigma for penetrating another man.[82] He was viewed as doing what he was supposed to do: penetrate. Of course, the penetrated male in this sex act could be viewed negatively.[83] Women could only be penetrated.[84] This is why same-sex relations between women were unacceptable.[85] In such situations, at least one of the women needed to function as a penetrator, that is, like a male.[86]

The terms *penetrator* and *penetrated* are probably the best labels to describe the roles in the sex act. Often the terms *active* and *passive* have been used in the history of this discussion.[87] Although the euphemistic nature of these terms makes them

---

anally, or orally (although the latter had some stigma attached to it in some contexts). See the discussion in Parker, "Teratogenic Grid," 48, 50–53.

73. Jennifer A. Glancy, *Slavery in Early Christianity* (Oxford: Oxford University Press, 2002), 21; Cantarella, *Bisexuality*, 101–4; Skinner, *Sexuality in Greek and Roman Culture*, 281.

74. Skinner, *Sexuality in Greek and Roman Culture*, 280.

75. Glancy, *Slavery*, 27.

76. Glancy, *Slavery*, 21; Andrew Lear, "Ancient Pederasty: An Introduction." In Hubbard, *Companion*, 117.

77. Skinner, *Sexuality in Greek and Roman Culture*, 158.

78. Parker, "Teratogenic Grid," 54–55. Parker's term "active" is common, but "penetrator" is preferred.

79. Parker, "Teratogenic Grid," 55.

80. Parker, "Teratogenic Grid," 55.

81. Parker, "Teratogenic Grid," 55.

82. Cantarella, *Bisexuality*, viii.

83. Skinner, *Sexuality in Greek and Roman Culture*, 280. Parker discusses men who desire to be penetrated (Parker, "Teratogenic Grid," 56–58).

84. Parker, "Teratogenic Grid," 56–58. As with "active" above, Parker uses the term "passive," which is imprecise and will be refined below.

85. Parker notes that women should not even desire sex ("Teratogenic Grid," 58–59).

86. Brooten, *Love between Women*, 241.

87. Active/passive terminology is imprecise and not sufficiently nuanced to reflect ancient reality. Thus it is best abandoned. A good representative and detailed example of this active/passive model can be found in Parker, "Teratogenic Grid." (Cantarella also uses the active/passive terminology [*Bisexuality*, xviii].) For an excellent critique of the model, see Kamen and Levin-Richardson, "Lusty Ladies in Roman Imaginary," 232–38.

attractive for labeling the primary dichotomy, such terms are not quite accurate. A penetrator will always be active. However, one penetrated is not necessarily always passive.[88] Passivity suggests one simply does nothing while another does something to him or her. Passivity thus essentially means "inaction."[89] However, such is not the case. One penetrated can be actively involved in sex. Deborah Kamen and Sarah Levin-Richardson find Holt Parker's grid of "active" and "passive" to be insufficient and further refine their terminology to facilitate more preciseness: penetrator, active penetrated, passive penetrated.[90] They retain the "active" and "passive" terminology, but these words no longer describe the main binary opposition. Rather, these labels are subordinate to the penetrator/penetrated contrast of the paradigm. They fall within a "secondary axis of agency (activity versus passivity) in the sexual act."[91] Kamen and Levin-Richardson challenge the assumption that one cannot be both *active* and *penetrated* by describing three types of women who when engaged in sex were both.[92] Thus, in this paradigm, the male citizen penetrator can only be active; those penetrated, however, may be either active (agent) or passive (see table 1).

Table 1: Kamen and Levin-Richardson's Modified Penetration Paradigm	
Penetrator	**Penetrated**
Active (agent)	Active (agent)
	Passive

Jews and the Penetration Model

One might wonder whether the Jews shared such a paradigm of sexuality. Or were they more like us today, viewing sexuality through grids such as heterosexual, homosexual, and bisexual? I believe that the Jews shared the view of their neighbors; however, the influence of the marital example in Genesis 2:18–25[93] and the strong prohibition against various types of sexual expression outside of male-female

---

88. Kamen and Levin-Richardson, "Revisiting Roman Sexuality," 449.
89. Amy Richlin, "Not before Homosexuality: The Materiality of *Cinaedus* and the Roman Law against Love Between Men," *Journal of the History of Sexuality* 3, no. 4 (1993): 531; see also Kamen and Levin-Richardson, "Revisiting Roman Sexuality," 449.
90. Kamen and Levin-Richardson, "Revisiting Roman Sexuality," 450–56. In this article, among other issues, Kamen and Levin-Richardson examine the Latin vocabulary for the participants and sexual activities and organize these in helpful tables. Their discussion of Latin vocabulary is rather nuanced and not necessary for the purpose of this chapter. The labels "penetrator," "active penetrated," and "passive penetrated" are sufficient for our purposes.
91. Kamen and Levin-Richardson, "Revisiting Roman Sexuality," 449.
92. Kamen and Levin-Richardson, "Lusty Ladies in the Roman Imaginary," 238–48.
93. An example of the influence from Genesis can be seen in the New Testament in Mark 10:6–9 (parallel Matt. 19:4–6); 1 Cor. 16:6; Eph. 5:31.

marriage, including same-sex sexual acts (Lev. 18:22; 20:13) and bestiality (v. 23), resulted in what looks today like our modern binary view of opposite-sex sexuality.[94] The text of the Hebrew Bible is the grid from which our "homosexuality" and "heterosexuality" contrast has arisen. Again, it must be stressed that there are many modern notions associated with the labels "heterosexuality" and "homosexuality" that were not present in the ancient context. Thus these labels are inaccurate for describing the first century's opposite- and same-sex sexual acts. Further, the prohibitions against these sexual expressions suggest that they were at some point viewed as options by the Jews. Such prohibitions served not only to keep a certain form of "purity" or "morality" but also as a way of keeping the Jews distinct from their neighbors (18:3). Such separatism certainly was the case in Roman times.

PEDERASTY

One final aspect of ancient Greek and Roman sexuality must be addressed—namely, the sexual relations between adult men and male children (usually adolescent boys, probably between the ages of twelve and twenty).[95] Such man-child sexual practice was called pederasty and was widely practiced in the Greek and Roman worlds.[96]

Acknowledging that there is much uncertainty over the practice in classical Athens, Andrew Lear and Eva Cantarella state, "The basic fact remains: [pederasty] was practiced on a more widespread basis and with greater public approval than any other form of homosexual relations at any time in any Western culture."[97] Pederasty was acceptable to Romans, but, as is to be expected, they were more restrained in their practice. Pederasty was simply an extension of Roman views on proper sexual activity for an individual in his or her social relationship to others: socially superior people could penetrate socially inferior people.[98]

---

94. It should be reiterated that the penetration model (or any model for that matter) is not an issue of the institution of marriage. My conclusion, which suggests that the Jews shared this view with their neighbors, must be understood within this context. In other words, the observation that the Jewish view looked more like our contemporary model is likely due to the biblical restrictions on sexual activity that limit such activity to married couples with the potential to bear children. It is less likely that their paradigm of sexuality differed from their neighbors.

95. Christian Laes, *Children in the Roman Empire: Outsiders Within* (Cambridge: Cambridge University Press, 2011), 264–68. However, it is possible that much younger boys were so used (especially slaves) (Amy Richlin, "Reading Boy-Love and Child-Love in the Greco-Roman World," in Masterson, Sorkin Rabinowitz, and Robson, *Sex in Antiquity*, 359–68). For a helpful chronological overview and introduction, see Lear, "Ancient Pederasty."

96. Lear, "Ancient Pederasty"; Andrew Lear and Eva Cantarella, *Images of Ancient Greek Pederasty: Boys Were Their Gods* (New York: Routledge, 2008); Skinner, *Sexuality in the Greek and Roman Culture*, 10–16. On terminology, see Laes, *Children in the Roman Empire*, 222–23. For a brief history of modern discussion, see Richlin, "Reading Boy-Love and Child-Love," 353–55. On Jews, see below.

97. Lear and Cantarella, *Images of Ancient Greek Pederasty*, xv. The subtitle of the volume is worth noting: *Boys Were Their Gods*.

98. Laes, *Children in the Roman Empire*, 239, 242.

Thus, as suggested above, an adult male citizen could have sexual relations (as the penetrating partner) with women, children, and slaves. Yet the fact that such practices were socially acceptable does not mean all sexual activity of a male with any women, children, and slaves was acceptable. For example, it was unacceptable for a man to have relations with another man's wife, nor was it acceptable (or legal) for an adult male to penetrate a citizen male child.[99] This was because boys grew up to be citizens and would exercise power and authority. Thus, to have experienced penetration was problematic given the importance of status and its relationship to the sexual act.[100] Even classical Greek culture, which permitted such activity, saw an apparent problem with young citizens being penetrated.[101] Such a contradiction concerning the social status of penetrated boys was resolved by Greeks and Romans differently: for Romans, only boys who were noncitizens were available for sex; for Greeks, the boys were not supposed to enjoy the act.[102] In Rome, however, even citizen boys were objects of desire and, despite safeguards, may at times have been used in a sexual manner (although such acts were not culturally acceptable).[103]

The acceptance of pederasty was one practice about which Jews (and Christians) strongly differed and disagreed with their first-century neighbors. As with same-sex relations described above, such a practice was not an option for Jews or Christians.[104]

Although modern readers often wish to distance themselves emotionally from cultures in which they are not a part in order to maintain some type of nonjudgmental objectivity, it is very difficult to read about this practice without having a sense of moral outrage. And such outrage is actually how we should respond. On this subject, Amy Richlin refreshingly states that

---

99. Laes, *Children in the Roman Empire*, 242; Lear, "Ancient Pederasty," 117.

100. Laes, *Children in the Roman Empire*, 242.

101. Laes, *Children in the Roman Empire*, 242.

102. Laes, *Children in the Roman Empire*, 242.

103. Richlin, "Reading Boy-Love and Child-Love," 352, 355–56.

104. In addition to the Old Testament, other Jewish texts condemn adultery, same-sex intercourse, pederasty, and other sex-related practices. See, e.g., the Old Testament pseudepigraphical book the Sibylline Oracles 3.185–87 (mid second century BC); 4.33–34 (late fourth century BC; redaction late first century AD); Philo, *Decalogue* 168–69 (mid first century AD) and the discussion in Loader, *Making Sense of Sex*, 132. Concerning pederasty specifically, the Jews explicitly forbade it and condemned non-Jews for practicing it (see, e.g., Sibylline Oracles 3.596–600 [mid second century BC]; 5.166; 5.430 [late first century to early second century AD]; Philo, *Special Laws* 3.37–42) ([Mary R. D'Angelo, "Sexuality in Jewish Writings from 200 BCE to 200 CE," in Hubbard, *Companion*, 536, 539, 542]). Of course, it is likely that some Jews viewed male sexuality in the same manner that the wider world did (536). Loader believes Jesus is warning against pederasty in Mark 9:42 (*Sexuality and the Jesus Tradition* [Grand Rapids: Eerdmans, 2005], 23–27; *Making Sense of Sex*, 138). Dates for passages in the Sibylline Oracles in this note are from John J. Collins, "Sibylline Oracles," in *The Old Testament Pseudepigrapha*, vol. 1, *Apocalyptic Literature and Testaments*, ed. James H. Charlesworth (New York: Doubleday, 1983), 355, 382, 390.

"pederasty did overlap with what we now call pedophilia; in discussing it as a social practice we can now no more view it through the lens of cultural relativism than we can slavery."[105] Further, Richlin's statement should also challenge us to consider another custom of the first century that is still practiced today in some places—namely, the forced marriages of girls of around the same age as the boys involved in pederasty. Most of us do not condone or even like this practice; nevertheless, we may accept it as a cultural phenomenon. We need to examine ourselves and ask why we do not have the same sense of moral outrage over child marriages.

CONCLUSION

Despite (1) the differences from our modern culture, (2) the options for sexual expression for males, and (3) the practice of pederasty, overall the picture of ancient sexuality is rather restrained. I do not intend to minimize the double standard or the horrible practice of pederasty. These are serious issues. Nevertheless, the portrayal of a culture obsessed with sexual excess that we often associate with ancient Rome is inaccurate. The orgies popularized by Hollywood did exist, but on a much smaller scale than we have been made to believe. In fact, considering the empire as a whole, I suspect that the orgy was a rare occurrence and may have been more due to the excesses associated with power than with the Roman people's view of sex or their values.

We must remember that our own society has its share of excessive sexual practices. Yet the existence of such practices does not suggest we all share in them or that our society generally approves of them. Given what has been said above about moderation and self-control, it is likely the Romans would be shocked at the modern evangelical approach to the topic of sex. Our dress, marriage books, and sermons on love, sex, and marriage would probably be seen by them as improper for honorable people.

It is my hope that this brief survey has demonstrated that our view of sexuality differs considerably from the view of those living in the Roman Empire during the first century. Our sources are minimal and come mainly from the elite segment of society. We do not really know what took place in any bedroom. It is likely many other sexual activities occurred that vanished with the people who practiced them. Nevertheless, we have seen a glimpse of what was considered "normal" at the time of the earliest Christians. And careful use of this knowledge should enable us better to understand the New Testament and thus apply the Scriptures in a more accurate and relevant manner in our lives and ministries.

---

105. Richlin, "Reading Boy-Love and Child-Love," 368. For a similar but slightly different (or more nuanced) approach, see Christian Laes, "When Classicists Need to Speak Up: Antiquity and Present Day Pedophilia-Pederasty," in *Aeternitas Antiquitatis: Proceedings of the Symposium Held in Skopje, August 28 as Part of the 2009 Annual Conference of Euroclassica*, ed. Valerij Sofronievski (Skopje, Macedonia: Association of Classical Philologists ANTIKA and Faculty of Philosophy in Skopje, 2010), 30–59.

FOR DISCUSSION

1. What was the main purpose of ancient marriage? Where does sex fit within this purpose?

2. How did the ancient Greeks and Romans classify sexual practice? Did they have the binary homosexual-heterosexual paradigm that we assume today? What are some of the factors contributing to the difference between their classifications and ours? How does such a difference affect our interpretation of Scripture? Give a specific example.

3. Compare ancient Roman views and physical expressions of their sexuality with modern evangelical views and practices. Is the common Hollywood portrayal of Roman society as a debased culture accurate? What do you believe ancient Romans would think of modern evangelical discussions of sex, modern dress, and marriage books?

FOR FURTHER READING

Hubbard, Thomas K., ed. *A Companion to Greek and Roman Sexualities*. Blackwell Companions to the Ancient World. Chichester, UK: Wiley-Blackwell, 2014.

Loader, William. *Making Sense of Sex: Attitudes towards Sexuality in Early Jewish and Christian Literature*. Grand Rapids: Eerdmans, 2013.

————. *The New Testament on Sexuality: Attitudes towards Sexuality in Judaism and Christianity in the Hellenistic and Greco-Roman Era*. Grand Rapids: Eerdmans, 2012.

Skinner, Marilyn B. *Sexuality in Greek and Roman Culture*. 2nd ed. London: Wiley-Blackwell, 2014.

CHAPTER 4

MALE AND FEMALE IN THE GENESIS CREATION ACCOUNTS: A MISSION, AN IDEAL, AND A TRAGIC LOSS

ROBERT B. CHISHOLM

The relationship between the sexes is fundamental to human life and experience. It is not surprising, then, that Scripture addresses the subject early and often. From the very beginning, the Bible reveals God's primary purpose for man and woman, presents God's ideal for marriage, and tells how sin has disrupted and even jeopardized the man-woman relationship. In this chapter I will discuss each of these themes as they are developed in Genesis 1–3.

GOD'S PRIMARY PURPOSE FOR MAN AND WOMAN (GENESIS 1:26–28)

In the first of the two creation accounts, the crowning achievement of God's creation comes on the sixth day, after God has made all the animals. He issues a call to action: "Let us make humankind in our image, after our likeness, so they may rule over the fish of the sea and the birds of the air, over the cattle, and over all the earth, and over all the creatures that move on the earth" (Gen. 1:26 NET). The text associates the divine image in humankind with rulership. Following the first-person verb form "let us make," the third-person verb form ("and let them rule") indicates purpose ("in order that they may rule") or result ("so that, as a consequence, they may rule").[1] This implies that the imparting of the divine image gives humankind the capacity and authority to rule over the animals and the earth.

God next carries out his call to action by creating humankind (*'adam*) in his own image (1:27a). The term *'adam*, which refers in the second creation account to the man as distinct from the woman (see Gen. 2:7, 18–23), is here used generically for humankind, which is composed of male and female (1:27b). If there is any doubt about this, Genesis 5:1b–2 settles the matter: "When God created humankind [*'adam*], he made them [literally, "him"][2] in the likeness of God. He created *them male and female*; when *they* were created, he blessed *them* and named *them 'humankind'* [*'adam*]" (NET). There is both unity and diversity here. God creates an entity, which he names "humankind," but it is apparent that humankind contains within it a plurality composed of male and female. The terms "male" (*zakar*) and "female" (*neqebah*) focus on biological sex. They are not mere synonyms for "man" and "woman." Usage makes this apparent, for the terms can be used of animals as well as human beings.[3]

Having created the male and female as his vice-regents, God blesses them and commands them, "Be fruitful and multiply! Fill the earth and subdue it! Rule over the fish of the sea and the birds of the air and every creature that moves on the ground" (1:28 NET). Of the five commands given here (all of which are plural in form) the prime directive is the last: "rule." The four preceding commands tell how the prime directive is to be achieved. The male and female must first reproduce, multiply, fill the earth, and subdue it. To this end, God "blessed" them. In this context, just prior to his command to reproduce, "bless" means "to endue with procreative power."[4]

To summarize, God creates the male and female as an entity called "humankind" and commissions them to rule on his behalf as his image bearers.

---

1. The verb forms are best taken as volitional, despite their morphological ambiguity. The first verb form is most likely a cohortative, issuing a call to action, "let us make," while the second, with prefixed nonconsecutive *waw*, is likely a jussive, "and let them rule." In such sequences, especially when there is a shift in person, the second volitional form often indicates logical consequence (purpose or result). See Emil Kautzsch, ed., *Gesenius' Hebrew Grammar*, rev. A. E. Cowley, 2nd English ed. (Oxford: Clarendon, 1910), 322 (par. 109f). For other examples of a jussive (third-person form) indicating purpose or result after a cohortative (first-person form), see, among others, Gen. 19:20; 34:23; 2 Sam. 3:21.

2. The third masculine singular pronoun agrees grammatically with the masculine singular noun *'adam*, but, as verse 2 makes clear, this need not mean that an individual male is the referent.

3. See Ludwig Koehler and Walter Baumgartner, eds., *The Hebrew and Aramaic Lexicon of the Old Testament*, rev. Walter Baumgartner and Johann Jakob Stamm, trans. and ed. under the supervision of Mervyn E. J. Richardson (Leiden: Brill, 2001), 271, 719 (hereafter abbreviated *HALOT*).

4. "Bless" has this same nuance in Gen. 17:16, where God promises to bless Sarah by enabling her to bear a son. Similarly, Gen. 27:27 speaks of a field (cf. also v. 28) that the Lord has blessed by making it fertile and productive.

They are to act in unison toward a common end.[5] Their prime directive is to rule over the earth and animals, but to do this they must reproduce. Elsewhere, the Bible speaks of the romantic dimension of human sexuality (see, e.g., Prov. 5:15–23 and Song of Songs), but Genesis 1:26–28 reminds readers that human sexuality is also foundational to God's purpose for the world. In short, God imparts sexuality, and the procreative power inherent in it, to the first male and female (and, by extension, to their offspring) so they can fulfill their God-given commission to rule on his behalf.

GOD'S IDEAL FOR MARRIAGE (GENESIS 2:18–25)

The second creation account, like the first, describes the creation of man and woman, but there are significant differences between the accounts. Viewed at the larger conceptual level, the first account assumes the unity of the man and woman from the outset and envisions them acting in unison to establish the rule of humankind over the earth. The second account focuses on the man and woman as distinct individuals. It is concerned with their relationship and depicts them becoming unified in response to the man's need. Additionally, the second account contains an etiological element, for it purports to explain present reality in light of what transpired at the beginning in Eden (see 2:24). When one looks closely at details, the two accounts vary considerably.

In Genesis 1:26–28 God creates the male and female, designated humankind, seemingly simultaneously and as a unified entity. As noted above, their common task as "humankind" (*'adam*) is to reproduce and spread out so they can rule the earth and animals on God's behalf. But in Genesis 2 the male, who is designated "the man" (*ha'adam*), is created before the female (who is called "[the] woman") and given the task of caring for the orchard of Eden (v. 15). Nothing is said about ruling over the earth. Despite his having this designated task, from the Lord God's perspective "it is not good for the man to be alone" (v. 18a NET). The man's need prompts the Lord God to make a companion for him (v. 18b). An initial attempt to find this companion from among the animals fails (vv.19–20). Nothing is said about the man ruling over the animals, though his naming them (vv. 19–20a) might imply that he has authority over them.

As the quest to make a companion for the man continues, the Lord God extracts a body part from the man's side (traditionally understood to be a rib) and makes a woman, who proves to be exactly what the man needs (vv. 21–25). But nothing is said about the couple reproducing, filling the earth, and ruling it. In fact, in the aftermath of their rebellion, their expulsion from Eden is presented as tragic, for it cuts them off from the life-giving tree (3:23–24; cf. 2:9b) and means eventual death (see 2:17). This prompts one to ask: How would they have carried out the mandate to fill and rule the earth (1:28) if they

---

5. See Richard M. Davidson. *Flame of Yahweh: Sexuality in the Old Testament* (Peabody, MA: Hendrickson, 2007), 22.

had remained in Eden? In short, the second creation account seems unaware of the first. Harmonization is, of course, possible, though inevitably speculative and even strained. For example, one might assume the mandate of Genesis 1:28 was given following the couple's expulsion from Eden. But, if so, the first account's theme of fertility and reproduction and the second account's focus on death stand in tension, which is relieved to some degree, though not fully, when the man names his wife Eve in anticipation of her becoming "the mother of all the living" (3:20).

The second creation account (2:18–25) highlights two dimensions of the man-woman relationship. First, we see that the woman's distinct purpose is to be the man's indispensable companion. After observing that the man's being alone is "not good," the Lord God declares, "I will make a companion for him who corresponds to him" (v. 18 NET). The word translated "companion" is *ezer*, sometimes defined as "helper." Because of its ambiguity, "helper" is not the best English term to use.[6] The term *ezer* refers to one who delivers another from a crisis, not to a subordinate who does menial tasks for a superior. In fact, God himself often appears in this role.[7] The accompanying phrase (Hebrew *kenegdo*, literally, "corresponding to the front of him") suggests agreement or similarity, not subordination or inferiority. The woman is man's indispensable companion.[8] She is not meant to be a servant, nor is she intended to function independently. Her role and purpose are in relation to the man.[9] This complements the theme of 1:26–28, where she is co-ruler with the man over God's created order and, together with him, is to populate and subdue the earth.

Is male headship implied here? Since the man was created before the woman, one might think this implies he has authority over her. After all, she derives her existence from him and she was created to be *his* companion, not vice versa. But if chronological priority is significant, then what do we make of the animals being created before the woman? The fact that the man names the woman might suggest his authority over her, since naming sometimes has this connotation. For example, when "a name is called *over*" an object, the one whose name is "called over" the object possesses or has authority over it.[10] But otherwise, naming expressions convey no such notion. Often names are given simply because they

---

6. A helper is sometimes thought of as an assistant. One definition offered by Merriam-Webster is "a relatively unskilled worker who assists a skilled worker usually by manual labor." Such notions suggest subordination and even inherent inferiority—ideas that the Hebrew word does not convey or connote.

7. See Exod. 18:4; Deut. 33:29; 1 Sam. 7:12; Pss. 20:2; 33:20; 70:5; 124:8.

8. See Davidson, *Flame of Yahweh*, 29–30.

9. See Susan T. Foh, *Women and the Word of God* (Phillipsburg, NJ: P&R, 1979), 60; Stanley J. Grenz, *Sexual Ethics: An Evangelical Response,* 2nd ed. (Louisville: Westminster John Knox, 1997), 32.

10. See Deut. 28:10; 2 Sam. 12:28; 1 Kings 8:43; 2 Chron. 6:33; 7:14; Isa. 4:1; 63:19; Jer. 7:10–11, 14, 30; 15:16; 25:29; 32:34; 34:15; Dan. 9:18–19; Amos 9:12.

are appropriate descriptions of the object being named.[11] Any idea of ownership or authority must be derived from the context (as when a conqueror renames a town, Judg. 1:17); it is not inherent in the expression itself. This means that the man's naming the animals (Gen. 2:20) and the woman (Gen. 2:23; 3:20) does not in and of itself reflect or establish his authority over them. That notion, if present, must be derived from the context, not from the mere use of a phrase for naming.[12] Yet the context views them as a unified entity (1:26–28) and focuses on the correspondence between them (2:18).

A second key element in the man-woman relationship emerges in verses 23–25. Although they are distinct individuals, this first, divinely orchestrated marriage creates a tight bond between them. When the Lord God brings to the man the newly built woman,[13] the man declares, "This one at last [or "this time"] is bone of my bones and flesh of my flesh; this one will be called 'woman,' for she was taken out of man" (v. 23 NET). He immediately recognizes that she, in contrast to the menagerie paraded before him earlier, derives from him physically and is a perfect match for him, so he names her accordingly. He is man (*'ish*); she is woman (*'ishah*). The sound-play mirrors the correspondence between them.

At this point the narrator interrupts the main story line in order to comment on the significance of this scene: "That is why a man leaves his father and mother and unites with his wife, and they become one family" (v. 24 NET). This is an etiological note, which links present reality with the historical event (note *'al-ken*, "therefore" or "that is why").[14] The statement is descriptive, not prescriptive, as usage of the Hebrew construction indicates. Elsewhere when *'al-ken* is followed by an imperfect verb form in a narrative framework, as in Genesis 2:24, the verb describes what is customary or habitual. In other words, it describes, from an ancient Israelite perspective, what is typical in human

---

11. See, e.g., Gen. 16:13; Ruth 4:17; 1 Sam. 9:9; 2 Sam. 18:18; Prov. 16:21; Isa. 1:26; 32:5; 35:8; 62:4, 12; Jer. 19:6.

12. See George W. Ramsey, "Is Name-Giving an Act of Domination in Genesis 2:23 and Elsewhere?," *Catholic Biblical Quarterly* 50, no. 1 (1988): 24–35; Davidson, *Flame of Yahweh*, 31–34.

13. The verb used in verse 23 (*banah*, "build") is different from the one used earlier (*yatsar*, "to form") regarding the creation of the man and the animals (vv. 7, 19). It pictures God constructing the woman according to an architectural design, as one would a building, tower, or altar. The man and animals are "formed" from soil, but the woman is "built" from the bodily part extracted from the man.

14. As Tosato points out, the introductory "therefore" "certifies beyond any doubt" that the author "intends here *to explain* something, presenting it as a consequence of what has been narrated in the preceding verses" (emphasis in original). See Angelo Tosato, "On Genesis 2:24," *Catholic Biblical Quarterly* 52, no. 3 (1990): 398. Collins states, "The marriage of Adam and Eve (Gen. 2:23–25) is taken as the paradigm for any sound future marriage of human beings. The comment makes clear that this is programmatic for human life." See C. John Collins, *Did Adam and Eve Really Exist? Who They Were and Why You Should Care* (Wheaton, IL: Crossway, 2011), 60.

experience.[15] In 2:24 the narrator observes what is typically the case: When a young man reaches a certain age, his focus shifts from his parents to a member of the opposite sex, whom he marries.

The statement about the man "leaving" his parents is hyperbolic. Elsewhere the verb (*'azab*), when used of one human being "leaving" another, has the nuance "forsaking, abandoning." But in an ancient Israelite context, an adult son was to honor his parents (Exod. 20:12)[16] and, in actual practice, remained close to them within the extended family structure.[17] Nevertheless, the exaggerated language accentuates the radical change in focus that typically occurs when a young man reaches puberty. It refers to a psychological change in perspective, not to a geographical change of residence.

The young man's attraction to his wife is vividly depicted. He clings to her, hugging her so tightly that they become, as it were, "one flesh."[18] Probing more deeply into the word picture, we see that the phrase "one flesh," while likely depicting the sex act, also points to the man and woman forming a new family, or becoming "kin," as it were.[19] The phrase "one flesh" occurs only here in the Old Testament. Its significance should be informed from the context, where the man recognizes that the woman is "bone of my bones and flesh of my flesh" (v. 23). This statement appears to reflect the idiom "bone and flesh," which is used of blood relatives, or kin (see Gen. 29:14; Judg. 9:2; 2 Sam. 5:1; 19:13–14).

The narrator's logic can be paraphrased as follows: What happened at the time of the first marriage explains the otherwise mysterious experience of a

---

15. See Gen. 10:9; 32:32 [v. 33 in Hebrew]; Num. 21:14, 27; 1 Sam. 5:5; 19:24; 2 Sam. 5:8. Lawton acknowledges that this "grammatical analysis is flawless," but he objects that this interpretation of the statement in 2:24 makes it trite. Defying usage, he suggests the imperfect verb form may have a potential force, expressing divine intention. See Robert B. Lawton, "Genesis 2:24: Trite or Tragic?," *Journal of Biblical Literature* 105, no. 1 (1986): 97–98, and also Davidson, *Flame of Yahweh*, 43n113. But once one understands the significance of the etiological statement, it is anything but trite. Indeed, it explains reality as we know it! Krueger asserts that the grammatical evidence is "not conclusive here" and suggests that the statement may refer to an obligation. He calls this a "moral reading" that contains an "implied command." But the grammatical evidence cannot and should not be so easily dismissed. See Paul Krueger, "Etiology or Obligation? Genesis 2:24 Reconsidered in the Light of Text Linguistics," in *Thinking towards New Horizons*, ed. Matthias Augustin and Hermann Michael Niemann, Beiträge zur Erforschung des Alten Testaments und des Antiken Judentums 55 (New York: Peter Lang, 2008), 44.
16. See Charlie Trimm, "Honor Your Parents: A Command for Adults," *Journal of the Evangelical Theological Society* 60, no. 2 (2017): 247–63.
17. Philip J. King and Lawrence E. Stager, *Life in Biblical Israel*, Library of Ancient Israel (Louisville: Westminster John Knox, 2001), 36–40.
18. The Hebrew construction used here for the man's action has the primary meaning "cling to, stick to." See *HALOT*, 209. It is used of Ruth hugging Naomi tightly, in contrast to Orpah, who simply gives Naomi a goodbye kiss (see Ruth 1:14).
19. Gordon J. Wenham, *Genesis 1–15*, Word Biblical Commentary (Waco, TX: Word, 1987), 71.

young man when he reaches puberty. Initially, his relationship with his parents is primary, but when he reaches a certain age, his focus radically shifts and he establishes a new relationship with his wife. Since the blood relationship between the first man and his wife was the first human relationship the Lord God established, marriage subsequently has priority over the parent-child relationship, even though this seems to go counter to experience, where the young man's relationship to his parents is genetic and chronologically prior.

Having explained present reality in light of the historical event of the first marriage, the narrator returns to what transpired in Eden. He informs readers that "the man and his wife were both naked, but they were not ashamed" (v. 25 NET). An imperfect verbal form is used (literally, "they were not feeling shame"), drawing attention to the continuing nature of the condition, rather than just stating the fact (which the perfect verbal form would have done). In light of present experience, this is surprising to read. The first couple's unabashed nakedness reflects their innocence and unity. A first-time reader is forced to ask: Why do man and woman no longer experience such unashamed intimacy?

PARADISE LOST (GENESIS 3:7–16)

Unfortunately, the idyllic scene depicted at the end of chapter 2 is shattered in the next episode as the story takes a decided turn for the worse. The serpent convinces the woman that eating the forbidden fruit will elevate her and the man to divine status (3:1–5).[20] She eats some of the fruit and shares it with her husband (v. 6). They become aware of their nakedness and make coverings for themselves (v. 7). In stark contrast to the scene depicted in 2:25, they feel alienated from each other and, worse yet, from the Lord God (vv. 8–10). In fact, when the Lord God asks what has happened (v. 11), the man deflects the blame: "The *woman*, whom *you* gave me, *she* gave me some fruit from the tree and I ate it" (v. 12 NET). The man does not make himself the subject of a verb until the very end of the statement. It is clear that he considers the woman primarily and the Lord God secondarily responsible for his action. When the Lord God questions the woman, she too points the finger elsewhere: "The *serpent* tricked me, and I ate" (v. 13 NET).

But the Lord God does not accept their self-defense. After announcing the serpent's punishment (vv. 14–15), he turns to the woman and says,

> I will greatly increase your labor pains;
> with pain you will give birth to children.
> You will want to control your husband,
> but he will dominate you. (v. 16 NET)

---

20. In verses 1–5 the serpent uses the plural in addressing the woman, as if anticipating she will tell the man what he has said. Indeed, one might even assume that the man was a silent observer to the conversation, though this cannot be proved from the syntax of verse 6.

It is then the man's turn. Because he listened to his wife, rather than the Lord God, the ground will resist his efforts to make things grow and will produce thorns and thistles (vv. 17–18). The man will have to work hard to grow food, and then he will die and return to the soil of the ground (v. 19). Conflict will be the order of the day—conflict between the serpent and the woman that will extend to their offspring (v. 15), between the man and the woman (v. 16b), and between the man and the ground (vv. 17b–19a). Furthermore, pain will characterize human experience, as the woman agonizes in pain to produce new life from her womb (v. 16a) and the man painfully produces crops from the hostile soil (v. 17b).

Verse 16b is of particular interest to our study, for it now characterizes the relationship between the man and woman as a power struggle. The statement reads literally, "Toward your husband (will be) your desire, but he will rule over you." Interpreters have debated the meaning of *teshuqah*, "desire," which is used only three times in the Old Testament. Because it refers to a man's romantic desire for a woman in Song of Songs 7:10, some see a sexual connotation as well in Genesis 3:16, even though the woman, not the man, is the subject of the desire here. But Genesis 4:7, because of its contextual proximity, is a better guide to the meaning. There the Lord God warns Cain that sin's "desire" is to control him, but he must "rule" over it. The "desire" refers to dominating and imposing one's will, as the exhortation to "rule" over it indicates. In 3:16 the verb "rule" (*mashal*) appears as well. The woman has exerted authority over her husband (cf. v. 17a) and will now want to continue to do so, but he will resist her efforts and rule over her.[21]

There is a deeper theological dimension to this power struggle. Like the hostility between snakes and humans (vv. 14–15) and the man and the ground (vv. 17–19), marital conflict is a reminder of the chaos that sin produces in relationships. The theological significance of 2:24 also comes into sharper focus.

---

21. See Susan T. Foh, "What Is the Woman's Desire?," *Westminster Theological Journal* 37 (1975): 376–83; Victor P. Hamilton, *The Book of Genesis Chapters 1–17*, New International Commentary on the Old Testament (Grand Rapids: Eerdmans, 1990), 202; and C. John Collins, *Genesis 1–4: A Linguistic, Literary, and Theological Commentary* (Phillipsburg, NJ: P&R, 2006), 159–60. Walton objects that Song 7:10 "cannot be reconciled to the domination concept." See John H. Walton, *Genesis*, NIV Application Commentary (Grand Rapids: Zondervan, 2001), 228. But the primary meaning, "dominate, control," is present in Song 7:10, where the girl is delighted that her lover is overwhelmed with her charms and wants to have his way with her sexually. Condren has recently called into question Foh's view that Genesis 3:16 depicts a struggle between the sexes. He surveys how the rare term *teshuqah* has been interpreted down through the years and suggests that it means "return," not "desire." In this case, the woman returns to her husband for "sexual intimacy" and "for the relational harmony and naked vulnerability forfeited by disobedience." See Janson C. Condren, "Toward a Purge of the Battle of the Sexes and 'Return' for the Original Meaning of Genesis 3:16B," *Journal of the Evangelical Theological Society* 60, no. 2 (2017): 227–45. But this more positive understanding of the statement does not coincide with the theme of conflict that is present in the judgment oracles that precede (3:15) and follow (3:17) it.

The natural attraction of a young man for his wife reflects an ideal, but it also serves as a foil for the harsh reality pictured in 3:16b. The strong attraction that characterizes the early romantic phase of the relationship, when juxtaposed with the conflict that inevitably mars a marriage, gives tragic testimony to what has been lost in the male-female relationship.

CONCLUSION

The Genesis creation accounts lay the foundation for a biblical theology of gender relationships and marriage. The first creation account reveals God's primary purpose for humankind, composed of male and female. In unison they are to reproduce and populate the earth, so they can rule over it as God's vice-regents (Gen. 1:26–28).

The second account, which differs considerably in detail and perspective from the first, focuses on the relationship between the man and woman. It is clear that the woman was created to be the man's indispensable companion, delivering him, as it were, from his isolation, which the Lord God regarded as "not good" (2:18). This account also reveals the Lord God's ideal. As the fundamental human relationship established by the Lord God, marriage creates a bond between man and woman where they enjoy intimacy, free of any shame (2:23–25).

Unfortunately, the ideal is shattered by sin. The second episode within the second creation account tells how sin disrupts unity and intimacy, as the man and woman cover their nakedness in fear, and the man then accuses the woman of causing him to sin. Sin brings conflict—between serpents and human beings (3:14–15), between the man and the accursed ground (3:17–19), and, tragically, between man and woman (3:16). The woman now desires to control the man, as when she gave him the forbidden fruit to eat, but the man in turn dominates her.

Fortunately, the biblical story does not end here. God resolves this tragic plot complication through his redemptive intervention. He urges the woman to surrender her desire for control and challenges the man to follow the self-sacrificial, loving example of the Redeemer himself (Eph. 5:21–33).

FOR DISCUSSION

1. Regarding Genesis 1:26–28, has the command to reproduce been essentially fulfilled by the human race? What implications, if any, does the command have for notions of population control? Is it appropriate for married couples to view the command as directly applicable to them and, consequently, to seek to produce as many children as possible?

2. Regarding Genesis 2:24, in light of what was said above, how would you assess interpretations that understand the verse prescriptively? Proponents of this view stress that a man *should* leave his parents and cling to his wife, and they *should* in turn become one flesh. Is this really the point of the passage?

3. Regarding Genesis 3:16, how does Paul in Ephesians 5:21–33 provide an antidote of sorts for the fallen-world reality described in Genesis 3:16?

FOR FURTHER READING

Collins, C. John. *Genesis 1–4: A Linguistic, Literary, and Theological Commentary.* Phillipsburg, NJ: P&R, 2006.

Davidson, Richard M. *Flame of Yahweh: Sexuality in the Old Testament.* Peabody, MA: Hendrickson, 2007.

Foh, Susan T. *Women and the Word of God.* Phillipsburg, NJ: P&R, 1979.

CHAPTER 5

GENDER: MALE AND FEMALE IN INTERPERSONAL EXPRESSION

SANDRA L. GLAHN

GENDER AS A USEFUL CATEGORY

In the not so distant past, the word *gender* referred only to grammatical fields.[1] But in 1955, sexologist John Money introduced the terminological distinction between biological sex and gender as a role. Another fifteen to twenty years passed before his idea caught on. In the 1970s, the academic field of gender studies emerged, and people began to define *gender* as the social construction of biological difference. So *sex* was the word to describe biological difference such as "male and female," and *gender* referred to the social outworking of that difference—"masculine and feminine behavior." That is, sex is ontology (who a person is), and gender is ethology (what a person does).

One of the limitations that had been inherent in women's studies was a too-narrow focus on the physical differences of men and women outside of cultural construction. Recognizing this weakness, Joan Scott wrote a seminal essay, "Gender: A Useful Category of Historical Analysis," published in *The American Historical Review*.[2] In it, Scott called for a shift from "women" to "gender" as a historical category of analysis. She emphasized the definition of gender favored by social historians—the social organization of the relationship between the sexes. Scott's interest lay in more than sexual differentiation; it was in exploring

---

1. See Benj. Ide Wheeler, "The Origin of Grammatical Gender," *Journal of Germanic Philology* 2, no. 4 (1899): 528–45. https://www.jstor.org/stable/27699089.
2. Joan Scott, "Gender: A Useful Category of Historical Analysis," *American Historical Review* 91, no. 5 (December 1986): 1053–75.

relationships of power. Such a shift, she felt, would broaden the field to include exploration of the historical and cultural construction of roles assigned to the biological differences and attributes of *both* men and women. Although people on both the left and the right challenged her, Scott's idea caught on, and the emphases and scope of historical research underwent significant shifts.

With the expansion in focus from only sex/biology to include gender/social outworking of sex difference, historians broadened the conversation to such questions as, How have people through time viewed masculinity? and What have they considered feminine? and especially, What have been the power relationships between men and women?

A recognition that culture shapes views of masculinity and femininity has led contemporary scholars to read ancient texts more critically to delineate the difference between representation and reality. For example, when reading a writer such as Cicero, who used "woman" imagery to insult Antony in *The Second Philippic*, a contemporary scholar might—instead of taking Cicero's commentary on women at face value—consider how Cicero was using gender as part of a rhetorical strategy to insult Antony's enemies.[3] Consequently, the scholar might ask, "What were the actual norms of femininity?"

More recently, we have come to understand that much of what we once attributed to "women's intuition," such as knowing the best time to talk to the boss (e.g., after he has had coffee), is now understood by many as something not innate to women. Rather, it is mainly due to a social-power difference. Women, who have been historically lower in social power, have spent more time observing and scrutinizing those in power, and become more attuned to their nonverbal cues.[4]

The shift from "women" to "gender" also caused scholars to do more reading between the lines as an emphasis on political history in the academy broadened to include more social history. For example, since the emperor Octavian passed laws allowing exemption from *manus* (male supervision) for mothers who birthed three or more children, the contemporary historian might observe that "exemption as incentive" suggests that many women preferred autonomy over being under male authority.

The distinction between sex/biology and gender as the social construction of sex difference helped provide language to explore the dynamic behind why when a woman in Kenya puts a roof on a house, she's doing women's work, while in America, most would consider a female roofer as doing work that is "unfeminine."

---

3. See Nancy Myers, "Cicero's (S) Trumpet: Roman Women and the Second Philippic," *Rhetoric Review* 22, no. 4 (2003): 337–52.
4. Ronald E. Riggio, "Women's Intuition: Myth or Reality?," *Psychology Today*, July 14, 2011, https://www.psychologytoday.com/us/blog/cutting-edge-leadership/201107/women-s-intuition-myth-or-reality.

My friend Musa is a member of the Pokot tribe in Kenya's Rift Valley. He stands about six foot two, and he is what many Americans would consider masculine. Several years ago, he came to the United States to attend a pastor's conference, and after spending a day in workshops, he sat bewildered with my husband and me.

"What is wrong with pink here?" he asked. He motioned to the pastel pink watch he was wearing. "All day people give this strange looks."

"Ah," I said. "In America, men usually don't wear pink watches."

He looked at me with furrowed brow. "Why not?"

"Most Americans associate pink with females," I told him.

He scoffed. "You can't wear some colors because they are for male or female?" Then he said basically that was the dumbest thing he had ever heard.

"You don't associate certain colors with men or women in your country?" we asked.

"No. Pink is just a beautiful color."

In America the husband is often the one who drives the car when a family is together; in other countries, the wife is more likely to serve by driving. And while pink is often considered the "girl" color in the United States, in ancient Rome, yellow was the color for girls. "Masculine" men at Versailles in the eighteenth century wore lace, high heels, hose, and long, flowing hair; today, such dress would not generally rank as "masculine." These examples suggest there's a fluidity to how we define masculine and feminine behavior and how we socially construct our ideals of gender. And it was the influences behind these sorts of behaviors and the desire to study them that led to distinguishing between "sex" and "gender" for the sake of studying social behavior.

BIBLICAL MASCULINITY AND FEMININITY

A Principle

The past few decades have seen a rise in the number of Christian small groups and curricula designed around discovering gender differences with the goal of conforming to biblical gender norms. The question such studies has sought to answer is, What is biblical masculinity and femininity and how do we conform to such behaviors? More to the point, such discussions have tended to revolve around exploring what social differences God designed to flow from sex difference. And whereas women's ministry in the past tended to focus on older women teaching wives how to love their husbands and children (based on Titus 2:3–4), many of today's evangelical churches are now also teaching women how to act like women and men to act like men.

Christians are generally unified in believing that God made male and female different by beautiful design.[5] A problem arises, however, when we seek to list

---

5. Complementarians frequently describe egalitarians as not believing in the complementary relationship of men and women. In response, a group of evangelical egalitarian

the sex-specific *behaviors* male and female should adhere to in order to become their true selves. Statements such as "man is *sacrificial* worker" versus "woman as *submissive* worker"[6] take commands given to husbands and wives and extrapolate to make them representative of something innate in all males and females. Such an approach also requires overlooking biblical calls for men to submit to others (e.g., Eph. 5:21) and for women to love sacrificially (e.g., 1 John 3:16). Some even speak of the need for men and women "to be faithful to their genders" and refer to the existence of the "male and female soul."[7]

In many cases evangelical teaching about what constitutes masculine and feminine behavior has followed Western cultural stereotypes. Consequently, we risk teaching essentialism as "biblical gender roles." And we also reveal race bias, class bias, and geographical bias in doing so. For example, in 1950s middle-class America, the idea that "God designed women to stay home and care for children, and God made men to work outside the home to support their families" was viewed by many White Protestant Americans as divine design for gender. But what about women who chose celibacy—were they going against design by leaving the home and working to survive? And wasn't life better for children when *both* parents were home and often accessible to their children throughout the day, as is still the case in agrarian societies? if sex-specific actions are innate, why had women-at-home men-in-the-workplace not applied to female domestic workers leaving their children for survival? Or why was it okay for women in the developing world to sell vegetables in the market instead of staying in the hut? Such observations lead us to a fundamental principle: If a practice cannot be applied in all cultures across the lines of race, class, and gender, it must not be a "biblical" expression of gender. That is not to say such practices are *un*biblical. They should just not be exported as a scriptural, universal ideal.

Defining Biblical Masculinity and Femininity
Perhaps the best known definitions of masculinity and femininity among evangelicals come from John Piper in his work *Recovering Biblical Manhood and Womanhood: A Response to Evangelical Feminism*:

---

scholars published Ronald W. Pierce, Rebecca Merrill Groothuis, and Gordon D. Fee, eds., *Discovering Biblical Equality: Complementarity without Hierarchy* (Downers Grove, IL: IVP Academic, 2005), putting the very word in the title to emphasize that they believe in complementarity—they just don't equate the innate gender differences with hierarchy of roles.

6. Robert L. Saucy, and Judith K. TenElshof, eds., *Women and Men in Ministry: A Complementary Perspective* (Chicago: Moody Press, 2001), 186, 188, 192. Such references raise the question of what the basis is for making such statements. Is there such a thing as an intersex or "born-eunuch" soul?

7. Saucy, and TenElshof, *Women and Men in Ministry*, 186, 188, 192.

At the heart of mature masculinity is a sense of benevolent responsibility to lead, provide for, and protect women in ways appropriate to a man's differing relationships. At the heart of mature femininity is a freeing disposition to affirm, receive, and nurture strength and leadership from worthy men in ways appropriate to a woman's differing relationships.[8]

These definitions of masculine and feminine raise some questions. First, what is the basis of authority for the creation of these definitions?

Second, if these definitions are correct, can men and women be their gendered selves only when accompanied by members of the opposite sex? If a woman is alone or in the company of only women, does she lose her "biblical femininity" because she has no man to affirm, receive, and nurture? And when a husband is only with other guys, does he stop being masculine because there is no female present to lead, protect, and provide for?

The husband-and-wife team George and Dora Winston self-identify as complementarians who served for decades at Belgian Bible Institute. They observe, "The problem [with these definitions] is that this premise, by grounding human authority in 'manhood' that is in *essence* and *being*, goes against the general teaching of Scripture that grounds leadership in *relationship* and *function*."[9]

Hermeneutical Approaches to Finding Masculine and Feminine Ideals

Having established that masculinity and femininity (gender) are the social outworking of embodiment as male and female (sex), we turn to Scripture to see if there are behaviors that represent "biblically masculine and feminine" behavior. But we must first consider how best to approach doing so. One way might be to observe what all the men and women of the Bible are described as doing. But that would lead us to conclude that being a sinner is part of God's design for biblical masculinity and femininity—for all have sinned (Rom. 3:23).

We could also extrapolate something about innate manhood and womanhood from sex-specific commands. But in doing so, we might read a verse such as 1 Timothy 2:8 ("Therefore I want the men everywhere to pray, lifting up holy hands without anger or disputing" [NIV]) and conclude that demonstrating anger and arguing are innate to manhood.

Indeed, even looking only at seemingly sex-specific commands does not necessarily lead to a biblical view of gender. One blogger writes something that is taught often, especially at Christian marriage conferences with accompanying

---

8. John Piper, "A Vision of Biblical Complementarity: Manhood and Womanhood Defined according to the Bible," in *Recovering Biblical Manhood and Womanhood: A Response to Evangelical Feminism*, ed. John Piper and Wayne Grudem (Wheaton, IL: Crossway, 1991), 35–36.

9. George Winston and Dora Winston, *Recovering Biblical Ministry by Women: An Exegetical Response to Traditionalism and Feminism* (Longwood, FL: Xulon, 2003), 41.

proof text: "Christian men are called to provide for their families. Paul uses some of the strongest language in the New Testament to warn those who do not provide: 'But if any man does not provide for his own, and especially for those of his household, he has denied the faith and is worse than an unbeliever' (1 Timothy 5:8). Whatever a man thinks he is 'called' to, this much is clear—he is called to provide for his family."[10]

After reading this verse, one might think the word "man" and the presence of three male pronouns would make it clear that providing is a man's—or at least a husband's—role. Some have, based on their reading of this passage, even gone so far as to say that a wife whose income exceeds that of her husband threatens his sense of manhood.[11] But if we were to translate woodenly, paying close attention to gender in the original, the verse would look more like this: "If someone does not provide for one's own, especially one's own family, that person has denied the faith and is worse than an unbeliever." Indeed, no male is referenced here, and the pronouns are not meant to suggest that they refer only to males. Indeed, verse 16 is the only sex-specific command in the entire pericope: "If any woman who is a believer has widows in her care, she should continue to help them and not let the church be burdened with them, so that the church can help those widows who are really in need." Some Christian scholars in the past even thought that the passage did not speak at all to men, applying only to women caring for widowed relatives.[12] So even if we sought to include only verses with sex-specific commands, we might end up including verses that have been wrongly placed in a male or female category, leading us to reach faulty conclusions.

Another approach to determining a biblical view of manhood and womanhood would be to look at how the Bible's much-respected men and women lived. But even when doing so, we tend to see only those details that fit our own culture's gender norms. For example, commentators have often observed that the excellent wife of Proverbs 31 is at home, while overlooking that she buys a field—which probably required going out to see it before purchasing it (v. 16). Also, she is physically strong (v. 17), probably generates more income than her husband (v. 16, 23), spends her own money (v. 16), and teaches torah (v. 26). We miss other examples that don't fit Western cultural norms too, such as Jesus cooking fish—in his postresurrection body, no less (John 21:9)—and male deacons, not the women's ministry, serving food to Greek widows (Acts 6:1–6). So, from observed behaviors of good men and women, we might conclude that serving tables is really men's work. Clearly, when it comes to gender, our hermeneutics need some help.

---

10. J. D. Gunter, "Men as Providers," Council on Biblical Manhood and Womanhood, November 11, 2013, https://cbmw.org/topics/leadership-2/men-as-providers/.
11. Interestingly, Jesus and the disciples relied on the generosity of women who brought in more income than they did—see Luke 8:1–3.
12. See Sandra Glahn, "Manhood vs. Grandma?" bible.org, *Engage* (blog), April 2, 2012, https://blogs.bible.org/engage/sandra_glahn/manhood_vs_grandma.

Both of these approaches have resulted in imposing social constructs on the text and therefore misconstruing "biblical manhood" and "biblical womanhood." So perhaps a better approach is to go back to the beginning and see what God actually said about his design for male and female social behavior—not what might be implied or even read into silence. But observing what he actually said.

Genesis 1–2

When one considers a biblical view of the social outworking of sex difference, the starting point must be Genesis 1. And because we are looking for the ideal manifestation of embodiment as male and female, we explore a question directed at social behavior: What were man and woman made to *do?* The first clue comes in verse 26: "Then God said, Let us make [*'adam*] in our image, after our likeness. And let them have dominion" (ESV).

Before we move to exploring dominion, it is worth pausing to note that *male and female are made in God's image.* On the first day of a class I was teaching on the role of gender in the home, church, and society, I thought through the material I planned to cover. I feared that some of what I'd prepared was too elementary for seminary students. Did they really need to hear again the teaching from Genesis 1:26–27 that says both male and female were made in the image of God? Yet despite my doubts, I determined to cover even the very basics. So, as I taught, I repeated what I assumed they all knew. But sure enough, a woman sitting in the front row sat stunned. "Are you saying I myself am made in the image of God—without having to be married?" she asked.

"*I'm* not saying that. Genesis says so."

She turned to face all her classmates. "Did you know that?" she exclaimed. They all nodded. She looked back at me and burst into the tears of joy. She did not have to marry to *fully* image God. Nor did she have to bear children to *ultimately* image him.

In the days that followed, this student changed her focus from trying to "become complete" through finding a husband to equipping herself for ministry. Her church had warned her of the dangers of radical feminism but had never told her *who she was.*

Male and female bear the image of God, and they need each other.

At the time of our creation, humans bore God's image—simply by being. Today that image is marred but not erased (James 3:9). Humans bear God's image by virtue of being his creations. As those who image God, we were given a job: to have dominion over the earth. "Have dominion" (Gen. 1:28). A bestselling Christian writer tells men that God gave dominion to Adam and his sons after him. But actually God originally gave dominion to the man and the woman. The idea that women co-rule and were made to do so did not find its origin in radical feminism. Indeed, the first purpose we see for both man and woman—and we find it in the mind of God even before their creation—is to share dominion over the earth and its creatures.

Man and woman were also given a mandate to fill the earth—a subject I will address in a later chapter. Indeed, male and female were differing creatures, but God, nevertheless, gave them the same purposes and mandates. The emphasis in Genesis so far has been on how similar male and female are in their mandated task, and not how different. They need each other, and what each uniquely brings to the partnership is not outlined.

After establishing that the humans bear the divine image and are created to rule together, the author goes back to retell the creation story from a different perspective. And readers see that the man is described as alone (not good, 2:18), and given a helper ('ezer) corresponding to him (v. 18, making the two together very good). So the woman is given not to solve the need for an assistant, but to solve the problem of man's aloneness. And Adam's exclamation of joy comes from his delight that finally there is one not *different* from him but *like* him (v. 23).

The woman is a helper—an 'ezer-warrior. Now, sadly, many read "helper" and think of a plumber's helper, or Hamburger Helper or "mother's little helper"—an adjunct or assistant capable only of accomplishing menial tasks. Yet 'ezer is used elsewhere in the Old Testament to refer to nations to whom Israel turns for military assistance when under attack. And even more significantly, the word is used in reference to God sixteen times.[13] When we pray, "God, help me," surely we don't have a junior assistant in mind. Indeed, in every other use of 'ezer in the Old Testament, we find military language involved.

God is his people's helper, sword and shield, and deliverer. He is the ever-present rescuer from trouble. He is better than chariots and horses. He keeps watch like a guard over his people, and with his strong arm he overthrows their enemies. That's the kind of help Genesis describes. So based on the consistent use of this term in the Hebrew Bible, it only makes sense to conclude that God created the woman to be a strong ally—a warrior. Battle is not just for males; females are called to put on armor too (see Eph. 6). The personification of Lady Wisdom in Proverbs 31 similarly has battle connotations, with words throughout such as "valor," "strength," and "prey."[14] Woman is a co-regent and co-heir. Woman, as a partner to man (and not only in the context of marriage), is designed to be a force to be reckoned with on the battlefield of life.

Genesis 3

Yet sadly, only three chapters into the narrative, disaster comes. The text begins with an observation not about the weakness of woman's nature, but

---

13. Carolyn Custis James, *Half the Church: Recapturing God's Global Vision for Women* (Grand Rapids: Zondervan, 2010), 112–13.
14. See Thomas McCreesh, "Wisdom as Wife: Proverbs 31:10–31," *Revue biblique* 92, no. 1 (1985): 25–46; Murray H. Lichtenstein, "Chiasm and Symmetry in Proverbs 31," *Catholic Biblical Quarterly* 44, no. 2 (1982): 202–11; Bruce K. Waltke, "The Role of the 'Valiant Wife' in the Marketplace," *Crux* 35, no. 3 (September 1999): 25–29.

about the shrewdness of her adversary (3:1). The serpent tempts her, and she tastes the forbidden fruit.

Much has been extrapolated about females' nature from the fact that Eve was deceived and Adam was not. Yet the Bible does not teach that vulnerability to deception is an innately female trait—it is a human trait. (Note that when warning the Corinthians, Paul tells both men and women that he is concerned they will be deceived as Eve was by the evil one; see 2 Cor. 11:3.) Indeed, the Bible does not teach that because Eve was deceived, all women are more easily deceived than men. Nor do the Scriptures teach, as some say they do, that women's nature makes them seducing and deceiving. (Ironically, being deceived yet excelling at deception are mutually exclusive.) Elsewhere in Scripture when Paul references Eve's deception (1 Tim. 2:14), he is not making a statement about how God made all women with a design flaw; the apostle is probably appealing to the Jewish creation story as a corrective to a gentile creation story in which the woman came first and was preeminent.[15] Indeed, Eve cannot be both fully responsible for the fall due to innate female weakness, while not responsible for the fall, because man, being male, was fully responsible. The Genesis story actually spells out not gender differences but what man and woman had in common: both rebelled against God.[16]

What this means to those embodied as male and female is that brokenness entered the world and introduced a power struggle into how male and female relate (3:16)—that is, unless they are controlled by the Spirit. Since the entry of sin in the world, all creation has been groaning (Rom. 8:22). Death and grief, for which humans were not designed, entered their experience. Sickness and violence became common. As did genetic mutations. And a world that began in the garden with only male and female has, in the words of our Lord, those who are born eunuchs (Matt. 19:12). While all humans are made in God's image, bodies often bear the effects of a creation yet to be redeemed.

But Christ . . .

Nevertheless, Christ is victor! And through the Holy Spirit man and woman can be reconciled—we do not have to wait for the eschaton to live in harmony. In Christ, all believers—whether male or female—are priests (1 Peter 2:9), together offering sacrifices of praise (Heb. 13:15) and bringing people to God (Matt. 28:19–20), with a final destiny of reigning together (Rev. 5:10; 22:5).

I read a description not long ago of what it looks like to be a Spirit-filled woman:

---

15. See Sandra L. Glahn, "The Identity of Artemis in First-Century Ephesus," *Bibliotheca Sacra* 172, no. 687 (July–September 2015): 316–34; also Glahn, "The First-Century Ephesian Artemis: Ramifications of Her Identity," *Bibliotheca Sacra* 172, no. 688 (October–December 2015): 450–69.

16. On Eve, see Glenn Kreider, Eve: The Mother of All Seducers in *Vindicating the Vixens: Revisiting Sexualized, Vilified, and Marginalized Women of the Bible,* ed. Sanra Glahn (Grand Rapids: Kregel Academic, 2017), 129–46.

She'll do the Father's work; not seek her own success/desires; be filled with the Spirit; walk in God's ways; share the gospel; focus on eternal pursuits; live a life of holiness and obedience; turn from sin; walk in love; seek to meet others' needs; be others-focused; sacrifice her desires for others; be unselfish, gentle and courageous; have confidence, and zeal; not be wishy-washy or afraid; lead God's disciples; not be a follower when she shouldn't be; show initiative when appropriate instead of waiting on someone else to do right; confront when necessary; not be a people-pleaser; be decisive according to God's revealed will; fulfill commitments; be a worker, not lazy or a quitter; be humble; serve and listen to others in Christian leadership; not lord it over others; glorify another—the Father; not be greedy for recognition.

Actually, I confess—I borrowed this list from a "chart of Christ-like character qualities" that will "help explain authentic manhood more specifically."[17] I merely changed the pronouns from "he" to "she." Clearly, none of the qualities listed is actually exclusive to males or females. Both are called to be like Christ. The more like Christ a man or woman becomes, the more they are living out the biblical social ramifications of life embodied as male or female.

Jesus, Paul, and Gender Norms

Men and women are different by divine design. And sometimes men and women are given different commands based on differing responsibilities (e.g., wives, husbands, fathers, mothers). But if we're honest, we must concede that the Bible outlines no definition of universal masculine or feminine behavior other than the fruit of the Spirit lived out in male and female bodies. And at this point, it is instructive to note how Jesus and Paul responded to gender norms in their day.

Roman Sexualities, a collection of essays published by Princeton University Press, offers a major contribution to our understanding of sexuality in the Mediterranean world in Jesus's time.[18] And in it we find an explanation for why gladiator, actor, and prostitute were considered dishonorable professions: people who engaged in these occupations had their bodies subjected to public observation. And in that culture, enduring such scrutiny was dishonorable. A real man had complete agency over his body.

In one chapter, readers learn that the honor/status-driven culture of Rome defined a truly masculine man in part by his class, the sign of which he wore on his garments. And class was broader than economic status. Class carried with it

---

17. Stuart Scott, "Profiling Christian Masculinity," *Journal for Biblical Manhood and Womanhood* (Fall 2004): 13–14, http://cbmw.org/wp-content/uploads/2013/05/9-2.pdf.
18. Judith P. Hallett, and Marilyn B. Skinner, eds., *Roman Sexualities* (Princeton, NJ: Princeton University Press, 1997).

bodily rights. An adult male citizen got his man card in part from his lack of subjection to sex on demand (required of slaves) and from exemption from beatings or violence without a trial (also something slaves endured). To an ancient male Roman, a big part of his macho power came from having the freedom to say, "You must leave my body alone."

Yet Jesus voluntarily endured beatings and violence. Knowing this, we can better appreciate that from a Greco-Roman perspective, Jesus exchanged the cultural norm of masculinity for shame when he gave himself up for humanity. In Jesus's value system, love trumped the culture's gender roles. Indeed, Jesus let the cultural norm of his masculinity be violated for the glory of God. He voluntarily endured the humiliation of nakedness. And earlier, in a context in which "real men" didn't cry, Jesus wept (John 11:35). Additionally, in a world in which masculine men didn't characterize themselves as women, Jesus compared himself to a hen (Luke 13:34); and God, figuratively speaking, was a woman who lost a coin (15:8–10). Elsewhere, in a weapon-wielding world, Jesus told Peter to put away his sword (Matt. 26:52). If we step back and look at our Lord, we see that he himself is a misfit when it comes to conforming to gender norms. For him character always trumped them. Later, Paul looked to this very example of Jesus when describing what the Spirit-filled male householder should look like. Not only was the Christian husband to offer up his bodily rights (1 Cor. 7), but he was to sacrifice his very life (Eph. 5).

This is in no way to suggest that unisex or neutering is the ideal. Males and females do uniquely reflect God's image. But how exactly they do so often falls within the realm of mystery. And considering the above examples, it appears that seeking to establish ideals of masculinity and femininity so we can pursue them is not the best way. Perhaps doing so is like pursuing happiness, which we find on the road to elsewhere. It appears that we become our true masculine and feminine selves—becoming transformed into the people God intended us to be—as we focus on pursuing Christ and his likeness, walking in the Spirit. And sometimes our obedience may even look culturally unmanly or unfeminine. Yet we must imitate Jesus, not the culture—not even the Christian subculture.

What does this mean for how Christ followers interpersonally relate with one another as distinct yet fully equal image bearers of God, where our distinctiveness is not defined by behaviors or roles? Perhaps a helpful parallel is in thinking about fathers and mothers. Both are parents in sexed bodies; both are charged with caring for children. But rather than constantly focusing on whether a mother is acting too fatherly or a father is acting too motherly, we ask what is the best way to act "parently" toward the child or children. And that takes us back to how we embody the fruit of the Spirit in the role of parent.

God made male and female different, by beautiful design, to complement each other. But he did not lay out a chart for how they differ socially. The study of how male and female differ is a fascinating scientific and social study, but nowhere in the Bible do we find the suggestion that we are to figure out what the innate differences are so we can conform to them.[19] Rather, the ideal laid out for the social outworking of our embodiment is conformity to Jesus Christ. Indeed, we are called and predestined to be conformed to his image. And that image is love, joy, peace, patience, goodness, kindness, gentleness, faithfulness, and self-control (Gal. 5:22–23). Living out these qualities embodied as male and as female is Spirit-empowered biblical manhood and womanhood.

---

19. An exploration of the interpersonal dynamics of the roles of husband and wife in heterosexual marriage is beyond the scope of this work. But you can find my treatment of the topic elsewhere: Sandra Glahn, "A Word to Wives," in *Sexual Intimacy in Marriage*, by William Cutrer, Sandra Glahn, and Michael Sytsma, 4th ed. (Grand Rapids: Kregel, 2020), 185–201.

FOR DISCUSSION

1. What are some ways we see the terms *sex* and *gender* used interchangeably? Why do you think we often conflate them?

2. What are some of the differing qualities that you typically hear attributed to men and to women? How might exhibiting the fruit of the Spirit challenge some social norms of masculinity and femininity?

3. What does it look like to image God embodied as male and female?

FOR FURTHER READING

James, Carolyn Custis. *Malestrom: Manhood Swept into the Currents of a Changing World.* Grand Rapids: Zondervan, 2015.

Pearcey, Nancy. "How Women Started the Culture War." In *Total Truth: Liberating Christianity from Its Cultural Captivity*, 325–48. Wheaton, IL: Crossway, 2004.

Storkey, Elaine. *Origins of Difference: The Gender Debate Revisited.* Grand Rapids: Baker Academic, 2001.

C H A P T E R   6

ETHICS AT THE BEGINNING OF LIFE: CONCEPTION AND ABORTION

RICHARD L. VOET

For more than two thousand years, the Hippocratic Oath[1] served as the basis for medical ethics. The oath provided guidelines for physician behavior and prohibitions against abortion and assisted suicide. In 1803, Sir Thomas Percival, an English physician and devout Christian, published the first modern code of ethics.[2] Percival's work served as the main source for the American Medical Association Code of Ethics, adopted in 1847.[3] The development of modern technology such as hemodialysis, respirators, cardiopulmonary resuscitation, intensive care units, and organ transplantation introduced decision-making dilemmas that previously did not exist in the field of medical ethics. The study of ethical issues relating to biomedical technology, medical research, and the provision of health care from both an individual and a societal perspective is often referred to as *bioethics*. Many bioethical issues relate to decisions occurring at the edges of life. This chapter will concentrate on ethical issues at the beginning of life.

1. Ludwig Edelstein, *The Hippocratic Oath: Text, Translation and Interpretation* (Baltimore: Johns Hopkins University Press, 1943).
2. Thomas Percival, *Medical Ethics; or a Code of Institutes and Precepts, Adapted to the Professional Interests of Physicians and Surgeons* (Manchester: Russell, 1803).
3. American Medical Association, *Code of Ethics, Adopted 1847* (Philadelphia: T. K. and P. G. Collins, 1848).

WHEN DOES LIFE BEGIN?

Ethical decisions at the beginning of life require a definition of when life and personhood begin. Decisions involving abortion, in vitro fertilization, stem cell research, cloning, and genetic engineering all depend on this definition.

Historical Background

Among early Greek philosophers, the Pythagoreans were unique in their belief that the embryo was an animate being from the moment of conception.[4] Pythagoras believed that the male sperm contained all the characteristics of a human, while the female menses served as a substrate for growth. In this view, known as *preformationism*, humans develop from a miniature version of themselves (homunculus). Those who hold that sperm contain the homunculus are known as *spermists*, while *ovists* believe it is within the egg.[5] Aristotle believed an embryo developed from an unformed mixture of menstrual blood and semen, and was then animated by a succession of souls.[6] The first was a nutritive soul, followed by sensitive soul, and finally the rational soul when the human embryo was formed at forty days for a male and at ninety days for a female.[7] This formation coincided with the first movement of the fetus (later referred to as quickening). Thomas Aquinas was strongly influenced by Aristotle and held the same view of *delayed animation* (also referred to as *delayed hominization*), although Aquinas taught that Christ's incarnation was an exception.[8] Aquinas felt that there could never be a point in time in which the physical substance of the incarnate Christ was without animation. The early church, through a series of creeds, settled the doctrine that the incarnate Christ was one person with two natures at the moment of conception (i.e., fertilization).

Beginning in the second century BC, Greek thought had a strong influence on Judaism. The translation of the Jewish Scriptures from Hebrew into Greek, known as the Septuagint, shows some evidence of this influence. The Septuagint rendering of Exodus 21:22–25 describes a difference between the unformed and formed embryo that is not in the original Hebrew text:[9]

> And if two men strive and smite a woman with child, and her child be born *imperfectly formed*, he shall be forced to pay a penalty: as the

---

4. Ludwig Edelstein, *Ancient Medicine* (Baltimore: Johns Hopkins University Press, 1967), 17–20.
5. Clara Pinto-Correia, *The Ovary of Eve: Egg and Sperm and Preformation* (Chicago: University of Chicago Press, 1998).
6. Aristotle, *On the Generation of Animals* 2.3, 736b 2–5.
7. Aristotle, *The History of Animals* 7.3, 583b 3–5.
8. Thomas Aquinas, *Summa Theologiae* III, q. 27, a. 2 ad 2.
9. Translation from Charles Lee Brenton, *The Septuagint*, 1884, http://qbible.com/brenton-septuagint/exodus/21.html.

woman's husband may lay upon him, he shall pay with a valuation. But if it be *perfectly formed*, he shall give life for life, eye for eye, tooth for tooth, hand for hand, foot for foot, burning for burning, wound for wound, stripe for stripe.

The concept of delayed animation is also found in the Talmud:[10]

Surely, it was taught: If a priest's daughter was married to an Israelite who died, she may perform her ritual immersion and eat *terumah* [food offerings made to the priests] the same evening! R. Hisda replied: She performs the immersion but may eat *terumah* only until the fortieth day. For if she is not found pregnant she never was pregnant; and if she is found pregnant, the semen, until the fortieth day, is only a mere fluid.

The Stoics believed that human life began at birth, when the infant began to breath air.[11] The toleration of infanticide in the ancient world might imply that a child did not have full human status until long after birth.

Christian Views of Ensoulment

Three main views of the origin of the soul developed.[12] The first is known as *preexistence*. In this view, a person's immaterial soul already existed prior to uniting with the body. In the early church there were few followers of this position, but one such follower was Origen of Alexandria. Others who held this position were Plato, who was followed by the ancient gnostics. Add to these modern-day Mormons and the New Age adherents. The second view is known as *creationism*. Adherents to this view hold that a new soul is created for every human being and is infused into an embryo at a certain time. Infusion at the point of fertilization is the view held by most Roman Catholics. The third view is known as *traducianism*. Its adherents maintain that when God breathed life into Adam (Gen. 2:7), all future humans, both their material and immaterial aspects, were present in him (1:27). Traducianism allows for an unbroken chain of life that began with Eve, coming directly from Adam (2:21–24) and continuing through the procreation of males and females. Traducianism explains how the soul can be transmitted through nonsexual reproduction such as twinning and reproductive cloning.

---

10. *Babylonian Talmud; Tractate Yebamoth* 69b, trans. Israel W. Slotki, ed., Isidore Epstein, http://halakhah.com/yebamoth/yebamoth_69.html.

11. David Albert Jones, *The Soul of the Embryo: An Enquiry into the Status of the Human Embryo in the Christian Tradition* (London: Continuum, 2004).

12. J. Lanier Burns et al., "Passages to Master," in *Exploring Christian Theology*, ed. Nathan D. Holsteen and Michael J. Svigel (Bloomington, MN: Bethany House, 2014), 2:36–37.

Personhood

Modern embryology reveals that a new human zygote with a unique genetic code exists after fertilization.[13] The human zygote's development into a fetus is known as *epigenesis*. The current debate centers on the concept of personhood. A variety of theories have developed regarding the beginning of personhood, some of them similar to the concept of ensoulment and animation. The earliest concept of personhood is at fertilization (conception), when the sperm enters the egg, or a few hours later when the chromosomes unite (syngamy). Another view is that personhood begins at implantation (when the embryo attaches to the uterine wall), which occurs at six to seven days. It is interesting to note that beginning in the 1960s, the medical definition of conception began to shift from the point of fertilization to the point of implantation.[14] This definition allows the term *contraception* to refer to any method of birth control that prevents pregnancy up to the point of implantation. Day fourteen after fertilization is often used as a cutoff point for embryo research, since it is prior to the occurrence of the *primitive streak* (after which twinning is no longer possible). This led to the so-called *fourteen-day rule*, which was an international ban on embryo research after this point.[15] In May of 2016, two research groups reported sustaining human embryos in vitro up to thirteen days, causing some scientists to challenge the fourteen-day rule.[16]

From the ancient world through the time of English common law, personhood was often thought to begin at quickening (awareness of fetal movement), which occurs around seventeen to twenty weeks. The point of viability was used in the *Roe v. Wade* Supreme Court decision. And the moment of birth is used by many Western courts to assign full human personhood. Some have also suggested that personhood occurs sometime after birth.[17]

The Christian Medical and Dental Associations (CMDA) have developed a detailed position statement on the beginning of life:

> A living human being is a self-directed, integrated organism that possesses the genetic endowment of the species *Homo sapiens* who has the inherent active biological disposition (active capacity and potency) for ordered growth and development in a continuous and seamless maturation process,

---

13. Keith L. Moore, T. V. N. Persaud, and Mark G. Torchia, *The Developing Human: Clinically Oriented Embryology* (Philadelphia: Elsevier Saunders, 2013), 30–31.
14. Christopher M. Gacek, "Conceiving Pregnancy: U.S. Medical Dictionaries and Their Definitions of Conception and Pregnancy," *National Catholic Bioethics Quarterly* 9, no. 3 (2009): 543–57.
15. D. Joy Riley, "Applying Pressure to the 14-Day Rule," Christian Medical and Dental Associations, *The Point* (blog), June 15, 2017, https://www.cmda.org/resources/publication/applying-pressure-to-the-14-day-rule-2.
16. Insoo Hyun, Amy Wilkerson, and Josephine Johnston, "Revisit the 14-Day Rule," *Nature* 533 (May 12, 2016): 169–71.
17. Peter Singer, *Practical Ethics* (Cambridge: Cambridge University Press, 2011), 153.

with the potential to express secondary characteristics such as rationality, self-awareness, communication, and relationship with God, other human beings, and the environment.

Thus, a human being, despite the expression of different and more mature secondary characteristics, has genetic and ontological identity and continuity throughout all stages of development from fertilization until death.

A human embryo is not a potential human being, but a human being with potential.[18]

ABORTION

The term *abortion* usually refers to the spontaneous or induced expulsion of an *embryo* (first eight weeks of pregnancy) or *fetus* (after eight weeks) prior to the point of viability. A spontaneous abortion is often referred to as a *miscarriage*. Historical references to abortion date back as far as the Code of Hammurabi (1760 BC).[19] According to the Ebers Papyrus (1550 BC), an abortion could be induced with the use of a plant-fiber tampon coated with a compound that included honey and crushed dates.[20] Abortion and infanticide were tolerated in ancient Greece and Rome, despite the prohibition in the Hippocratic Oath. Ludwig Edelstein holds that the oath was written not by Hippocrates but by the Pythagoreans, who believed that human life begins at conception.[21] The earliest Christian reference that directly addresses abortion comes from the Didache (or The Lord's Teaching Through the Twelve Apostles to the Nations) from the first century AD.[22] Chapter 2 of the Didache states, "You shall not murder a child by abortion nor kill that which is born." Although Augustine and Aquinas held to the Aristotelian view of delayed animation, both were opposed to early abortion. There continue to be references to Aquinas in the contemporary Christian debate on the human embryo.[23]

In the United States, abortion was prohibited with few exceptions until 1973, when the decision was rendered by the US Supreme Court in *Roe v. Wade*.[24] The following is a summary of the decision taken from the opinion of Justice Harry Blackmun:

---

18. Christian Medical and Dental Associations, "Beginning of Human Life Ethics Statement," https://www.cmda.org/library/doclib/the-beginning-of-human-life-concfert.pdf.

19. *The Code of Hammurabi, King of Babylon*, trans. Robert Francis Harper (Clark, NJ: Lawbook Exchange, 2010), sec. 209–12.

20. John M. Riddle, *Contraception and Abortion from the Ancient World to the Renaissance* (Cambridge, MA: Harvard University Press, 1994), 69–72.

21. Edelstein, *Ancient Medicine*, 18–19.

22. Jones, *Soul of the Embryo*, 57.

23. David Albert Jones, "Aquinas as an Advocate of Abortion? The Appeal to 'Delayed Animation' in Contemporary Christian Ethical Debates on the Human Embryo," *Studies in Christian Ethics* 26, no. 1 (2013): 97–124.

24. Roe v. Wade, 410 U.S. 113 (1973).

1. For the stage prior to approximately the end of the first trimester, the abortion decision and its effectuation must be left to the medical judgment of the pregnant woman's attending physician.

2. For the stage subsequent to approximately the end of the first trimester, the State, in promoting its interest in the health of the mother, may if it chooses, regulate the abortion procedure in ways that are reasonably related to maternal health.

3. For the stage subsequent to viability, the State in promoting its interest in the potentiality of human life may, if it chooses, regulate and even proscribe abortion, except where it is necessary in appropriate medical judgment for the preservation for the life or health of the mother.

Prior to these words in his decision, Justice Blackmun wrote,

> With respect to the State's important and legitimate interest in potential life, the "compelling" point is at viability. This is so because the fetus then presumably has the capability of meaningful life outside the mother's womb. State regulation protective of fetal life after viability thus has both logical and biological justifications. If the State is interested in protecting life after viability, it may go so far as to proscribe abortion during that period, except when it is necessary to preserve the life or health of the mother.

A subsequent decision, *Doe v. Bolton*, defined maternal health so broadly ("all factors—physical, emotional, psychological, familial, and the woman's age—relevant to the well-being of the patient")[25] that it essentially permitted abortion on demand at any stage.[26]

It is interesting to read a policy statement issued by the American College of Obstetricians and Gynecologists in 1975, two years after the landmark decision of *Roe v. Wade*. The following excerpt is from their statement "Some Ethical Considerations in Abortion":

> The College recognizes that situations of conflict may arise between a pregnant woman's health interest and the welfare of her fetus. Both legally and ethically this conflict can lead to a justification for inducing abortion. The College affirms that the resolution of such conflict by inducing abortion in no way implies that the physician has an adversarial relationship towards the fetus and therefore the physician does not view the destruction

---

25. Doe v. Bolton, 410 U.S. 179 (1973).
26. Megan Best, *Fearfully and Wonderfully Made: Ethics and the Beginning of Human Life* (Kingsford, Australia: Matthias Media, 2012), 154.

of the fetus as the primary purpose for abortion. The College consequently recognizes a continuing obligation on the part of the physician towards the survival of a possibly viable fetus where this obligation can be discharged without additional hazard to the health of the mother.[27]

This position has changed significantly, and the American College of Obstetricians and Gynecologists now supports *feticide* (intentional killing of the fetus), euphemistically referred to as *fetal reduction*.[28] There are proposed ethical guidelines for abortion and feticide.[29] And there is acknowledgment by some that there is no distinction between feticide and infanticide.[30] In 2005, an article was published in the *New England Journal of Medicine* describing a protocol for infanticide in the Netherlands.[31] Infanticide has also been referred to as an "after-birth abortion."[32]

In 2001, the US Congress passed the Born Alive Infant Protection Act.[33] The act specifies that infants who are born alive, at any stage of development (and regardless of the circumstances of their birth), are persons who are entitled to the protections of the law. Although the act defines all live births as persons, it does not mandate medical treatment where none is indicated. In 2003, the US Congress passed the Partial-Birth Abortion Ban Act.[34] This act states that any physician "who knowingly performs a partial-birth abortion and thereby kills a human fetus shall be fined under this title or imprisoned not more than two years, or both." Recent guidelines for feticide reference this act, since "many abortion providers have begun to induce and document fetal demise before an abortion begins, to avoid any potential accusations of intending to violate the law."[35] The American Academy of Medical Ethics with the support of the Ethics Committee of the Christian Medical and Dental Associations has developed a position statement on abortion:

---

27. American College of Obstetricians and Gynecologists, (ACOG) Executive Board, "Some Ethical Considerations in Abortion," ACOG statement of policy, December 12, 1975.
28. ACOG Committee on Ethics, "Multifetal Pregnancy Reduction," ACOG committee opinion, 719 (2017).
29. Frank A. Chervenak and Laurence B. McCullough, "An Ethically Justified Practical Approach to Offering, Recommending, Performing, and Referring for Induced Abortion and Feticide," *American Journal of Obstetrics and Gynecology* 201 (2009): 560.e1–6.
30. Henrik Friberg-Fernros, "Clashes of Consensus: On the Problem of Both Justifying Abortion of Fetuses with Down Syndrome and Rejecting Infanticide," *Theoretical Medicine and Bioethics* 38, no. 3 (2017):195–212.
31. Eduard Verhagen and Pieter J. J. Sauer, "The Groningen Protocol—Euthanasia in Severely Ill Newborns," *New England Journal of Medicine* 352 (2005): 959–62.
32. Alberto Giubilini and Francesca Minerva, "After-Birth Abortion: Why Should the Baby Live?," *Journal of Medical Ethics* 39 (2013): 261–63.
33. Born Alive Infant Protection Act of 2001, Pub. L. No. 107–207, 116 Stat. 926 (2002), https://www.congress.gov/bill/107th-congress/house-bill/2175/text.
34. Partial-Birth Abortion Ban Act of 2003, Pub. L. No. 108–105, 117 Stat. 1201 (2003), https://www.congress.gov/bill/108th-congress/senate-bill/3/text.
35. Justin Diedrich, Eleanor Drey, and Society of Family Planning, "Induction of Fetal Demise before Abortion: Clinical Guidelines," *Contraception* 81, no. 6 (2010): 462–73.

1. As healthcare professionals dedicated to saving and protecting human life, we affirm that all human life has special value derived from being a part of the human family.
   A. The value of human life is independent of an individual person's genotype, developmental stage, age, sex, ethnicity, place of origin, disability, or perceived worth.
   B. The value of human life is continuous throughout lifetime, from fertilization to death.

2. Abortion results in the death of a human life. Elective abortion is an unnatural termination of pregnancy through intentional trauma, be it pharmacologic or surgical. Abortion may also be traumatic to the mother, resulting in lifelong physical and emotional sequelae.
   A. Elective abortion is not consistent with ethical health care as it violates the tenet that healthcare professionals "do not harm."
   B. Some medications and devices used as contraceptives can also be lethal to the developing child.
   C. In rare circumstances when a pregnancy puts the mother at substantial risk of dying, abortion can be ethical in order to save the life of the mother.
   D. In pregnancies that result from rape or incest, we support efforts to:
      1. encourage the mother to bring her child to term,
      2. protect the woman and her child from contact by the rapist or the incest perpetrator.

3. We oppose the practice of elective abortion and encourage life-honoring alternatives such as:
   A. parenting with family and community support,
   B. adoption,
   C. and foster care.[36]

ASSISTED REPRODUCTIVE TECHNOLOGIES

In 1978, Louise Joy Brown was the first child born after the use of in vitro fertilization (IVF). Since then, many women have overcome infertility by using this and other assisted reproductive technologies. In addition, IVF led to cloning and stem-cell research, which brought to light new ethical concerns at the beginning of life. Scott Rae and Joy Riley have written an excellent review of this subject.[37] The CMDA have developed guidelines for the use of assisted reproductive

---

36. American Academy of Medical Ethics, position statement on abortion, https://www.ama-assn.org/delivering-care/ethics/abortion.

37. Scott B. Rae and D. Joy Riley, *Outside the Womb: Moral Guidance for Assisted Reproduction* (Chicago: Moody Press, 2011).

technologies that uphold the sanctity of life and acknowledge that life begins at fertilization.[38] The CMDA consider the following consistent with God's design for reproduction: medical and surgical intervention to assist reproduction, artificial insemination by husband, embryo adoption, in vitro fertilization using wife's egg and husband's sperm with subsequent embryo transfer to wife's uterus, and cryopreservation (freezing) of sperm or eggs. The CMDA consider that the introduction of a third party may be problematic. This includes the use of donor egg or sperm, including components of a donor egg (the three-parent embryo).[39] Gestational surrogacy (third party carries child produced by wife's egg and husband's sperm) should preferably be reserved for extenuating circumstances (such as the loss of wife's uterus or a major medical problem) or for embryo adoption.[40] CMDA guidelines state that cryopreservation (freezing) of embryos should be done with the sole intent of future transfer to the genetic mother. The number of embryos produced should be limited to eliminate cryopreservation of excessive numbers of embryos. There should be agreement that all frozen embryos will be eventually transferred back to the genetic mother. Should it become impossible to transfer the frozen embryos to the genetic mother, embryo adoption or gestational surrogacy should be pursued.

The CMDA oppose discarding or destroying embryos; uterine transfer of excessive numbers of embryos; selective abortion (embryo reduction); destructive experimentation with embryos; true (or traditional) surrogacy (third party provides the egg and gestation); routine use of pre-implantation genetic diagnosis; and pre-implantation genetic diagnosis done with the intent of discarding or destroying embryos.

In November of 2017, a baby born at a Texas hospital became the first in the United States to come from a transplanted uterus. The mother, who was born without a uterus, received the transplant a year earlier from a live donor. In 2014, a woman in Sweden was the first in the world to deliver a child from a transplanted uterus. Like most new medical technologies, uterus transplantation has its ethical challenges.[41] In April 2017, researchers at the Children's Hospital of Pittsburgh published their results of an artificial womb used to sustain premature lambs for up to four weeks until they could survive on their own.[42]

---

38. Christian Medical and Dental Associations, "Assisted Reproductive Technology Ethics," https://www.cmda.org/resources/publication/assisted-reproductive-technology-ethics-statement.

39. Christian Medical and Dental Associations, "Three-Parent Human Embryos Ethics," https://www.cmda.org/resources/publication/three-parent-human-embryos-ethics-statement.

40. See the Snowflakes Embryo Adoption Program website, https://www.nightlight.org/snowflakes-embryo-adoption-donation/embryo-adoption/.

41. Ruby Catsanos, Wendy Rogers, and Mianna Lotz, "The Ethics of Uterus Transplantation," *Bioethics* 27, no. 2 (2013): 65–73.

42. Emily A. Partridge et al., "An Extra-Uterine System to Physiologically Support the Extreme Premature Lamb," *Nature Communications* 8 (2017): https://doi.org./10.1038/ncomms15112.

The premature lambs were placed in a synthetic Biobag filled with synthetic amniotic fluid. The umbilical cord was attached to a circulating pump acting as a heart-lung machine for oxygenation. The hope of the investigators is to eventually use a similar device to sustain extremely premature human infants born nineteen to twenty-two weeks' gestation, which is currently at or below the threshold of viability.[43] The use of artificial wombs was first coined *ectogenesis* in 1924 by the British scientist J. B. S. Haldane.[44] Haldane's concept of ectogenesis was a complete in vitro pregnancy from fertilization until birth. He predicted that by 2074, more than over 70 percent of births would be by ectogenesis. The ability to support in vitro embryos beyond fourteen days, coupled with artificial wombs, raises concerns regarding ectogenesis.[45] Others see the artificial womb as an opportunity to reduce the number of abortions.[46]

GENETIC INFORMATION AND TECHNOLOGY

The prominent Greco-Roman gynecologist Soranus of Ephesus (AD 98–138) gave instructions on how to recognize whether an infant was worth rearing, based on size, physical appearance, and anomalies.[47] A significant contributing factor that led to the Holocaust in Nazi Germany was the concept of *eugenics*. Eugenics was first introduced by Sir Francis Galton,[48] a cousin of Charles Darwin. It is based on the concept of selective breeding in humans. "Positive eugenics" promotes the reproduction of those couples who have desirable or "superior" traits that would be transmitted to their offspring. "Negative eugenics" advocates preventing reproduction of those who have undesirable or "inferior" traits. Eventually such a line of reasoning led to forced sterilization and ultimately euthanasia. It was in essence "a war against the weak." The physically and mentally disabled were targeted as well as ethnic groups that were thought of as socially undesirable. Unfortunately, some American religious leaders were also involved in the early stages of this movement.[49]

Although the Nuremberg trials condemned the Nazi eugenic practices as war crimes, controversy continues regarding the treatment of the disabled. In 1963, an infant with trisomy 21 (Down syndrome) and duodenal atresia (a blockage

43. Jeffrey L. Ecker et al., "Periviable Birth," *Obstetrics and Gynecology* 130, no. 4 (2017): e187–199.

44. J. B. S. Haldane, *Daedalus; or, Science and the Future* (New York: Dutton, 1924), 63–68.

45. C. Ben Mitchell, "Ectogenesis and the Future of Procreation," *Ethics and Medicine: An International Journal of Bioethics* 33, no. 3 (2017): 133–32.

46. I. Glenn Cohen. "Artificial Wombs and Abortion Rights," *Hastings Center Report* 47, no. 4 (2017): inside back cover, doi:10.1002/hast.730.

47. Owsei Tempkin, *Soranus' Gynecology* (Baltimore: Johns Hopkins University Press, 1956), 79–80.

48. See Nicholas Wright Gillham, *A Life of Sir Francis Galton: From African Exploration to the Birth of Eugenics* (Oxford: Oxford University Press, 2001).

49. See Christine Rosen, *Preaching Eugenics: Religious Leaders and the American Eugenics Movement* (Oxford: Oxford University Press, 2004).

in the intestines) was admitted to the Johns Hopkins Hospital.[50] The usual treatment would be a surgical repair of the blockage. The parents and physicians requested that it not be performed because of the developmental handicap of the child. The physicians assumed the parents had a right to make this decision, and the court was never asked to intervene. The child was not treated, and so the child died. In 1973, physicians at the Yale New Haven Hospital reported on a series of forty-three patients who were allowed to die without treatment.[51] The Johns Hopkins case and the Yale series became the focus of numerous commentaries and debates about the role of parental decision and the right of infants who had developmental disabilities.

The current availability of genetic testing provides an extensive amount of information that can lead to complex ethical dilemmas. Current rhetoric sounds similar to the writings of Soranus of Ephesus in describing a *principle of procreative beneficence*, which states that "couples who decide to have a child have a significant moral reason to select the child who, given his or her genetic endowment, can be expected to enjoy the most well-being."[52] An interesting program has been developed to reduce and eliminate the incidence of genetic disorders common to Jewish people. The program was developed by Rabbi Josef Ekstein and is called Dor Yeshorim (upright generation), based on Psalm 112:2.[53] Jewish children are tested anonymously and given a PIN linked to their sample. When a couple contemplates marriage, they contact Dor Yeshorim and enter their PINs to see if they are compatible. Infertility clinics routinely offer in vitro pre-implantation genetic testing on the embryo, and obstetricians routinely offer screening for genetic disorders for pregnant women.

On October 28, 2016, a team of scientists in China became the first to inject a person with cells that contained genes edited using the new CRISPR-Cas9 technique as part of a clinical trial to treat lung cancer.[54] CRISPR is an abbreviation of Clustered Regularly Interspaced Short Palindromic Repeats. Its simplified version, CRISPR-Cas9, is a rapid, accurate, and inexpensive technique to modify genes. Ten months later, an international team of researchers published their use of CRISPR-Cas9 gene editing to correct a disease-causing mutation in viable human embryos.[55] Although they did not transfer any of

---

50. Robert J. Boyle, "Paradigm Cases in Decision Making for Neonates," *NeoReviews* 5 (2004): 477–83.

51. Raymond S. Duff and A. G. M. Campbell, "Moral and Ethical Dilemmas in the Special-Care Nursery," *New England Journal of Medicine* 289 (1973): 890–94.

52. Julian Savulescu and Guy Kahane, "The Moral Obligation to Create Children with the Best Chance of the Best Life," *Bioethics* 23, no. 5 (2009): 274–90.

53. See the website for Dor Yeshorim at http://www.doryeshorim.org.

54. David Cyranoski, "CRISPR Gene-Editing Tested in a Person for the First Time," *Nature* 539 (November 24, 2016): 479.

55. Hong Ma et al., "Correction of a Pathogenic Gene Mutation in Human Embryos," *Nature* 548 (2017): 413–19, https://doi.org/.1038/nature23305.

the embryos, their work raises the ethical question of modifying the human germ line, which would permit unintentional genetic change to be passed on to future generations. The CMDA have developed guidelines regarding genetic information and technology.[56]

CONCLUSION

This chapter reflects a sanctity-of-life perspective based on scriptural principles. Scripture indicates that the fetus is created by God and seen by him (Ps. 139:13–16), considered worthy to be called by name (Isa. 49:1, 5), and set apart for specific tasks (Jer. 1:4–5). Old Testament passages that affirm the personhood of the unborn include Job 3:3–4; Psalm 95:6–7; 100:3; 119:73; and Isaiah 44:2, 24. The encounter between Mary and Elizabeth recorded in Luke 1:41–45 implies that even three months before birth, John was fulfilling his prophetic role;, and that early in gestation, Jesus was a person, and worthy of honor. Every human being is a person made in the image of God from fertilization until death. This principle should guide Christians with their decisions regarding beginning-of-life topics.

---

56. Christian Medical and Dental Associations, "Use of Genetic Information and Technology Ethics Statement," https://www.cmda.org/library/doclib/use-of-genetic-information-and-technology.pdf.

FOR DISCUSSION

1. Should a woman be forced to have a cesarean section to save the life of the baby? Why or why not?

2. A married couple who both suffer from a form of hereditary deafness decide to undergo in vitro fertilization. Should they be permitted to use pre-implantation genetic diagnosis to select an embryo who will also be deaf?

3. A twenty-five-year-old male has transitioned to a transgender female and desires a uterus transplant to have a child. Is this ethically permissible?

FOR FURTHER READING

Best, Megan, *Fearfully and Wonderfully Made: Ethics and the Beginning of Human Life*. Kingsford, Australia: Matthias Media, 2012.

Kilner, John F. *Dignity and Destiny: Humanity in the Image of God*. Grand Rapids: Eerdmans, 2015.

Rae, Scott B., and D. Joy Riley. *Outside the Womb: Moral Guidance for Assisted Reproduction*. Chicago: Moody Press, 2011.

CHAPTER 7

ADOLESCENT SEXUALITY

JESSICA N. McCLEESE AND CHELSI A. CREECH

A discussion on adolescent sexual behaviors is best understood by first determining how to define an adolescent. Such defining is important, because, generally speaking, adults consider adolescence as the "tween to teen" years. But from a research standpoint, adolescence includes children as young as eleven up to the young adult age of twenty-one. It is imperative that adults who work with those falling in this age group gain an understanding of adolescents' developmental levels in order better to understand the many nuances involved in discussing and teaching on sexuality. The idea that "knowledge is power" is especially true if one wants effectively to work with youth.

DEVELOPMENTAL LEVELS

Adolescence can be divided into three age categories: early adolescence (ages 11–14), middle adolescence (15–17), and late adolescence (18–21).[1] Significant differences exist between children eleven to twelve years old and young adults ages twenty to twenty-one. This means that sexuality education will vary based on stage of adolescence.

---

1. See "Stages of Adolescence," American Academy of Pediatrics, 2017, https://www. healthychildren.org/English/ages-stages/teen/Pages/Stages-of-Adolescence.aspx.

Early Adolescence (11–14)[2]

Physical development

Children in early adolescence are in the puberty stage. Those in this stage will typically have heightened awareness of physical appearance, comparing their physical selves to those of their peers. They will also typically have a growing awareness of physical attraction toward others.

Intellectual development

At this age, children transition from concrete thinking (things are either black or white) into abstract thinking (gray areas exist in many situations). They are also starting to think and reason more effectively and can understand that their current actions will have consequences later. Even so, they typically stay more present-focused than future-focused, often believing that bad things will not likely happen to them.

Emotional development

As children enter into puberty, their hormones rapidly change. This means that their emotions also change and intensify. At the same time, the children are maturing emotionally and learning how to handle emotions such as rejection, fear, and frustration. They are also growing in empathy.

Social development

At this age, adolescents are starting to individuate and turn more toward peers than to their parents. These youth want to be accepted by peers and are starting to figure out their identity by how they present themselves to others. They are exploring clothing and hairstyles that will tell the world around them who they are. Grown-ups may also find that their teens vacillate between wanting to spend time with parents and wanting to isolate themselves.

---

2. Sutter Health Palo Alto Medical Foundation, "Parents and Teachers: Teen Growth and Development, Years 11–14," 2001, http://www.pamf.org/parenting-teens/health/growth-development/pre-growth.html; Healthlink BC, "Growth and Development, Ages 11–14," 2017, https://www.healthlinkbc.ca/health-topics/te7233; Janelle Stewart, "15–17-Year-Olds: Ages and Stages of Youth Development," State Adolescent Health Resource Center, Michigan State University Extension, 2013, http://msue.anr.msu.edu/news/15_to_17_year_olds_ages_and_stages_of_youth_development; K. Teipel, "Understanding Adolescence: Seeing through a Developmental Lens," State Adolescent Health Resource Center, Konopka Institute, University of Minnesota, http://www.amchp.org/programsandtopics/AdolescentHealth/projects/Documents/SAHRC%20AYADevelopment%20LateAdolescentYoungAdulthood.pdf.

Middle Adolescence (15–17)[3]

Physical development
By the ages of fifteen to seventeen, especially near the end of this stage, teens have completed puberty and are sexually mature. Concerns about the body can grow during this time, and eating disorders can become a problem.

Intellectual development
By this time, teens have learned to reason well and are more likely to give logical answers to questions. They have a more defined sense of right and wrong and have developed personal convictions that might differ from those of their parents.

Emotional development
Youth at this stage are more at risk for struggling with feelings of sadness or depression. Many are starting to feel more confident about their own unique personalities, while still seeking some level of acceptance from peers. They are more likely to consider their futures, and they will start moving toward planning for future jobs and education with both excitement and a healthy level of apprehension. They need less supervision to complete tasks and are more self-motivated than they were in early adolescence.

Social development
Teens at this stage are growing even more interested in romantic and sexual relationships and have further differentiated from their parents. They can have an unrealistic view of relationships, seeing them as more ideal than they actually are. Such youth are far more interested in connecting with peers and significant others than they are in connecting with their parents. While they show this independence, they also often find that less conflict exists with their parents.

Late Adolescence (18–21)[4]

Physical development
Physical maturity has leveled off by this stage. Young people in this age range have a firmer understanding of their identity and feel more secure in regard to who they are individually. They are beginning to have more acceptance of their physical appearance.

---

3. Centers for Disease Control and Prevention, "Teenagers (15–17 Years of Age)," 2018, https://www.cdc.gov/ncbddd/childdevelopment/positiveparenting/adolescence2.html; Education.com, "Teenage Growth and Development: 15–17 Years," 2009, https://www.education.com/reference/article/teen-development-fifteen-seventeen-years (accessed August 14, 2018; article discontinued).
4. Hunter College of Social Work, "Late adolescence (18–21 Years Old)," http://www.hunter.cuny.edu/socwork/nrcfcpp/pass/learning-circlcs/four/Late%20Adolescence.pdf.

Intellectual development

Late adolescence brings with it an ability to make decisions and reason well, and teens in this stage are more idealistic and philosophical than they were previously. They hold on to several viewpoints at one time and see situations from several perspectives. They now better understand underlying principles and apply these to new and separate situations. These new intellectual abilities can cause them to have a greater concern for issues of diversity and social justice and can make them more empathetic to others.

Emotional development

While same-aged peers are still important, teens at this stage also seek more adult input regarding decisions or relationship development. They find that they are not in as much need of acceptance from peers; instead, they are becoming more willing to find acceptance within themselves. They are ready to take on adult responsibilities and are increasingly future-oriented. Often, there is some renegotiation of roles with regard to the adolescent and the parents, and the teen is much more likely to value the input of parents.

Social development

Intimate relationships are important and may become a greater focus. In this stage, the adolescent will begin self-assessment: "Am I who I need to be to have a serious relationship?" Most at this stage believe that love and fidelity are necessary for a committed relationship, and most are at least somewhat sexually experienced. Relationships become more about shared values than shared interests.

ISSUES OF SEXUALITY

Because of all the changes occurring biologically, socially, and psychologically at this time, teens tend to become interested in romantic and sexual relationships. Peer pressure and media often leave them feeling like sexual activity is a normal part of being an adolescent, and that not engaging in these activities makes them weird or abnormal in some way. To combat the myth that "everyone is doing it," it can be helpful to review the statistics regarding teen sexual activity to get a better idea of what teens are actually doing and saying about having sex. Such information can lead to more open and honest conversations about the issues related to teen sexuality and sexual activity.

What Statistics Reveal

In many junior-high and high-school hallways, cafeterias, and classrooms, teens discuss romantic and sexual activity with their peers in a way that leads most to believe that all teens are sexually active. In reality, though, this is not the case. According to data from 2016, the most recent year available, only 41 percent of high schoolers have ever been sexually active—and this is a decrease from previous years. While 41 percent is a lot, just a few years earlier close to 50 percent of high-school teens surveyed had already had sex. The decrease by nearly 10 percent has led some researchers to conclude that teens today are more willing to hold off on sexual intercourse. Teens who remain abstinent cite religious beliefs as one of the most important factors in their decision to abstain. Additionally, there is further cause for hope in that few teens are becoming sexually active at younger ages. Down from a few years ago, only about 4 percent of teens now have had sex by age thirteen. Following the trend of decrease in sexual activity, only 11.5 percent of teens report having four or more partners, again a decrease from previous years. To summarize, fewer teens are reporting any sexual activity, and sexually active teens are waiting longer and having fewer partners.[5]

Premarital Intercourse

While the numbers are trending in a positive direction, there is clearly still work to do in promoting healthy sexuality in teens. One way to do so is to recognize what makes it more likely for teens to become sexually active before marriage. As with most areas of adolescent development, much starts at home. Teens need to feel supported at home and need to feel heard. When teens approach their parents with questions, with concerns, or just to talk, moms and dads need to respond with love and warmth. Teens who report feeling misunderstood or unsupported by their parents are more likely to report being sexually active.

While parental influence is key, however, same-age peers often supplant parents as the most influential people in a teen's life. A desire to fit in and avoid standing out means teens are more likely to engage in behaviors they believe their friends are also engaging in. If their friends get a certain haircut or use a certain catch phrase, teens will often adapt their own personas to incorporate such behaviors. Similarly, what teens *believe* about their peers' sexual activity will have a great deal of influence on their own sexual behaviors. Notice, though, that it is less important what a teen's peers are *actually* doing—only what teens *believe* they are doing. If a teenager is convinced his or her friends are having sex, that teen is about 2.5 times more likely to become sexually active.

This all leads to the third factor that influences teens' decisions to become sexually active—that is, education. Overall, teens engaging in sexual activity usually are not hearing the message of Christian sexuality. They do not hear it at home, and they rarely hear it at church. In such scenarios parents generally are not setting up prescriptions of behavior for their children by making statements such as, "We want you to wait for sex until you are married." At church, when teens dress in inappropriate clothes or clothes that bear inappropriate messages, youth pastors tend to ignore the behavior. When young people don't hear what the expectations are for their behavior, or worse, don't receive correction when

---

5. Centers for Disease Control and Prevention, Youth Risk Behavior Surveillance—United States 2016," Morbidity and Mortality Weekly Report, June 10, 2016, https://www.cdc.gov/healthyyouth/data/yrbs/pdf/2015/ss6506_updated.pdf.

they fall short of expectations, they are left to figure out guidelines on their own. But because the adolescents' brains do not have fully developed frontal lobes, teens are literally incapable of fully evaluating the consequences and implications of their choices. Thus, letting these young people go it alone is an abandonment of responsibility as parents and pastors. The adolescents may not like correction at thirteen, fifteen, nineteen, or even twenty-one. Yet behind all the eye rolls and uncomfortable seat shifting, adolescents really do appreciate guidance on these big matters, as opposed to silence.

Gender Identity

The discussion of premarital sex has been part of parent-child relationships for decades. A newer dimension to this, though, is the addition of gender identity. *Sexual* identity, one's preference for another as a sexual partner—whether man, woman, both, or neither—has been part of the conversation longer, and has more often been the topic of church teachings, blog posts, and sermons. *Gender* identity, however, is one's self-perception as male, female, neither, or both. Gender identity is a new avenue of discussion that even those who devote their lives to studying it are still trying best to understand and explain. Unfortunately, teens, parents, and church leaders are learning about gender identity simultaneously, with little to no time for grown-ups to discern what to say before the children in their care have questions.

Gender dysphoria or transgenderism, the terms for a feeling of disconnect between one's biological sex and how one perceives his or her gender, is on the rise among all people, including teens. (See the chapter on gender dysphoria in this volume by Mark A. Yarhouse and Julia A. Sadusky.) As stated earlier, teens are still developing their decisional capacity, so shades of gray are hard to navigate. They may find different labels a way to explore such shades, but many who initially report struggles with gender identity will not adopt cross-gender identification. Current statistics show that approximately 12 percent of teens who initially report gender dysphoria will continue to experience it into adulthood; in other words, approximately 88 percent of cases will remit. With this in mind, one of the best things parents and pastors can do in the face of gender dysphoria is offer love and support as teens learn to discern between gender and stereotype. That is to say, a teenage boy may say, "I might be 'trans' because I like to draw and play music, and don't like sports much." In this instance, it is helpful to help the teen to see how wide the spectrum of masculinity can really be—some of the greatest artists and musicians have been men, for example. For teen girls, showing that traditional femininity is not the end-all and be-all of being a woman is equally important. Helping teens see a spectrum of "gray" rather than limiting life to black-and-white thinking is key.

Social Media Influence

Overall, one of the biggest complicating factors is the constant presence of social media to influence teens. The near limitless availability of technology and internet access leads to a lot of unsupervised time. With this time, teens often encounter pornography, sex-chat lines, and strangers online that used to be difficult to find.[6] Even when parents try to supervise discretionary time and use protective filters, new sites develop faster than filter software can keep up. Vigilance is good, but teaching healthy boundaries around technology is ultimately the better route. One of the most important factors in this regard is reminding teens that the internet is not real life—an idea that many adults may need reminders of occasionally too. With social media, it can feel like one's entire life is on display constantly. And that sense of life on display fosters feelings of inadequacy and depression when teens inevitably compare their online lives to those of their peers. As discussed earlier, it is not so much what a teen's peers are *actually* doing that influences behavior; it is much more what teens *believe* their peers are doing. When the highlight reels run constantly in front of their eyes, it can be hard for them to form an accurate perception of what is *actually* happening in real life. Instead, the bits and pieces of carefully worded status updates, filtered pictures, and videos that supposedly will disappear instantly become their whole world. Remember, again, teens are not able to fully comprehend the results of their actions, so this all seems quite reasonable to them—until the consequences are too large to ignore. All of this combines to create an atmosphere in which teens are left almost defenseless without parents, pastors, and reliable adults to help them make decisions. As with guidelines about premarital sex, teens need guidance in making decisions about social media.

HOW TO MINISTER TO AND HELP ADOLESCENTS

As already noted, there are three age categories of adolescence, which means that the help we offer is somewhat dependent on the stage of the adolescent in view. In general, we are working to move teens from concrete thinking regarding sexuality to more logical thinking. To better understand this concept, Timothy Jennings's teachings on moral decision-making will be used. Specifically, levels four and five of the seven-level model will be noted here.[7]

Level-four thinking is categorized by law and order—the belief is that if one obeys the rules, he or she can avoid punishment. In this stage, people may choose to look for "legal loopholes" that allow them to *not quite* break the rules. This might be seen in adolescents who engage in sexual behaviors, but not sexual intercourse.

Level-five thinking is based on a love for others—decisions made based on how they will affect another person. Jennings says that "this was Jesus healing on the Sabbath, socializing with tax collectors, and teaching lepers. Also, the

---

6. Raychelle Cassada Lohmann, "Sexting Teens," *Psychology Today*, March 30, 2011, https://www.psychologytoday.com/us/blog/teen-angst/201103/sexting-teens.

7. T. R. Jennings, "God and Your Church: Preparing People to Meet Jesus." Come and Reason Ministries, 2015, http://www.comeandreason.com/index.php/en/media-center/column1/god-and-your-church-seminar/seven-levels-of-moral-decision-making.

story of the Good Samaritan, apostles picking grain on the Sabbath, David and the showbread."[8]

Working with teens from early to late adolescence requires the process of moving them from level-four thinking to level-five thinking. In many ways, teens are already in the process of making this transition. Remember that teens in the early stages are starting to want to rebel a little against the rules that have always been set for them. They are beginning to question whether the adults in their lives have the right answers, because these teens are now trying to determine their own beliefs about right and wrong. It is no longer acceptable for parents to say, "because I said so." Instead, teens want to know adults' reasoning. Let's look at how we can help teens make the transition from level-four thinking to level-five thinking in a way that leads them into a Christ-centered manner of decision-making with regard to sexuality.

Put Some Protections in Place

Brain scans have shown that the frontal lobe of the brain, the part responsible for logical processing and understanding possible consequences of actions, is not fully formed until about the age of twenty-five.[9] In fact, adults use their frontal lobe when making decisions, and teens use the amygdala. Because teens are using the emotional center of their brains, adolescents can get wrapped up in the here and now and find it difficult to make decisions or fully understand what in-the-moment decisions can mean in the long term.

While discussions about teens' ability to make wise choices are important (and will be explored here shortly), it is also practical to put protections on teens that help them make wise decisions. For example, since it is known that teens are going to be using their devices often and that internet access can be a gateway to accidental porn exposure or porn addiction, parents can limit the time that their teens spend online. The producers of the film *Screenagers* created a list of resources to monitor the time spent online, and these resources can be found on their website.[10]

It is also noteworthy that many phone companies will allow parents to mirror their teens' devices onto their own phones. This means that the parents' screens will show exactly what web pages and apps their teens have visited, as well as any texts that have been sent or received. Those who choose this option must make sure that they do this with their teens in the early to middle stages, and that they have conversations with their teens about taking this step. It is good to remind the teen that the monitoring is intended not as a lack of trust but rather designed to protect them, keeping them from accidental exposure to unsafe people and sites.

---

8. Jennings, "God and Your Church," slide 84.
9. University of Rochester Medical Center Health Encyclopedia, "Understanding the Teen Brain," 2018, https://www.urmc.rochester.edu/encyclopedia/content.aspx?ContentType ID=1&ContentID=3051.
10. See "Screentime Management Apps," Screenagers, www.screenagersmovie.com/parent-ing-apps.

In addition to apps that will help with monitoring screen time, doing a quick search on the app store for "parenting apps" or for "monitoring apps" will reveal a number of programs that aid parents in creating rating systems for allowable content, block web pages of apps, and set time limits. Since specific apps are rapidly changing, none will be included in this essay. Instead, parents are encouraged to do searches and explore which programs seem most appropriate for accomplishing their goals.

Create a Supportive Environment for Teens

It has been said that raising kids takes a village. This has become even more true as teens are more readily exposed to harmful images online and in every advertisement imaginable. One of the most effective ways to increase communication with one's teen is to have talks about what interests them. Teens desperately want to be known, so learn their story. Let them know they are important.

Parents often have some difficulty withholding correction of their teens when their thought processes seem incorrect and illogical. And, in many ways, parents need to provide correction when it comes to faulty theology or beliefs that could ultimately hurt their teens. But teens want to know that their opinions are respected, and they want to feel that they are allowed to differ in their beliefs from those of the adults around them. When talking to teens, it is good to ask them about themselves. Parents can consider the following: What does your teen like to do? What interests your teen? What are your teen's thoughts on sexuality and faith? What does your teen believe about God?

We advise parents to ask questions and refrain from too much correction. Then, as you hear out your teen, explain your thoughts on who God is and how we live sexually pure lives. Your teen needs to know that you trust him or her to make good decisions. Practice conversation with your teen that encourages him or her to continue thinking through issues while gently providing some guidance into the decisions that will bring the most positive results long term. Remember, you are stepping away from level-four, rule-based thinking into level-five thinking, which looks at how these actions show a God-like love to others over the long term.

In a supportive community, we're called to love as Christ loved the church. Scripture teaches that others should know who we are by the love we show one another. Supportive community does not require that we agree with someone's choices, but simply that we love them well and have a willingness to know them.

Help Teens Understand the Bigger Picture of Sex

In their book *Soul Virgins*, Doug Rosenau and Michael Todd Wilson describe the concept of 3D sexuality, in which single young adults can grow to understand that they are sexually whole beings with body, soul, and spirit. While this book emphasizes young adult behaviors directed toward dating, it is clear that teens could also benefit by seeing themselves for more than just their physical appearance. Recall that teens transition from greater focus on their own physical appearance to an interest in the physical attraction of others. It is healthy and appropriate to notice and appreciate members of the opposite sex; however, it is important that our young people learn to see themselves and others as beings with a body, heart, and soul. All pieces come together to make a whole person. Focusing on other aspects of the person (their soul and the heart of who they are) can help teens to have a relationship-centered focus as opposed to a sexually centered focus. Importance and value come from being made in the image of God, not the image that might be shown on social media.[11]

In his book *Sex in a Broken World*, Paul David Tripp preaches a similar message when he encourages his readers to have a big-picture view of sex. He notes that a small-picture view of sex is self-focused, self-seeking, and immature. On the other hand, a big-picture understanding of sex can happen only when someone realizes that sex is connected to God's existence. Even if someone is unaware that God is connected to sex, Tripp says, "The way you express your sexuality will either recognize God's existence and honor him or deny his existence and rebel against his authority."[12] Helping teens understand this basic principle can give them the ability to see that decisions today can affect them in the future and in their immediate relationship with God.

Dispel the Myth That "Everybody Is Having Sex"

Alison Calabia, writing for *Psychology Today*, notes that teens are 2.5 times more likely to have sex if they believe that their friends are having sex.[13] So simply letting teens know that most teens are *not* having sex can serve as a protective factor against engaging in sexual behaviors. Even when teens have had sex in the past, they can be taught that abstinence from this point forward is possible. Teens can create boundaries in their relationships, even if their new boundaries are more limiting than the boundaries they had in the past. Remember, statistics are actually showing us a decrease in recent years regarding the percentage of teens involved in premarital sex.

Seek to Involve Parents or Adult Members of the Church in Work with Teens

In ministry, there will often be opportunity to help parents better understand their teens. It's a wonderful thing when the church is able to team up with parents and their community to support kids and teens. Hoping for change

---

11. Douglas E. Rosenau and Michael Todd Wilson, *Soul Virgins: Redefining Single Sexuality* (Grand Rapids: Baker Books, 2006).

12. Paul David Tripp, *Sex in a Broken World: How Christ Redeems What Sin Distorts* (Wheaton, IL: Crossway, 2018), 91.

13. Alison Calabia, "Teens and Sex," *Psychology Today*, July 1, 2001, www.psychologytoday. com/us/articles/200107/teens-and-sex.

through sermons or ministry alone may not be enough. When teens return to their home environment from church or youth group, they can be surrounded by other messages and will need adults to come around them to support them.

Teach parents how to engage their teens in communication around sexual topics as well as how to ask questions that will help such parents better understand their teens. Encourage them to practice "take-nology," in which everyone in the house sets aside all forms of technology to spend time together as a family. Use this time to open up dialogue that allows a teen to ask questions or express concerns. For conversation starters, see the references at the end of this chapter.

Make Communication Comfortable[14]

Being comfortable discussing sexual topics is absolutely necessary if you're going to show teens that they can have these conversations with you. Practice having these conversations in your adult circles. Make sure that you communicate your values, but do so without getting overly preachy. Try using the Socratic method, asking several questions that get others thinking. Instead of saying directly, "God designed sex for after marriage, and you should be abstinent while you're single," try asking questions that let teens think this out for themselves: "What would it be like to save yourself for marriage? What would it mean to you if you were able to hold to your own convictions instead of letting society say what is best? Do you believe your faith affects your decisions when it comes to sexuality? What do you believe is God's best plan for sex?" Questions such as these invite dialogue and show teens that you are comfortable with their thoughts and questions.

CONCLUSION

Engaging teens can help them see a bigger picture of the gospel as well. These dialogues teach them that the gospel isn't just the words we read from Scripture or what we hear on a Sunday morning. The gospel is lived out in one's entire existence, including how a teen treats others and lives life. Teens can learn that the behaviors they engage in or don't engage in all indicate what they believe about God. As stated earlier, God cannot be separated from sexuality.

---

14. For more information about having conversations with teens about sex, see Sara Villanueva, "Teens and Sex," *Psychology Today*, February 11, 2016, https://www.psychologytoday.com/blog/how-parent-teen/201602/teens-and-sex.

FOR DISCUSSION

1. A common myth for adults and adolescents is that "everyone is doing it."
    What information and what approach are needed to combat this myth?
    Why is this important?

2. Moral decision-making has been described to occur at level four and
    level five for adolescents. What are the processes for each of these levels?
    Why is it important to transition from level four to level five? How does
    an adolescent transition to level five in moral decision-making?

3. What does it mean for an adolescent to get a "bigger picture of the gos-
    pel" as it relates to personal sexuality? How can you as a parent facilitate
    that bigger picture with your teen?

FOR FURTHER READING

Jones, Stan, and Brenna Jones. *What's the Big Deal? Why God Cares about Sex.* Colorado Springs: NavPress, 2007. Also see the authors' four-book series specific to different age groups, God's Design for Sex.

Villanueva, Sara. "Teens and Sex." *Psychology Today*, February 11, 2016. https://www.psychologytoday.com/blog/how-parent-teen/201602/teens-and-sex.

CHAPTER 8

ADOLESCENT AND YOUNG ADULT SEXUALITY

DOUGLAS E. ROSENAU

Wouldn't you agree that the church can do a better job of dealing with single sexuality? If 50 percent or more of the people attending church are single, why haven't we helped them negotiate this exciting and difficult time in their lives with a solid Christian ethic? The place we have to start in creating such a Christian sexual ethic for singles is with the symbolic concept of chastity. I have often been asked by single adults, "Why would I want to be chaste? Why would I want sexual purity and to discipline my sexual urges?" What I reply is this: "If you don't believe there is a creator God who made us, and if you don't believe that he really wants a love relationship with us through Jesus, and if you don't believe that he gave us instructions and guidelines through his Word for creating personal intimate love relationships—I'm not sure why you want to be chaste."

And so, when it comes to a sexual ethic and exploring sexual integrity, chastity, and wholeness, it all revolves around who God is and what I refer to as God's "sexual economy." We usually look at the word *economy* as something to do with finances, but actually the word *economy* comes from two Greek words: οἶκος and νόμος. Οἶκος is the idea of a house or household, and νόμος means rules or guidelines. God has a sexual economy, household guidelines, revealed in Scripture. God gives us an economy to follow, and that is what I want to unfold and look at in this chapter through three illustrations: the inside-out approach, the sexual boxes of social and erotic sexuality, and the relationship-continuum bridge.

THE INSIDE-OUT APPROACH TO
SEXUAL INTEGRITY AND WHOLENESS

The bottom line when it comes to sexual ethics is ultimately this: the intimate Trinity has given humans their sexuality as a primary vehicle for creating and enriching intimacy. The Creator has also given us a sexual ethic through his Word that works and helps humans to build and protect intimate relationships.

Sexually, the church has usually operated with an outside-in approach. That is, we have tended to teach that if we work hard to avoid certain "sinful" sexual behaviors, we will create attitudes that will help us be more Christlike. The problem with such an approach is that this is not the way Jesus taught. He didn't say, "Fight sin, my children, and you'll be more like me." He said, "Come have a love relationship with me and with the Father, and my light will drive out the darkness." What Jesus offers is illustrated in figure 1.

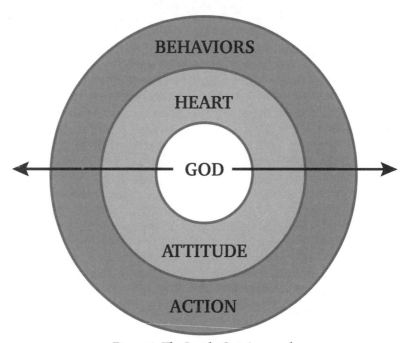

Figure 1. The Inside-Out Approach

Yet, sadly, our outside-in approach has deteriorated into a sexual ethic of chastity that is based on controlling one behavior: penis-in-vagina intercourse. And we can see in the present Christian culture in many parts of the world that such a sexual ethic hasn't resulted in pure lives. I often tell young single adults, "If all you are doing is trying to keep from sleeping with your girlfriend or boyfriend, you are in trouble. Let's let Jesus help you be unselfish and cast a vision of sexual chastity that will help you and your girlfriend or boyfriend grow into the sexual person God intended you to be." What a fun job description that is: Helping someone grow into their full sexual potential.

An inside-out theology starts with God and a motivating personal relationship with him through Jesus and the empowering Holy Spirit. Then our ethic is built on his Word and his sexual economy. As we take the inside-out approach as seen in the circles in figure 1, God truly touches our hearts and our minds and that work of the Spirit in turn truly touches our actions and our behaviors. What if we really let Jesus put an unselfish love into our hearts rather than simply trying to avoid certain behaviors? Such an approach is so important that Jesus came to create a new covenant, and this covenant is not going to be based on works and Levitical laws. This covenant relationship will be internally motivated with a changed mind and heart—not based only on regulating behaviors:

> This is the covenant I will make with them
> > after that time, says the Lord.
> I will put my laws in their hearts,
> > and I will write them on their minds. (Heb. 10:16 NIV)

My conservative Christian background focused on banning behaviors and going outside-in. You can see how such an approach was effective only if the "sex police" were out to keep an eye on everyone's actions. Ethics, if they're not internally motivated, will ultimately have little effect on us. That is why it is crucial to define virginity and chastity as much more than behaviors we abstain from. I like to define a virgin—and remember that this is not about what your body has done or not done—as a heart attitude, as *someone who values, celebrates, and protects his or her sexuality and that of one's brothers and sisters.*

So, an effective sexual ethic begins with a personal relationship with Jesus and his transforming power. And then it involves inviting him to guide you: "Okay Lord, help me understand your sexual economy better."

Using such a grid, let's choose a behavior—let's say masturbation—and apply an inside-out, internally motivated ethic. I'm never going to start with a simple assessment of something as "a right or wrong behavior." Jesus always got personal; so I imagine he would ask, "How is masturbation affecting you in your relationship with me and with your brothers and sisters—or the person you are dating?"

We can take any sexual behavior and start inside-out rather than outside-in. So, let's be careful as Christians to refrain from basing our ethics on banning behaviors. Instead, let's go inside-out; let's be internally motivated. And let's really try to think through how we value, celebrate, and protect our sexuality and that of another. Let's invite God to help us achieve a sexual integrity and chastity that can build sexual wholeness. So that is the starting ethic—go inside-out.

SOCIAL AND EROTIC SEXUALITY

Part of creating a Christian sexual ethic is considering semantics and fashioning a language to convey the various concepts. In thinking through sexuality and an ethic for singles, we can see two types of sexual expression. The late Stanley Grenz, in his book *Sexual Ethics*,[1] and William Kraft, in *Whole and Holy Sexuality*,[2] called these two sexual expressions "affective" and "genital" sexuality. Marva Dawn in *Sexual Character*[3] labeled the two modes "social" and "genital" sexuality. Many years ago, I called affective sexuality "platonic" sex, and in my book *Soul Virgins*,[4] I labeled it "gender" sexuality. I feel "social" best expresses the concept of gender sexuality, while "erotic" communicates a broader concept than merely "genital."

Defining Social and Erotic Sexuality

All relationships include social sexuality, and some include erotic sexuality. The concept of social sexuality would be that of gender and family, while erotic sexuality would have more to do with genital, libido, sexual arousal, and romantic sexuality. The two are rooted in the two ways that God loves:[5] God loves inclusively and expansively, with a communal intimacy; and God loves exclusively and permanently through Jesus with a covenantal intimacy. Social sexuality is where singles and marrieds alike spend most of their relational time, while perhaps still having a yearning to enjoy and be truly known through erotic sexuality.

Social sexuality demonstrates God's communal love as most arrive in a world with parents of both sexes who love us in ways expressed through their unique genders. When I interact with males or females, I always carry my masculinity with me. It is always a unique and richer interaction because of the way my masculinity interacts with the masculinity or femininity of the other person. My gender weaves a vital thread into the tapestry of all my interactions, as does yours. It's not what we do but who we are—a man or woman adding a rich dimension to all of our relationships and reflecting the very image of God:

> So God created human beings in his own image.
> In the image of God he created them;
> male and female he created them. (Gen. 1:27 NLT)

---

1. Stanley J. Grenz, *Sexual Ethics: An Evangelical Perspective* (Louisville: Westminster John Knox, 1990), 98–102, 196, 219.
2. William Kraft, *Whole and Holy Sexuality: How to Find Human and Spiritual Integrity as a Sexual Person* (Eugene, OR: Wipf & Stock, 1998).
3. Marva J. Dawn, *Sexual Character: Beyond Technique to Intimacy* (Grand Rapids: Eerdmans, 1993), 9–11.
4. Douglas E. Rosenau and Michael Todd Wilson, *Soul Virgins: Redefining Single Sexuality* (Grand Rapids: Baker Books, 2006).
5. Grenz, *Sexual Ethics*, 98–102, 196, 219.

We also must remember that nearly everyone has the ability to experience sexual attraction and arousal. Sexual arousal and attraction, or libido, add the erotic to relationships. In addition to an inclusive communal interaction, God also wants to create an exclusive relationship with his children through Jesus Christ. Marriage and the genital erotic expression of becoming one with our beloved is a profound metaphor for the love Christ has for his bride, the church. The eternal God, being neither male nor female, is not sexual, but he does use our physical erotic feelings and marriage to reflect and reveal the way he pursues and loves us exclusively in a unique, personal love relationship. We see this reflected in his invitation to humans: "Here I am! I stand at the door and knock. If anyone hears my voice and opens the door, I will come in and eat with that person, and they with me" (Rev. 3:20 NIV).

The erotic can always add color and excitement to living life fully and experiencing intimacy, but it can also become a frustrating nuisance, especially for the single adult. In the same way we always take our gender into our relationships, our sex drive is with us, adding energy and complexity to every one of our social interactions. Since God wants us to wisely put boundaries around erotic expression with an exclusive member of the opposite sex, single adults have to learn how to embrace their libido and find ways to manage this erotic component of their lives. Singles can learn to cultivate and discipline meaningful social and erotic intimacy, but doing so requires many wise choices.

The Boxes of Social and Erotic Sexuality
To help explain the place of social and erotic sexuality within single relationships, picture three sealed boxes that exist as a box within a box within a box (see figure 2).

SOCIAL & EROTIC SEXUALITY

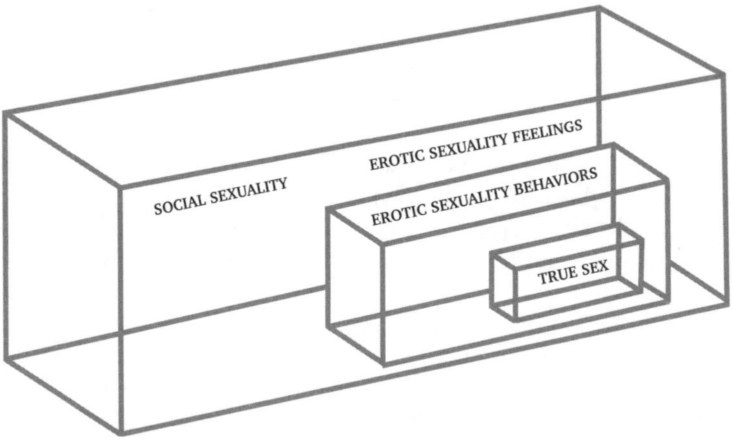

Figure 2. The Boxes of Social and Erotic Sexuality

We can open each of these boxes and have its space as a place in which we live out our lives. The largest box, where we all spend most of our time, is "social sexuality." And then within this the largest of boxes, I have placed two smaller boxes: erotic sexual behaviors (dating and marriage); and within that box, true sex (genital sexual expression within marriage).

We live mostly in the fun box of social sexuality, where we have healthy gendered interactions. Such interactions begin in infancy as we are involved with parents of both sexes, grandparents, and other relationships. How awesome that God created humans male and female in his image for a reason. As I stated before, gender weaves beautiful, enriching threads into the tapestry of every one of our relationships.

Within social sexuality is what I call righteous flirting. Righteous flirting is the ability for men and women to build each other up and affirm their masculinity or femininity. The person I have enjoyed flirting with most was my ninety-four-year-old mother-in-law, who passed away last year. She grew up with four brothers and just loved men. When she was in the nursing home in her late eighties and nineties, some of it would almost get embarrassing. I visited her once in the summertime and she said, "Doug, you know, you are just so handsome. I didn't remember your legs were that hairy, and they really are nice looking." I said, "Well thank you, Kay." She would also affirm what a good grandpa and son-in-law I was. I would comment on her hair and femininity—we would build each other up and were enriched by this righteous flirting.

What's really difficult at times is that in the middle of our gendered social interaction, God still hasn't eliminated erotic sexual feelings. We still have hormones; we still have that ache; we still have erotic desires and attractions that come up. One young lady came to me recently and said, "Dr. Doug, I've been married only eight months, but there's this guy at work, and he is really hot." She was almost crying.

I asked, "Did you think that when you got married, you would never be attracted—no one else would ever be hot again?"

"Well, I think I hoped so," she said.

I shook my head. "No, no. You are going to have sexual feelings, you're going to notice other men besides your husband, and that's where the discipline comes in." I told her that there would always be relationships she would have to treat more carefully and place boundaries around more tightly, because there is more attraction.

Please notice that the "erotic sexual feelings" rectangle placed within our social sexuality box. The relationship with my mother-in-law was not erotically charged, but women closer to my own age might have that erotic attraction. Whether single or married, within your social sexuality there are some relationships that you have to "boundary" a little better. It's a good tension. But always that tension of "Mercy, that person is attractive to me; he's kinda hot.

She's—yeah, wow, you know." We can learn how to discipline our sexual feelings and steward them in healthy ways.

The second box to consider as we develop social and erotic sexuality is erotic sexual behaviors (and thoughts). With singles, these are dating relationships. Often these adults ask, "If I'm dating someone exclusively, how far can I go? What exactly are the erotic boundaries? Where can I go with the erotic part of my sexuality? I'm in love with this person; I really enjoy him." Or "I find that we have a great deal of chemistry. What is permissible to us sexually?" Of course, I often will tell singles that "How far can I go?" is a pretty selfish question.

I think we should be asking, "I'm dating this guy, and I may not marry him" or "I'm dating this gal, and I may not marry her," and "How could I influence this person so if we end up breaking up and not getting married that her future husband or his wife could come to me and say, 'Thank you for dating my mate. My spouse is so much more sexually whole and mature because they dated you'?" That would be a testimony to what I call "soul virginity." When I am defining chastity and trying to think through making out, allowing arousal, and enjoying that chemistry, it's not a *wrong* question to ask, "How far should we go?" That question can encourage wisely setting boundaries and stewarding erotic sexual thoughts and behaviors.

How do people sort all this out? It goes back to our inside-out ethic. Allow me an example of how hypocritical and complex this becomes if we don't base our sexual ethic solidly on a chastity that values, celebrates, and protects our own sexuality and the sexuality of those with whom we are in relationship.

A young lady was feeling intimidated and guilt-ridden because her brother and his fiancée had chosen to wait to kiss until their wedding day. That was their boundary. You can imagine how the sister was feeling tremendously guilt-ridden, since she had a troubled sexual past with guys. About three months into the marriage, her sister-in-law came to her and said, "I'm really feeling guilty. I see all the shame that we've created for you because of your past and our boundary not to kiss. I do hope you can work it through better with the Lord, but I don't want to create false guilt. Your brother I didn't kiss until our wedding day, but we actually were naked and had oral sex. We realize now what an arbitrary boundary that was to not kiss until our wedding day."

As we explore the meaning of erotic sexual thoughts and behaviors and the box of true sex, there will have to be a better understanding of chastity that is not based on behaviors. One can be single and sexually whole. One can place boundaries around genital erotic sexuality and still be sexually whole. We must think through and keep in mind why God created our sexuality. The creative Trinity wanted humans to be able to reflect the loving intimacy the Triune God experiences, and sexuality was God's chosen grand metaphor. This can be demonstrated through the relationship-continuum bridge.

THE RELATIONSHIP-CONTINUUM BRIDGE

My last illustration, the relationship-continuum bridge, pulls together social and erotic sexuality and helps us sort out the whole dating experience. The bridge can be looked at as a sexual ethic for dating, and it can show the place of social and erotic sexuality within all our intimate relationships. See figure 3.

THE RELATIONSHIP-CONTINUUM BRIDGE

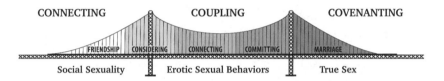

Figure 3. The Relationship-Continuum Bridge

The bridge explores three types of relationships: connecting, coupling, and covenanting. Connecting stands for friendships; coupling stands for dating, romantic relationships, and becoming an "item"; and covenanting stands for the commitment of marriage. Connecting is a place where singles are on solid ground in social sexuality; they are building meaningful intimate friendships that may or may not turn romantic. Singles within connecting friendships may be looking across to the land of marriage and saying, "I would like some day to be married. I'm going to get on the bridge with someone at some point and walk over the bridge into marriage." They realize that the covenanting-partnership vows ("I do") do not represent a simple contract, but a lifetime promise of sexual fulfillment and fidelity.

In thinking through a Scripture-based sexual ethic, it is worth restating that "erotic" sexuality always comes with wise boundaries. Connecting social sexuality that has erotic sexual feelings present must be carefully stewarded to value, protect, and celebrate intimate friendships. Coupling relationships have boundaries around "How far can I go?" within the romance and sexual excitement. Dating relationships guard genital expressions that are reserved for marriage and true sex.

Important parts of the bridge continuum in guiding relationships as they move toward marriage are what I call the three *Cs* of considering, confirming, and committing, which describe the progression of coupling/romantic dating relationships. The two posts of the bridge illustration are critical: they represent dating exclusively and saying "I do," making the sacred commitment of a lifetime together.

As the illustration makes clear, considering dating starts from the place of connecting friendship, before one even reaches that post of exclusively dating. Dating sites such as eHarmony would say they can put people on the bridge. But actually, that's not quite accurate. eHarmony can help people obtain a lot of compatibility and information, but eHarmony can only put someone in the place of a connecting friendship, from where they can consider getting on the bridge.

Getting on the bridge, however, is still something people must make choices about. And when someone is actually on the bridge, the three *Cs* represent different and important stages. The considering stage begins before one even chooses to get on the bridge, and it continues within exclusive dating until a person has traveled to the middle of the bridge and is connecting. That, in my opinion, is where a couple should start doing premarital therapy, rather than waiting until there's a ring on the finger and invitations have been sent. Connecting is where the heavy lifting of courtship takes place and the couple takes enough time to search out deal breakers. The third part of the bridge, committing, ideally should last only two or three months—not a year or eighteen months.

The Bridge with Dating and Sexual Ethics

Courtship should provide clarity in the relationship and increase the satisfaction. I appreciate an article by Scott Stanley, Galena Rhoades, and Howard Markman that talks about "sliding versus deciding."[6] Singles need to *decide* on a good marriage and not *slide* into such a commitment. And to me, the bridge is all about deciding, not sliding. The present cultural practice of living together can become a decision based on constraint rather than a loving commitment. After living together, people can think, "Now we have a mutual mortgage note or rent" or "Now we actually have a child," so they feel that they need to stay together. Such additions can be constraints that lead to commitment rather than a dedicated decision that says, "I love you unselfishly. I really want to be with you for a lifetime." So the bridge is important in doing more than defining sexuality; it actually helps a couple in growing and defining their relationship—in working toward that critical post of exiting the dating bridge and entering marriage.

In addition to sliding, sex can also sabotage the bridge process as couples try for instant intimacy by taking shortcuts. Members of a college group with whom I talked recently told me that they try to take shortcuts to sexual intimacy because they think hooking up and getting naked is going to make them really known, accepted, and intimate. I told them if they really wanted to be known and close to someone, go with that woman or man to Starbucks for three hours and really listen to their heart. That takes a whole lot more courage than just getting naked.

---

6. Scott M. Stanley, Galena K. Rhoades, and Howard J. Markman, "Sliding versus Deciding: Inertia and the Premarital Cohabitation Effect," *Family Relations* 55, no. 4 (October 2006): 499–509.

The bridge helps summarize social and erotic sexuality and their place in relationships, especially in building a healthy sexual ethic for singles. Connecting friendships involve navigating social sexuality with carefully managed erotic sexual feelings. Coupling relationships happen when the considering stage has moved onto the "exclusive" bridge heading toward marriage, incorporating erotic sexual thoughts and behaviors that are kept unselfish. True sex begins after the "I do" post and a covenant commitment.

One of my friends knows the bridge, and in her casual-connecting (considering) dating, she does not engage in erotic sexual behaviors. So I asked her about a first date recently with a guy she considered "dreamy."

I asked, "Did you kiss him?"

She said, "He probably dropped more than one hundred fifty dollars on a steak dinner, a bottle of wine, and a movie. I'm really attracted to him. Yeah, I kissed him."

I know her well enough to tease a little. "Wow," I said. "That sounds like you compromised some of your values because he was attractive and you felt some sense of obligation."

She almost punched me, but she remembered our discussions about how singles navigate social sexuality and the considering stage of dating, in which we're really saying, "I'm going to put boundaries completely around the erotic." It comes down to the sexual ethic that asks, Why does God want us to "boundary" erotic sexuality and true sex? Why does he want us, especially in dating relationships, to carefully steward sexuality?

When trying to sort out the erotic part of humanness and singleness, there's another question to consider in creating a practical sexual ethic: What needs are you trying to meet with your erotic sexual behaviors? Sometimes I'll say to friends in my men's group who have acted out sexually, "Were you just bored? Or possibly lonely?"

When I look at the bridge, I can wonder about deeper meaning and what is really going on. I can ask, What part of the bridge is simply infatuation? What part of this was loneliness or a desire to be married because you're thirty-two years old?

All who marry do so for some wrong reasons, but the good reasons really need to be there too. We need to think wisely as we sort through those strong feelings—that's part of why God is saying, "Let's 'boundary' the sexual." In the dating experience, because feelings are so powerful, they can easily take over.

Singles need to collect a lot of data when they're on the bridge. I tell them, "You need to see him with his friends, see her with her mom and dad. You need to see them in church and worshiping. You need to see them getting a traffic ticket. You need to see them angry or tired. The bridge is a time of growth and decision-making."

Making Ethical Decisions

Singles have to be careful to avoid blurring the stages of a healthy dating relationship. Peer pressure often encourages couples to move in together after they've dated for only three to six months. One area that often gets violated in Christian dating is the lack of intentionality in actively pursuing the possibility of marriage, proposing marriage, and getting married. Christian men especially have created this "Christian" way of living together within a pseudo-romantic relationship that has some sexual interaction and friendship with no real commitment or intention of moving toward marriage.

It's also difficult at times to think through that middle part of confirming a relationship. This is the point at which, for many, that box of erotic sexual behaviors appears with the question "How far can I go?" Ethical decisions can depend on attitude and situation rather than rigid rules.

Here's an example of what I mean by ethics relating to attitude, even within a married relationship. There are some things I could do with my wife sexually on Monday that would be perfectly God-honoring and intimacy-inducing. Yet I could do the same thing on Thursday and the action would be sin, because of my attitude. Because on Thursday, I'm just objectifying rather than truly making love.

Sorting through the questions of how far we can go and what we can do when dating will also depend on one's experiences and relationships. One of my friends was a child of the seventies with free love, hippies, and the sexual revolution. Consequently, for this person, any type of physical contact was arousing, requiring a physical-contact boundary. So he and his girlfriend had to come up with an alternative to develop the erotic in a way that was safe for them. They were both writers and singers, so instead of physical touch, they wrote love poetry and steamy letters to each other. When he told me this, I thought, "Steamy love letters would probably turn me on more than kissing someone." Each couple, with the help of the Spirit, must determine what righteous living looks like for them. So, when we get on the bridge and are trying to sort out ethical behavior, we realize that "How far can I go?" sometimes really depends.

Wouldn't it be refreshing if a couple was open enough and transparent enough in that confirming part of coupling that the guy could come over to pick up his almost-fiancée at her apartment and have her say to him, "You know, I am really aroused tonight. We were going to come back to my apartment and watch a movie. But we don't dare come back to my apartment and watch a movie. Let's go out and watch a movie together and get supper, and then you drop me off at the door." Wouldn't that kind of transparency be a far better sexual ethic than having to ask, "How did we end up going too far?"

CONCLUSION

There is a sexual ethic for the single who desires to live holy. It starts inside-out and is based on God's truth about sexuality. It takes into consideration the erotic and how it intersects with social sexuality. We must be careful when we're on the bridge of coupling, and we're thinking, "This could be my future mate, and I really enjoy this person, and there's chemistry." With any romantic involvement, setting limits will depend at times on the unique nature of the relationship and the current level of libido.

The relationship bridge can be useful in ethically navigating the dating world. A key idea is to understand the progression of romantic involvement and God's desire for humans to create meaningful courtship relationships that lead to marriage.

There are ways that we can, with God's help, think through single sexuality and dating as we set effective boundaries. We can learn lovingly to value, celebrate, and protect each other's sexuality.

FOR DISCUSSION

1. How would you explain the inside-out model compared to the outside-in model? How does this model become useful when applied to single sexuality?

2. How would you explain the model based on boxes of social and erotic sexuality? How does this model become useful when applied to single sexuality?

3. How would you explain the model of the relationship-continuum bridge? How does this model become useful when applied to single sexuality?

FOR FURTHER READING

Dawn, Marva J. *Sexual Character: Beyond Technique to Intimacy*. Grand Rapids: Eerdmans, 1993.

Stanley, Scott M., Galena K. Rhoades, and Howard J. Markman. "Sliding versus Deciding: Inertia and the Premarital Cohabitation Effect." *Family Relations* 55, no. 4 (2006): 499–509.

Winner, Lauren F. *Real Sex: The Naked Truth about Chasity*. Grand Rapids: Brazos, 2005.

C H A P T E R   9

CELIBACY ACCORDING TO JESUS AND PAUL

JAY E. SMITH

Voluntary celibacy has elicited a number of conflicting responses over the centuries. Referring to the "voluntarily celibate," Martin Luther maintained that "such persons are rare, not one in a thousand, for they are a special miracle of God."[1] The Council of Trent (1545–1563), in its counter to the Reformation, announced, "If anyone says that the marriage state excels the state of virginity or celibacy, and that it is better and happier to be united in matrimony than to remain in virginity and celibacy, let him be anathema."[2]

The Babylonian Talmud could not be any more different, equating celibacy with murder and defacing the image of God.[3] And Danish philosopher Søren Kierkegaard (1813–1855), sounding all too contemporary, notes that, to the non-Christian, celibacy "for the kingdom of heaven's sake (Matt 19:12) . . . constitutes [an] offence to the natural man . . . is mere madness . . . infinitely worse than the disease."[4]

---

1. Martin Luther, "The Estate of Marriage, 1522," in *Luther's Works*, vol. 45, *The Christian in Society II*, ed. Walther I. Brandt (Philadelphia: Muhlenberg Press, 1962), 21. This text can also be found in Martin Luther, *The Annotated Luther*, vol. 5, *Christian Life in the World*, ed. Hans J. Hillerbrand (Minneapolis: Fortress, 2017), 46.

2. H. J. Schroeder, trans., *Canons and Decrees of the Council of Trent* (St. Louis: Herder, 1941; repr., Rockford, IL: Tan Books, 1978), session 24, canon 10 (p. 182).

3. *Babylonian Talmud: Tractate Yebamot*, trans. Israel W. Slotki, ed. Isidore Epstein, 63b, http://halakhah.com/yebamoth.

4. Søren Kierkegaard, *Training in Christianity and the Edifying Discourse Which "Accompanied" It*, trans. Walter Lowrie (Princeton, NJ: Princeton University Press, 1941), 113.

Yet our concern is not with such reactions to voluntary celibacy—however provocative—but with the most important responses, that is, biblical responses, particularly the pivotal responses of Jesus and Paul. It comes as no surprise that Jesus (via Matthew) and Paul are responsible for the central passages on celibacy in the New Testament—and for that matter in the entire Bible. Matthew, alone among the Gospels, records Jesus's teaching on celibacy (Matt. 19:10–12), and Paul's treatment is found in 1 Corinthians 7. So we begin with the passage in Matthew.

CELIBACY IN MATTHEW 19:10–12

Jesus addresses the issue of celibacy in Matthew 19:3–12 and in particular in verses 10–12.[5] We begin here with a text of the individual clauses of Matthew 19:10–12.[6]

> [10] The disciples said to him,
>> "If this is the situation between a husband and wife,
>> it is better not to marry."
> [11] Jesus replied,
>> "Not everyone can accept this word, but only those to whom it has been given.
> [12a] For there are eunuchs who were born that way,
>> and
> [12b] there are eunuchs who have been made eunuchs by others—
>> and
> [12c] there are those who choose to live like eunuchs because of[7] the kingdom of heaven.
> [12d] The one who can accept this should accept it."

The context immediately preceding verses 10–12 concerns Jesus's teaching on divorce and remarriage and climaxes with the famous exception clause: "I tell you that anyone who divorces his wife, *except* for sexual immorality, and marries another woman commits adultery" (v. 9). In this, Jesus apparently permits divorce on the sole ground of sexual immorality (πορνεία); and remarriage likewise is apparently permitted on the same, singular ground.[8] In this, Jesus adopts a more stringent position on divorce and remarriage than either of the two main Pharisaic views of his day, that of Hillel and Shammai.[9] In short, Jesus maintains that liberal or permissive divorce and remarriage rights do not exist.[10]

---

5. Verses 10–12 are not paralleled in the other gospel accounts.
6. Scripture quoted in this chapter is from the NIV unless otherwise indicated.
7. I depart from the NIV and have substituted "because of" (with the CEB, CSB) for "for the sake of"—an issue to be discussed below (note 30).
8. See the essay by W. Hall Harris in this volume.
9. The classic text is Mishnah tractate Gittin 9:9–10.
10. *Pace* Heinrich Greeven, "Ehe nach dem Neuen Testament," *New Testament Studies* 15, no. 4 (1968–1969): 379; Günther Bornkamm, "End-Expectation and Church in

This rigor explains the disciples' reaction:[11] "It is better not to marry" (v. 10). The specter of being trapped in a difficult relationship means that marriage has lost some of its luster, and the disciples' response reveals a measure of their dismay.[12] Jesus takes their comment seriously, yet offers a qualification: "Not everyone can accept this word [τὸν λόγον τοῦτον],[13] but only those to whom it has been given" (v. 11).[14] "This word" refers to the disciples' assessment, "it is better not to marry" (v. 10), and not to Jesus's teaching on divorce and remarriage in verses 4–9.[15] Not only is verse 10 the nearest referent, but also this identification is confirmed by Jesus's explanation ("for," γάρ, v. 12a) of his immediate reply, "not everyone can accept this word, but only those to whom it has been given" (v. 11), in that he outlines three "classes" of eunuchs

Matthew," in *Tradition and Interpretation in Matthew*, ed. Günther Bornkamm, Gerhard Barth, and Heinz Joachim Held, New Testament Library (Philadelphia: Westminster, 1963), 25–26; Richard B. Hays, *The Moral Vision of the New Testament: Community, Cross, New Creation; A Contemporary Introduction to New Testament Ethics* (San Francisco: HarperSanFrancisco, 1996), 353; J. Carl Laney, *The Divorce Myth* (Minneapolis: Bethany House, 1981), 68; Ethelbert Stauffer, *Die Botschaft Jesu: Damals und Heute*, Dalp-Taschenbücher 333 (Bern: Franke, 1959), 78.

11. If Jesus's position is no stricter than the house of Shammai, the disciples' reaction is difficult to explain fully. Meier expresses it well: "If Jesus had simply championed the position of Shammai over that of Hillel, there would hardly be cause for such a shocked exclamation that the unmarried state is preferable" (*A Marginal Jew*, vol. 1, *Rethinking the Historical Jesus*, Anchor Yale Bible Reference Library [New Haven, CT: Yale University Press, 1991], 216). See also Craig Blomberg, *Matthew*, New American Commentary (Nashville: Broadman, 1992), 294; Osborne, *Matthew*, 706; cf. Leon Morris, *The Gospel according to Matthew*, Pillar New Testament Commentary (Grand Rapids: Eerdmans, 1992), 484; David L. Turner, *Matthew*, Baker Exegetical Commentary on the New Testament (Grand Rapids: Baker Academic, 2008), 463.

12. As W. D. Davies explains, "They virtually make the attractiveness of marriage contingent upon the possibility of divorce, and that on easy terms" (*The Setting of the Sermon on the Mount* [Cambridge: Cambridge University Press, 1964], 393).

13. Reading τοῦτον (this) with the NA[28] and the preponderance of the external evidence.

14. The universal proposition of the disciples (v. 10)—not Jesus's teaching in vv. 3–9—is qualified. This qualification does not distinguish between unbelieving outsiders and Jesus's true disciples, but distinguishes between disciples with and without a special gifting. This is consistent with the qualifications in vv. 11–12: "not everyone can," "only those," "those who chose," and "the one who can." See W. D. Davies and Dale C. Allison, *The Gospel according to Saint Matthew*, 3 vols., ICC (Edinburgh: T&T Clark, 1988–1997), 3:21.

15. So, e.g., Carson, "Matthew," in *The Expositor's Bible Commentary*, vol. 9, *Matthew and Mark*, ed. Tremper Longman III and David E. Garland, 23–670, rev. ed. (Grand Rapids: Zondervan, 2010), 474; Davies-Allison, *Gospel according to Saint Matthew*, 3:20; R. T. France, *The Gospel of Matthew*, New International Commentary on the New Testament (Grand Rapids: Eerdmans, 2007), 723; Craig S. Keener, *A Commentary on the Gospel of Matthew* (Grand Rapids: Eerdmans, 1999), 470–71; Meier, *Marginal Jew*, 1:343, 367n74; John Nolland, *The Gospel of Matthew*, New International Greek Testament Commentary (Grand Rapids: Eerdmans, 2005), 776; Eduard Schweizer, *The Good News according to Matthew*, trans. David E. Green (Atlanta: John Knox, 1975), 383.

"who can accept this word": (1) those by birth, (2) those by castration,[16] and (3) those who voluntarily choose that lifestyle[17] "because of the kingdom."[18] In other words, since those who "can accept this word" are various classes of eunuchs, this suggests that the antecedent of "this word" is the disciples' affirmation of celibacy in verse 10. Still further, if "this word" refers back to verses 4–9, Jesus immediately undermines his prohibition of divorce. D. A. Carson explains, "After a strong prohibition, it is highly unlikely that Jesus's moral teaching dwindles into a pathetic 'But of course, not everyone can accept this.'"[19] Carson continues, "It helps little to say that those to whom the teaching is given are Christians [vis-à-vis unbelieving outsiders] who must follow Jesus's moral standards but that others cannot accept what he says, for Jesus's appeal has been to the creation ordinance [Gen. 1:27; 2:24], not to kingdom morality."[20] In summary, Jesus responds to the disciples' appraisal by pointing out that not all of his *disciples* can (or should) live with this abstinence from marriage—"but only those to whom it has been given" (v. 11).[21]

One expects the pericope to end at this point[22]—with the sober realization that one enters into marriage with no "easy" way out. Yet Jesus adds what is, for "mainstream" Judaism, a final and startling statement: "The one who

---

16. Pace Constantin Daniel, "Esséniens et Eunuques (Matthieu 19:10–12)," *Revue de Qumran* 6 (1968): 353–90, esp. 363–64. He argues that the second category does not refer to castration but to those who, like the Essenes, abstained from marriage because of doctrinal conviction. This ethical interpretation is unlikely and has not generally been adopted.

17. See T. W. Manson, *The Sayings of Jesus* (London: SCM, 1949), 215–16. He argues decisively for a figurative interpretation and dispels any doubt that this third class of eunuch might involve a literal self-castration.

18. On the import of this explanatory γάρ, see France, *Gospel of Matthew*, 723; also Francis W. Beare, *The Gospel according to Matthew* (San Francisco: Harper & Row, 1981), 391; Morris gives this sense: "In the next verse [v. 12] he [Jesus] goes on to look at them"— those for whom "it is better not to marry" (*Gospel according to Matthew*, 485).

19. Carson, "Matthew," 474.

20. Carson, "Matthew," 474. Similarly, Craig L. Blomberg, "Marriage, Divorce, Remarriage, and Celibacy: An Exegesis of Matthew 19:3–12," *TJ* 11 (1990): 183; Davies-Allison, *Gospel according to Saint Matthew*, 3:20; Jean Galot, *Theology of the Priesthood*, trans. Roger Balducelli (San Francisco: Ignatius, 1985), 233–34; Ulrich Luz, *Matthew*, trans. James E. Crouch, 3 vols., Hermeneia (Minneapolis: Fortress, 2001–2007), 2:501; Grant R. Osborne, *Matthew*, Zondervan Exegetical Commentary on the New Testament (Grand Rapids: Zondervan, 2010), 706.

21. As Robert Stein points out, Jesus "appears to distinguish between two groups of Christians" rather than between unbelieving outsiders and Jesus's true disciples (Robert H. Stein. *The Method and Message of Jesus's Teachings*, rev. ed. [Louisville: Westminster John Knox, 1994], 93).

22. For the authenticity of v. 12 (excluding v. 12d) as a genuine logion of Jesus, see Heinrich Baltensweiler, *Die Ehe im Neuen Testament: Exegetische Untersuchung über Ehe, Ehelosigkeit und Ehescheidung*, ATANT 52 (Zurich: Zwingli-Verlag, 1967), 51–52, 103, 106–7.

can accept this should accept it" (v. 12d).[23] The referent of "accept this"[24] is probably "this word" in verse 11,[25] which in turn refers to the disciples' claim in verse 10, "it is better not to marry." Confirmation comes from (1) the structure of the argument in that verses 12a–c are an explanatory aside interrupting the flow of the discourse and thus isolating verse 12d, so that "this" refers back to verse 11 in a classic ABA' chiastic pattern[26] and (2) the repetition in verse 12d of "accept" from verse 11:

> verse 11: "Not everyone can *accept* [χωρέω] this word."
> verse 12d "The one who can *accept* [χωρέω] this should *accept* [χωρέω] it."

In keeping with this connection between verse 12d and verse 11, verse 12d and verse 12c are not explicitly linked;[27] nevertheless, the implication from (1) the juxtaposition of their lines "because of the kingdom" (v. 12c) and "should accept it" (v. 12d) and from (2) the escalation of the argument to this climatic point[28] is that "those to whom it has been given" (v. 11) should voluntarily "choose to live like eunuchs because of the kingdom" (v. 12c).[29] The phrase "because of the kingdom" does not mean, as Carson rightly points out, "'for the

---

23. Startling in that marriage and procreation were, in general, viewed as religious obligations within "mainstream" Judaism. See, e.g., Craig S. Keener, "Marriage," in *The Dictionary of New Testament Background,* ed. Craig A. Evans and Stanley E. Porter (Downers Grove, IL: InterVarsity Press, 2000), 681–83; and George Foot Moore, *Judaism in the First Centuries of the Christian Era: The Age of the Tannaim* 3 vols. (Cambridge, MA: Harvard University Press, 1927–30), 2:119–20, 270. Moore writes, "Marriage was regarded not only as the normal state, but as a divine ordinance. . . . Celibacy was, in fact, not common, and was disapproved by the rabbis" (119).

24. The Greek text of v. 12d does not have an expressed direct object for the first occurrence of the verb "accept" (nor for the second occurrence of the verb). The object is rightly supplied by "this" (ESV, NASB, NIV) or "it" (ASV, CEB, CSB, NKJV). Cf. REB, which does not supply the direct objects: "Let those accept who can."

25. Blomberg, "Marriage," 185; Carson, "Matthew," 474; France, *Gospel of Matthew,* 726.

26. So Charles H. Talbert, *Matthew,* Paideia (Grand Rapids: Baker Academic, 2010), 234. A = v. 11; B = v. 12a–c; A' = v. 12d (see the textual layout at the beginning of this section). Cf. Rudolf Schnackenburg, *The Gospel of Matthew,* trans. Robert R. Barr (Grand Rapids: Eerdmans, 2002), 185.

27. An asyndeton isolates v. 12d from v. 12c.

28. The argument develops as follows:
    1. it is better not marry (v. 10).
    2. not everyone can accept this (v. 11).
    3. some voluntarily accept it because of the kingdom's claims and interests (v. 12c).
    4. the one who can accept this—because of the kingdom's claims and interests—should accept it (v. 12d).

29. The traditional reading sees a call or invitation (exhortation): those who are able should voluntarily choose a life of celibacy. So Blomberg, "Marriage," 185; Carson, "Matthew," 474. Jesus's words here are a call to acceptance and action, much like his words, "He who has ears to hear let him hear."

sake of attaining it,'" but "'because of its claims and interests.'"[30] Thus, marriage is not renounced *for* the kingdom, that is, to gain the kingdom, or for ascetic reasons to acquire merit,[31] rather it is waived *because of* the kingdom—because of the kingdom's all-consuming importance and value (see below). In the words of Thaddée Matura, "The decision to live as a eunuch is connected to this new situation, to the kingdom . . . *because* the reality of it opens new perspectives and offers new possibilities."[32] At its most basic level, then, celibacy does not have the kingdom as its *goal* but as its *foundation*. As Josef Blinzler puts it, "The kingdom of God is not so much the goal [*Ziel*], but the reason [*Grund*] for the action of those people"[33]—it is "what lies behind and energizes" celibacy.[34] And while this understanding is not necessarily incompatible with the notion that marriage is waived for the kingdom (i.e., for greater usefulness in the kingdom),[35] it seems inconsistent with the supreme importance of the kingdom to view celibacy as simply a decision "arrived at by cool calculation from a number of equal options,"[36] resulting in what Adolf Schlatter calls a "wavering renunciation

---

30. Carson, "Matthew," 474. The expression "because of" represents the preposition διά, and Carson handles it deftly. The usual meaning of διά with an accusative object, as here, is causal—so without exception in Matthew's twelve other occurrences of this construction (10:22; 13:21, 58; 14:3, 9; 15:3, 6; 17:20; 24:9, 22; 27:18, 19). That marriage should be renounced in order to gain entrance into the kingdom is foreign to every impulse of biblical revelation—Rev. 14:4 notwithstanding.

31. So Wolfgang Schrage, *The Ethics of the New Testament*, trans. David E. Green (Philadelphia: Fortress, 1988), 93; *pace* Lagrange, who indicates that the celibate "may gain great merit" (*The Gospel of Jesus Christ*, trans. English Dominican Province, 2 vols. [London: Burns, Oates & Washburn, 1938], 2:91).

32. Thaddée Matura, *Gospel Radicalism: The Hard Sayings of Jesus*, trans. Maggi Despot and Paul Lachance (Maryknoll, NY: Orbis, 1984), 58 (emphasis added).

33. Josef Blinzler, "'Zur Ehe unfähig . . .' Auslegung von Mt 19:12," in *Aus der Welt und Umwelt des Neuen Testaments: Gesammelte Aufsätze 1*, SBB (Stuttgart: Katholisches Bibelwerk, 1969), 28n27. Similarly, Jerome Kodell, "The Celibacy Logion in Matthew 19:12," *BTB* 8 (1978): 21. Cf. Nolland, who notes that in this view, which he does not favor, the kingdom is "what lies behind and energizes" celibacy (*The Gospel of Matthew*, 777).

34. Nolland, *The Gospel of Matthew*, 777.

35. See Carson, "Matthew," 474; and esp. Davies-Allison, who note that "διά has not final but causal sense: 'because of the kingdom' (in order to serve it)" (*Gospel according to Saint Matthew*, 3:23n115). For F. W. Beare, "'For the sake of' (διά) is more naturally taken to mean 'to serve,'" and this service to the kingdom is probably the "standard" understanding of this construction (*Gospel according to Matthew*, 391–92). Cf. Harrington, who understands the eunuch saying, "on account of the kingdom of heaven" as supplying "the proper motivation for celibacy—*dedication to the kingdom of God*" (274 [emphasis added]); similarly, Galot, who adds that celibacy is "motivated" by "zeal *for the kingdom* of God" (*Priesthood*, 236 [emphasis added]).

36. Adapted from Kodell, "Logion," 22. Similarly, Roger Balducelli, "The Decision for Celibacy," *TS* 36 (1975): 227. Cf. Karl Barth who adds, "Celibacy . . . cannot be chosen capriciously" (*Church Dogmatics*, trans. Geoffrey W. Bromiley, ed. Geoffrey W. Bromiley and Thomas F. Torrance 4 vols. [Edinburgh: T&T Clark, 1956–75], III/4, 185–86).

that struggles with the desire for marriage."[37] Instead, "the flow of causality runs rather in the opposite direction,"[38] making Jerome Kodell's assessment attractive and perhaps closer to the truth: "Some people, Jesus is saying, have been so seized by the kingdom that all their attention and energy is consumed by it. They no longer have the capacity to commit themselves to the demands of the marriage relationship. They are 'eunuchs because of the kingdom of heaven.' . . . Celibacy is a response to an experience of the kingdom, being seized, grasped, swept away by Christ."[39]

Similarly, Blinzler indicates that "indescribable joy has overpowered the celibate and he can no longer direct his thoughts and aspirations [to anything other than] the kingdom of God, to which he has abandoned all."[40]

And finally, Heinrich Baltensweiler suggests that Jesus did not speak of celibacy (*Ehelosigkeit*) or renunciation of marriage (*Eheverzicht*) but of an unfitness (*Eheuntauglichkeit*) for marriage: "Jesus tells his opponents that he and his disciples are so grasped by the reality of the kingdom of heaven that they are 'unfit' [*untauglich*] for marriage. . . . There are people for whom the joy of the kingdom of God and the overwhelming character of its message were so great that they are not fit [*nicht taugen*] for marriage, for the kingdom of heaven completely absorbs them, and their thoughts and aspirations are completely satisfied."[41]

Unsurprisingly, such "eunuchs" who are "so seized by the kingdom" and whose "attention and energy is consumed by it" do indeed advance the kingdom through their greater service in it and for it.[42]

HIDDEN-TREASURE PARABLES
It is also worth noting that Jesus's teaching in Matthew 19:10–12 has a clear resonance with the twin parables of the hidden treasure and the valuable

---

37. Adolf Schlatter, *Das Evangelium nach Matthäus*, in Erläuterungen zum Neuen Testament 1 (Stuttgart: Calwer, 1961), 293. His full line is "Jesus does not permit a wavering renunciation that struggles with the desire for marriage." Cf. Carson, who notes, "Those who would impose this discipline on themselves must remember Paul's conclusion: it is better to marry than burn with passion (1 Cor 7:9)" ("Matthew," 474).
38. Balducelli, "Celibacy," 227. The movement is not from deliberation over celibacy to decision, but from the affirmation of God's lordship to its consequence—"disablement from marriage" (Balducelli's words).
39. Kodell, "Logion," 21–22. With reference to "prophetic figures" (John the Baptist, Jeremiah, Moses after God began to speak to him) in ancient Judaism, Meier notes, "An all-consuming commitment to God's word in one's whole life precludes the usual path of marriage and child-rearing" (*Rethinking*, 341). Cf. Rabbi Ben 'Azzai's explanation of his singleness: "My soul is in love with the Torah; the world can be carried on by others" (Babylonian Talmud, tractate Yebamot 63b; similarly, Tosefta, tractate Yebamot 8:7).
40. Blinzler, "Auslegung von Mt 19:12," 30, with adaptation.
41. Baltensweiler, *Die Ehe*, 109, 107. Matura adds that "because of religious motivations (the kingdom), [they] seem to be unsuited for marriage" (*Radicalism*, 58).
42. See Kodell, "Logion," 22; Leopold Sabourin, "The Positive Values of Consecrated Celibacy," *The Way Supplement* 10 (1970): 52.

pearl (13:44–46). In these parables Jesus claims that the supreme value of the kingdom means that no sacrifice is too great for one to be a part of it. Although the emphases slightly differ,[43] in both cases (Matt. 19:10–12 and the parables of chap. 13), the kingdom and its supreme value supersedes all rivals; that is, it is worthy of any sacrifice, even the forgoing of marriage.

Similar is Jesus's teaching on "abandoning" wife and family: "If anyone comes to me and does not hate father and mother, wife and children, brothers and sisters—yes, even their own life—such a person cannot be my disciple. . . . Truly I tell you . . . no one who has left home or wife or brothers or sisters or parents or children for the sake of the kingdom of God will fail to receive many times as much in this age, and in the age to come eternal life" (Luke 14:26, 18:29–30).[44]

Jesus demands unqualified allegiance and makes the claim that the kingdom of God takes precedence over familial relationships. No sacrifice is too great "for the sake of the kingdom of God" (Luke 18:29 // Matt 19:29 // Mark 10:29, with Matthew reading "for my sake," and Mark reading "for me and the gospel"[45]). On Jesus's scale of priorities, the kingdom and its king are worthy of uncompromising loyalty, dedication, and commitment—even to the extent of forgoing marriage and conventional family life. F. F. Bruce says it well: "The interests of God's kingdom must be paramount with the followers of Jesus, and everything must take second place to them, even family ties. . . . There [can] be no matter of greater moment than the kingdom of God."[46] Edward Schillebeeckx agrees: "The kingdom of God makes sovereign claims which take precedence over everything else."[47] Although both Bruce and Schillebeeckx are absolutely correct, their statements are perhaps too "heroic" to be appreciated fully. In this sense, Martin Dibelius does a better job pricking our consciences: "Jesus did not require self-mutilation, but rather the risk and sacrifice even of things that seemed indispensable . . . *things that displaced concern for the Kingdom*."[48]

---

43. The concern of the parables is the supreme value of the kingdom and hence the need to be a part of it or to gain entry into it (see, e.g., Carson, "Matthew," 375–77; Morris, *Gospel according to Matthew*, 359–61). The issue in Matt. 19:10–12 is the "claims and interests" of the kingdom, and thus it is likely directed toward service within the kingdom rather than entrance into the kingdom.

44. Parallels: Luke 14:26–27, 33 // Matt. 10:37–38. Parallels: Luke 18:29–30 // Matt. 19:29 // Mark 10:29–30. See also Gospel of Thomas 55, 110, which repeats the substance of Matt. 10:37 and Luke 14:26.

45. The expression "for the sake of" in Luke 18:29 // Matt 19:29 // Mark 10:29 is the preposition ἕνεκεν. It is causal (Frederick W. Danker et al., *Greek-English Lexicon of the New Testament and Other Early Christian Literature*, 3rd ed. [Chicago: University of Chicago Press, 2000], 334.1) and, as Carson suggests for Matt. 19:12, means something close to "because of my claims and interests" (glossing Matt. 19:29).

46. Walter Kaiser et al., *Hard Sayings of the Bible* (Downers Grove, IL: InterVarsity Press, 1996), 475.

47. Edward Schillebeeckx, *Marriage: Human Reality and Saving Mystery*, trans. N. D. Smith (New York: Sheed & Ward, 1965), 123.

48. Martin Dibelius, *The Message of Jesus Christ: The Tradition of the Early Christian Communities*,

SUMMARY OF JESUS AND CELIBACY

Jesus unabashedly commends celibacy to "those [among his disciples] to whom it has been given" (v. 11). As Maurice Goguel puts it, "This introduces a leading idea which is the key to the moral teaching of Jesus, that is, the idea of *vocation*. There is no question here of different degrees of holiness or of optional duties. Here the idea is of duties which vary from man to man, according to the *gifts* each has received"—a point that Paul will exploit in 1 Corinthians 7:7 ("each of you has your own gift").[49]

Consequently, "the one who can accept this should accept it" (v. 12d); that is, they should accept the notion that "it is better not to marry" (v. 10). Again, this is no counsel "for an élite which was determined to attain an ideal of superior holiness."[50] Instead, it is grounded in divine gifting and is intended for greater usefulness in the kingdom. In 1 Corinthians Paul not only echo will this line of thought, but also will expand on it.

CELIBACY ACCORDING TO PAUL

Introduction

Paul's key treatment of celibacy is scattered across 1 Corinthians 7—a text that bristles with some of the most difficult challenges found anywhere in the New Testament. Therefore, with due caution we come first to 1 Corinthians 7:1–2.

Celibacy in 1 Corinthians 7:1–2

Paul addresses the issue of celibacy in 1 Corinthians 7, particularly in verses 1–2, verse 7, and verses 25–35. We begin with a textual layout of the individual clauses of 1 Cor 7:1–2.

> [1a] Now for the matters you wrote about:
> [1b] "It is good for a man not to have sexual relations with a woman."
> [2a] But since sexual immorality is occurring,
> [2b] each man should have sexual relations with his own wife,
>   and
> [2c] each woman with her own husband.

This text presents interpretive challenges owing to the abbreviated nature of the interchange between Paul and the Corinthians. Specifically, it is difficult to discern precisely what the Corinthians have proposed (or what question or questions

---

trans. Frederick C. Grant (New York: Scribner's Sons, 1939), 164, with slight adaptation and emphasis added.

49. Maurice Goguel, *Jesus and the Origins of Christianity*, trans. Olive Wyon, 2 vols. (New York: Macmillan, 1933; repr., New York: Harper & Brothers, 1960), 2.583 (emphasis added).

50 Goguel, *Jesus*, 2.582.

they have asked). Paul merely acknowledges their concern. Each knows the other and the specific issues at stake, so communication is abbreviated. And Paul's response is brief and rather puzzling at that (see below). My goal then is modest, and at numerous points my arguments and conclusions will be tentative.

At one level, the issue here is singular and resolved nicely by many modern English translations, including the NIV given above. Yet the issue has a long history and persists in tradition or even "folklore"—probably as a result, among other things, of older English renderings, and it needs to be addressed. The 1973, 1978, and 1984 editions of the NIV are representative of the problem:[51]

> [1a] Now for the matters you wrote about:
> [1b] It is good for man not to marry.
> [2a] But since there is so much immorality,
> [2b] each man should have his own wife,
> and
> [2c] each woman her own husband.

In these (mis)translations, the problem is threefold:

1. Verse 1b is presented as a Pauline statement; it is not. Rather, it represents a Corinthian slogan[52]—a summary given by Paul of a view held and promoted by the Corinthians.

2. This same line is understood as a reference to marriage; it is not. It reads literally, "It is good for a man not to touch a woman" and represents a euphemism for sexual relations.[53]

3. Verse 2b–c is understood as a recommendation to marry; it is not. Rather, it represents "Paul's rebuttal of the position espoused in the slogan"[54] and

---

51. For a brief overview, see Raymond Collins, *First Corinthians*, Sacra Pagina 7 (Collegeville, MN: Liturgical Press, 1999), 252; David E. Garland, *1 Corinthians*, Baker Exegetical Commentary on the New Testament (Grand Rapids: Baker Academic, 2003), 247.

52. Roy E. Ciampa and Brian S. Rosner, *The First Letter to the Corinthians*, Pillar New Testament Commentary (Grand Rapids: Eerdmans, 2010), 272–73; Collins, *First Corinthians*, 252–53; Gordon D. Fee, *The First Epistle to the Corinthians*, rev. ed. NICNT (Grand Rapids: Eerdmans, 2014), 306–7; Jane F. Gardner, *Family and* Familia *in Roman Law and Life* (Oxford: Clarendon, 1998), 296–97; Garland, *1 Corinthians*, 248–51; Anthony C. Thiselton, *The First Epistle to the Corinthians*, New International Greek Testament Commentary (Grand Rapids: Eerdmans, 2000), 498–500.

53. Collins, *First Corinthians*, 257–58; Fee, *First Epistle to the Corinthians*, 305–6, esp. n33; Garland, *1 Corinthians*, 254, 256; Thiselton, *The First Epistle to the Corinthians,* 500.

54. Collins, *First Corinthians*, 258; see also 253. Similarly, Fee, *First Epistle to the Corinthians*, 307–10; Gardner, *Family and* Familia, 298; Garland, *1 Corinthians*, 249–51,

is an admonition for a man or woman to "have" his or her own spouse, that is, "to have sexually" one's spouse. The point is not "to find" or "to get" a spouse but "to possess sexually" one's existing spouse.[55]

The NIV, along with most modern versions, is a better rendering on all these fronts, and for convenience and clarity the two versions (interpretations) can be briefly summarized in tabular form (see table 2).

Table 2. Differing NIV translations of 1 Corinthians 7:1–2		
	NIV 1973 / 1978 / 1984	**NIV 2011**
v. 1a	Now for the matters you wrote about:	Now for the matters you wrote about:
v. 1b	It is good for man not to marry. = Pauline statement. = Advocates singleness.	"It is good for a man not to have sexual relations with a woman." = A Corinthian slogan. = Advocates celibacy (continence).
v. 2a	But since there is so much immorality,	But since sexual immorality is occurring,
v. 2b-c	each man should have his own wife, and each woman her own husband. = Pauline advocacy of marriage (finding a spouse) because of sexual immorality.	each man should have sexual relations with his own wife, and each woman with her own husband. = Pauline response urging sex within marriage because of sexual immorality.

Whether the earlier versions of the NIV (1973–1984) or the most-recent edition (2011), one point remains constant: πορνεία is the problem (literally, "but because of sexual immoralities," διὰ δὲ τὰς πορνείας). Since Paul

---

255, 257; Thiselton, *The First Epistle to the Corinthians,* 498–501. In line with their understanding of the Corinthians' slogan, Ciampa-Rosner suggest that Paul offers "minor qualifications" (*First Letter to the Corinthians,* 275).

55. Ciampa-Rosner, *First Letter to the Corinthians,* 276–77; Fee, *First Epistle to the Corinthians,* 309–10; Garland, *1 Corinthians,* 256; Thiselton, *The First Epistle to the Corinthians,* 502. Collins befogs the issue (*First Corinthians,* 258); cf. Gardner, *Family and* Familia, 299.

encourages marital relations solely because of sexual immorality (πορνεία),[56] it would seem that celibacy is acceptable as long as immorality is not an imminent threat. Yet at precisely this point—Paul's tacit endorsement of celibacy[57]—things start to become very interesting, or, as I already noted, "puzzling."

Given our modern cultural context, Paul does not respond as we might expect. Our expectations probably run something as follows: You Corinthians say, "It is good for a man not to have sexual relations with a woman." Yes, this is quite true, but it only applies to the unmarried; the married should enjoy full conjugal rights. Sex within marriage is a good thing—a gift from the Lord—and is to be freely enjoyed.

Paul's line of thought is quite different, however. Leaving the principle of celibacy in place, Paul seems to reject its application solely because of (the prevalence and danger of) sexual immorality. He seems to imply that in the absence of this threat, celibacy is "good"—even within marriage. This is startling and suggests that Paul might, if all things were equal, prefer celibate marriage. But all things are not equal, and so he encourages (acquiesces to?) sexual relations within marriage because of (the risk of) immorality. In short, if it were not for (the threat of) immorality, no reason is given that precludes the application of the Corinthian slogan to the married couple—for a married couple not to be celibate.[58]

In his response to the Corinthians' slogan, Paul, rather oddly, does not draw a distinction between the married and unmarried with regard to celibacy. In fact, he passes over the unmarried[59]—the assumption apparently being that celibacy is the rule for them. It would seem, then, that the Corinthians' slogan would rightly apply to both groups if it were not for existing or recurring sexual immorality. Thus he advocates marital relations only as a deterrent to immorality. He has a near-perfect opportunity to emphasize the divinely sanctioned goodness of sexual relations within marriage, yet he declines and prefers to paint the act merely as a prophylactic against immorality. His focus is singular, and he presents sex solely as a curb to sin.[60]

It might be countered that "because of immoralities" is just one reason among many for marital relations—and it alone is raised because it is the

---

56. See Fee, who comments, "*The reason* for this lies with the *porneia* just spoken to. . . . Again *the reason* . . . is the instances of *porneia*" (*First Epistle to the Corinthians*, 304 [emphasis added]).

57. That Paul corrects the Corinthians' viewpoint without rejecting celibacy in principle is widely recognized. See, e.g., Fee, *First Epistle to the Corinthians*, 305, 307; Garland, *1 Corinthians*, 250, 255; Max Thurian, *Marriage and Celibacy*, trans. Norma Emerton (London: SCM, 1959), 68–69.

58. See Garland, *1 Corinthians*, 257.

59. Garland, *1 Corinthians*, 255.

60. So, e.g., Hans Conzelmann, *1 Corinthians*, trans. James W. Leitch, Hermeneia (Philadelphia: Fortress, 1975), 116; and Garland, who suggests that Paul's exposition is limited by and to the present context (*1 Corinthians*, 257). See further in the next note.

most contextually relevant reason.[61] Yet this is not what Paul's words seem to indicate.[62] In fact, in the immediate context (v. 5) Paul seems to view abstinence as a way to enhance one's prayer life and perhaps even suggests that marital relations are a hindrance to prayer:[63] "Do not deprive each other except perhaps by mutual consent and for a time, so that you may devote yourselves to prayer."

And then when he encourages the resumption of sexual relations, the reason given is not the wholesomeness of the relationship, but the risk of temptation—now a recurrent theme in the passage: "Then come together again so that Satan will not tempt you because of your lack of self-control" (v. 5).

As Günther Bornkamm notes, "In the detailed discussions of 1 Corinthians 7, one looks in vain for a positive appreciation of love between the sexes or of the richness of human experience in marriage and the family."[64] And in the end, rearguard actions defending Paul against those who would "berate" him for what he does not say positively about sexuality and marriage are not entirely satisfying.[65] Added to all this is the possibility—quite strong in the minds of some—that Paul endorses so-called spiritual marriage.[66]

---

61. So, e.g., Gardner, *Family and* Familia, 299; Thiselton, *The First Epistle to the Corinthians*, 501; cf. Garland, *1 Corinthians*, 256n16. This is plausible (note the repetition of the term πορνεία, which is probably an anaphoric reference), but not particularly satisfying in that it seems to beg the question. Moreover, it lacks compelling Pauline evidence from other passages.

62. See, e.g., Johannes Weiss, who argues, "Paul actually considers sexual intercourse as something which draws man from God and is degrading to him" (*The History of Primitive Christianity*, trans. Frederick C. Grant, 2 vols. [New York: Wilson-Erickson, 1937], 2:582).

63. Cf. Exod. 19:10–15; Lev. 15:16–24; 1 Sam. 21:4–5, where sexual relations hinder or exclude fellowship with God. See Alfred Marx, who understands 1 Cor 7:5 as an extension of this thought ("Les racines du célibat essénien," *Revue de Qumran* 7, no. 3 [1970]: 326–27). The extrabiblical evidence also points in this direction. See Josephus, *Against Apion* 2.8 §§103–4; *Jewish War* 5.227; Philo, *On the Life of Moses* 2.67–69; 1 Enoch 83.2; 85.3; CD XII, 1–2; 11Q19 (Temple Scroll) XLV, 7–12; Babylonian Talmud, tractate Shabbat 87a; Sifre on Num. 12:1 (99.2). Geza Vermes suggests that the sect at Qumran "appears to have made an institution of celibacy . . . in order to be always in a condition to take part in worship" (*Jesus the Jew: A Historian's Reading of the Gospels* [Philadelphia: Fortress, 1981], 99).

64. Günther Bornkamm, *Paul*, trans. D. M. G. Stalker (New York: Harper & Row, 1971), 208. David R. Cartlidge adds, "The reason that Paul gives in 7:2 for the fulfillment of sexual relations in marriage is not . . . a positive expression of sexual joyfulness. . . . At the most, it is a negative reason for sex and is hardly a smashing blow in favor of marital bliss" ("1 Corinthians 7 as a Foundation for a Christian Sex Ethic," *Journal of Religion* 55, no. 2 [1975]: 224).

65. See Garland, who does as good of a job as anyone defending Paul (*1 Corinthians*, 257–58).

66. So, e.g., Greg Peters, "Spiritual Marriage in Early Christianity: 1 Cor 7:25–38 in Modern Exegesis and Earliest Church," *Trinity Journal* 23 (2002): 211–24. This practice is usually referred to as *virgines subintroductae* and is reflected in the NEB: "a partner in celibacy," i.e., "roommate."

In sum, it would seem that Paul does indeed value celibacy perhaps even to the point of expressing reticence about sex within marriage. Interestingly, in this he is not far removed from a number of his contemporaries who restricted sex within marriage to procreation alone.

Here perhaps is the solution to Paul's puzzling response in 7:2: the Corinthians are arguing that marital relations are solely for procreation.[67] Recreational sex—so to speak—is forbidden within marriage and must be sought outside marriage.[68] Such a view is commonly thought to be reflected as early as the fourth century BC by Apollodorus in Demosthenes's *Against Neaera*: "Mistresses we keep for the sake of pleasure, concubines for the daily care of the body, but wives to bear us legitimate children and to be faithful guardians of our households."[69]

Demosthenes is not alone. Plutarch (ca. AD 50–120) reports his approval of the Persian custom that resonates strongly with Demosthenes:

> The lawful wives of the Persian kings sit beside them at dinner, and eat with them. But when the kings wish to be merry and get drunk, they send their wives away, and send for their music-girls and concubines. In so far, they are right in what they do, *because they do not concede any share in their licentiousness and debauchery to their wedded wives.* If therefore a man in private life, who is incontinent and dissolute in regard to his pleasures, commit some peccadillo with a paramour or a maidservant, his wedded wife ought not to be indignant or angry, *but she should reason that it is respect for her which leads him to share his debauchery, licentiousness, and wantonness with another woman.*[70]

In the same vein, Lucius Aelius Caesar (ca. AD 104–138), "when his wife complained about his amours with others," responded, "Let me indulge my desires with others; for wife is a term of honour, not of pleasure."[71]

---

67. As Collins points out, "sexual asceticism was 'in the air' in first-century Corinth" (*First Corinthians*, 253–54). Similarly, Richard B. Hays, *First Corinthians*, Interpretation: A Bible Commentary for Teaching and Preaching (Louisville: John Knox Press, 1997), 114. A number of social-cultural factors likely contributed to this. See the careful survey by Garland, *1 Corinthians*, 263–66; and esp. Ciampa-Rosner, *First Letter to the Corinthians*, 267–68, 270, 273–75. By suggesting that the Corinthians restricted the purpose of sexual relations to procreation, I do not mean to offer *the* exclusive explanation. Contributing factors and allied explanations are quite possible, not necessarily mutually exclusive, and even likely.

68. For a similar line of thought, see Ciampa-Rosner, *First Letter to the Corinthians*, 270.

69. Demosthenes, *Against Neaera* 122 (*Oration* 59) (Murray, LCL, with slight adaptation); ca. 373–339 BC (although probably pseudo-Demosthenic and written by Apollodorus himself).

70. Plutarch, *Conjugalia Praecepta* (*Advice to Bride and Groom*) 16 (= *Moralia* 140B) (Babbitt, LCL) (emphasis added).

71. "Aelius," 5.11–12 in *Scriptores Historiae Augustae* (LCL, Magie). The *Augustan History*, as the whole work is commonly known, is believed to have been written toward the end of the fourth century AD (see *Oxford Classical Dictionary*, ed. Simon Hornblower and Antony Spawforth, 4th ed. [Oxford: Oxford University Press, 2012], 691).

The Hellenistic-Jewish world, as represented by Philo and Josephus, likewise concurs. Philo writes, "But those who sue for marriage with women whose sterility has already been proved with other husbands, do but copulate like pigs or goats, and their names should be inscribed in the lists of the impious as adversaries of God. In the end, they are 'the most lecherous of men' and are in a quest for 'mere licentious pleasure.'" Later, he adds, "They [murderers of their own children] are pleasure-lovers when they mate with their wives, not to procreate children and perpetuate the race, but like pigs and goats in quest of the enjoyment which such intercourse gives."[72] He is seconded by Josephus: "The Law recognizes no sexual connections, except the natural union of man and wife, and that only for the procreation of children."[73]

If this reconstruction captures the basic viewpoint of a group within the Corinthian community, Paul can be seen as breaking with the traditional values that represent their perspective (and that encourage their aberrant behavior). Instead, Paul is perhaps advocating (encouraging?) so-called pleasure-seeking or recreational sex within marriage because of the threat of immorality.[74]

Such a reconstruction not only has precedent in the larger Greco-Roman milieu but also goes a long way in explaining the problem of prostitution in 1 Corinthians 6:12–20.[75] Prostitutes apparently served as a sexual outlet for those who eschewed martial intercourse.[76] Still further, it makes good sense of the fact that the Corinthian slogan of 7:1 is most likely directed exclusively (and most surprisingly) to married couples. Several observations point in this direction. First, there was little need for the Corinthians to craft and direct this slogan to the *unmarried*, for most of the Corinthian believers would have probably understood and accepted such a position, despite their practice of not measuring up to their understanding.

---

72. For Philo see, in order, *On the Special Laws* 3.6 §36; 3.6 §36; 3.20 §113 (Colson, LCL).
73. Josephus, *Against Apion* 2.24 §199 (Thackeray, LCL).
74. Whether Paul holds the same basic view as the "ascetic" Corinthians (with the threat of πορνεία forcing an accommodation to his preferred position) or whether he holds a less "puritanical" view with regard to marital relations (with the threat of πορνεία providing an additional reason for marital relations) is unclear. OT antecedents and Paul's Jewish heritage would suggest the latter. Cf. 1 Cor. 7:2–4; Col. 2:20–23; 1 Tim. 4:1–5; 5:11–15.
75. See Ciampa-Rosner, *First Letter to the Corinthians*, 275; Fee, *First Epistle to the Corinthians*, 301, 303–4, 306–7, 309; Gardner, *Family and* Familia, 298–99; Garland, *1 Corinthians*, 256n16; Gregory J. Laughery, "Paul: Anti-marriage? Anti-sex? Ascetic? A Dialogue with 1 Corinthians 7:1–40," *Evangelical Quarterly* 69 (1997): 118–21; Thiselton, *The First Epistle to the Corinthians*, 501.
76. It is perhaps likely that some believing wives thought of themselves as "eschatological women," who claimed to be "spiritual beings" above marital intercourse and thus who shunned sexual relations. Nevertheless, these women may have acquiesced to bearing legitimate children and managing the household. See S. Scott Bartchy, *ΜΑΛΛΟΝ ΧΡΗ-ΣΑΙ: First-Century Slavery and 1 Corinthians 7:21*, Society of Biblical Literature Dissertation Series 11 (Missoula, MT: Society of Biblical Literature, 1973), 131–32. Assuming the presence and influence of "eschatological women" does not rule out other possible motivations for the Corinthians' behavior.

(Sexual purity was surely a staple of initial Pauline catechesis.)[77] Second, applying this principle of celibacy to married couples vis-à-vis the unmarried is clearly the harder case, and this difficulty suggests a plausible origin for the Corinthians' sloganizing—the need to develop a motto or rallying cry to make or press this "unusual" case. Third, this is the direction that Paul takes the matter in his response (vv. 2–4). In fact, as noted above, Paul merely passes over the unmarried in silence.

In sum, my reconstruction offers a historically plausible explanation for a number of the "puzzling" details of 1 Corinthians 7:1–2: (1) It explains how the Corinthians can advocate celibacy yet run the risk of and ultimately fall prey to πορνεία—because they advocate marital celibacy, rejecting nonprocreative intercourse while apparently approving extramarital dalliances; and (2) it explains why Paul directs all his attention exclusively to the married (the real target of the Corinthians in their deployment of the slogan), advocating marital relations as a safeguard against πορνεία. In other words, it explains what is on the surface rather ironic—Paul's response suggests that the Corinthians applied the slogan to married couples rather than to the single, which in turn perhaps explains why Paul, oddly enough, never expresses approval for the slogan as it might be applied to the unmarried. Again, we might expect Paul to argue, "You Corinthians say, 'It is good for a man not to have sexual relations with a woman.' Yes, this is quite true, but it only applies to the unmarried; the married should enjoy full conjugal rights."

But he never does, and our proposed historical reconstruction makes good sense of this (since it was only nonprocreative marital relations that were being rejected).

Yet, why does Paul not elevate marital relations to a wholesome, God-given gift? Why does he instead apparently reduce them to a prophylactic against immorality?[78] At least two possible reasons can be suggested.

The first reason Paul does not elevate marriage as a God-given gift is that by focusing explicitly on πορνεία and marital relations, Paul directly confronts the incongruity of the Corinthians' thinking: "You say that it is not good to touch a woman (wife), but what do you do? Turn around and touch a woman!" The celibacy-minded Corinthians are in danger of not only violating their principle of celibacy but are running the risk of doing so in a way that raises the specter of πορνεία. In short, they advocate marital celibacy, rejecting God-sanctioned relations, all the while falling prey to (approving?[79]) extramarital liaisons with presumably non-Christians. Paul reverses and corrects the logic: "It is not good to have extramarital dalliances; turn instead to your spouse."

---

77. See esp. Acts 15:20, 29; 21:25, as well as the Pauline texts on sexual immorality (Rom. 1:24–27; 1 Cor.; 6:12–20; Eph. 5:3–7; Col 3:5–8; 1 Thess. 4:3–8) and Paul's vice lists that contain the term(s) πορνεία/πόρνος (traditionally, "fornication/fornicator") or words in the same or a similar semantic domain.

78. Whether this exhausts Paul's understanding of the purpose of marriage and sex is a separate question. It seems unlikely that it encompasses Paul's entire vision.

79. It seems likely that this was the Corinthians' thinking; cf. 1 Cor. 6:12–20.

The second reason Paul does not elevate marriage as a God-given gift is that, for Paul, πορνεία is unequivocally wrong—sinful. In fact, in his thinking it is so much so that in the preceding paragraph (1 Cor. 6:12–20), the *locus classicus* on πορνεία, he never really argues this, and he offers no explanation or analysis of πορνεία per se. Instead, he appears to operate from (what should be) accepted premises ("Do you not know," vv. 15, 16, 19) and to assume the sinfulness of πορνεία.[80] It is one of Paul's most basic assumptions, as evidenced by his vice lists. So with his expression "since sexual immorality is occurring" (1 Cor. 7:2), Paul can safely table all other arguments. There is little need for elaborate theologizing. The implementation among married couples of the Corinthians' slogan (v. 1) has led to πορνεία, and marital relations are an excellent remedy for this intolerable situation. The solution of marital relations (vv. 2b–c) is obvious, and Paul's appeal to it forms a decisive rejection of the Corinthians' use of the slogan.[81] This is all too easy for Paul—low-hanging fruit, if you will. There is no need to elaborate on the wholesomeness or the God-givenness of marital relations. The alternative (πορνεία) is unthinkable.

All that said, certain assumptions and "inside" information shared only between Paul and the Corinthians are unknown to us. Although historical reconstruction, mirror-reading, and the like are fraught with difficulty and risk, Robert Mounce's paraphrase of 1 Corinthians 7:1–2 coupled with my reconstruction may be the way forward: "Now regarding some of the issues you brought up in your letter: You said, 'It is good for a man not to have sexual contact with a woman.' Yes, but not the way you meant it. Some of you men are practicing chastity, but unable to control the urge you have turned to prostitutes. It would be better for you and your wife to maintain normal sexual relationships with one another."[82]

In the final analysis, Paul approves of celibacy—perhaps even to the point of viewing sexual relations within marriage with a bit of ambivalence. Perhaps he can take them or leave them, provided that πορνεία is avoided. One wonders whether Paul's less-than-positive assessment of marital relations does not betray a certain sympathy for marital celibacy. In this regard, Roy Ciampa and Brian Rosner note, "[Paul] would certainly not object to married people who were happy to refrain from sex except for the purposes of procreation."[83] Yet

---

80. Brian S. Rosner suggests that "Paul's instructions, it appears, are designed to underscore the severity and weight of the sin of *porneia*, and not so much to show that it is sin" (*Paul, Scripture and Ethics: A Study of 1 Corinthians 5–7*, Arbeiten zur Geschichte des antiken Judentums und des Urchristentums 22 [Leiden: Brill, 1994], 124). See also Traugott Holtz, who argues precisely the same point, namely, that Paul presupposes that πορνεία is wrong ("The Question of the Content of Paul's Instructions," in *Understanding Paul's Ethics*, ed. Brian S. Rosner [Grand Rapids: Eerdmans, 1995], 54–55).

81. Not necessarily the slogan itself.

82. Robert H. Mounce, *Letters of Paul to the Early Church: A Contemporary Translation* (Eugene, OR: Cascade, 2017), 25.

83. Ciampa-Rosner, *First Letter to the Corinthians*, 275.

he certainly prefers to endorse sexual relations in the face of the Corinthian alternative: sexual immorality (6:12–20). Yet 7:1–2 is a curious text and difficult to understand with certainty. In the end, perhaps it should remind us, rather jarringly, of the need to read Scripture and to read our theology and ethics out of it rather than into it.

Celibacy in 1 Corinthians 7:7

As with the other text that we have considered, we begin with a textual layout of the individual clauses, this time of 1 Corinthians 7:7.[84]

> 7a I wish that all of you were as I am.
> 7b But each of you has your own gift from God;
> 7c one has this gift,
> 7d another has that.

Here in verse 7a Paul is referring to his unmarried, celibate condition. This is made clear from the present context of 7:1–7 and from verses 8–9, immediately following.[85] His wish is that all persons were single, but he recognizes that not all are suited for celibacy. Such an existence is a matter of a "gift from God" (v. 7b)—almost certainly an allusion to Jesus's statement, "not everyone . . . only those to whom it has been given" (Matt. 19:11).[86] So Paul's wish is one thing, but he realizes that it is only that—his preference or desire—and that ultimately the decision rests with God, specifically his gifting.

Verse 7c–d does not contain the word "gift" and reads more literally:[87]
> 7c the one thus,
> 7d the other thus.

Paul's wording is a bit cryptic, and what he means is not entirely clear. Perhaps verse 7c–d should be understood generally, not referring specifically or exclusively to the

---

84. Although not without some relevance to our discussion, we bypass 1 Cor. 7:8–9. Paul almost certainly addresses widows and widowers, introducing a significant new variable. Moreover, with most commentators, unlike Garland, we see a paragraph break beginning at v. 8.

85. So most interpreters.

86. John Calvin notes that "Paul is therefore an interpreter of our Lord's words here" (*The First Epistle of Paul to the Corinthians*, trans. John W. Fraser, Calvin's Commentaries [Edinburgh: Oliver and Boyd, 1960], 141).

87. See Thiselton, *The First Epistle to the Corinthians*, 513; cf. Danker et al., *A Greek-English Lexicon*, 742.1b. The complementary expressions "the one" and "the other" probably refer to persons, as v. 7b ("each of you") leads one to expect, and not to gifts. So rightly CEB, CSB, GNB/TEV, NIV, NRSV; *pace* ESV, NABR. Note that in the preceding clauses of vv. 7a and 7b, Paul leads with a reference to persons ("you") and follows with a reference to gifting ("as I am"; "gift from God"). So probably here as well.

gift of celibacy: "one having one kind of gift and another a different kind."[88] Still the explicit contrast in the immediately preceding lines between Paul's preference for celibacy and God's unique gifting ("I wish . . . as I am. But each of you has your own gift [χάρισμα] from God") suggests that Paul does indeed have a gift of celibacy in mind[89]—or perhaps better, the gift of ἐγκράτεια, or "self-control" (v. 9).[90] Perhaps Paul contrasts the gift of celibacy (v. 7c) with any other special endowment from God—and not specifically a gift of marriage (v. 7d), which some maintain. As G. G. Findlay suggests, the expression "another has that" (v. 7d) does not refer to marriage as a gift but "to any special endowment for service in Christ's kingdom other than that stated."[91] However, the juxtaposition of the two lines in verses 7c–d *would seem to suggest* that the referent of the second or corresponding element of the pair is (or includes) the counterpart of celibacy (if that is indeed in view in v. 7c), namely, marriage.[92] It is difficult to be certain. If Paul does have a gift of marriage in view, what is not clear is whether Paul is being exhaustive, that is, whether each and every Christian falls into one of the two camps: gifted for celibacy or gifted for marriage.

As for the gift of celibacy, one can improve little on the contextually sensitive definition offered by James Dunn: "To restrain the sexual appetite when unmarried, Paul regards as something given by God. It is not the celibate state which is the charisma, but the enabling to say 'No' to sexual passions—an enabling which Paul experienced as something not in his own strength but as given from beyond."[93] Ciampa and Rosner summarize the point: "The issue is whether

---

88. NRSV; similarly, ESV, NABR, NLT. See Jeremy Moiser, "A Reassessment of Paul's View of Marriage with Reference to 1 Cor 7," *JSNT* 18 (1983): 106–7. Alternatively, "the one exercises his gift, whatever it is, in one way—i.e., while single; the other exercises his gift, whatever it might be, in another way—i.e., while married. However, this seems less likely in that Paul seems to be referring specifically to "gifts" (χάρισμα, v. 7b) rather than "states" or "conditions" in which gifts operate.

89. So Collins, *First Corinthians*, 256; James D. G. Dunn, *Jesus and the Spirit* (London: SCM, 1975; repr., Grand Rapids: Eerdmans, 1997), 206–7; Fee, *First Epistle to the Corinthians*, 316; and Garland, *1 Corinthians*, 271.

90. Conzelmann, *1 Corinthians*, 120; Kurt Niederwimmer, *Askese und Mysterium: Über Ehe, Ehescheidung, und Eheverzicht in den Anfängen des christlichen Glaubens*, Forschungen zur Religion und Literatur des Alten und Neuen Testaments 113 (Göttingen: Vandenhoeck and Ruprecht, 1975), 96n70; Roy Bowen Ward, "Musonius and Paul on Marriage," *New Testament Studies* 36, no. 2 (1990): 284.

91. G. G. Findlay, "St. Paul's First Epistle to the Corinthians," in *The Expositor's Greek Testament*, ed. W. Robertson Nicoll (London: Hodder and Stoughton, 1897; repr., Grand Rapids: Eerdmans, 1983), 2:824. Similarly, C. K. Barrett, *The First Epistle to the Corinthians*, Black's New Testament Commentary (London: Black, 1968), 158–59.

92. So Collins, *First Corinthians*, 256; Fee, *First Epistle to the Corinthians*, 316; Thiselton, *The First Epistle to the Corinthians*, 513. Cf. Moffatt: "He has a gift for one way of life or the other." *Perhaps*: "the one in one way [celibacy]; the other in *the alternative* way [marriage]."

93. Dunn, *Jesus and the Spirit*, 206. Similarly, Victor Paul Furnish, *The Moral Teaching of Paul*, 3rd ed. (Nashville: Abingdon, 2009), 41; Weiss, *Primitive Christianity*, 2:580.

an individual . . . can concentrate on living a life worthy of the gospel *to the glory of God* without being distracted by sexual desires."[94]

A gift of or for marriage is more problematic. Marriage does seem to be humankind's "natural" estate—a default position so to speak, and hence many deny the existence of any special gifting from God. As Richard Lenksi puts it, "No grace and no special gift of grace is needed for that, the constitution of our nature suffices entirely."[95] Yet, as indicated above, Paul's parallel wording (vv. 7c–d) plausibly suggests some special endowment from God for the married life. At least Karl Barth so thinks: "Marriage is a matter of freedom, not of routine, not of a supposedly sacred ethical custom, not even of normal biological maturity. . . . It is a matter of the Holy Ghost freeing man for this in no sense ordinary but highly extraordinary fulfillment of the relation between man and woman. . . . A fundamental question [is] whether a man has the κλῆσις [call] and χάρισμα [gift] for this in every way extraordinary venture."[96] Perhaps this gifting, if it is indeed a gift, is some sort of God-given "adaptation and capacity"—beyond the natural human condition—for the married state.[97] And perhaps some are gifted neither for celibacy nor for marriage. Yet on all this, Paul is not particularly clear.

In sum, Paul presents a clear preference for singleness. Yet it is merely that—a preference—not a requirement, since such is a matter of gifting from God. As Raymond Collins puts it, "It is not Paul's wish but God's gift that is normative in these matters."[98] And Paul provides no hint here that singleness is in any way superior to the married state.

Celibacy in 1 Corinthians 7:25–35

In interpreting 1 Corinthians 7:25–35, Jerome Murphy-O'Connor's assessment is worth bearing in mind: "This is probably the most difficult and controverted section of the letter."[99] Indeed, this paragraph is something of an exegetical nightmare. In light of this complexity and the overall length of verses 25–35, I will alter my approach. Although I will again provide a textual layout, my focus will be narrowed to the reasons given by Paul for singleness, bypassing some of the more difficult—and for our purposes, tangential—issues in the paragraph.

---

94. Ciampa-Rosner, *First Letter to the Corinthians*, 285n73 (emphasis added).
95. R. C. H. Lenski, *The Interpretation of Paul's First and Second Epistles to the Corinthians* (Minneapolis: Augsburg, 1937), 282.
96. Barth, *Church Dogmatics*, III/4, 184. Others also see gifting for marriage as a special God-given endowment.
97. For some possibilities of what this gift might include, see Gardner, *Family and Familia*, 304; cf. Thiselton, *The First Epistle to the Corinthians*, 513–14.
98. Collins, *First Corinthians*, 261. Similarly, Conzelmann: "The wish is not made into a principle" (*1 Corinthians*, 118); Schrage, *Ethics*, 229.
99. Jerome Murphy-O'Connor, *1 Corinthians*, New Testament Message 10 (Collegeville, MN: Liturgical Press, 1979), 71.

Up to this point our concern has been more or less on the gift of celibacy (esp. Matt. 19:10–12; 1 Cor. 7:7). Now the focus changes to the more general question—irrespective of gifting: Should one marry or remain single? Here Paul's advice—and that is what it is, advice, but trustworthy advice and not merely personal preference (v. 25)[100]—is summarized in verse 26. And this advice is exactly what it was in the explanatory aside of 7:17–24, namely, the admonition to *remain in whatever social situation one was in when called.*[101]

Traditionally Paul is understood as presenting two reasons for remaining single:[102]

1. Marriage is of little positive meaning or purpose in light of the times. In other words, since the parousia is imminent, there is little point in inviting the additional trouble of marriage when so precious little time remains (vv. 28b–31).

2. Singleness simplifies and streamlines life, allowing one to prioritize better its commitments and demands, "to put first things first." In other words, singleness is the better option, as the married are (or can be) especially burdened with "the affairs of this world" (v. 33 and v. 34b) and thus distracted from the priority of "undivided devotion to the Lord" (v. 35c).

With some important qualifications, these reasons point in the right direction. To these points, and some key qualifications, we now turn, after my own "explanatory aside" of a textual layout of 1 Corinthians 7:25–35.

---

100. So Fee, *First Epistle to the Corinthians*, 362–63, 365, 368; Garland, *1 Corinthians*, 321–22. Verse 25: "I have no command from the Lord but I give a judgment [γνώμη] as one who by the Lord's mercy is trustworthy." Not mere "opinion" (e.g., CEB, CSB, NABR, NASB, NET, NJB, NRSV, REB), for this advice comes from someone "who by the Lord's mercy is worthy of trust" (v. 25). The term (γνώμη) has a slightly more authoritative nuance that is better captured by "judgment" (ASV, ESV, NIV). See Ciampa-Rosner, *First Letter to the Corinthians*, 333–34; Collins, *First Corinthians*, 289–90: "authoritative opinion." Paul uses this term again in v. 40 in much the same way that he does here—with a touch of authority: "I too have the Spirit of God."

101. Jean-Jacques von Allmen, *Pauline Teaching on Marriage* (London: The Faith Press, 1963), 14; Ciampa-Rosner, *First Letter to the Corinthians*, 334; Fee, *First Epistle to the Corinthians*, 298, 358–59, 365; Gardner, *Family and* Familia, 344; Ben Witherington III, *Jesus, Paul, and the End of the World* (Downers Grove, IL: InterVarsity Press, 1992), 27. The principle, remain in whatever social situation one was in when called, is reflected in 7:17, 20, 24. Barrett points out that throughout vv. 17–24, "Paul is not thinking primarily of a vocation *to* which a [person] is called, but the condition *in* which a [person] is when the converting call of God comes to him [or her] and summons him [or her] to the life of Christian faith and obedience" (*First Epistle to the Corinthians*, 168; similarly, Fee, *First Epistle to the Corinthians*, 343).

102. See, e.g., Morton Scott Enslin, *The Ethics of Paul* (New York: Harper & Brothers, 1930), 190.

[25] Now about virgins:
> I have no command from the Lord,
>> but
> I give a judgment as one who by the Lord's mercy is trustworthy.

[26a] Because of the present crisis,

[26b] I think that it is good for a man to remain as he is.

[27] Are you pledged to a woman?
> Do not seek to be released.
> Are you free from such a commitment?
> Do not look for a wife.

[28a] But if you do marry,
> you have not sinned;
>> and
>>> if a virgin marries,
> she has not sinned.

[28b] But those who marry will face many troubles in this life,
>> and
> I want to spare you this.

[29a] What I mean, brothers and sisters, is that the time is short.

[29b] From now on
> those who have wives should live as if they do not;

[30] those who mourn, as if they did not;
> those who are happy, as if they were not;
> those who buy something, as if it were not theirs to keep;

[31a] those who use the things of the world, as if not engrossed in them.

[31b] For this world in its present form is passing away.

[32a] I would like you to be free from concern.

[32b] An unmarried man is concerned about the Lord's affairs—how he can please the Lord.

[33] But
> a married man is concerned about the affairs of this world—how he can please his wife—

[34a] and
> his interests are divided.

[34b] An unmarried woman or virgin is concerned about the Lord's affairs:
> Her aim is to be devoted to the Lord in both body and spirit.
>> But
> a married woman is concerned about the affairs of this world—how she can please her husband.

[35a] I am saying this for your own good,

[35b] not to restrict you,
> but

[35c] that you may live in a right way in undivided devotion to the Lord.

Paul presents one primary reason for singleness—*the eschatological world-view and existence of the Christian.* He also gives secondary reasons, related to both the primary reason and to each other: *additional trouble and the divided interests of the married.* These will be explored below.

The Christian's eschatological worldview and existence

Paul's "radical new understanding of our relationship to the present world" (vv. 29–31)[103] relativizes the value of marriage vis-à-vis singleness. In other words, the "eschatological urgency of our present existence" renders marriage optional and raises the price of celibacy's stock.[104] This urgency, this worldview, means that the Christian's existence in the present is determined by the future that has already been inaugurated—already been set in motion—by Christ.[105] It is not that Paul necessarily expects the parousia in a very short time[106] and counsels singleness as a result,[107] but he understands that he is living in the last days, the days between Christ's first and second comings.[108] For the Christian this means that a definite future ("the time is short,"[109] "this world in its present form is passing away," vv.

---

103. Fee, *First Epistle to the Corinthians*, 380.

104. Fee, *First Epistle to the Corinthians*, 298.

105. For the thought and some of the wording, see Fee, *First Epistle to the Corinthians*, 372. Cf. Barth, *Church Dogmatics*, III/4, 147.

106. For a vigorous rejection of the idea that the parousia "is expected within a few years or months," see Arthur L. Moore, *The Parousia in the New Testament*, Supplements to Novum Testamentum 13 (Leiden: Brill, 1966), 114–17. The quotation in the first sentence is taken from C. H. Dodd, *New Testament Studies* (New York: Scribner's Sons, 1968), 112–14.

107. Allmen rightly notes, "In short, it is not because of an imminent *parousia* that St. Paul accords a very positive virtue to celibacy: the constant imminence of the *parousia* prevents neither work, nor trade, nor cultural pursuits, and marriage, even if obliging the partners to live for one another, is nevertheless not an insurmountable obstacle to Christian watchfulness" (*Marriage*, 19–20). If imminence were Paul's argument, one might draw the opposite conclusion—get married promptly and wring the most out of the time remaining (see Leander E. Keck and Victor Paul Furnish, *The Pauline Letters*, Interpreting Biblical Texts [Nashville: Abingdon, 1984], 85). Cf. also G. B. Caird: "The one appeal he [Paul] never employs is that they should be ready for the *parousia*" (*New Testament Theology*, ed. L. D. Hurst [Oxford: Clarendon, 1994], 254).

108. The "last days" encompasses the whole period beginning with Christ's first advent and continuing to his second coming. See Leon Morris, "Last Days," in *Evangelical Dictionary of Biblical Theology*, ed. Walter A. Elwell (Grand Rapids: Baker, 1996), 464–67; and esp. Acts 2:17; Heb. 1:1–2; 1 Peter 1:20; 1 Cor. 10:11; also Heb. 9:26; James 5:3; 2 Peter 3:3; 1 John 2:18; cf. 1 Tim. 4:1; 2 Tim. 3:1.

109. Precisely what Paul intends by the expression "the time is short" is not entirely clear. In light of his choice of words and his "radical," "contradictory," even "absurd" argument in vv. 29–31 (Fee's terms, *First Epistle to the Corinthians*, 375–76), Fee reproduces Paul's thought more or less as follows: this present era has been "compressed, foreshortened" so "that God's people stand at the end of history, as it were." In this way, "the future . . . is now in plain view" (374). In other words, with the death and resurrection of Christ, the decisive event has taken place. The last days have begun. The corner has been turned, and the "Corinthians are in the final stretch of history"

29, 31) conditions their present existence, including the question of whether to marry. As David Garland points out, "choices in life" and "decisions in mundane matters of this world" should be evaluated from "the perspective of the end," seeing that "the new age has invaded the present."[110] No better explanation of this perspective can be given than that offered by Gordon Fee:

> We catch a glimpse of the man himself [Paul], and what makes him run. . . .
> He is thoroughly eschatological. . . . For him it means that the future (Christ's return and reign) has been determined by the past (Christ's death and resurrection), and that that certain future (guaranteed by the gift of the Spirit) determines the present. The resurrection of Jesus from the dead was not a matter of creed for him; it was the singular reality that conditioned his entire existence. But not his alone. By way of the resurrection the eternal God had set the future inexorably in motion; the "coming" of Christ and subsequent "judgment" are inevitable corollaries, as sure as life itself. For

---

(Ciampa-Rosner, *First Letter to the Corinthians*, 345). Thus the present era has been compressed in that the time is limited and that the final consummation is now staring the Christian in the face (both temporal and perspectival foreshortening). The image painted by E.-B. Allo, in keeping with the nautical term συστέλλω ("has been shortened"), is that of a ship that has its sails furled because its voyage is ending (*Corinthiens*, 179). Garland offers an alternative metaphor: "The future outcome of this world has become crystal clear . . . Christians stand on a mountaintop, as it were, where distances are foreshortened. From this vantage point, they can see the termination of history on earth and its goal. They can discern what really matters, and they should conduct their lives accordingly" (*1 Corinthians*, 329; cf. Witherington, *End of the World*, 28–29). Thus this *radically new* perspective leads, in turn, to a *radically new* stance concerning one's relationship to the world and to a *radically altered* set of values (vv. 29–31; cf. Ciampa-Rosner, *First Letter to the Corinthians*, 345; Fee, *First Epistle to the Corinthians*, 374–76; Witherington, *End of the World*, 28–30).

A number of English translations, along with the NIV, render the verbal construction in v. 29 as "is short" (NET, NKJV, NLT; see also the CSB: "is limited"), implying that Paul expected the Lord's return very soon (cf. also ESV, NJB, NRSV, REB). However, this not only seems to mistranslate the verbal construction—it should almost certainly be rendered as a verb phrase, i.e., "has been/is shortened" (NASB; cf. NABR) rather than with an adjective as in "is short" (correctly Barrett, *First Epistle to the Corinthians*, 176; Ciampa-Rosner, *First Letter to the Corinthians*, 344–45; Fee, *First Epistle to the Corinthians*, 374n303; Thiselton, *The First Epistle to the Corinthians*, 581–83)—but also suggests quite wrongly that a "*theology* of eschatological imminence" presupposes a "*chronology* of eschatological imminence" (Thiselton, *The First Epistle to the Corinthians*, 578; see also Ciampa-Rosner, *First Letter to the Corinthians*, 345). Leopold Sabourin captures the point: "It is often objected that this interpretation makes Paul share the erroneous belief that the end of the world is imminent. Not chronology, however, but theology is here directly involved. For the New Testament writers, this is the last period of the world, however long it may be, and the expectation of the *parousia* colors the values that belong to it" ("Consecrated Celibacy," 56). In other words, *Paul is not operating with an eschatological timetable but from an eschatological perspective.*

110. Garland, *1 Corinthians*, 317.

Paul, therefore, those sure events radicalize present Christian existence. All merely human judgments [and values, including marriage and singleness] are nothing in light of the final judgment.[111]

Marital status is not the main issue; rather, it is one's relationships to the world. Indeed, everyday matters of this world, including the possibility of marriage, are finally not "the determining factor" in how one orders his or her life.[112] "Escapism is by no means an option, but this world's occupations should not absorb the Christian's life."[113] "The kingdom of God is not a matter of eating and drinking, but of righteousness, peace and joy in the Holy Spirit" (Rom. 14:17). As Barth notes, "The light of the resurrection of the dead . . . shines already in the present. Is it right to proceed as though nothing had happened?"[114] Ultimately then for Paul, his eschatological worldview and focus, in conjunction with the "present crisis" (v. 26) and the additional and "divided" interests of the married (v. 34), means that celibacy is preferable to marriage, but not mandatory. And contrary to Paul's Jewish heritage, marriage is merely an option—and one he does not particularly encourage.

In short, 1 Corinthians 7:29–31 appears to be Paul's expression of a dominant theme found in Jesus's life and teaching—the supreme value of the kingdom of God. For Jesus, the kingdom superseded and relativized all earthly relationships and activities.[115] They are no longer the fulcrum on which all of life pivots. That place is reserved for the kingdom of God (on all this, see above).

With his "as if . . . not" clauses in verses 29–31, Paul makes a similar point. Marriage, mourning, rejoicing, buying, and possessing/consuming are not rejected or negated, only realigned—relativized.[116] The five realities in the "as if . . . not" clauses no longer (need to or should) dictate or determine the Christian's relationship to the world, for "this world in its present form is passing away" (v. 31b).[117] That place is reserved for the kingdom of God, which has been inaugurated—set in motion—by the crucified and risen Lord.

In a word, it is a matter of priorities. With the dawning of the new age, marriage is not a given. Other variables are now a part of the equation. The

---

111. Fee, *First Epistle to the Corinthians*, 170 (bracketed comments added). Weiss writes, "Paul certainly has a different viewpoint than we: he must be thought of as an eschatologically-minded Christian" (*Primitive Christianity*, 2:583–84).

112. For a helpful summary, see Garland, *1 Corinthians*, 317–18.

113. Gardner, *Family and* Familia, 348.

114. Barth, *Church Dogmatics*, III/4, 147.

115. In referring to Jesus's viewpoint, Barth notes, "Marriage is obviously relativized" (*Church Dogmatics*, III/4, 144).

116. Thiselton notes that "Paul counsels not withdrawal from the world but 'relativizing' it" (*The First Epistle to the Corinthians,* 601).

117. Barrett correctly points out that "Paul's point is not the transiency of creation as such, but the fact that its outward pattern, in social and mercantile institutions, for example, has no permanence" (*First Epistle to the Corinthians*, 178).

Christian's worldview is now (or should be) dominated by kingdom priorities, and this, for many individuals, elevates celibacy to a position of practical—not moral or spiritual—superiority.[118]

As noted above, an eschatological perspective radically alters one's relationship to the world and its institutions, sorrows, joys, affairs, and activities. The routine affairs of the present world have been relativized. They have been set within a much larger, grander context. Just as the "call-up" for active duty in the time of war alters the soldier's priorities and perspective, so it is with those who are "gripped by God's eschatological activity."[119] For those so gripped it is no longer business as usual—the present age no longer lays ultimate claim on our lives.[120] To this realignment of priorities and perspective, Paul calls for deliberate assent (vv. 29–31). For some, this will mean a life of celibacy. In all this, Paul is merely echoing Jesus's sentiment—that some voluntarily forgo marriage "because of the kingdom of heaven" (Matt. 19:12 CEB, CSB).

This decisive role for the kingdom of God seems borne out by the observation that Paul's illustrations and wording in the "as if . . . not" clauses do not seem to be haphazard or random but rather seem to take their cue from the supreme value that Jesus himself placed on the kingdom of God. In short, conceptual and terminological parallels[121] found in the Gospels (esp. Luke) to Paul's five "as if . . . not" categories suggest that he has in fact learned an important lesson from Jesus: with the dawn of the kingdom of God everything has changed.[122] Old wineskins cannot hold new wine. In sum, Paul understood that the kingdom of God is the

---

118. See Philippe Menoud, "Marriage and Celibacy according to Saint Paul," in *Jesus Christ and the Faith*, trans. Eunice M. Paul, PTMS 18 (Pittsburgh: Pickwick, 1978), 4–5. He notes and then illustrates that "it is on the practical level and not the theological level that celibacy is better in relation to marriage," but only "for those who have received the gift of the ability to live alone." See further, Allmen, *Marriage*, 15; Furnish, *Moral Teaching*, 39–40, 42; Erhard S. Gerstenberger and Wolfgang Schrage, *Woman and Man*, trans. Douglas W. Stott (Nashville: Abingdon, 1980), 179; Thurian, *Marriage and Celibacy*, 78–83.

119. Christian Wolff, "Humility and Self-Denial in Jesus's Life and Message and in the Apostolic Experience of Paul," in *Paul and Jesus: Collected Essays*, ed. A. J. M. Wedderburn, Journal for the Study of the New Testament Supplement Series 37 (Sheffield: JSOT Press, 1989), 154. I neither recall the origin of the illustration nor the immediately preceding wording. It was unearthed from my lecture notes and so is perhaps original with me.

120. See Furnish, *Moral Teaching*, 37.

121. Although not pervasive or overwhelming in isolation, collectively the parallels present a plausible case for Pauline dependence on Jesus:
   1. wives (Luke 14:26–27, 33 // Matt. 10:37–38 // Gospel of Thomas 55, 110; Luke 18:29–30 // Matt. 19:29 // Mark 10:29–30);
   2. mourning (Luke 9:59–62);
   3. rejoicing (Luke 10:20);
   4. buying and possessing (Luke 12:22–32 // Matt. 6:25–34; Luke 14:15–23; 16:19–31; 17:26–36).

122. The inauguration of the kingdom of God and its priorities goes a long way in explaining why Gen. 1:28 is no longer imperative in this new era. In short, the inauguration of the kingdom of God trumps the mandate to "be fruitful and multiply and fill the earth" (ESV).

supreme joy and priority in life and so aligned his priorities and structured his life accordingly, as did Jesus.[123] For both, this meant a life of singleness.

Having established his primary reasons in favor of celibacy, Paul goes on to give two secondary ones.

Paul's two secondary reasons for singleness

The first of Paul's secondary reasons in support of singleness is additional trouble: "Because of the present crisis" (v. 26), the married will experience "many troubles in this life" (v. 28b)[124]—something "that will not be experienced as fully by single people."[125] Leon Morris notes, "When high seas are raging it is no time for changing ships."[126]

The identity of the "present crisis" is disputed and, despite extended debate, is not entirely certain.[127] And although it is probably instrumental in

---

123. See the insightful interview with John Stott in the appendix to Albert Hsu, *Singles at the Crossroads: A Fresh Perspective on Christian Singleness* (Downers Grove, IL: InterVarsity Press, 1997), 176–81.

124. Paul is probably referring primarily back to the "present crisis" (v. 26), not forward to the anxieties that a husband and wife regularly experience in the ebb and flow of marital life (vv. 32–35).

125. Ciampa-Rosner, *First Letter to the Corinthians*, 342.

126. Leon Morris, *The First Epistle of Paul to the Corinthians*, rev. ed., Tyndale New Testament Commentary (Leicester, UK: Inter-Varsity Press, 1985), 113.

127. Two basic views have dominated the literature (see Danker et al., *Greek-English Lexicon*, 61.2; 337.2–3). (1) The expression should be translated "impending distress" (NET, NRSV) and refers to the imminent coming of Christ and the great distress that will accompany the events of his return. (2) The expression should be translated "present distress" (CEB, CSB, ESV, NABR, NASB, NIV, NJB, REB) and refers to some calamity or trial already being experienced by the Corinthians. Despite the fact that the eschatological language of vv. 29, 31, points in the direction of the first view, linguistic considerations probably tip the balance in favor of the second view (see, e.g., Ciampa-Rosner, *First Letter to the Corinthians*, 336; Fee, *First Epistle to the Corinthians*, 363–64; Garland, *1 Corinthians*, 323–24).

The precise identification of this "present distress" is uncertain, but several plausible suggestions have been proposed: (1) persecution; (2) a famine or famines that occurred in Greece around AD 51 during the reign of Claudius (Acts 11:28); (3) the suffering and trouble that is the common experience of all Christians (Fee, *First Epistle to the Corinthians*, 364; Garland, *1 Corinthians*, 323–25). Finally, it should be noted with Garland (*1 Corinthians*, 324) that it is difficult to "deny the apocalyptic tenor of the whole passage with its references to 'compressed time' (7:29) and 'the form of this world passing away' (7:31)." Thus it is most likely that Paul "has in view a present crisis (perhaps the famine) interpreted as an end-time event" (Garland, *1 Corinthians*, 324; similarly, Barrett, *First Epistle to the Corinthians*, 175; Ciampa-Rosner, *First Letter to the Corinthians*, 327; Gardner, *Family and Familia*, 344–45; Moore, *Parousia*, 116n1; Thiselton, *The First Epistle to the Corinthians*, 575; Bruce Winter, *After Paul Left Corinth* [Grand Rapids: Eerdmans, 2001], 224–25). Hays also presents an attractive third option: the phrase should be translated "present necessity" and refers to "the urgent imperative of proclaiming the gospel and doing the work of the Lord in the short time that remains" (*First Corinthians*, 129).

introducing "many troubles in this life" (v. 28) for the married, which the single are spared (to a degree), it is questionable whether all such "troubles" can be reduced to this singular cause.[128] In other words, "present crisis" or not, the married "will face many troubles in this life." And in light of dominating kingdom priorities, these are problems that the Christian living in the last days can well do without.

The second secondary reason Paul gives is that of divided concerns. The married, because of additional concerns "about the affairs of this world" (vv. 33, 34b), find that their "interests are divided" (v. 34a). Yet Paul does not condemn those in this situation. Rather, he is concerned to promote celibacy but at the same time "to remove any anxiety [v. 32a] that marriage might be thought wrong or 'unseemly' in itself. Different, yes; more involved in the present world, yes; but inferior or sinful, no."[129] So he neither denies the importance of marital responsibilities that create competing interests, nor does he criticize the Christian for meeting these obligations. His comments are merely a statement of fact, not an indictment against marriage.[130] As Victor Furnish notes, "There is not the slightest hint that he regards their married status as *compromising* their commitment to the Lord or their labors on the Lord's behalf."[131] He simply acknowledges that "married people have to work out their devotion to the Lord in the context of a very demanding this-worldly commitment."[132]

Since Paul indicates that the married person's "interests are divided" (v. 34a) and that he (Paul) is trying to promote "undivided devotion to the Lord" (v. 35), he implies that the married have less opportunity for service—less time, energy, and freedom to be "concerned about the Lord's affairs" (vv. 32b, 34b)—than that which is available to the single. Although Paul's concern seems to be driven by his desire that the Corinthians be "free from concern" (v. 32a) and rightly devoted to the Lord (v. 35)—whether single or married—it is difficult to escape the conclusion that Paul sees (the gift of) celibacy as providing "extraordinary opportunity for single-minded investment in ministry for Christ."[133] Here lies the fundamental purpose of the gift of celibacy, for as Jesus himself said, "There

---

128. See Joseph A. Fitzmyer, *First Corinthians*, Anchor Yale Bible 32 (New Haven, CT: Yale University Press, 2008), 316; cf. Gardner, *Family and* Familia, 347; Thiselton, *The First Epistle to the Corinthians*, 578.

129. Fee, *First Epistle to the Corinthians*, 380.

130. Furnish, *Moral Teaching*, 40.

131. Furnish, *Moral Teaching*, 41 (emphasis added to the operative word).

132. David Wenham, "Marriage and Singleness in Paul and Today," in *Readings in Christian Ethics*, vol. 2, *Issues and Applications*, ed. David K. Clark and Robert V. Rakestraw (Grand Rapids: Baker, 1996), 147; repr. from *Themelios* 13 (1988).

133. John Piper, "For Single Men and Women (and the Rest of Us)" in *Recovering Biblical Manhood and Womanhood*, ed. John Piper and Wayne Grudem (Wheaton, IL: Crossway, 1991), xix. The commentators on 1 Corinthians seem reluctant to express this "opportunity" for service too strongly, presumably so as not to imply that celibacy is superior to marriage (see, e.g., Fee, *First Epistle to the Corinthians*, 380; Garland, *1 Corinthians*, 334).

are those who choose to live like eunuchs for the sake of the kingdom of heaven"
(Matt. 19:12). In short, the gift "is given by God for the building up of the body
of Christ."[134]

SUMMARY OF PAUL AND CELIBACY

Paul's preference for celibacy does not also make it a superior existence, as if those
who are married should feel like second-class citizens. Still, it is hard for some
to accept Paul's preference for celibacy. Yet our real failure is to take Paul's main
point seriously enough, namely, that we are to live out our lives in the present
age, whether married or not, as those who have been determined (gripped) by the
"foreshortened time." Being eschatological people is to free us from the grip of the
world and its values. We are to live "as if . . . not" (7:29–31), that is, fully in the
world, but not controlled by its systems or values. Such freedom, which comes
only from Christ, both removes one from the anxiety about which existence might
be better (7:32–34) and liberates one from societal and familial "demands" for
marriage. Whichever existence one is called to—or gifted for—is better for him
or her, as long as it is appropriate and allows for unhindered devotion to the Lord
(7:35). And thus, although eschatology is the driving force behind Paul's thought,
Christology—devotion to the Lord—is front and center in his thinking.[135]

---

134. Ciampa-Rosner, *First Letter to the Corinthians*, 285.
135. I owe much of my conclusion to Fee, *First Epistle to the Corinthians*, 384, as well as in-
    sights from Schrage, *Ethics*, 229.

FOR DISCUSSION

1. Think about the messages you have heard both in and outside of the church relating to celibacy. How do they align with the teaching of Jesus and Paul?

2. Compare and contrast celibacy with marriage. What are the costs unique to each?

3. In what ways can you make the focus of your own marital status—whether celibate or married—more christological?

FOR FURTHER READING

Carson, D. A. "Matthew." In *The Expositor's Bible Commentary*, vol. 9, *Matthew and Mark*, edited by Tremper Longman III and David E. Garland, 23–670. Rev. ed. Grand Rapids: Zondervan, 2010.

Ciampa, Roy E., and Brian S. Rosner. *The First Letter to the Corinthians*. Pillar New Testament Commentary. Grand Rapids: Eerdmans, 2010.

Fee, Gordon D. *The First Epistle to the Corinthians*. Rev. ed. New International Commentary on the New Testament. Grand Rapids: Eerdmans, 2014.

CHAPTER 10

CELIBACY AND THE GOSPEL

ABRAHAM KURUVILLA

In 2016, in the United States, there were about 115 million adults eighteen years and older who were single—never married, married but separated, widowed, and divorced—making up about half of all US adults in that age group (see table 3).[1]

Table 3. 2016 Statistics for US Singles (in 1000s)			
	TOTAL (percent)	**MALES (percent)**	**FEMALES (percent)**
Total 18 and older	244,544 (100.0)	118,350 (100.0)	126,194 (100.0)
Total single	115,780 (47.3)	53,915 (45.6)	61,866 (49.0)
Never married	70,218 (28.7)	37,592 (31.8)	32,627 (25.9)
Separated	5,212 (2.1)	2,169 (1.8)	3,043 (2.4)
Widowed	14,839 (6.1)	3,462 (2.9)	11,377 (9.0)
Divorced	25,511 (10.4)	10,692 (9.0)	14,819 (11.7)

1. Data are from United States Census Bureau, "America's Families and Living Arrangements: 2016," https://www.census.gov/data/tables/2016/demo/families/cps-2016.html. The 2010 Census showed a total US population of 308,745,538 (United States Census Bureau, "By Decade," https://www.census.gov/programs-surveys/decennial-census/decade.2010. html) and, in 2016, the population was estimated to be 325,000,000 (United States Census Bureau, "U.S. and World Population Clock," https://www.census.gov/popclock/).

This reality makes it vital for any Christian organization or ministry to comprehend the issue of what it means to be single *and* Christian. This essay, however, will focus not so much on the question of singleness until marriage, or between marriages, or even after marriage, but rather on what it means to be single apart from the possibility of marriage. While most works on this subject see singleness as a problem to be countered, an oppression to be overcome, a burden to be relieved, and an agony to be suffered, I am taking a different tack. I'd like to emphasize three core elements of celibacy that, strikingly enough, parallel the three core elements of the Christian gospel.

CELIBACY AND GIFT

While there may be varieties of singleness, in this essay I'd like to focus on *ecclesiological* singleness, singleness for the church—a Christian form of committed singleness. I define ecclesiological singleness with four parameters: it is by choice (unforced and deliberate); it is for life (not a temporary measure or state); it is unto Christ (in order to serve him and his body, the church); and it is in community (not living in isolation, but fully entrenched in the corporate fellowship of Christians). Only this ecclesiological variety of singleness demands abstinence from sex, for an orthodox biblical Christianity does not permit extramarital sexual activity. So, again, ecclesiological singleness is by choice, for life, unto Christ, and in community.

Ecclesiological singleness is a countercultural response from the inside to a personal calling. By "calling," I mean the recognition of a gift, a sense of its givenness. Paul declares in 1 Corinthians 7:7, "Yet I wish that all men were even as I myself am. However, each has his own gift from God, one this way, and another that way."[2] Thus both marriage and celibacy are gifts. Both need a giftedness to maintain their respective states faithfully to God, the gift giver. And in a discussion with his disciples, where Jesus labeled any divorce for reasons other than immorality as adultery, they responded that if that were the case, "it is better not to marry." To which Jesus observed, "Not all can accept this statement, but those to whom it has been given" (Matt. 19:9–11).[3] And, as with all the gifts of God, this one, too, is given for "the common good" to the church (1 Cor. 12:7), that the body of Christ might be served (1 Peter 4:10). Hence, celibacy of this sort is rightly ecclesiological.

Because of this "givenness," because ecclesiological singleness is a gift, permit me to make another distinction: celibacy is not merely abstinence. Although celibacy is nowadays defined as the renunciation of sexual activity for a lengthy

---

2. Unless otherwise indicated, all translations of Scripture are my own.

3. From an entirely subjective basis, I would bet—if I were a betting man, that is—that there are more people to whom the gift of celibacy has been given than we realize or acknowledge. I think there are more people with the gift of celibacy who end up being married (because that's the default pathway) than the other way around—people with the gift of marriage remaining single.

period of time (= abstinence), such a usage is a twentieth-century development. In fact, *celibacy* comes from the Latin *caelebs*, "alone" or "unmarried/single." My preference is to retain celibacy as a synonym for ecclesiological singleness, and to use "abstinence" simply to refer to the relinquishment of sexual activity by singles or by marrieds. Thus abstinence is a response on the outside to a circumstance of some sort, resulting in the renunciation of sex. On the other hand, celibacy is a response from the inside to a calling and gifting and goes beyond just the giving up of sex.[4] Most of the early church fathers recognized celibacy as having a transcendent aim. In the fourth century, Gregory of Nyssa argued that celibacy defined simply from a mere physical praxis held no value: celibacy was more than just abstinence:

> [Celibacy] is not a single achievement, ending in the subjugation of the body, but that in intention it reaches to and pervades everything that is, or is considered, a right condition of the soul. That soul indeed which in virginity cleaves to the true Bridegroom will not remove herself merely from all bodily defilement; she will make that abstention only the beginning of her purity, and will carry this security from failure equally into everything else upon her path.[5]

The philosopher Max Scheler declared that "Christian asceticism . . . had as its goal not the suppression of the natural drives or even their extermination, but only power and control over them and their complete integration with soul and spirit [spiritualization]. It is positive, not negative, asceticism—and essentially aimed at the liberation of the highest powers of personality from the inhibitory automatism of the lower drives."[6] Indeed!

In a world besotted with sex, the church unfortunately has lost her way. She too has fallen into the trap of conceiving of this drive and its fulfillment as one of the greatest goods and ends of humanity. The evangelical wing of Christendom gives scant regard to sexual abstinence, let alone celibacy and singleness. This despite the biblical and historical emphases on this singular course of life. In the following sections, I show how celibacy reflects the Christian gospel in three distinct ways.

---

4. See Gabrielle Brown, *The New Celibacy: A Journey to Love, Intimacy, and Good Health in a New Age*, rev. ed. (New York: McGraw-Hill, 1989), 1. This is, of course, not to make celibates (who are by definition abstinent) asexual, for sexuality relates to ontology (who a person is) rather than to ethology (what a person does).
5. Gregory of Nyssa, *On Virginity* 14, in *The Nicene and Post-Nicene Fathers*, series 2, ed. Philip Schaff (repr., Peabody, MA: Hendrickson, 1994), 5:360. While I recognize that some, such as Christopher Yuan, urge listeners to use "chastity" instead of "celibacy," as the latter is not found in the Bible, I still prefer celibacy.
6. Max Scheler, *Vom Umsturz der Werte: Der Abhandlungen und Aufsätze zweite durchgesehene Auflage: Volume 1* (Leipzig: Der Neue Geist, 1919), 181 (my translation).

CELIBACY AND THE GOSPEL AS SELF-SACRIFICE

As Pope John Paul II said, "[Celibacy] for the sake of the kingdom of heaven" is characterized by "successive self-sacrifices"—"a conscious and voluntary renouncement of that [marital] union and all that is connected to it."[7] Such sacrifices include those of family life and legacy as well as sex and companionship—with the concurrent sacrifice of time and abilities, and energy and resources, that are, instead, directed toward and for the church.

And, of course, the gospel, in its broadest sense, is also characterized by self-sacrifice. As Jesus exhorted, " If anyone wishes to come after Me, he must deny himself, and take up his cross and follow Me" (Mark 8:34 NASB). So here is the first way in which celibacy reflects the gospel (in its broadest sense): both are characterized by self-sacrifice. Celibacy as self-sacrifice reflects the gospel.

On the other hand, the world cannot conceive of giving up sex, which is viewed as a biological imperative that cannot—nay, should not!—be resisted. At an International AIDS Conference in Bangkok in 2004, Congresswoman Barbara Lee, a Democrat from California, declared, "An abstinence-until-marriage program is not only irresponsible, it's really inhumane." Andy Rooney said similarly, "The fact is, sex isn't something a person can decide to have or promise not to have. . . . They might as well have ordered church bells not to ring when struck."[8] Unfortunately, Christians are not exempt from such attitudes either. In fact, Rooney's sentiments echo those uttered by Martin Luther half a millennium ago: "The person who wants to prevent [the conception of children] and keep nature from doing what it wants to do and must do is simply preventing nature from being nature, fire from burning, water from wetting, and man from eating, drinking, or sleeping."[9] More recently, when asked if celibacy was a realistic alternative to marriage, Tim LaHaye replied, "I really don't think so. It is an idealistic and unnatural standard." He opined that celibacy may be in the will of God for those with lower sex drives![10]

---

7. John Paul II, *The Redemption of the Body and Sacramentality of Marriage (Theology of the Body)* (Vatican: Libreria Editrice Vaticana, 2005), 198–99, http://www.catholicprimer. org/papal/theology_of_the_body.pdf (site discontinued).

8. Lee's remarks were reported in the *Chicago Tribune*, "AIDS Delegates Slam U.S. Policy," July 13, 2004, http://articles.chicagotribune.com/2004-07-13/news/0407140098_1_ condoms-abstinence-until-marriage-international-aids-conference. Andy Rooney, "Those Rotten Apples," *60 Minutes*, CBS, March 31, 2002, https://www.cbsnews.com/ news/those-rotten-apples. Both Rooney's and Lee's comments were cited in Christine A. Colón and Bonnie E. Field, *Singled Out: Why Celibacy Must Be Reinvented in Today's Church* (Grand Rapids: Brazos, 2009), 23. I am grateful to Colón and Field for their perceptive tome, from which I have liberally harvested.

9. Martin Luther, "Against the Spiritual Estate of the Pope and the Bishops Falsely So Called, 1522," in *Luther's Works*, vol. 39, *Church and Ministry I*, ed. Eric W. Gritsch and Ruth C. Gritsch (Philadelphia: Fortress, 1970), 297.

10. In Barry Colman, ed., *Sex and the Single Christian: Candid Conversations* (Ventura, CA: Regal, 1985), 109.

But sex is *not* a biological imperative like eating and drinking—not having sex does not kill a person. On the other hand, if sex and marriage were absolute essentials and integral to holistic humanity, they would persist into the eternal state. But they do not, as Jesus averred: "For when they arise from the dead, they neither marry nor are given in marriage, but are like angels in the heavens" (Mark 12:25). Marriage is not an eternal institution, and that in itself tells us that marriage is not the summum bonum, the greatest good, of the Christian life.

Now one might ask: What about Genesis 2:18, where we read that Yahweh declared, "It is not good for the man to be alone"? While this verse does commend the goodness of "man + woman," it is not merely telling us about the goodness of marriage. What is "not good" is *aloneness*, being by oneself, separateness—the lack of community, without which individuals are incomplete. And when there is only Adam on the scene, for community to be formed, a marriage is essential. Hence Genesis 2:18. It is to fulfill the important mandate to humanity to "be fruitful and multiply, and fill the earth" (1:28) that God instituted marriage—not an end in itself, but a means to an end, the formation of community. Of course, one does not necessarily have to be married and have a family to be part of community. As I noted, ecclesiological singleness is characterized by being integrated into community.

The emphasis on community in the New Testament is considerable, perhaps even prioritized over the family (see Mark 3:33–35). So much so, upon nearing death, Jesus handed over the care of his mother, not to his biological relatives (6:3), but to John, a beloved one among his spiritual relatives, the community of believers: "Seeing his mother and the disciple whom he loved standing [by], he said to his mother, 'Woman, behold your son!' Then he said to the disciple, 'Behold, your mother!' And from that hour, the disciple took her into his own [house]" (John 19:26–27). The underscoring of the importance of community is obvious. Add to this Jesus's statement about "hating" one's parents, spouse, and children, if one wished to become his disciple (Luke 14:26)—certainly not an aphorism congruent with modern family values. The late Stanley Grenz wrote, "The New Testament indicates that the primary community for the Christian is to be the believing community, the church. And the primary bond is the covenant with God in Christ, and by extension with the covenant community. While this is to be true for all Christians regardless of marital status, the single Christian often experiences this primary bonding in a more vibrant way. . . . Single believers readily look to their congregation to be 'family' in the primary sense and discover within the church membership their deepest friends."[11]

In fact, for the current post-fall dispensation, the New Testament seems to be more inclined toward singleness than marriage as an ideal. As Paul confessed, "I wish that all men were even as I myself am" (1 Cor. 7:7). Other biblical

---

11. Stanley J. Grenz, *Sexual Ethics: An Evangelical Perspective* (Louisville: Westminster John Knox, 1990), 191. Indeed, "God settles the lonely in families" (Ps. 68:6).

characters in Paul's mold include Jeremiah (Jer. 16:1–2), John the Baptist, the four virgin daughters of Philip who prophesied (Acts 21:8–9), and possibly Timothy, Luke, Barnabas, and others.[12] There was also, of course, Jesus himself.[13]

So, in short, the first reason celibacy reflects the gospel is because at its core celibacy is self-sacrifice, as is true of the gospel.

CELIBACY AND THE GOSPEL AS GOD-DEPENDENCE

What is characteristic of all of the remarkable celibate persons—biblical, ancient, and modern—is their resonance with Jeremiah's sentiment: "Your words were found and I ate them, and Your words became to me a joy and the delight of my heart; for I have been called by your name, O Lord, God of hosts" (Jer. 15:16 NASB). This verse reminds us that, Song of Songs notwithstanding, "the key to a joyful life is found not in our family arrangements but in our relationship with God"—in utter God-dependence.[14]

And, of course, the gospel, in its broadest sense, is also characterized by God-dependence. As Jesus asserted, "I am the vine, you are the branches. The one who abides in me and I in him, he bears much fruit, for apart from me you can do nothing" (John 15:5). So here is the second way in which celibacy reflects the gospel (in its broadest sense): both are characterized by God-dependence. Celibacy as God-dependence reflects the gospel.

It is only in God-dependence, and not in spousal and familial arrangements, that humans will find ultimate fulfillment. In the words of Henri J. M. Nouwen, "No human being can understand us fully, or give us unconditional love, or offer constant affection that enters into the core of our being and heals our deepest brokenness."[15] In other words, if you are seeking satisfaction in a human spouse, you can be sure that Hauerwas's law will prove itself true: "You always marry the wrong person."[16] One never finds the "right person"—that species doesn't exist. Or, as Erma Bombeck noted wryly, "Marriage has no guarantees. If that's what you're looking for, go live with a car battery."[17] Celibacy, then, is a refusal to over-romanticize marriage; it is a recognition that nothing—not things, persons,

---

12. Among the ancients, almost all the church fathers were celibate. Among moderns are John Stott, Amy Carmichael, Isaac Watts, Corrie ten Boom, Florence Nightingale, Charles Simeon, William Cowper, Ida Scudder, and Dietrich Bonhoeffer, to name a few.

13. Unfortunately, the evangelical church has lost its testimony against all manner of sexual aberrations and excesses. Where can it point to its celibates to proclaim and affirm, *contra mundi*, that sex is not the end-all and be-all of human life?

14. Carrie A. Miles, *The Redemption of Love: Rescuing Marriage and Sexuality from the Economics of a Fallen World* (Grand Rapids: Brazos, 2006), 168.

15. Henri J. M. Nouwen, *Clowning in Rome: Reflections on Solitude, Celibacy, Prayer, and Contemplation* (New York: Image, 1979), 39–40.

16. Stanley Hauerwas, "Sex and Politics: Bertrand Russell and 'Human Sexuality,'" *Christian Century*, April 19, 1978, 421.

17. Cited in Debra A. Schwartz and Ralph Rivas, "Humor," in *Encyclopedia of American Journalism*, ed. Stephen L. Vaughn (New York: Routledge, 2008), 216.

places, or actions—can fully satisfy one's deepest needs. Only God can, and it is on him, and on him alone, that all humans—single and married—should depend. No, humans were not made with a spouse-shaped lacuna that only a wife or husband can occupy. We were made for *God*. As Søren Kierkegaard reflected, "Only the married are genuine citizens in this world, the single person is an alien (which is precisely what Christianity wants the Christian to be—and what God wants the Christian to be, in order to love him). Consequently, God wants the single state because he wants to be loved."[18]

Celibacy thereby becomes an acknowledgment that we have offered ourselves to God completely—a God-dependence that reflects the gospel. In dealing with the monastic life and the attendant sacrifices of self (by living under the guidance of a superior), of family (by living as a celibate person), and of things (by living in simplicity/poverty), Thomas Aquinas calls for the celibate one to be "empty for God": *Deo vacetur*—a vacancy for God, as it were.[19] Nouwen agrees, saying that celibate people "live out a holy emptiness by not marrying, by not trying to build for themselves a house or a fortune, by not trying to wield as much influence as possible, and by not filling their lives with events, people, or creations for which they will be remembered. The hope is that by their 'empty' lives, God will be more readily recognized as the source of all human life and activity. It is an openness to being loved first by God."[20]

So, in short, the second reason celibacy reflects the gospel is because at its core celibacy is God-dependence, as is true of the gospel.

CELIBACY AND THE GOSPEL AS ETERNITY-FOCUS

Ironically, sex and death are allies. Sex is necessary because of death, in order for the human race and community to continue. So sex is, at least in this sense, an acknowledgment of death. By contrast, writes Rodney Clapp, "confident Christian celibacy, based on the hope of the resurrection of a then undying body, was a bold witness to the total defeat of death."[21]

The Christian *can* be single. One does *not* have to procreate. Because there *is* a resurrection. And the Christian *will* live eternally. Celibacy, I submit, is therefore a symbol of our eternal state: it has, at its core, an eternity-focus. For the celibate person, there is no safety net of children, whether for expectation of support, for enactment of legacy, or for the extension of memories. The celibate one is *alone*—the core meaning of *caelebs*. The resurrection is the only hope for ecclesiological single persons, that they will live on. And

---

18. Søren Kierkegaard, *Journals and Papers, Volume 3: L–R*, ed. and trans. Howard V. Hong and Edna H. Hong (Bloomington: Indiana University Press, 1975), 142.

19. Thomas Aquinas, *Summa contra gentiles* III.130.

20. Nouwen, *Clowning in Rome*, 47, 50.

21. Rodney Clapp, *Tortured Wonders: Christian Spirituality for People, Not Angels* (Grand Rapids: Brazos, 2004), 58.

the church is the only hope for ecclesiological single people, that they will be remembered.[22]

The gospel, of course, in its broadest sense, also looks forward keenly to an eternity with God: "For God so loved the world, that he gave his only begotten Son, that whoever believes in Him shall not perish, but have eternal life" (John 3:16). So here is the third way in which celibacy reflects the gospel: both are characterized by an eternity-focus. Celibacy, maintaining an eternity-focus, reflects the gospel.

Raniero Cantalamessa, preacher to the papal household (the only person permitted to preach directly to the pope) for more than twenty-five years, affirmed that celibacy "is not *ontologically* (that is, in itself) *a more perfect* state, but it is an *eschatologically more advanced* state, in the sense that it is more like the definitive state toward which we are all journeying." And this celibacy "shows what the final condition of men and women will be: one that is destined to last forever." Cantalamessa therefore labels the celibate state "a prophetic existence."[23]

So, in short, the third reason celibacy reflects the gospel is because at its core celibacy has an eternity-focus, as does the gospel.

FREEDOMS OF CELIBACY

In addition to reflecting the gospel, celibacy also offers some freedoms. *Biological* freedom releases one from the societally decreed compulsion to have sex and, instead, to live limiting one's sexual drive in the spiritual discipline of abstinence. *Provisional* freedom allows the celibate person to focus on God's total provision for needs. *Sociological* freedom relieves one from the pressures of family activities and allied interests, permitting the ecclesiologically single person to focus on the ecclesia, the body of Christ.[24] *Passional* freedom gives the celibate person room to suffer for Christ without putting loved ones in danger. And *emotional* freedom enables the celibate person to demonstrate inclusive (nonexclusive) love to the eternal family of God, the wider community of fellow believers.

There is, of course, no doubt that in another sense marriage, too, pictures the gospel, particularly in its symbolic portrayal of the relationship of the church with her bridegroom, the Lord Jesus Christ. Marriage comes with its own corresponding set of freedoms—for instance, the freedom to demonstrate fidelity

---

22. Rodney Clapp, *Families at the Crossroads: Beyond Traditional and Modern Options* (Downers Grove, IL: InterVarsity Press, 1993), 101.

23. Raniero Cantalamessa, *Virginity: A Positive Approach to Celibacy for the Sake of the Kingdom of Heaven*, trans. Charles Serignat (New York: Alba, 1995), part 1, chap. 1, para. 9 (Kindle; emphases original). Cyprian of Carthage (200–285) encouraged the first Christian virgins, pronouncing, "That which we shall be, you have already begun to be" (*On the Dress of Virgins* 22).

24. This, of course, does not necessarily mean that celibate people have more time on their hands than married people. The numerous responsibilities of maintaining a household, sustaining daily life, caring for parents, and so on cannot be shared with a partner when one is single.

and exclusive love to one's spouse; the freedom to suffer for one's family, sacrificing self-interest; the freedom to be hospitable; the freedom to intensely disciple the next generation; and so on. All this substantiates the fact that one state is not any better than the other: both celibacy and marriage are valid platforms for ministry and service to Christ and his church. This is to say that the church needs both the married state and the single state to fully portray the gospel. The marriage metaphor depicts God's exclusive love for his people (reflected in the faithful love between spouses); the celibacy metaphor depicts God's all-inclusive love that invites all to enjoy (reflected in the freedom celibate persons have to love those in the family of God). Both marriage and celibacy are essential for a complete picture of God's love; either by itself is inadequate.[25]

On a related note, there is a surprising reference to the suffering servant's "offspring" recorded by the prophet Isaiah (53:10). Who are these messianic "offspring"? Since Jesus was unmarried, "offspring" must refer to the church, the body of believers, the children of God. Interestingly enough, in the Gospels, Jesus refers to disciples as "sons" (Matt. 9:2 // Mark 2:5), as "daughters" (Matt. 9:22 // Mark 5:34 // Luke 8:48), and as "children (Mark 10:24; John 13:33; 21:5). Indeed, for the one following Jesus, the abandonment of siblings, parents, and *children* ensures the reception (a hundred times over) of all of the above (Mark 10:29–30 // Luke 18:29–30). In like fashion, Paul frequently refers to himself as the parent of the churches he planted or of individuals he mentored (1 Cor. 3:1–2; 4:15; 2 Cor. 6:13; 12:14; Gal. 4:19; Phil. 2:22; 1 Thess. 2:7, 11; 1 Tim. 1:2, 18; 2 Tim. 1:2; 2:1; Titus 1:4). All this bespeaks a "fruitfulness of the spirit, not of the body. And since human beings are spirit as well as flesh, it is also a supremely human fruitfulness."[26] Thus celibacy is also a liberation to be fruitful, though in a different sense from that of physical reproduction.

One can understand when the world with its materialism and antispirituality fails to grasp these nuances. But the church should deeply comprehend these truths.

CELIBACY AND THE CHURCH

If you ask me to describe the status of celibate people in the body of Christ, my tongue-in-cheek answer would be that they are "saved, single, and second-class."[27] Ever since a celibate monk, Martin, broke away from the Catholic Church and married a celibate nun, Katerina, Protestants have looked askance at celibacy as a way of life to serve Christ.

Evangelicals have traditionally viewed marriage as the cure for aloneness/ temptation. Such thinking in the church probably began with the Reformation,

---

25. Colón and Field, *Singled Out*, 168, 171, 195.
26. Cantalamessa. *Virginity*, part 1, chap. 1, para. 21.
27. From the title of an essay by Joseph Bayly, "Saved, Single, and Second-Class," *Eternity*, March 1983, 23–26.

when Luther asserted that "marriage may be likened to a hospital for incurables which prevents inmates from falling into a graver sin."[28] Such thinking permeates sermons and Christian literature, and is the very ethos of evangelical churches, unfortunately. Speaking of this reality, Stanley Hauerwas asserted darkly, "Just about every time Christians make a fetish of the family, you can be sure they don't believe in God anymore."[29] Such a sentiment may go a bit too far, but I have to agree with Clapp: "To put it strongly, there is at least one sure sign of a flawed vision of the Christian family: it denigrates and dishonors singleness."[30] Luther went so far as to proclaim that what celibate people do is less pleasing to God than even an out-of-wedlock birth of a child to a woman.[31] For Luther, sex, even outside of marriage, is apparently preferable to continence in the context of celibacy.

Several years ago, the academic dean then serving at the institution where I currently teach organized faculty and spouses for get-togethers in different parts of town. Those who lived in a particular area would congregate in a local home for fellowship over a meal, with the dean's office providing the meat, and the attendees delivering the carbs and greens and the rest. The dean's program was called "Dinner for Eight." Except when I, a celibate man, was present, making it "Dinner for Seven [or Nine]." Clearly, the single person was the oddball, the anomaly. While I'm certain there was no malice aforethought in such a label, the point is that evangelical Christians generally don't even think of the presence of single people in their midst—they are invisible: saved, single, second-class.

Gary Thomas, while recognizing the irony of his comment that "marriage is the preferred route to becoming more like [Christ (himself celibate)]," nonetheless confesses to having advised his brother, "If you want to become more like Jesus, I can't imagine any better thing to do than get married."[32] In the same vein,

---

28. Martin Luther, "A Sermon on the Estate of Marriage, 1519," in *Luther's Works*, vol. 44, *The Christian in Society I*, ed. James Atkinson (Philadelphia: Fortress, 1966), 9. Actually, such a bias existed way before the Reformer. An ancient Sumerian proverb from the third millennium BC goes, "He that has no wife, he that supports no son, may his misfortunes be multiplied" (cited in W. G. Lambert, "Celibacy in the World's Oldest Proverbs," *Bulletin of the American Schools of Oriental Research* 169 [1963]: 63). As well, the Talmud: "Any man who has no wife is no proper man" (Babylonian Talmud, tractate Yebamot 63a).

29. Stanley Hauerwas, "On Bonhoeffer and John H. Yoder" (lecture, theology conference: Sermon on the Mount, Center for Applied Christian Ethics, Wheaton College, November 7, 2005 (http://espace.wheaton.edu/cace/audio/05SOMhauerwas.mp3 [audio]).

30. Clapp, *Families at the Crossroads*, 89.

31. Martin Luther, "The Estate of Marriage, 1522," in *Luther's Works*, vol. 45, *The Christian in Society II*, ed. Walther I. Brandt (Philadelphia: Muhlenberg, 1962), 41.

32. Gary Thomas, *Sacred Marriage* (Grand Rapids: Zondervan, 2000), 21–22. And Thomas writes, "Our God, who is spirit (John 4:24), can be found behind the very physical panting, sweating, and pleasurable entangling of limbs and body parts. He doesn't turn away. He wants us to run into sex, but to do so with his presence, priorities, and virtues marking our pursuit. If we experience sex in this way, we will be transformed in the marriage bed every bit as much as we are transformed on our knees" (225). Sacramental sex?

Albert Mohler boldly submitted, "In heaven, is the crucible of our saint-making going to have been done through our jobs? I don't think so. The Scripture is clear that it will be done largely through our marriages."[33] It needs hardly be said that any argument making either marriage or singleness the *primary* means of God's sanctification of his children is, at best, naïve, and, at worst, reprehensible. John Piper boldly goes against this grain:

> I am declaring the temporary and secondary nature of marriage and family over against the eternal and primary nature of the church. . . . This is not trivial; this is huge. And I fear that we have settled into our land and our culture and idolized the family, idolized marriage. We are here for a vapor's breath, and then we are gone. What happens here is relatively minor compared to what will be after the resurrection. . . . Marriage is a temporary institution, it stands for something that lasts forever, namely, our relationship with Christ—Church and Bridegroom. . . . So I say it again to all singles in Christ who will be that way long-term: God promises you blessings in the age to come that are better—far better—than the blessings of marriage and children.[34]

Amen!

CONCLUSION

Celibacy, like the gospel, is characterized by self-sacrifice. Celibacy, like the gospel, is marked by God-dependence. And celibacy, like the gospel, is typified by an eternity-focus. And until that dispensation of eternity, in the words of Paul, "I have learned to be content in whatever situation I am. . . . And my God will fulfill all your needs according to his riches in glory in Christ Jesus" (Phil. 4:11, 19). Whether we are celibate or married, we need have no doubt about God's ability to provide. Yes, "the young lions lack and hunger; But those who seek Yahweh shall not be in want of any good thing" (Ps. 34:10). No, celibate people will not be in want, "for your husband is your Maker, Yahweh Sabaoth is his name; And your Redeemer, the Holy One of Israel, called the God of all the earth" (Isa. 54:5).

Therefore, I can be celibate, because being so reflects the gospel in self-sacrifice, God-dependence, and eternity-focus.[35]

---

33. R. Albert Mohler Jr., "The Mystery of Marriage, Part 2" (talk delivered at the New Attitude Conference, 2004), https://albertmohler.com/2004/08/01/the-mystery-of-marriage-part-2/ (audio).

34. John Piper, "Single in Christ: A Name Better Than Sons and Daughters" (sermon preached at Bethlehem Baptist Church, Minneapolis, MN, April 29, 2007), https://www.desiring-god.org/messages/single-in-christ-a-name-better-than-sons-and-daughters.

35. An expanded version of this essay may be found on http://homiletix.com under "Ecclesiological Celibacy."

FOR DISCUSSION

1. If you are currently single, before you decide to get married or remain single, have you considered what your gifting from God might be?

2. What can you, as a married or as a single person, do to help move evangelicalism toward a more biblical view of celibacy?

3. What are some ways your church could do so?

FOR FURTHER READING

Colón, Christine A., and Bonnie E. Field. *Singled Out: Why Celibacy Must Be Reinvented in Today's Church.* Grand Rapids: Brazos, 2009.

Hsu, Albert. *Singles at the Crossroads: A Fresh Perspective on Christian Singleness.* Downers Grove, IL: InterVarsity Press, 1997.

Nouwen, Henri J. M. *Clowning in Rome: Reflections on Solitude, Celibacy, Prayer, and Contemplation.* New York: Image, 1979.

CHAPTER 11

THE MARRIAGE BED: THE FULLNESS OF GOD'S DESIGN

J. SCOTT HORRELL

George was my drug dealer. He was also the sound engineer in the band I hung out with."[1] Thus Debra Hirsch begins the story of George in jail reading his mother's big Greek Orthodox Bible, and then believing in Jesus. His drug customers soon became his evangelism "hit list." Out of the most unlikely people grows a community of new Christians, as Hirsch recounts her own story of healing and eventual marriage in *Redeeming Sex*. And so it is. Through history, through cultures, and today, the gospel fertilizes our heaps of failure. God transforms our sexual compost stations into something that flourishes.

When asked, "Why get married?," according to the Pew Research Center, 88 percent responded for "love," 81 percent for "lifelong commitment," and 76 percent for "companionship."[2] For most people, it seems, marriage continues to offer the ideal. Indeed, surprising sociological demographers, multiple surveys find the highest sexual satisfaction among married Christian couples.

Paradoxically, in contemporary culture, ideals of sex and marriage are at odds with each other. God's design as seen in Genesis 1–2 is ignored by many who assert they can do better—that sex and coupling need not be constrained

---

1. Debra Hirsch, *Redeeming Sex: Naked Conversations about Sexuality and Spirituality* (Downers Grove, IL: InterVarsity Press, 2015), 11.
2. Abigail Geiger and Gretchen Livingston, "8 Facts about Love and Marriage in America," Pew Research Center, February 13, 2019, https://www.pewresearch.org/fact-tank/2019/02/13/8-facts-about-love-and-marriage/.

by divine standards. They say the bed stimulates, but marriage—well, it ruins it all. For many unmarried people, a Christian marriage is not even on the horizon. Assumptions of sex as priority and sex for fun are endemic in culture. Our youth say, "Why can't I watch that movie with my friends?" "A lot of kids already have sex. Why does God say it's bad?" Single adults opine, "Hey, you don't really know someone until you have sex with them. Then you know *everything!*" "What, wait to get married? I want to make sure sex with that person is good." Some argue, "Animals aren't monogamous. Neither am I. Why hold back natural attractions?" "For me, marriage destroys love. Love has to be free." For many in a society inundated with sex, if the bed intoxicates, then marriage is the hangover in which the headache only gets worse. Yet the Creator's design is precisely the opposite—and far more beautiful than even many Christians imagine.

What exactly is that design? Why marriage? What is the purpose of marriage? What is the meaning of sexual intercourse? If sex is so exciting, why does Scripture protect it so carefully? Such questions lead to responses more majestic than we might imagine. Rightly understood, the bed and marriage beautify and dignify male and female created in the image of God.

We begin by acknowledging that God made humans as embodied creatures. Our study takes us to the very core of who we are as persons—to that which is both universal and intensely intimate; we are "sexed" creatures in every cell of our being. Thus we begin by considering what it means for humans to image God. Like the Triune God himself, what we are as humans is a mystery we approach from multiple angles. So, after building a theological framework for sexuality, we will explore marriage patterns in Scripture, the boundaries and limitations of conjugal union, the place of procreation, and the public dimension of marriage.

SEXED BODIES AND MARRIAGE IN CONTEXT

As we begin, let's place biblical marriage in global perspective. On the one hand, all traditional societies recognize some form of marriage. When we sweep through historical world cultures, husband-wife relationships appear everywhere. On the other hand, the roles of spouses reveal considerable divergence, over both time and place. The following distinctions are intended not as demeaning but as reflective of broad historical realities shaped by religious or secular worldviews: In older traditions of East Asia shaped by Confucianism, the husband is revered and served by the wife and offspring, especially the girls; husband-wife affection and father-child tenderness appear far from the norm. Among tribal religions in Africa, wealthy chieftains have taken as many wives as they chose or could afford, often having dozens of children; wives have been purchased or taken, and female children have brought the riches of dowry. The teaching of Islam permits men to have up to four wives, with minimal rights for females, while male offspring vie for inheritance; the beauty of girls and women must be covered lest men be tempted. Meanwhile, in the contemporary West, Hollywood housewives' affairs, multiple liaisons in LGBTQ communities, and the open sexual freedom of those with no religious affiliation have failed to improve on the normative cultural ideal of marriage. What Jesus declared to be the original design for matrimony is still what we see most often: one man and one woman in covenanted, ordered parity. When such a relationship is in order, whatever the religion or culture, then spousal love can best mature and children flourish.

As biblical marriage informs the global scenario, so consideration of our individual selves as sexed beings equally serves to orient our thinking. In the holistic sense, the mystery of our sexuality—long before we have thoughts of sex as an action—invokes the need both to accept ourselves and to embrace others. If we do not accept ourselves as God made us, our discontent hinders us from loving others well. Every person needs friendships with those of the same as well as opposite sex. Within proper guidelines, opposite-sex relationships foster wholesomeness and ballast to every human being—to those single, married, widowed, divorced, orphaned, young, middle-aged, or aged. For those struggling with sexual identity, strong friendships with those of both sexes help encourage godly choices. Far from asexual, Jesus himself exemplifies both purity and compassion to females—little girls (presumably among the children he blessed), his under-sixty female followers (both single and married), and the older women (not a few of whom he healed). Rather than a "restricted or compartmentalized segment of our lives," our embodiment as sexual beings stands "at the center of our response to life."[3]

In biblical faith God proclaims marriage as the normative foundation for mutually beneficial wife-husband unions, satisfying sexual relationships, wholesome family structures, and the fruitfulness of the human race. Spoiling erotic "fun" is not the divine intent. Rather, God designs us for healthy relationships expressed through sexed bodies, thus channeling our human desires in ways that enhance and safeguard both male and female. To that end the writer of the Epistle to the Hebrews sets before readers both the positive and the safeguard: "Marriage should be honored by all, and the marriage bed kept pure." The conjugal relationship—including our most intimate sexual expression—flourishes when the marriage bed is guarded in righteousness. Then comes the warning: "for God will judge the adulterer and all the sexually immoral" (Heb. 13:4).[4] The consequences of sexual disorder, greed, and deceit not only affect this life but also bring judgment in the life to come.

Particularly in the West, but universally as well, the increasing abandonment of ethical norms for sex has brought about a social void into which Scripture speaks beautifully and powerfully. And grounded in God's Word, the church has the opportunity to proclaim the good news of cleansing in Jesus Christ, exemplify vibrant, healthy community, and make known the divine

---

3. James B. Nelson, *Embodiment: An Approach to Sexuality and Christian Theology* (Minneapolis: Augsburg, 1978), 104.
4. Unless otherwise noted, all Scripture quotations in this chapter are from the NIV.

design for lasting intimate relations between a woman and man. We will find that, created in the *imago Dei*, as human beings with sexed bodies, we fit in this world of the trinitarian God's design.

IMAGE OF GOD, SEXUAL RELATIONS, AND MARRIAGE

Genesis 2:21–24 establishes the Creator's template for male and female uniting in "one flesh," a norm reaffirmed by our Lord Jesus and supported by broader biblical teaching.[5] God's intent is male-female monogamy and lifetime faithfulness.[6] But why? What gives reason and attractiveness to sexual relations exclusively within biblical monogamy?

Our response begins when we see how the story begins, one chapter earlier—in Genesis 1. Before uniting the man and woman,

> God said, "Let us make mankind in our image, in our likeness." . . .
>   So God created mankind in his own image,
>   in the image of God he created them;
>   male and female he created them. (1:26–27)

Multiple lenses inform the meaning of this text, but one perspective articulated from the earliest church fathers is that God's "let us" suggests the doctrine of the Trinity.[7] That both male and female are created in the *imago Dei*, that together male and female reveal something about God, implies unity and diversity within the Godhead—equality of nature yet distinction of persons. While God reveals himself as Father, Son, and Holy Spirit, the Trinity itself, as infinite spirit, transcends gender distinctions.[8] Nevertheless,

---

5. See Matt. 19:4–6; Mark 10:6–9; 1 Cor. 7:2–5; Eph. 5:31; Heb. 13:4.

6. In the biblical record, alternative forms of conjugal relations begin several generations after Cain, with Lamech, who "took two women" (Gen. 4:19). While polygyne (multiple wives) and concubinage are not directly forbidden, and while levirate marriage to a widowed sister-in-law is in fact sanctioned, multiple wives are neither normative nor generally encouraged—the consequences sometimes underscored this reality. See Ken Stone, "Marriage and Sexual Relations in the World of the Hebrew Bible," in *The Oxford Handbook of Theology, Sexuality, and Gender*, ed. Adrian Thatcher (Oxford: Oxford University Press, 2015), 174–80.

7. As canonically informed, so also Gen. 1:1–2. The text in 1:26, however, does not define the exhortative verb "let us." Some interpret "us" as heavenly "sons of God," i.e., angels. However, neither creation nor the forming of the *imago Dei* is ever attributed to angels (cf. Isa. 40:14; 44:24; Zech. 12:1); the pronouns "us," "our," "he," "him" seem to rule out other agents or reference to a divine council. So Umberto Cassuto, *A Commentary on the Book of Genesis*, trans. Israel Abrahams (Jerusalem: Magnes, 1961), 1:55.

8. All trinitarian analogies have limits: human creation was of two persons, not three; moreover, Trinity transcends sex and gender. Bonaventure saw the image of Trinity mirrored in the family of husband, wife, and the fruit of their love as Spirit. But almost all theologians avoid such direct analogy, many preferring to see the family as broadly reflective of the Trinity yet without assigning sex-specific or familial roles. See Ouellet, *Divine Likeness*, 20–37.

the creation of man and woman as expression of the divine image is rich with implications.

If human beings are the *imago* (image), then what is the *Dei* (God)? Five relationships within the Godhead are reflected in human relationship, especially in the context of sexual intimacy.[9]

1. Humans, Like God, Have an Essential Nature.

Certainly God has attributes no human possesses, such as eternality, omniscience, and omnipresence. But humans do reflect God's *communicable* attributes, which include virtues such as love, holiness, wisdom, goodness, and justice. God is much more than a collection of attributes; nevertheless, God's attributes reflect *what* he is—that is, the divine *nature*. As God is constituted by *Godness* (the divine nature), so he has created humankind with a human nature, our "material" reality, which diversifies in biological sex and a multitude of other features. All of us are human, yet no one of us is identical to another. For this reason, Christians defend the inherent dignity of every human being from conception to death. As God is defined by Godness, so we are created as embryos with an innate humanness, a nature designed to flourish, albeit now subjected to a fallen world. And different from the infinite God, our conception as finite human beings is genetically coded for diversity in sex, ethnicity, and a plurality of individual features that make each of us unique. As the DNA that defines humanity is universal, so every person's genetic makeup, our genome map, is individually distinct.

2. Humans, Like God, Have Self-Consciousness.

A "person" is characterized by self-consciousness. In the Bible, God defines himself as the "I AM" (*Yahweh*). The Father declares "I AM," the Son declares "I AM," and the Spirit speaks in first person terms "I" and "me" (Acts 13:2). Each is fully God, yet each reflects a distinct personal consciousness in relation to the other.[10] Our humanity, while beginning on a biological level, is created to develop into a self-conscious person. The "I am" of the newborn infant soon cries out for nourishment. Self-consciousness integrates the whole of our individual reality: my toe throbs, the night is cold, my heart is happy, I fear death. Our physical bodies contribute to self-understanding, one with dark skin, another light, one with a vagina, another a penis, one with alabaster muscles, another with skin flaccid with age. Yet unifying all humankind, our inner structure of who we are as persons—that

---

9. A multitude of works seek to define *imago Dei* typically dividing in (or combining) three categories: ontological (personhood, nature), relational, and functional (dominion, reproduction). These three dimensions of personality, relationality, and functionality coalesce remarkably in the man and woman becoming one flesh (Gen. 2:24).

10. Although God is singularly the "I AM," thus with unity of consciousness, the Trinity manifests itself with a threefold personal consciousness—the tension that frames the mystery of Trinity. The revelation of the Trinity in creation (*ad extra*) reflects indirectly the Godhead in itself (*ad intra*) beyond creation.

I think, speak, will, and have emotions—finds mooring in a trinitarian God who in Scripture also "reasons," "speaks," "wills," and manifests "emotions." The divine Being surely differs from ourselves; yet the language ascribing intensely personal traits to each member of the Godhead is striking. God further defines himself as sovereign, the acme of righteousness, everlasting, abundantly creative, and so on. Therefore, to be *imago Dei* implies our role as vice-regents of creation, endowed with moral conscience, a sense of immortality, and inclined to creativity. If the Holy Trinity reveals itself in such personal terms, then human self-consciousness (who "I am") finds grounding in God's tripersonal being; our inner ontology reflects our Creator.[11] As a consequence, when our self-understanding rests in the I AM, then we move toward being more deeply *personal* ourselves—reflective of and authentic to our innermost being. In a day when the concept of person has been reduced to chemicals and conditioning, classical Christianity proclaims that the self-consciousness of human beings is not a mirage or ghost in the machine; rather our "I" as *imago Dei* reflects the "Let us" of the Creator.

3. Humans, Like God, Have I-Thou Relationality.
Especially visible in the Gospels, Jesus's relationship with God the Father led the early church to confess both the Son and the Father as God. The two persons stand in I-Thou loving kinship, yet not as two Gods but one God (John 1:1–2). The Son further describes the Spirit as "another advocate" (John 14:16), one like himself yet personally distinct from himself and the Father. Each member of the Godhead is defined in relationship to the other, defined in the Nicene-Constantinopolitan Creed (AD 381) as the eternal *generation* of the Son and eternal *procession* of the Spirit. Analogous to how each member of the Trinity is defined by the divine nature, self-consciousness, and I-Thou relationship, so our personal identity derives from our material human nature and self-awareness together with the I-thou relationships around us at every point in our lives. We are defined as "persons" both by our individual self-consciousness and our social interactions with others. Neither the individualism of the West (Descartes's "I think, therefore I am") nor the self-transcendence (or nonself) of Eastern thought can capture the complexity of what we are as persons, as images of God. Our "I" and the other's "thou" create a mutual acknowledgment—of acceptance, status, or fear. In the case of friends and all the more of lovers, the I-thou consciousness draws forth reciprocal attraction and engagement.

---

11. Discussions of similarities between personhood in God and human beings recognize the necessity of anthropomorphism, i.e., the Triune God reveals himself in categories understandable by finite beings. God has no need of linear reasoning, yet he invites us to reason together; biblical emotions of God (jealously, anger) sometimes bristle, yet Jonathan Edwards's calmer references to divine *affections* surely point toward something correspondent but not univocal to what we know of emotions. Always the Trinity stands beyond our comprehension, yet God comes to us truly and personally so that we may know and love him.

As the intratrinitarian relations from all eternity are constituted, in part, by each divine person loving the other, so the *imago Dei* of Genesis 1 unfolds immediately in Genesis 2 with the man and woman each uniquely created and defined by their relationship to the other.[12] Adam's loneliness finds satisfaction in Eve, his counterpart. "Far from being a mystical loss of selfhood, the appropriate union between embodied creatures is the union of presence."[13] Their I-thou sexual differences enable them to become one flesh and so to obey the mandate to populate the earth with their offspring. The man and woman's marriage in the garden, through love's consummation, generates the human race.

4. Humans, Like God, Are Made to Be Indwelled.

The I-Thou within the Christian Godhead suggests a greater depth of unity intended in Eden's sexual union and designed for all human marriage. Jesus declares, "I am in the Father, and . . . the Father is in me" (John 14:10; cf. 10:38)—a mutual spiritual indwelling or reciprocal habitation. In these contexts Jesus clearly distinguishes himself as Son from the Father. And equally striking, Jesus invites and prays that believers also participate in this habitation by the Son and the Father "that all of them may be one, Father, just as you are in me and I am in you. May they also be in us so that the world may believe that you have sent me . . . that they may be one as we are one—I in them and you in me" (John 17:21–23; cf. 14:20). In similar language, the Savior speaks of the Spirit who comes forth from the Father, is sent by the Son, and "will be *in* you" (14:17; 15:26). With time, the Greek fathers developed the concept (later defined as *perichoresis*[14]) to denote both the identical divine essence permeating the three persons and a truly personal communion,[15] a dynamic, reciprocal cohabitation, each inviting and each invited by the other.

This trinitarian doctrine interpreted analogously regarding the *imago Dei* affirms three intriguing, forceful truths. (1) Every human being is created with a capacity to be indwelled. As *imago Dei*, we are structured to be spiritually inhabited (different, it seems, from angels). For this reason, Christian conversion requires regeneration within by the Spirit. This same perichoretic capacity explains how a person can be indwelled by a demonic spirit, thereby usurping

---

12. If Gen. 1 affirms male and female as equally designed to reflect God (with no distinctions), Gen. 2 describes the process as God creates the woman from the man's side and presents her to his son as would a father.

13. Robert Miner, *Thomas Aquinas on the Passions* (Cambridge: Cambridge University Press, 2009), 134.

14. The interpersonal co-inherence of the Greek *perichoresis* and Latin *circumincessio* complement the more static Latin *circuminsessio* (with an "*s*" versus "*c*"), which denotes the full reality of the divine nature equally present in the three.

15. Khaled Anatolios, "Personhood, Communion, and the Trinity in Some Patristic Texts," in *The Holy Trinity in the Life of the Church*, ed. Khaled Anatolios (Grand Rapids: Baker, 2014), 147–64.

the place of God. (2) By analogy, the I-thou sexual oneness of the man and woman appears designed to reflect the dynamic, cohabitational oneness of the Trinity. The marriage bond culminates in "one flesh," the conjoining of two in the most intimate of sexual love. As it was in the beginning, so today sexual intercourse—a kind of human perichoresis—is not to be casual but covenantal. Even as a purely human act, it intimates the greater mutual indwelling of the Godhead. Conjugal intimacy, therefore, is sacred and to be safeguarded by the vows of marriage. (3) Out of the mutual love within the Godhead the world was created, so marital love constitutes an act of creation. Conjugal intimacy envisions fruitfulness, procreation, a reproduction of ourselves. In the words of Genesis, "God blessed them and said to them, 'Be fruitful and increase in number; fill the earth and subdue it'" (1:28). God ordained marital intercourse as the means for populating the world, eventuating in the promised Offspring (3:15). Contrary to Christian traditions that insist the *primary* purpose of sexual intercourse is to bear children, however, a trinitarian theology suggests that the mutual indwelling of husband and wife is itself expressive of the divine design for the *imago Dei*. Children, if permitted, evidence that love in fruition. Said again, the joy of sexual intercourse reflects something of the transcendent unity of the tripersonal God; therefore, the Creator has deemed it not only special but in some sense sacred as well, protected within the covenant of marriage.

5. Humans, Like God, Are Capable of Self-Giving.
The Holy Trinity is rightly denominated the "self-giving God," the one who freely created and sustains the entirety of creation by grace. In the New Testament, this self-giving manifests in the love between the Son and the Father: the Father has given all things to the Son—all judgment, all authority, "all things" (Matt. 28:18; John 5:22; 13:3). Yet after Christ destroys all enemies and establishes his kingdom, then he "the Son" will hand over "everything" to the Father, "so that God may be all in all" (1 Cor. 15:28; cf. 15:20–28). God's glory is a shared glory, even as each person of the Trinity works within creation in distinctive ways.

Christian life is the divine invitation to self-giving. "We love because he first loved us" (1 John 4:19). In all the Bible, only Ephesians 5 directly summons believers to "be imitators of God, as beloved children. And walk in love, as Christ loved us and *gave* himself up for us" (5:1–2 ESV). Paul warns against any hint of sexual immorality (v. 3) and admonishes believers to "submit to one another out of reverence for Christ" (v. 21). In the weightiest passage on marriage in the Bible (vv. 22–33), Paul then exhorts husbands and wives to give of themselves to one another. This self-giving expresses itself in both similar yet different ways by husband and wife, the husband as Christ and the wife as the church—sacrificer and responder. We imitate the Trinity by giving of ourselves in different ways to those around us, most tangibly for those who enter into the bond of marriage to their spouse, in free, mutual, self-conscious I-thou unity. God has no obligation to give to creation, yet he has structured every person as *imago Dei* such that we *must* give of ourselves to be filled with God's life. Jesus, the perfect image of God, declares, "For whoever wants to save their life will lose it, but whoever loses their life for me will save it" (Luke 9:24). There is no other way to be fulfilled, no other way for the Christian to radiate the life of God.

So the image of God is revealed in marriage and sex. Responding to the Pharisees' cunning question about divorce, Jesus returns to the divine template of Genesis 1:26–27 and 2:24 (Matt. 19:3–6), and so must we. Husband and wife express the *imago Dei* in (1) their sexed material nature, (2) the "I am" of their self-consciousness, (3) the I-thou magnetic relationship of two in love, (4) mutual indwelling, embodied in sexual intercourse, and (5) their obligation to give themselves to one another. Erotic mutual love is meant to provide, in the words of Pope Benedict XVI, "not just fleeting pleasure, but also a certain foretaste of the pinnacle of our existence, of that beatitude [blissful happiness] for which our whole being yearns."[16] Mutual and loving, sexual intercourse satisfies for the moment. But like other satisfactions of earthly existence, it wanes, pointing to something greater to which our Creator beckons.

If Christian belief in the Holy Trinity can be analogously applied to a man and woman in love, then the why of the marriage covenant as God's design for sexual intercourse receives a relevant, timeless, and commanding response. The Triune Maker designed the conjugal act as the acme of male-female love and therefore declares sexual intimacy as sacred. Multiple sources affirm that the highest sexual satisfaction, including the frequency of orgasm of both woman and man, is found among those who hold to the exclusivity of sex in marriage.[17] As Jewish and Christian marriage vows intend, "the commitment of romantic love calls for exclusivity."[18] Sex outside of covenant violates the Creator's intention. Conversely, within the bond of marital fidelity, conjugal intercourse approaches within our embodied framework the greater spiritual cohabitation into which we are invited by the Holy Trinity itself.

To the question of "Why not sex, Mom?" the Christian responds, "Because God created you and your sexuality for far more." Single or married, sexual purity is premised not just on "because the Bible says so" but on the very nature of the *imago Dei* and the Godhead's own perichoretic unity-diversity. In this sense, understanding God as Trinity provides the superstructure and theological center of human sexuality.

---

16. Benedict XVI, *Deus Caritas Est*, Encyclical Letter (Vatican: Libreria Editrice Vaticana, 2006), §4. See Christopher West, *Fill These Hearts: God, Sex, and the Universal Longing* (Cicero, NY: Image, 2013), 11.

17. See Dennis P. Hollinger, *The Meaning of Sex: Christian Ethics and the Moral Life* (Grand Rapids: Baker Academic, 2009), 135–36.

18. Alexander R. Pruss, *One Body: An Essay in Christian Sexual Ethics* (Notre Dame, IN: University of Notre Dame Press, 2013), 234.

MARRIAGE: PATTERNS, BOUNDARIES, FAMILY

While conjugal joy has its place, marriage constitutes a primary means, but not the only means, of expressing "the image of [our] Creator" (Col. 3:10). The church itself is elevated to familial value in the New Testament as the bride of Christ. Various expressions of the *imago Dei*—with Jesus Christ being the perfect image— have fulfillment in the local community of faith, which unites believers in love. Indeed, both conjugal unity in marriage and spiritual unity "in Christ" within the church portend a greater, future "marriage supper of the Lamb" promised for all "who hold to the testimony of Jesus" (Rev. 19:7–10 ESV).

Marriage Metaphors in Old and New Testaments

In both Testaments, marriage is the pattern of covenantal, intimate union between a man and a woman, and analogously between God and his people.[19] In the prophets, Israel is portrayed as Yahweh's chosen, cared-for wife—one he himself made beautiful. Consequently, her spiritual adultery of "breaking the covenant" (Ezek. 16:59; cf. 8–63) is finally cause for separation and judgment (Isa. 50:1; Hos. 2:14–20). The stark sexual images of Israel's prostitution with false gods contrast with the lovers' mutual desires for consummation in Song of Songs. "The intention of Yahweh was that Israel be like a virgin bride who gives herself willingly, continually, exclusively to her husband (Jer. 2.2) and thereby becomes his delight."[20] But Israel and Judah's adultery undermined the marriage bond (Jer. 3:1–10; Hos. 1:6–9)—even as the Lord God promises yet to restore what was once one (Isa. 54:5–8; Jer. 31:31–32; Hos. 1:10–11.).

In the New Testament we encounter fresh images, this time of the church as the bride of Christ. Sometimes the church appears as the chosen fiancée with dowry paid in full, awaiting the Bridegroom's return (see Mark 2:19–20; John 3:28–29; 2 Cor. 11:2; Rev. 19:7–9); other times the Christ-church union seems to mirror the husband and wife already in marital union (Eph. 5:22–33). Whether in the Old Testament or New, such metaphors for God's relationship with his people reinforce the hallowed place of marriage in conjugal relations and the intimate relationship that God himself desires with his people.

All the Bible's *divine-human* analogies of husband and wife reflect distinct roles of male love/head and female submit/body. Concluding one of the strongest New Testament passages of a wife's submission to her husband (modeled

---

19. If multiple wives were at times recorded in the Old Testament—for example with Jacob, who was deceived into marrying Leah before Rachel (his true love), as mentioned earlier—having more than one wife never appears encouraged nor is it presented as ideal. The Torah instructs a king "not [to] take many wives" (Deut. 17:17). Even if circumstances permitted a second wife (e.g., a levirate marriage where the brother is surrogate to a deceased, 25:5–6), Jesus and the New Testament reaffirm the original design of the one husband-wife union (Matt. 19:4–6; Eph. 5:31).

20. Stanley J. Grenz, *Sexual Ethics: An Evangelical Perspective* (Louisville: Westminster John Knox, 1990), 61.

by Sarah to Abraham), Peter exhorts husbands to sensitivity toward their wives, adding "Finally, all of you, be like-minded, be sympathetic, love one another, be compassionate and humble" (1 Pet. 3:8; cf. 3:1–7; Col. 3:18–19; Eph. 5:21). As the Trinity has revealed itself in creation, so in wedlock one recognizes equality of nature, distinction in ways of relating, and shared glory—albeit uniquely expressed in different cultures, contexts, and individual marriage relationships.

Boundaries and Directives of Sexual Expression

The philosopher Michel Foucault advocated the act of sex as a salvific nirvana, "a singular bliss, obliviousness to time and limits, the elixir of life, the exile of death and its threats."[21] For Foucault, erotic pleasure itself transcends this world, largely irrespective of with whom or what might be its context. In sharp contrast, the Bible does not excuse the individual from the objective context of sex—the partner, the place, the circumstances. Christians are neither materialists (as Foucault) for whom physical gratification is made ultimate, nor gnostics who detach soul from body as though a random sexual hookup has no effect on one's inner being. Rather, humans are whole, integrated persons. Paul warns, "The body . . . is not meant for sexual immorality but for the Lord" (1 Cor. 6:13). To have sex with another inescapably unites two in "one flesh." And in the words of Paul, "All other sins a person commits are outside the body, but whoever sins sexually, sins against their own body" (6:18), as well as against the Holy Spirit who indwells the believer (v. 19). For the Christian, sexual expression is never private.

In Genesis 2 the Creator presents the woman to the man (v. 22) so that both may be satisfied in friendship and innocent sexual expression, thus fulfilling their very design. In the garden, the covenantal bonding of man and woman vitalizes their full human potential. Complete acceptance encourages wholesomeness and free expression. The ancient Greeks rightly employed the term κοινωνία ("participation," "fellowship" of closest nature) to define, among other meanings, the marital relationship.[22] In the Edenic coupling of the two, God himself was also present, blessing their oneness, which would include (how could it be otherwise?) their sexual orgasm. The Creator stood as officiator and supporting Father of both the woman and the man. Even in our world marred by sin and shame today, God's presence in marriage facilitates the expression of the *imago Dei*—this in the union of two persons embodied as sexual beings each authentically expressing themselves, each recognizing their I-thou identity through the sexual act of becoming one, each fulfilled by giving themselves to one another and to God himself. The divine template for marriage satisfies and safeguards sexual expression.

---

21. Michel Foucault, *The History of Sexuality* (New York: Vintage, 1978), 1:57. Foucault (1926–1984) was the first public intellectual in France to die of HIV/AIDS.

22. Friedrich Hauck, "Κοινός, etc.," in *Theological Dictionary of the New Testament*, ed. Gerhard Kittel, trans. Geoffrey W. Bromiley (Grand Rapids: Eerdmans, 1967), 3:798.

To be sure, however, in our fallen world all marriages also suffer brokenness and "ungrace." The reality of conjugal relations often disappoints. As Stanley Hauerwas humorously says, "We always marry the wrong person."[23] If seen as primarily for satisfying one's own desires, marriage is robbed of its theological, indeed, trinitarian meaning. We search the Scriptures with difficulty to find an ideal married couple, perhaps as a reminder that marriage is designed to teach us—given our own imperfections—to love one another. Even if a spouse does not believe in Jesus Christ, our spousal responsibility to care for the other remains part of the marriage covenant (1 Cor. 7:2–14, 17). Amid the brokenness of life, our love for spouse and faithfulness in marriage ultimately demonstrate our love and obedience to our God and Savior. In Eastern Orthodoxy, the marriage ceremony includes literally placing a crown on each spouse as a form of testimony (μαρτυρία) to Christ, that is, ceding oneself sacrificially to the other in the Lord.[24] Nevertheless, we always yearn for something beyond, as though romantic satisfaction (and dissatisfaction) point toward a greater divine reality.[25]

Procreation, Family, and the People of God

The original man and woman were commanded, "Be fruitful and increase in number; fill the earth and subdue it" (Gen. 1:28). Conjugal relations envision children, a theme obvious to humankind and indigenous to the Old Testament. The Mosaic law provided parameters and protection for the wife, husband, and children, with ample passages warning of aberrant sexual behavior and their consequences—from incest and same-sex eroticism to bestiality. With few exceptions, childbirth was the primary purpose of marriage and sign of the blessing of God.

> Children are a heritage from the LORD,
>   offspring a reward from him. (Ps. 127:3)

Jewish sons and daughters not only *filled* the land but they also *tilled* the land and expanded the kingdom. Singleness was rare, and a woman's childlessness brought shame.

Whereas in the Old Testament God's covenant with Israel was tied directly to the Hebrew family and nation, the New Testament decidedly elevates the role of the celibate and single for the kingdom of God. John the Baptist, Jesus Christ himself, and Paul resound as unmarried examples, as do a multitude of "saints"

---

23. Stanley Hauerwas, *A Community of Character* (Notre Dame, IN: University of Notre Dame Press, 1981), 172.
24. Paul Evdokimov, *The Sacrament of Love: The Nuptial Mystery in Light of the Orthodox Tradition* (Crestwood, NY: St. Vladimir's Seminary Press, 1985), 80, cf. 78.
25. Elizabeth Stuart, "The Theological Study of Sexuality," in Thatcher, *Oxford Handbook*, 30, concludes that the modernist Christian "affair with sexuality" needs to move beyond glorified immediacy to "the dissatisfaction, disappointment, and boredom" of sex that urge us toward the greater "joy of death in which we will be making love with God."

(later church fathers would add the Virgin Mary). The "dispensation of grace" overturns the Hebrew social structure. Indeed, celibacy and singleness proclaim the Christian's freedom and self-determination in service to Jesus Christ rather than ceding to cultural insistence on a woman bearing children.[26] When Mary and Jesus's siblings came to correct him (saying, "He is out of his mind," Mark 3:21), Jesus himself declared, "Who are my mother and my brothers? . . . Whoever does God's will is my brother and sister and mother" (3:33–35; cf. Luke 14:26). For many New Testament believers, the local church itself became more family than their unbelieving natural families—thus the common address of "brothers" and "sisters." "Because human beings are made for communion with God and one another," writes David Jensen, "the trajectory of Christian life [married or single] evokes pilgrimage more often than a permanent home"[27]—a pilgrimage forward in becoming the bride of Christ.

Countercultural as the church became, the place of the Christian family in the New Testament remains equally important alongside singleness. Familial instructions abound (Eph. 5:25–6:4; Col. 3:18–21). Qualifications for local church leadership—men and, to some extent, women—include careful evaluation of family order and comportment (1 Tim. 2:8–3:13; Titus 1:5–9). Christian children came to populate and expand Christendom, together with the rescued children cast aside by pagan society. Never an end in themselves, parents with their offspring were now in service to the mission of the church. "Marriage is an expression of the expansive nature and outreach mandate of the church," writes Grenz, "and it functions quite naturally as a vehicle of that mission."[28] Parents learn to love beyond themselves. And children grow the church.

The *Catechism of the Catholic Church* declares that the procreation mandate of Genesis 1:28 continues obligatory today: "The spouses' union achieves the twofold end of marriage: the good of the spouses themselves and the transmission of life. These two meanings . . . cannot be separated without altering the couple's spiritual life. . . . The conjugal love of man and woman thus stands under the twofold obligation of fidelity and fecundity."[29] That is, licit copulation must envision conception. Historically, Augustine argued that all sexual intercourse involves lustful passion (hence loss of reason), justifiable only if motivated for

---

26. See Peter Brown, *The Body and Society: Men, Women, and Sexual Renunciation in Early Christianity*, rev. ed. (New York: Columbia University Press, 2008), 33–64. Radical asceticism also marked certain movements in Judaism, yet the onus to reproduce was ever present: "Human [sexual] desire, a child and a woman—the left hand should repulse them but the right hand bring them back" (Babylonian Talmud, tractate Sanhedrin 107b, quoted in Brown, *Body and Society*, 64. The Essenes (all men) were celibate, yet with a second order that practiced marriage.

27. David H. Jensen, *God, Desire, and a Theology of Human Sexuality* (Louisville: Westminster John Knox, 2013), 58.

28. Grenz, *Sexual Ethics*, 59.

29. *Catechism of the Catholic Church*, 2nd ed. (New York: Doubleday, 1995), part 3, ch. 2, art. 6.3, 2363 (p. 627).

procreation.[30] Aquinas allowed that the ecstatic passion of sexual intercourse, albeit with loss of reason, is not *necessarily* sinful any more than sleep (also with loss of reason); rather, sin is the pursuit of pleasure alone.[31] In either case, as codified in Roman Catholic instruction, conjugal ecstasy must not be separated from the prospect of procreation.

To insist, however, that connubial activity must prevision childbearing would seem to truncate the full-orbed design of the *imago Dei* for marital intimacy: sexual intercourse constitutes the indwelling of one in the other and the self-giving pleasuring of the other. Insisting that the sexual act anticipate procreation undermines its perichoretic meaning and beauty—not the least to those unable to have children, or to those whose later childbearing years raise dangers regarding the health of a newborn, or, again, to those whose childbearing years are behind them. While progeny has great value, depending on circumstances and calling in the church, contraception is not sin. Christian couples choosing not to have children are not necessarily disobedient to God's direction in their lives. Rather sexual intimacy itself is reflective of trinitarian mutual indwelling, and is hence an important aspect of the image of God and testimony to the powerful beauty of "the marriage bed kept pure" (Heb. 13:4).

The Public Nature of Marriage

In the gospel of John, Jesus's first public sign of "his glory" began at the wedding feast in Cana of Galilee (John 2:11; cf. 2:1–11). The Johannine canon ends with an infinitely greater "wedding supper of the Lamb," with Christ's bride ready, bright, and clean (Rev. 19:7–9). The new Jerusalem descends from heaven, "the bride, the wife of the Lamb" (21:9), and "the glory and honor of the nations will be brought into it" (21:26). Whatever else might be said, whether in Cana or on the new earth, these are formal, public events—the bigger the better.

Accordingly, truly biblical marriage is not merely the secretive "I do" of sexual intimacy. Nor is physical intercourse a prequel to a public pledge. As in all dimensions of life, inward commitment to another (and to God) should motivate proper outward social expression. In most countries, nuptial vows require juridical attestation with binding legal status. In the United States, recognized religious authorities have authority in a marriage ceremony to officiate both the civil and religious dimensions of nuptial agreements. A man and woman's one-time covenantal vow before witnesses seals a commitment then consummated and reenacted in a life of togetherness. Within these public, legal arrangements, children are born receiving rights and protection as heirs. Rather than merely

---

30. Augustine, *On Marriage and Concupiscence*, in *Nicene and Post-Nicene Fathers of the Christian Church*, series 1, vol. 5, *Anti-Pelagian Writings*, ed. Philip Schaff (Edinburgh: T&T Clark, 1902), 5:288; cf. Margaret D. Kamitsuka, "Sexual Pleasure," in Thatcher, *Oxford Handbook*, 507–8.
31. Thomas Aquinas, *Summa theologiae*, ed. and trans. T. Gilby (London: Blackfriars, 1968), 43:192–95; again, Kamitsuka, "Sexual Pleasure," 507–8.

a private affair, therefore, marriage extends far beyond the husband and wife to include children, solidify the church, and ultimately benefit all society.

So marriage and families serve as a gift to the world. In the eloquence of Nigerian sister Ifeyinwa Awagu, "The couple is the starting point, but it's a ripple that goes round wide. . . . Whatever I do in my marriage, the circle keeps increasing, keeps widening, until it covers the whole world. . . . Marriage is beyond us. It's about the society. It is your own project for the world."[32]

As the Creator presided over the first union of husband and wife, so "the original model of the family must be sought in God himself, in the Trinitarian mystery of his life."[33] As the Father, Son, and Holy Spirit enjoy the bond of infinite personal unity yet in their mutual love then create and sustain the entire universe, so marriage preserves the unity within yet effects creative good toward others. Love and goodness are self-diffusive. Increased affection in marriage strengthens a person's capacity for communion with believers and for kindness in the world. Thus the meaning of conjugal love prefigures a greater "social intimacy"[34] of believers and a final consummation in God's eternal community.[35]

CONCLUSION

The often-repeated comment of Andy Warhol that "sex is the biggest nothing of all time" is itself undone in light of God's Word. Rather, in God's design, the marriage bed is something precious that satisfies the core of our basic human constitution—not in its entirety, but in the greater purpose of meeting sexual longing and replenishing the earth. When torn away from the Maker's guidelines, when focused on selfish lust, sex does indeed become emptied of its mystery and beauty. The prostitute has no joy. The playboy's scarlet robe conceals the void.

From the beginning, two becoming one flesh hints at a greater spiritual significance reflective of the Triune God in whose image we are created. As the Godhead is constituted of a single divine nature, so we possess—whatever the ethnicity, sex, age, or differing ability—a human nature that unifies us all. As

32. Ifeyinwa Awagu, speaking in "The Humanum Series," Vimeo, posted by Humanum, April 25, 2016, https://vimeo.com/ondemand/humanum. See also Doug Mainwaring, "Your Marriage: You Have No Idea of the Good You Are Doing," *Public Discourse*, March 7, 2017, http://www.thepublicdiscourse.com/2017/03/18600/.

33. John Paul II, *Letter to Families* (Rome: Libreria Editrice Vaticana, 1994), §6.

34. Jonathan Grant, *Divine Sex: A Compelling Vision for Christian Relationships in a Hypersexualized Age* (Grand Rapids: Brazos, 2015), 147. "Jesus's announcement of the kingdom puts our present desire for sexual and relational fulfillment in its ultimate context. The urgency of God's mission to invite all who will come to the future wedding feast focuses the church on this most important goal," which in turn makes Christian marriage a vocation and frees others to serve God in singleness.

35. Helpful regarding the eschatological meaning of our sexuality is Gifford A. Grobien, "From Taboo to Delight: The Body, Sex, and Love in View of Creation and Eschatology," in *Ethics of Sex: From Taboo to Delight*, ed. Gifford A. Grobien (Saint Louis: Concordia, 2017), 201–20.

self-conscious personal beings we, too, form self-awareness and exist in part defined by I-thou relationships reflective of the Father-Son-Spirit relationship of Trinity. In the sacred covenant of marriage, we, too, indwell the other, analogous to the perichoresis of the Godhead. And we, too, are called to self-giving—a sacrificial love that fills rather than empties. Conjugal love replenishes. By grace, it generates love toward others, in babies born and children raised, in caring for others, in vibrant life in the church, in healthy communities. In all, we are debtors to the forgiveness and restoration promised for all who trust in Jesus Christ, the Son of God, the Bridegroom of the redeemed.

FOR DISCUSSION

1. According to a major US federal study conducted in 2015, about half of high-school seniors have had sexual intercourse.[36] How would you persuade Christian high school students to reserve sex for marriage? How do you persuade yourself?

2. What are five parallels between the trinitarian Creator and the human image of God? Why is this relevant to sex and the marriage covenant?

3. Compared to nonbiblical conjugal arrangements, what are the practical effects of a faithful, Christian marriage? In concentric circles, who is affected, and what is the effect on them?

---

36. Results for various sexual behaviors can be calculated at Centers for Disease Control and Prevention, https://nccd.cdc.gov/youthonline/App/Results.aspx.

FOR FURTHER READING

Allender, Dan B. and Tremper Longman III. *God Loves Sex: An Honest Conversation about Sexual Desires and Holiness*. Grand Rapids: Baker Books, 2014.

Grenz, Stanley J. *The Social God and the Relational Self: A Trinitarian Theology of the* Imago Dei. Louisville: Westminster John Knox, 2001.

Rosenau, Douglas E. *A Celebration of Sex*. Rev. ed. Nashville: Thomas Nelson, 2002.

CHAPTER 12

REPRODUCTION, CONTRACEPTION, AND INFERTILITY

SANDRA L. GLAHN

U nder the Spirit's inspiration, the author of Genesis describes the creation of male and female. God said, "Let us make *'adam* in our image, after our likeness." And the text goes on to say,

> So God created *'adam* in his own image,
>   in the image of God he created him;
>   male and female he created them. (1:26–27 ESV; cf. 5:2)

Thus the Bible's first stated purpose for God designing male and female was to reflect his own divine image and likeness.

The purpose for the first marriage also reveals itself in Genesis, where the text tells how God provides for the man's need. God pronounced something "not good" for the first time—man's aloneness (2:18), but after God crafted woman from man's side and brought man and woman together, God's updated assessment was that *this* creation was "very good" (1:31). The woman's presence with man reversed the negative assessment. As *ish* and *ishah*, husband and wife together, were purposed with bearing God's image and being "not alone."

MARRIAGE AND REPRODUCTION

Considering how many people think the purpose of marriage is procreation, it is interesting to see, as theologians George and Dora Winston observe, that "neither procreation nor motherhood are mentioned in Genesis 2:18–24, which is the foundational passage in Scripture on marriage." They go on to note, "The primary purpose of God's creating a wife for [the man] was not procreation but to help [man] out of his loneliness."[1]

Examining the creation account in Genesis 2, one finds no mention of multiplying—a significant omission. If procreation were the purpose of marriage, or even a primary purpose or a moral mandate for all time, one would expect to find reproduction at least mentioned in the husband-wife creation story. Certainly, part of God's design for marriage includes procreation, but based on the Genesis text in which marriage is established, reproduction is certainly less emphasized than bearing God's image and partnering together to subdue the earth.

The passage ends with an interesting observation: "For this reason a man will leave his father and mother and be united to his wife, and they will become one flesh" (Gen. 2:24 BSB). Rather than a command to leave parents, the original verb is in the future passive—not active—indicative form. That is, the husband is joined to his wife by an outside force. The implication is that God performs a divine amalgamation, fusing man and woman to each other so that they are rejoined as one. Indeed, centuries later when Jesus argues for the permanence of marriage, he quotes the Genesis account: "But at the beginning of creation God 'made them male and female.' For this reason a man will leave his father and mother and be united to his wife, and the two will become one flesh.' So they are no longer two, but one flesh. Therefore what *God has joined together*, let no one separate" (Mark 10:6–9 NIV, emphasis mine).

Mark records Jesus's statement about husband and wife as "no longer two" using a verb form (present active indicative) that emphasizes their oneness as an ongoing event—not an occasional event limited to the bedroom. Their oneness is constant. Indeed, God's design for oneness in marriage is more far-reaching than sexual intimacy. The author of Genesis says husband and wife are "united," and later Jesus himself says that they, the man and woman, "are no longer two."

Thus oneness is the central focus of biblical teaching on the purpose of marriage. Not only does the author of Genesis establish it, but—as mentioned—Jesus repeats this idea. And Paul develops it more thoroughly in Ephesians. There the apostle makes "two shall become one" the apex of his argument when speaking of the head-and-body, husband-wife relationship.

Readers focused on Paul's reference to head and body as an organization chart miss the beautiful oneness metaphor the apostle intends. Whereas the Genesis account evokes a *horizontal* image of two-become-one that brings to mind—though is not limited to—the marriage bed, Paul creates a *vertical* picture of two becoming one. In his analogy, a physical head is attached to the rest of a physical body. Interestingly, in all of Paul's teaching on marriage, nowhere does he mention reproduction, but he does emphasize oneness. And that oneness depicts the relationship between Christ and the church.

---

1. George Winston and Dora Winston, *Recovering Biblical Ministry by Women: An Exegetical Response to Traditionalism and Feminism* (Longwood, FL: Xulon, 2003), 213.

The rest of Scripture is consistent with the oneness emphasis when speaking of marriage. In Song of Songs, the one book of the Bible dedicated entirely to physical love, one might expect to find at least a passing reference to reproduction if multiplication were an essential component of physical intimacy. But instead, the only emphasis is on love's expression, on passion, and on pleasure. Solomon's beautiful poetry is complemented by observation of God's design of the human body: The very position of the clitoris, a woman's sexual pleasure center, suggests that a woman's sexual pleasure happens for most wives apart from reproductive potential. Indeed, "some studies report that as many as 70 percent of women . . . find themselves unable to achieve orgasm during sexual intercourse from penetration and thrusting alone."[2] Most wives need clitoral stimulation outside of intercourse—generally required for reproduction—to experience orgasm.

Continuing in our survey of Scripture, when the apostle Paul speaks about choosing marriage or the single life, he does not include reference to children as part of the consideration. To the married he provides this instruction:

> The husband must fulfill his duty to his wife, and likewise also the wife to her husband. The wife does not have authority over her own body, but the husband does; and likewise also the husband does not have authority over his own body, but the wife does. Stop depriving one another, except by agreement for a time, so that you may devote yourselves to prayer. (1 Cor. 7:3–5 NASB)

Several details are worth noting here. First, again in the context of instruction about marital sexual interactions, Paul makes no mention of reproduction. What he does stress as essential instead is doing the opposite of depriving one's spouse—which is to give, to bless, to prosper, and contribute to the other's flourishing. So it would appear that another purpose of marital relations is to give to one's spouse sexually.

From Genesis to Song of Songs to Jesus's words to 1 Corinthians, a brief survey of Scripture demonstrates that the purpose and focus of marriage is oneness. Two become one. Male and female need each other to more fully reveal God as image bearers, to serve as companions to one another, and, in the case of marriage, to give each other sexual pleasure. When two become one, they are stronger together. Indeed, they retain their unique identities, yet as a couple, they are united.

AFTER THE FALL AND THE FLOOD

From the beginning, humanity challenged God's intended oneness. It was not long before the man and woman chose to disobey their Sovereign. And after

---

2. See William Cutrer, Sandra Glahn, and Michael Sytsma, *Sexual Intimacy in Marriage*, 4th ed. (Grand Rapids: Kregel, 2020).

God sent them from the garden, the couple faced consequences that affected their ability to be united. God told the woman that he would multiply her work pain and her conception-related pain (Gen. 3:16). God told the man that the earth would fight him (v. 18). The couple's two shared responsibilities, to rule the earth together and to multiply image bearers, suddenly involved struggle. After leaving the garden, the first couple did procreate, but their son Cain killed his little brother. And before long, humanity had become so evil that God destroyed nearly everyone and started over.

When Noah emerged from his voyage with the animals, God repeated the original imperative to fill the earth: "Be fruitful and multiply" (9:1). Both times God tells humans to do so, the pronouncement comes at a critical juncture when those hearing the words are earth's only human inhabitants.

Back in the garden, *ish* and *ishah* had been charged with increasing from two to many. Following the flood, the surviving humans faced a similar task. If either the first couple or Noah and his family failed to procreate, the entire human race would have vanished.

Interestingly, after the flood the command to have dominion over the earth, or subdue it, is not repeated. And after God tells Noah and his sons to get busy, nowhere in the rest of Scripture do we find the creation mandate repeated. And while some consider "be fruitful and multiply" a timeless command, Jesus, John the Baptist, and Paul were unmarried. We find no reference to the creation mandate in the New Testament. And, in fact, the scriptural emphasis "seems to turn from a Jewish perspective of marriage to valuing celibacy for the kingdom of God."[3] All talk of multiplying at the time of the earliest Christians focuses on reproducing disciples—filling the earth with worshipers through sharing the good news. The lone exception to this is Paul's exhortation that younger widows in Ephesus marry and have children rather than depending on the church for support (1 Tim. 5:14). In the same epistle he disparages those who forbid marriage (4:3). He also reminds his protégé that God "richly provides us with everything for our enjoyment" (6:17 NIV). But in this letter he is speaking in a context of excessive asceticism,[4] and elsewhere he wants singles to remain as they are (1 Cor. 7:8, 20).

It would be simplistic, however, to conclude that the Old Testament emphasizes physical reproduction while the New Testament emphasizes spiritual reproduction. Although biological families do receive emphasis in the Old Testament, in its pages we still find a hint that kingdom living is about more than having children. Isaiah comforts believing eunuchs with the truth that leaving an eternal legacy will be even better than children (Isa. 56:4–5).

---

3. J. Scott Horrell, "The Covenant of Singleness: The Bible and Church History," *Kindred Spirit*, Spring/Summer 2015, 12.

4. Sandra L. Glahn, "The First-Century Ephesian Artemis: Ramifications of Her Identity," *Bibliotheca Sacra* 172, no. 688 (October–December 2015), 455.

With the coming of Christ, however, the emphasis overtly shifts from physical to spiritual reproduction. "Family" is introduced as a metaphor for the spiritual community. Calling nonrelatives "brother" and "sister" develops as a new habit, and Jesus responds to the news that his earthly family has arrived by saying those who do his Father's will are his brother, sister, and mother (Matt. 12:50). When a woman in a crowd says Mary is blessed for giving birth to and nursing Jesus, he rearranges priorities with, "Blessed rather are those who hear the word of God and obey it" (Luke 11:28 NIV).

So to summarize, the Scriptures demonstrate that the primary metaphor and focus of marriage in Scripture is oneness (Gen. 2:24; Mark 10:8; Eph. 5:31). Husbands and wives, being made in the image of God (Gen. 1:27), hold mutual authority over each other's bodies (1 Cor. 7:4). Man and woman are interdependent (11:11) and spouses were made to enjoy sexual pleasure (see Song of Songs). As best they can, husbands and wives are to give to each other sexually (1 Cor. 7:3). Two-become-one is a favorite reference to Genesis (Matt. 19:6), and ultimately marital oneness reflects a picture of Christ and the church (Eph. 5:32). While reproduction is a celebrated by-product of the marriage union, physical multiplication—or at least an attempt at such—does not appear to be the (or even *an*) essential requirement.

CHILDREN ARE A GIFT OR *THE* GIFT?

Yet some see in one Old Testament passage—Psalm 127—a statement that would suggest otherwise: "children are a gift from the LORD" (v. 3 NLT).

At the time of Solomon, to whom Psalm 127 is attributed, the family structure included members of all living generations, often inhabiting the same property. And the primary inheritance or "heritage" was passed to the eldest male; that is, he received a double portion compared to that of his siblings. The oldest father and his primary wife were central. If we think of this primary family as being like the hub of a wheel, each son with his wife and children form the spokes, as they are connected with the entire family on one single compound. Upon the patriarch's death, the preeminent position shifts to his eldest son.[5]

This concept of family in Old Testament times—all the male descendants of a living patriarch dwelling on a compound with dependents and their spouses and children—was true from early days, and persists today in some parts of the world. Often the tribal chief had (and has) multiple wives, as did Abraham and Jacob.

In the tenth century BC, when Psalm 127 was probably written, people understood "family" to mean something quite different from the Western nuclear structure of father, mother, 1.14 children, and their pets. Indeed, most today would define the husband-wife-children household as an independent unit. The contemporary norm is for nuclear families to live in their own homes, remote

---

5. Daniel Block, "Old Testament Perspective on Marriage" (lecture given to Colloquium at the Southern Baptist Theological Seminary, October 2001).

from parents. And once the children establish their own homes, they typically become independent.

Yet those in the ancient Near East lived in a much different cultural setting. And to say a certain structure existed in Bible times is not the same as saying such a structure reflected God's desire. Indeed, many confuse a biblical description of a cultural practice with a biblical mandate, as if the context in which a passage was written is as Spirit-inspired as the passage itself.

Such is the danger when taking the Old Testament's poetry, metaphors, and narratives and applying them directly as commands in completely different contexts. Neither the ancient Near East nor the modern North American structure is ideal. And this quickly becomes obvious when observing that one major difference between the two kinds of families is how parents in the ancient Near East would have viewed the announcement "It's a girl!" Today in the West, most families celebrate when a girl is born. But such was not the case in Solomon's day. Here's how the NASB renders his psalm:

> Behold, children are a gift of the Lord,
> The fruit of the womb is a reward.
> Like arrows in the hand of a warrior,
> So are the children of one's youth.
> How blessed is the man whose quiver is full of them;
> They will not be ashamed
> When they speak with their enemies in the gate. (Ps. 127:3–5 NASB)

The NLT and NASB translators—doubtless in a well-intentioned effort to be gender inclusive—chose to render the text as asserting that "children are a gift" (v. 3). But Solomon did not say "children" are a gift from the Lord. Rather, the word he chose was actually "sons." And as Robert Anderson Barclay, a theologian in the twentieth century, accurately observed, "As in most ancient societies, the real purpose of marriage [was] the procreation of lawful sons."[6] Note that Barclay said procreation was the ideal of most ancient *societies*—not necessarily the scriptural ideal.

A rendering that more accurately reflects the type of family Solomon had in mind would be "sons are an inheritance." And the reason for emphasizing males over females was that the psalmist had in view both economic prosperity and physical safety, which in his day depended on sons.

In the ancient Near East, sons would defend the family's assets through physical force. And in order to have an army of sons, a man needed a fertile wife. If the primary wife was unable to bear children, especially sons, an additional wife or wives might be acquired. One sees this in the case of Sarah and

---

6. Robert Anderson Barclay, *The Law Givers: Leviticus and Deuteronomy* (New York: Abingdon, 1964), 39.

Hannah, for example. And while never prescribed or even commended in the Old Testament, polygyny was also never clearly condemned and was certainly practiced. In the beginning, God had revealed his ideal for marriage as two becoming one. But only later did the people of God with any sort of consistency seem to comprehend this intention.

In the context in which Solomon wrote his psalm lauding God's provision through sons, villagers had no social security, 401(k) plans, nursing homes, health insurance, Meals on Wheels, or pensions. Instead, they had children. More to the point, there was no police force, and no federal, state, or local jail system. So when it came to protecting one's assets, a premium was placed on boys. This latter perspective on warfare and defense is what Solomon had in view. The words "arrows," "quiver," "warrior," and "opponents" (i.e., "enemies") bear this out. Certainly if a warrior ran out of arrows in the midst of a battle, he was in deep trouble.

The point of Psalm 127, then, is not that contemporary families should look like ancient Near Eastern families or that the blessing of God looks the same in both contexts. The main point of Psalm 127, which celebrates sons, is not—as some think—that every godly family should have numerous boys—a "quiver full." Nor is the point of the psalm even to suggest that a primary purpose of marriage is multiplication. Rather, the text is talking about the goodness of God through great provision. In Solomon's day, a major provision for safety was sons. As "arrows," male offspring provided protection in a world in which families, rather than police, enforced the law.

Moving from the specifics in Solomon's culture to the universal ideas in his poetry, one sees that contemporary 401(k) plans, nursing homes, health insurance, Meals on Wheels, pensions, police forces, jails that keep criminals off the streets, a strong national defense, and, yes, even daughters are all blessings from God that make the same point about his wonderful provision. The body of Christ is also a community that provides aid. So perhaps rendering "sons" as "children" in contemporary translations is appropriate after all, as doing so is consistent with the author's emphasis on God's blessing. Most who see the passage as requiring large families still understand the text as saying that daughters are blessings, but such readers can do so only by picking and choosing what specifics to keep from the original context.

Psalm 127 was written at a time when virtually no one—man or woman—remained unmarried. Yet compare such a cultural context with the marital status of Jesus, John the Baptist, Paul, and others, and then also to North America today, where the majority of people sitting in pews on Sunday mornings are either never-married youth or adults, divorced, separated, or widowed. Nevertheless, Psalm 127 applies to them (as it does to those with large families), because the timeless point of the passage is not about physical reproduction; rather, it is about God's rich blessing, his provision, and the human flourishing that comes only as a gift from God.

Having reviewed the purposes of marriage, one can see that procreation, while a wonderful part of God's design for married couples, is not mandated for all able married people in this age of grace. And Psalm 127 is not saying that godly people in all eras of human history must strive to have large families—nor that those who choose to have few or no children are somehow quenching the Spirit.

Having established the purpose of marriage, especially as it relates to reproduction, we turn now to consider biblical ethics as they apply to two reproduction-related subjects—contraception and infertility.

CONTRACEPTION

In light of the above-mentioned considerations about children and in the absence of other compelling passages to suggest otherwise, contraception would appear to fall on the list of liberties that couples may embrace within a context of seeking God's direction.

The history of contraception itself goes back nearly to the beginning. The first and perhaps only overt scriptural reference to preventing pregnancy appears in Genesis 38, with the story of Onan, grandson of Jacob. Many have seen in this story a biblical view of contraception as "unnatural." But providing general commentary on contraception is not the point of the author, as we shall see. The text says this:

> Judah got a wife for Er, his firstborn, and her name was Tamar. But Er, Judah's firstborn, was wicked in the LORD's sight; so the LORD put him to death. Then Judah said to Onan, "Sleep with your brother's wife and fulfill your duty to her as a brother-in-law to raise up offspring for your brother." But Onan knew that the child would not be his; so whenever he slept with his brother's wife, he spilled his semen on the ground to keep from providing offspring for his brother. What he did was wicked in the LORD's sight; so the LORD put him to death also. (Gen. 28:6–10 NIV)

The phrase "whenever he slept with his brother's wife" tells readers that Onan engaged in coitus interruptus not just once, but multiple times. He did so in order to keep from having to sire, provide for, and give an inheritance to a child who would bear his brother's name instead of his own. Had Onan impregnated Tamar, the offspring from his first wife would have received less of an inheritance.

Onan had apparently done the math. When Er, Onan's older brother, died, Onan benefited financially, as the double portion of Judah's estate allotted to the eldest son passed from Er to himself. This double portion would have increased Onan's inheritance from one-fourth to two-thirds of the estate. And Onan sought to keep all the property in his own name. Nevertheless, he was also willing to exploit Tamar, using her body while nearly guaranteeing she would be destitute in the future. And for Onan's wickedness God dealt with him as he had done with Er—he put him to death.

Onan had kept the letter of God's law by marrying Er's wife. But in doing so without seeking to give his brother a legacy, Onan violated the law's intent. And drawing on a long history of both Jewish and Roman Catholic commentators, Robert H. Brom explains what many have considered the reason God went so far as to kill Onan for spilling his seed: because his doing so violating natural law.[7]

Yet, interestingly, the text suggests that Onan did something far worse. He obeyed God's law in taking Tamar as his wife, but he used her. He helped himself to her body while refusing to fulfill the intent of the levirate marriage law. And such a refusal meant not only that his brother's name would be forgotten (a terrible fate in the ancient Near East) but also that without children Tamar would be destitute and further violated because she was prohibited from marrying anyone else. Those who have reasoned that the great evil in Onan's "spilling his semen" was a violation of natural law have missed that Onan's great evil was actually in violating a person. That victim was a woman bereaved of a husband. And God—who cares for the widow—defended her cause, as promised (see Deut. 10:18).[8]

In the absence of a biblical prohibition against family planning and in light of Scripture's emphasis on filling the earth with worshipers, some couples choose not to have children or to have few children in order to devote themselves more fully to gospel work. And such a decision is consistent with the Great Commission as a priority.

Some may limit family size for the sake of their testimony in lands where resources are limited. For example, a Christian physician ministering in Southeast Asia, where population is dense, wrote, "There have been many times when there was not enough food to go around. I don't believe, however, that we are near to having more people than the world can feed *if the resources are used efficiently.* There are many more people who could live in [my part of the world] if there were proper management of resources. I am of the opinion that prevention of conception beats abortion, so I do not push for unlimited conception."[9] While one can debate the reality of overpopulation, a case can be made for mismatch of resources. Many missionaries have significantly limited the size of their families, or chosen not to have children, for the sake of advancing the gospel in regions where they minister.[10] And a couple living in a place with a mismatch of people and resources may consider that having no children or a small family might best

7. Catholic Answers, "Birth Control," August 10, 2004, http://www.catholic.com/tract/birth-control.

8. For a more detailed account of this story, see Carolyn Custis James's chapter "Tamar: The Righteous Prostitute, in *Vindicating the Vixens: Revisiting Sexualized, Vilified, and Marginalized Women of the Bible*, ed. Sandra Glahn (Grand Rapids: Kregel Academic, 2017), 31–48.

9. Personal correspondence with the author, September 2015. Name withheld for security reasons.

10. William J. Webb, *Slaves, Women and Homosexuals: Exploring the Hermeneutics of Cultural Analysis* (Downers Grove, IL: InterVarsity Press, 2001), 43.

glorify God in such a context. Certainly, procreation remains a good value, but our world differs dramatically from that of the garden. So perhaps God's "creation pattern"[11] has been heavily modified to emphasize a "new-creation pattern" that looks to the eschaton.

Believing couples have many reasons for choosing to limit family size. And Christian charity says that others should not judge their actions as "unbiblical." Certainly a Christ-following couple who devote their lives to raising twelve or more sons and daughters can glorify Christ through their large family. But couples unable to have children or who have medical problems that leave them unsure whether they could reproduce should feel no obligation to use in vitro fertilization, pursue expensive medical treatment, or adopt in order to fulfill God's vision of marriage. And a couple who chooses to have no children in order to more fully serve Christ may—with the Spirit's guidance—choose to glorify God through their family of two. What is essential is that the couples in all of these scenarios—and more—are committed to oneness, discerning the Lord's leading, holding a high view of human life, and recognizing God's call on their lives, even as it relates to their most intimate choices. Although decisions about family size are often approached mindlessly, every married couple seeking to follow Christ should prayerfully entreat the Spirit to guide their choices.

Some Christians believe the Scriptures prohibit contraception, precluding even using natural family planning. Those holding such a view feel that any avoidance of pregnancy reveals an ungodly attitude toward children. But they tend to argue their case using different Scriptures. Many Roman Catholics argue against any means (other than "natural ones") of contraception on the basis of Onan's story. Most Protestants, however, accept a variety of types of family planning. Yet even those who eschew all forms of family planning typically tend to appeal not to Onan's story but to Genesis 1 and Psalm 127 to argue that believers who use contraception are refusing "to consider children an unmitigated blessing."[12]

Nevertheless, most Protestants and Catholics, while gravitating toward different means of controlling reproductive ability and/or timing, do see the Scriptures as allowing for responsible family planning. And if a couple does discern that the Lord is leading them to engage in family planning, there are some additional ethical concerns to consider before using any of the available methods.

One concern about natural family planning (NFP) is that it requires couples to abstain from sexual relations during the time when the wife is most fertile. She is more likely to desire and enjoy sexual relations at this time than at any other time of monthly cycle. Thus, while NFP is effective for preventing pregnancy when practiced correctly, the method is "natural" only in that it does not involve barriers or chemicals. One could argue, in fact, that NFP goes against nature in

---

11. Webb, *Slaves, Women and Homosexuals*, 125.
12. Mary Pride, *The Way Home: Beyond Feminism, Back to Reality* (Wheaton, IL: Crossway, 1985), 75.

that this method has the potential to limit the most pleasurable fulfillment of desire to the husband only. And because one of the purposes established for sex is to give to one's spouse through sexual expression, couples must be especially careful that they are united in mutual agreement when opting to practice NFP.

For those using methods other than NFP, an additional concern is the need for the chosen method to be consistent with biblical teaching on the sanctity of human life. A discussion of family-planning methods is beyond this essay. But suffice it to say that part of living biblically is to recognize the limits of human dominion when it comes to taking human life. Each human from the moment of fertilization is made in God's image and is thus of infinite value. And because of the eternal significance of human life, it is important that any method of contraception be consistent with this value.

In short, because the Scriptures are silent on the topic of contraception, although the practice of avoiding pregnancy has been around from the beginning, it would seem that the decision to use or not to use family-planning methods may be viewed as an area of Christian liberty. The parameters for making such a decision would fall within the boundaries of valuing human life at its earliest stages and engaging in mutual Spirit-guided decision-making.

Couples can be helped further in their decision-making by borrowing concepts from the field of ethics. First, there are four questions they might ask about the choices they face:

1. Beneficence: Does it do good (e.g., Is having a child a good goal? Is our choice to limit family size motivated by kingdom purposes or by materialism?)?
2. Nonmaleficence: Does it avoid doing harm?
3. Autonomy: Does it respect self-determination—a person's right to decide for himself or herself?
4. Justice: Does it give what is right or due?

With each decision, couples can be guided to ask these questions, which fall within three major systems of ethics. Each of these systems has merit, and each can also be viewed through a biblical grid:

1. Utilitarian ethics: Does it do the most good for the most people? As long as one keeps in mind the eternal perspective of God—that life extends beyond temporal existence and that we are called to love others as we love ourselves—believers can operate within utilitarian ethics.
2. Deontological ethics: Does the action conform to rule or law? In this case, does it conform to or violate God's law; and does it conform to or violate civil law?
3. Virtue-based ethics: What would a person of virtue do in this situation? Another way of asking this is, What would Jesus do?

INFERTILITY

At the other end of the spectrum from avoiding pregnancy is a couple's inability to have children when they want them—infertility. There are two categories of infertility—primary and secondary. Primary infertility is the inability to conceive after one year of unprotected intercourse and/or the inability to carry a pregnancy to term. Secondary infertility is when couples who have had one or more children are unable to conceive or carry to term again. (If the wife is over thirty years old, doctors recommend waiting only six months rather than one year to seek medical assistance.)

About 10 percent of women (6.1 million) in the United States between the ages of fifteen and forty-four have difficulty getting pregnant or staying pregnant, according to the Centers for Disease Control and Prevention. About 30 percent of the time the inability to conceive is due to factors in the female; 30 percent of the time it's due to factors in the male; and about 40 percent of the time it's a combination of both male and female factors or is unexplained. One of the myths associated with infertility is that it is a "woman's problem," but as these percentages demonstrate, men and women share infertility equally.

The Bible includes numerous stories about people who experience infertility (e.g., Sarah and Abraham, Rebekah and Isaac, Rachel and Jacob, Samson's mother, Hannah and Elkanah, Ruth in her first marriage). But the Bible is not an unabridged text on the subject, and pulling each "infertility story" out of context to create a "survey" of what the Bible says about infertility is a misguided hermeneutic. Such an approach can lead to such observations as "all the righteous women who prayed to have children were blessed with conceptions."

The inability to have children often brings with it marital, emotional, financial, spiritual, medical, and ethical crises. My focus here will be on the latter. In order to guide couples through the ethical landmines that accompany infertility, it is helpful to know about some of the procedures involved and the decisions that accompany them. Dr. Richard Voet in his chapter in this book on beginning-of-life issues considers some of the ethics associated with in vitro fertilization such as manipulating human embryos, so I won't repeat that information here. But suffice it to say, the sanctity of human life should be a high priority when considering any of the assisted reproductive technologies (ART).

For couples longing for children, a key question is when and/or whether to seek medical treatment. For those who in good conscience feel they should pursue treatment, below are some additional procedures and associated ethical considerations.

IUI (intrauterine insemination or artificial insemination)
IUI assumes the husband's sperm is used. With the aid of a catheter, a doctor places specially treated sperm directly into a woman's uterus. Associated ethical questions to consider are whether masturbation is used to retrieve sperm, and if so whether pornography is involved. Is it a sin to separate conjugal love from reproduction? And if so, is the couple open to using special condoms for collecting semen that involve the wife in the process?

Donor insemination and egg donation

When a sperm donor (either anonymous or known) is used, the procedure is called donor insemination (DI). Questions to consider are whether DI or egg donation violate the "one-flesh" marital relationship. Is using donor gametes wise? Would the couple tell their child(ren) the truth about parentage? Would keeping secrets violate their child's autonomy? Would telling others, even family members, violate their child's autonomy? Would having a child via a third party affect marital dynamics?

Some Christians argue that using a donor differs little from Sarah using Hagar as a surrogate. Weaknesses in this argument are that Sarah had received a direct promise from God that she herself would conceive, a promise that God has not given to everyone; that Hagar was a slave and treated as one; and that Abraham had sexual intercourse with Hagar—which clearly violates the one-flesh relationship. So the Sarah/Hagar/Abraham scenario is not the best example to follow for ethical guidance.

For those arguing that God never introduces a third party into the marriage, the levirate marriage laws indicate otherwise (Deut. 25:5–6). Nevertheless, such "inseminations" happened "within the family" and when the first husband was no longer alive.

Surrogacy

Surrogacy can either be traditional (using a donor's eggs and uterus) or gestational (using the couples' fertilized egg and "borrowing" only the uterus). News coverage of cases in which surrogates contest their contracts are familiar to most. But in reality, of greater risk than the surrogate's changing her mind is the infertile couple's changing their minds and leaving the surrogate with a child. Other issues are the same as mentioned above with DI/egg donation, with the major addition of the ongoing presence of a third party. Frozen-embryo adoption would fall into the surrogate category, but an additional consideration is that in frozen-embryo adoption, the couple are saving the lives of the embryos rather than allowing their destruction.

CONCLUSION

A biblical survey of the purpose of marriage and a look at a theology of reproduction reveal that oneness is the key purpose of marriage, and marital love is designed to flourish in a way that results in physical or spiritual reproduction or both. Contraception appears to be an area of Christian liberty, assuming that couples prayerfully seek God's guidance and are committed to valuing life even at the one-cell stage. Couples seeking to physically reproduce but who are unable to do so often face numerous ethical considerations, many of which focus on the need to value human life, as they pursue medical treatment. A compassionate shepherd will gently guide couples in these deeply personal areas, helping them discern the Spirit's guidance and ground all ethical decisions in Scripture.

FOR DISCUSSION

1. What are some of the purposes of marriage you see reflected in media and hear taught at conferences or in sermons? How well do they align with what Scripture says?

2. In what, if any, scenarios do you think a couple is justified in choosing not to have children?

3. What do you consider the most challenging ethical questions associated with infertility, and why?

FOR FURTHER READING

Cutrer, William, Sandra Glahn, and Michael Sytsma. *Sexual Intimacy in Marriage*. 4th ed. Grand Rapids: Kregel, 2020.

Glahn, Sandra L., and William Cutrer. *Control? A Couple's Guide to Contraception*. Plano, TX: Authenticity Book House, 2015.

———. *When Empty Arms Become a Heavy Burden: Encouragement for Couples Facing Infertility*. 2nd ed. Grand Rapids: Kregel, 2011.

CHAPTER 13

MARITAL SEXUALITY

MICHAEL R. SYTSMA

M y thirty years of listening to questions married couples ask about sexuality reveals three themes. First, the most common questions couples ask relate to normalcy: "How often do most couples have sex?" "How long should foreplay typically last?" "How long can most men have intercourse before they orgasm?" and "Don't most women orgasm during intercourse?" The underlying question in all of these examples seems to be, "Are we normal in our sexuality?"

Such a question suggests that the ethical framework for sexuality is normalcy. It assumes a practice in question is okay as long as it falls in alignment with what everyone else does. Certainly normalcy provides valuable information that can often teach us about God's design. For example, the fact that nearly 100 percent of men will experience some level of erectile dysfunction before the age of eighty teaches us something about how the human male "works." But while such information reveals a little bit about natural design, normalcy is not generally a good foundation for defining our own frame for sexuality (or any other behavior). As a general rule, what most people do doesn't equate to "good" or "healthy." Just because most men regularly view pornography doesn't make such behavior healthy or fit within a Christian ethic.

The second most common question I receive is, "Can we (fill in the blank)?" In context, individuals are typically asking, "Is [this practice] acceptable within a Christian ethic?" Occasionally, the question seems to be more naturalistic— "Did God design our bodies to [whatever practice], or do I believe a myth?" But more often questions about right and wrong relate to whether God permits a particular practice: "Can we watch porn together as a Christian couple if we both agree, and it's done within the marriage bed?"

The third type of question is more difficult to define, but it presents itself in the form of "Shouldn't . . . ?" Typically, the individual is questioning directives. "Shouldn't my spouse do (such and such)?" or "Isn't (such and such) the way it's supposed to be?" Usually the one asking this question is indirectly asking me to serve as the pry bar that moves his or her spouse's frame. The questioner is actually saying, "I want (some behavior or attitude in my spouse). Is there not some kind of biblical directive that tells my spouse they need to be who I want them to be?"

This third question reflects an often more sinister foundation for a sexual ethic. The question—"Shouldn't . . . ?"—suggests an egocentric foundation for an individual's sexual ethic. It's an approach that says, "This is what I want, so make Scripture fit it." The individual asking seems to see his or her desires as primary and right. While there is value in knowing what an individual wishes, elevating one's opinion above that of the spouse, a scriptural directive, or developed theology can destroy one's marriage (see Gal. 5:19–21).

The second approach identified above ("Can we . . . ?") gives the opportunity to place primacy on seeking God's design for the behavior, whether found in natural revelation, Scripture, wisdom, or developed theology. The following model of sexual response provides a structure within which to explore such a God-first framework (see figure 4).

The information here on David Reed's erotic pathway model[1] includes four stages: seduction, sensation, surrender, and reflection. To these I have added "setting" as an overall context, and it contains three elements: the "energizers to the process" of desire and intentionality; "spark" as an additional stage; and "mindfulness" and "desire" as facilitators. So we begin with setting.

SETTING

A couple's sexuality is embedded in a complex relational setting. Most couples only minimally explore and discuss their setting with each other, but the setting creates the context of their relationship. As such, it serves as the foundation for sexuality in their life and relationship. Just as a healthy plant cannot grow in improper soil or in the absence of nutrients and moisture, healthy sexuality cannot grow when the setting is unhealthy and unconducive to growth. Setting consists of components such as the couple's purpose for sex, sexual script, relationship dynamics, and personal dynamics. And each one of these helps to define the frame for sex in a relationship.

Purpose for Sex

If a husband believes the purpose for marriage is to have a wife who serves him, the marriage will look very different from a marriage in which the husband

---

1. William R. Stayton, "A Theology of Sexual Pleasure in Sexuality: A Theological Conversation," *American Baptist Quarterly* 8, no. 2 (1989): 94–108.

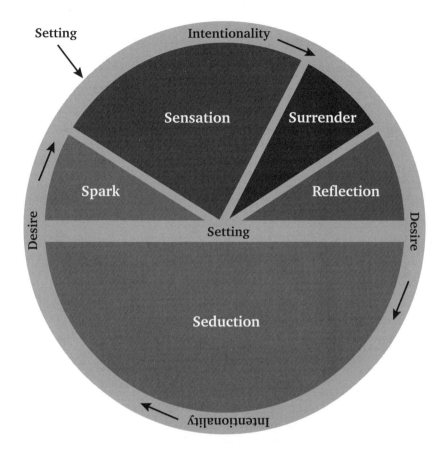

Figure 4. David Reed's Erotic Pathway Model Adapted by Michael R. Sytsma

believes God made his wife to walk beside and complement him as they serve one another. This same principle holds for marital sex.

What do you believe about sex? What is its purpose? Why did God make it the way he did? Disagreement between a couple about their setting can cause a high level of conflict. If one spouse does not hold to the ethic of covenantal monogamy, for example, he or she may seek to bring others into the marital setting through fantasy, image, affair, multiple partners, or partner swapping, to name a few. If the spouse of such a person holds to the ethic of covenantal monogamy, he or she will not be okay with bringing others into the setting of their sex life; such an experience will likely cause damage. Similarly, if a spouse views the purpose for sex as meeting a need, for procreation, or for pursuing pleasure, the whole context of sex shifts.

There is great value in couples articulating and sorting through their purpose for sex. For Christian couples, the purpose is not always clear. For much of history the church has taught procreation as the purpose for sex. Others point out that sex in Song of Songs was about celebrating each other. For others, the purpose may settle on pursuit of intimacy and oneness, or reflecting God.[2] Spouses don't need to fully agree, but a discussion and understanding of each other's is important in establishing a healthy setting for sex.

Sexual Script

Our sexual script is a way of talking about why we do what we do sexually.[3] Such a script consists of the set of beliefs that define our role and the role of the other (or others) in sexuality. One's sexual script includes messages about what should and shouldn't be taught through culture, experience, and our relationship with ourselves and others. Some aspects of our sexual script need to be agreed on; others need only to be communicated and understood.

Should the husband be the sexually aggressive one? Should the wife be seductive, resistant, accommodating, or indifferent? Who takes the lead once a sexual act begins? Does it matter? What are the rules for a couple's sex dance? Who is responsible for achieving orgasm—is one responsible for one's own, or is the spouse responsible for "giving me one"? These questions are typically answered by one's internal sexual script.

If one (or both) of the spouses have experienced sexual trauma, this spouse's sexual script is likely largely influenced by that traumatic experience. If either spouse grew up in a sexually repressed environment, their sexual script may be highly defined by that culture. Similarly, growing up in a family in which sex was an open topic—or even involved incest—greatly affects one's sexual script.

An important role for sex therapists is to help bring these sexual scripts to the surface so each couple can sort through them and decide whether they want to claim them or adjust them. Again, wrestling through sexual scripts is critical to creating a healthy setting.

Relationship Dynamics

Research has consistently demonstrated a strong connection between overall relationship dynamics and sexual satisfaction. Couples who communicate well, are satisfied with their marriage, manage finances as a team, problem-solve well, and generally like each other, for example, do better in their sex life. How the marriage is doing overall serves as a foundational part of the setting. If a couple cannot communicate well in other areas, they will struggle to communicate about

---

2. Douglas E. Rosenau and Michael R. Sytsma, "A Theology of Sexual Intimacy: Insights into the Creator," *Journal of Psychology and Christianity* 23, no. 3 (2004): 261–70.
3. John H. Gagnon and William Simon, *Sexual Conduct: The Social Sources of Human Sexuality*, 2nd ed. (New Brunswick NJ: AldineTransaction, 2005).

sexuality. If a couple wants to follow a Christian sexual ethic, it is important for them to follow a Christian marriage ethic.

Personal Dynamics

Healthy sexuality requires more than a healthy vision and partner relationship; it also requires a healthy individual, including a healthy relationship with one's self. An immature person cannot be a mature lover. Empathy, grace, kindness, curiosity, transparency, and other traits of a mature person provide a much healthier setting for sex than do their opposites. A selfish, demanding individual can deeply infect the setting for a couple's sexual intimacy. The fruit of the Spirit (Gal. 5:22–23) provides a healthier setting for good sex than the fruit of the flesh (vv. 19–21).

Similarly, knowing and accepting oneself is a critical part of creating a healthy setting. A husband or wife who feels uncomfortable with his or her body or sexuality will have difficulty maintaining a healthy setting. I spend a great deal of time in sex therapy helping individuals discover and embrace their own eroticism. Those able to feel comfortable with their own bodies, sensuality, and sexuality find it easier to openly share with a spouse.

How a couple sorts through setting and its four components (purpose for sex, sexual script, relationship dynamics, and personal dynamics) defines the largest portion of their framework for sexuality in marriage. Those who merely pursue normalcy or have a mentality of "Shouldn't . . . ?" have a warped ethic and will eventually experience unhealthy sexuality.

Energizing the Process

What keeps the sexual process energized? While the answer to this question is the subject of heated debates and more complex than what we will consider here, we can identify the energy for the sexual process by looking at desire and intentionality.

Desire

Conflict over sexual desire is the number-one sexual issue for which couples seek help. Most couples do so hoping to discover the one cure that will cause one, or one's spouse, to have the sexual desire they believe is right. North American culture has spent billions of dollars attempting to change sexual desire. And if we have learned anything in our studies, it's that sexual desire is complex, and we don't understand it. We don't understand direction or intensity of sexual desire. We don't understand why sexual desire is directed toward the opposite sex, the same sex, objects, animals, children, the elderly, or anything else. We don't understand why sexual desire for some people is quite intense, while for others it seems almost absent. And it is difficult to adjust what we don't understand.

Most conflict over sexual desire occurs as one spouse demands that the other be like one's self. Typically, the high-desire spouse wants the lower-desire spouse to have high desire. One with such a mentality thinks, "I want my low-desire spouse to be different from who they are. I want them to want the way I want," or "with the frequency that I want."

At other times spouses expect a different type of sexual desire: "She's very open to having a nurturing kind of sex, but I don't want a nurturing kind of sex. I want her to be hungry for it." Or "I want him to enjoy kissing and making out more, and maybe cuddle more after. Why does he only want the orgasm?"

Note that in both of the above conflicts, the point of view for the sexual ethic is the self. Those with such a perspective will often ask for the "normal" ethic, but conform to it only if it supports their own perspective. But a Christian ethic accepts the other (Rom. 15:7), whether they are like us or not. In following a Christian ethic, both spouses will seek to understand and serve each other (Eph. 5:21). It is likely they will have different types of desire. One may have a more initiating type of desire, the other a more receptive type of desire. And both are reflective of God's design.[4]

Intentionality

For many people, "desire" means "response to arousal." Thus desire may be absent until the individual decides to engage sexually and remains mindful during the act itself. So in chronological terms we have arousal, decision, and then desire.

Decision. I believe true desire is more about choice than biology. While we may want the surging that comes with physiological hunger, being intentional in our choice to pursue sex is an important part of healthy sexuality. For the high-desire spouse, the decision might be to keep their sexuality fully focused on their spouse in a way that cherishes him or her, not just pursues hunger. For the low-desire spouse, the choice may mean deciding to be open and receptive.

Mindfulness. The other aspect of intentionality, in addition to decision, is attention to our attention, or mindfulness. The more aroused we feel, the more desire grows. While we may want to become captivated by our desire and arousal, the reality is that desire often grows as we attend to being present with our spouse and the sensations we are experiencing. Being mindful in every stage of the lovemaking process provides energy and facilitates movement toward the next stage of the lovemaking process.

Much as in worship, being intentional with choosing to engage in the act while being mindful of our heart, body, and mind facilitates the enrichment and enjoyment of the act. When it comes to sexual intimacy, sometimes we cruise passively, along for the ride as our body and heart draw us forward; but more often than not, sex thrives on intentionality.

---

4. Michael Sytsma and Debra L. Taylor, "Current Thinking in How to Help Couples and Individuals Struggling with Low Sexual Desire," *Marriage and Family Therapy: A Christian Journal* 5, no. 3 (2002): 311–20.

Seduction

Within the setting and the energy that comes from desire and intentionality, we have the sexual act itself. The first stage of the sexual act is seduction. Individual acts of seduction take place within the larger context of living life in a way that draws one's spouse toward one's self (seducing him or her).

Many of the clients with whom I work spend a lot of time trying to encourage, push, or demand something from their spouse. Yet, as humans, the more we feel pushed, the more we tend to resist. To the contrary, seduction takes an invitational stance where we get to know our spouse first and then do all we can to draw them toward us. Doing so requires taking on Christlike character that mimics his inviting us to follow him and doing everything to make the path clear for us to accept him—including giving of himself (Eph. 5:25).

What would it take to live in such a way that continually seduces one's spouse—to live in such a way that is attractive, always being one's best self and drawing the other to intimacy? Seduction compels a partner to learn what fascinates and appeals to the spouse and then expending energy to show that to him or her. It communicates, "I love you, I care for you, I desire to be with you at all times."

Many have expressed their dislike for both the word and concept of *seduction*. Typically, such individuals are viewing seduction through a negative sexual lens. Indeed, the origin of the word is Latin meaning "to lead away or apart," and so seduction is often thought of in terms of leading someone away from what *is* good to what is *not* good. The key, however, is to have a vision of what one is leading another to. Enticing one's spouse to engage within the framework of honoring sexuality is good. If one thinks of drawing or charming his or her partner toward a mutually agreed-on goal for intimacy, oneness, adoration, and cherishing, seduction can serve as a welcome and valuable skill.

In most marriages a wife can easily seduce her husband with her body or sensuality. This is part of the power God gave to most females. Although many a wife will hesitate—for a variety of reasons—to use this power, most husbands are very much okay with their using it. However, husbands learning how to seduce their wives can be quite difficult. Wives talk about security, protection, consideration, focused attention, and caring for her children as possible ways men can seduce. Learning that the art of seduction begins when he wakes up in the morning, not when he is thinking about sex and ready for bed, can be a powerful lesson in seduction for many men.

Spark

Spark warrants its own stage. Why? Because (1) after we have spent time seducing our spouse, we still need to transition from attracting our spouse to starting the sex act itself; and (2) I spend a great deal of time helping couples problem-solve this stage. So, what works well in spark?

Couples report some creative, hilarious, playful, and pathetic ways they initiate sex in their relationship. "How do you know your spouse is in the mood?" is my typical starting question, followed by, "How well does that work for you?" The answers to the first vary widely, but the answer to the second is all too often negative.

One wife said, "You know, he comes in and says, 'So do you wanna?'"

I asked, "So does that work for you?"

"Not . . . not really, you know."

In terms of what is normal for couples, I haven't found a "normal" way of initiating sex. In terms of boundaries—or ethics—of what works, maintaining an honoring, seductive stance and learning what works for your marriage is the key.

I said to the husband, "It doesn't sound like what you are doing is working very well."

"That's been pretty obvious," he replied, chagrined.

"I wonder what might work better?" I asked.

He huffed. "Obviously, I don't know!"

"I bet I know who does," I invited. He looked at her. I encouraged him to lean in: "Go ahead and ask her with curiosity."

It took three full sessions to help this couple sort through a variety of ways to spark the process. Both had to explore a host of trappings that came with this stage of lovemaking.

Other aspects of spark that need defining include, "What specifically are you initiating?" (as intercourse isn't the only activity available), and "Who's responsible for it?"

I often hear the higher-drive spouse comment, "I am tired of being the only one who initiates sex. I really want my spouse to initiate more." We all want to be chosen; we all want to be pursued. I believe God himself wants to be chosen and pursued. So I invite seeing initiation as a role. We tend to take the lead role for areas we find important (such as heart talk, finances, social connecting, sex). The higher-drive spouse tends to be the one who initiates sex most often. Because the husband is the higher drive spouse in 80 percent of marriages, the husband typically has the role of initiating sex. Wives in such marriages are typically in the receptive role.

Scripture does provide a model for spark to be considered. In Revelation 3:20, we read that Christ identifies himself as the groom and speaks to his bride: "Behold, I stand at the door and knock." Notice he's not trying to bust down the door. He's not trying to force the door open. He's not standing there whining and moaning and complaining about how long it's been since she has opened the door. He's not storming off down the sidewalk saying, "If you don't open the door, I'll go find another door." He just stands there and politely invites: "You know I would love to come in and be with you. I'm ready when you are." He says, "If anyone hears my voice and opens the door, I will come in to him and we will have a sensual feast together." In response to his invitation, the bride draws in the groom as she opens the door and invites him into the house. God illustrated this principle even in how he designed our bodies: To have sexual intercourse the husband needs to be strong and erect and pursue. The wife has to be soft and open and inviting.

One of the ethical questions couples ask in this stage is, "Is it acceptable to say no to sexual initiation, even if it's done well?" I would answer by asking this: "If I don't allow my spouse to say no, will I ever know when she is really saying yes?" I want to be chosen. If it isn't safe for her to say no, she can't ever really choose yes. And freedom is a good thing.

Sensation

The next stage is sensation, as the couple moves into the deeper connection of physical and emotional arousal. Keys to this stage include focusing on the sensations and arousal in addition to communicating well with one's spouse. What feels good? What is in the way of the receiving partner fully attending to the sensations in his or her body? How does one communicate to the spouse what is happening in addition to perceiving what is happening for them?

Ethical boundaries

The sensation stage is where I hear the most questions prefaced by "Can we . . . ?" If we are going to work with couples in the arena of sexuality, we have to give them a rubric that helps them sort through whether a particular behavior is acceptable. I give couples three steps to work through in making such "can we" decisions: scriptural mandates, heart issues, and personal preference.

Scriptural mandates. Sometimes I wish Scripture had more "thou shalt" and "shalt not" directives pertaining to sexuality. In reality the list of behaviors prohibited by Scripture is quite short (see Lev. 18 for one list). The New Testament expands the law to include heart principles. The writer to the Hebrews says, "Marriage should be honored by all, and the marriage bed kept pure, for God will judge the adulterer and all the sexually immoral" (13:4 NIV). The word translated here as "kept pure" means "undefiled" or "unsoiled." One lexicon defines it as "free from that by which the nature of a thing is deformed and debased, or its force and vigor impaired."[5]

Sometimes couples will come in to my office and say, "I read someplace that anything done within the marriage bed is okay." They have in mind this verse from the book of Hebrews. But the passage actually states the opposite—that we can defile what God has set apart as sacred, and it seems that what is unholy is anything that robs married sex of force or vigor. The scriptural standard here isn't what others find acceptable or what one thinks "should" be okay. Rather, what is

---

5. Bible Study Tools, "Amiantos," https://www.biblestudytools.com/lexicons/greek/kjv/amiantos.html.

"pure" refers to what adds wholeness of life to the marital bed. The questionable behavior should not be acceptable if it robs the marriage bed of life, energy, force, or vigor.

Heart issues. The second ethical boundary in the marriage bed is limiting actions to those that honor the heart of sex for that couple. What is the purpose for sex, and are both husband and wife caring for each other? Is there a sense of respect in their behaviors? Any behavior that doesn't pursue intimacy and oneness likely belongs outside the frame.

Personal preference. During therapy, one wife was talking about how she loves a particular sexual position. "It gives us such great access to each other's bodies. I love the feeling when we are engaged in this position. I think everybody ought to do it all the time. It's just the best sexual position." The wife in my very next couples' session shared how her husband enjoys that same position, but she hates it: "I feel like I'm an animal in that position. I can't imagine why anybody would enjoy it."

I was struck by how differently each wife experienced the same position, both of which were in God-honoring marriages. One wife found the position to be life-giving—it added force, vigor, and energy to her sex life with her husband. For the other wife, that same position completely robbed their marriage bed of life force and anything that was good. We must attend to personal preference without pushing, *should*-ing, or attempting to coax by normalizing.

Surrender

After the sensation stage, the next is surrender. I like the language Reed uses, because it maintains focus on the goal. The goal is not a "bigger and better buzz." And the goal is not a whole string of number-ten-type sexual encounters. Rather, the goal is a unique quality of intimacy and oneness.

Orgasm is an internal shift from the parasympathetic nervous system to the sympathetic nervous system, a shift that requires surrender. I think God gave us an important message in this design. During this stage, we also experience a flood of different chemicals such that for five to thirty minutes post-orgasm, our bodies are in a completely altered biochemical state.

That being said, orgasm is not a requirement for good sex, and it's not even a great goal. Sometimes an orgasm isn't even a possible goal. I worked with a couple in their eighties. He's learning that, because of his medical issues, his body no longer responds like it did when he was twenty. He said, "I am reaching the point of grieving the loss of ever having an orgasm again, but that doesn't mean I have to give up on sex at least twice a week with my wife. Because I still enjoy having sex with her." If sex was just about the intercourse and orgasm, they would have stopped being sexually intimate a long time ago. Keeping sex about intimacy, enjoyment, and connection allowed this couple to continue to add life to their marriage.

Reflection

During the last stage, that of reflection, the sexually intimate couple is in the postsurrender chemical bath. The invitation is to simply bask in the moment. This is rich time to connect, especially if the goal of sex is truly about oneness. At this point, for example, his oxytocin, the bonding chemical, is elevated 500 to 600 percent. He is highly open to bonding even more deeply with his wife if he attends to her during this stage.

There is a sense of vulnerability in reflection that may feel uncomfortable for some. Many times couples put their walls back up and pull away almost immediately. Yet the invitation is simply to be mindful, to be present, and to bask in the moment. Attending well to reflection helps to feed the seduction and keeps the process moving forward. There's something about lying together, looking at each other, and saying, "You are an awesome lover. I am so glad you married me." "You are so beautiful. I enjoy being with you." Affirming each other in that state of vulnerability can lift up one's spouse and strengthen the relationship.

CONCLUSION

Understanding what is "normal" for other couples may be informative, but "what others do" is an unhealthy guide for establishing a good ethical framework. Focusing on self without fully honoring and serving one's spouse is a destructive frame. In contrast, a Christian ethic of marital sexuality is one that takes into account and respects the physiology of how God designed sex to work. A Christian ethic then attends to the setting within which the sexual relationship is embedded to ensure that setting is consistent with the framework to which God calls us. Finally, a Christian ethic for sex seeks to honor and serve each other through every stage of the lovemaking cycle.

FOR DISCUSSION

1. Can what is "normal" for couples in any group ever be the foundation for a healthy sexual ethic? Why or why not?

2. Is there ever a time when it would be okay for a spouse to push the other to adjust to his or her frame for sex because of a "should"? How does your answer fit with Paul's exhortation to "work out your own salvation with fear and trembling" (Phil. 2:12)?

3. The boundary for what should and shouldn't fit within an individual couple's sexual ethic comes from the word "undefiled" in Hebrews 13:4—free from anything that would rob it of force or vigor. What are the strengths and limits of this boundary?

FOR FURTHER READING

Cutrer, William, Sandra Glahn, and Michael Sytsma. *Sexual Intimacy in Marriage*. 4th ed. Grand Rapids: Kregel, 2020.

Penner, Clifford L., and Joyce J. Penner. *The Married Guy's Guide to Great Sex*. Colorado Springs: Focus on the Family Publishing, 2017.

Rosenau, Douglas E. *A Celebration of Sex*. Rev. ed. Nashville: Thomas Nelson, 2002.

CHAPTER 14

COHABITATION: RESEARCH TRENDS AND OBSERVATIONS

SCOTT M. STANLEY

The CDC's National Center for Health Statistics (NCHS) put out a report in May 2018 on the demographics of cohabitation, with interesting contrasts among adults who are cohabiting, married, or neither.[1] The report is based on a large, representative, national survey of US adults aged eighteen to forty-four, sampled between 2011 and 2015. To conduct the analyses, the authors (Colleen Nugent and Jill Daugherty) selected only adults who had sexual intercourse with a partner of the opposite sex. They did so to ensure the groups were comparable in some respects regarding their histories in intimate relationships. The groups reflect those who were currently cohabiting, married, or neither at the time of being surveyed.

COHABITATION, MARRIAGE, OR NEITHER

The report shows that, as of 2015,

1. 17.1 percent of women and 15.9 percent of men were cohabiting;
2. 44.9 percent of women and 43.5 percent of men were married; and
3. 38.0 percent of women and 40.6 percent of men were unmarried, and not cohabiting.

---

1. Colleen Nugent and Jill Daugherty, "A Demographic, Attitudinal, and Behavioral Profile of Cohabiting Adults in the United States, 2011–2015," *National Health Statistics Reports* 111 (2018): 1–11.

This type of data does not address pathways over time, such as how many among the current cohabiters will eventually marry or how many of those not currently residing with a partner will eventually do either or neither. The data do, however, provide estimates of the number of times people in the groups had cohabited outside of marriage up to the time they were surveyed.

Sixty-seven percent of those currently married had cohabited before marriage with one or more partners.[2] Many of those currently unmarried or not cohabiting had cohabited before. Fifty-one percent of the women in that group had lived with one or more partners before, and 43 percent of the men had done likewise. Doing a little math, we estimate from the report that 64.5 percent of the entire sample have cohabited with a romantic partner at some point outside of marriage. That's not the percent of people sampled who will cohabit outside of marriage at some point in their lives, however. The lifetime percent for this group would, of course, be higher. To get that number, you'd have to follow everyone in the sample until each person had either cohabited or died. That could be a long wait.

The data on premarital cohabitation history in this sample will be an underestimate because the marrieds make up a higher percentage of the older people in that age range, and there is every reason to believe that the youngest nonmarrieds in the sample are more likely to cohabit prior to marriage than those who are older. Other estimates not based on this specific report are that the percentage of people living together before tying the knot is now at an all-time high of more than 70 percent.[3] We believe this figure will go higher still. There remain some groups, particularly the more traditionally religious,[4] who will not live together before marriage; but otherwise, cohabitation is common, and there is little stigma associated with it.

---

2. It cannot be determined from these data if this means that 67 percent would have cohabited before marriage with their spouse, but presumably that is a reasonable estimate for those doing so.

3. Paul Hemez and Wendy D. Manning, "Thirty Years of Change in Women's Premarital Cohabitation Experience," National Center for Marriage and Family Research, *Family Profiles* 5 (2017), https://www.bgsu.edu/ncfmr/resources/data/family-profiles/he-mez-manning-30-yrs-change-women-premarital-cohab-fp-17-05.html. That's for the United States, but the rates are similarly high in all industrialized nations. In a recent address to the Population Association of America, I believe Manning put that number at around 75 percent.

4. There is a nuance here for this new report. The group that is excluded by the selection criteria (about having had sexual intercourse with someone of the opposite sex) are those in that age range who have neither married nor had sexual intercourse up to this point in their lives. Because of that, the estimate of 67 percent living together before marriage for this particular age range at that point in history would be a little high. We cannot say how high, but do not doubt that the percent who will live together before marriage is now over 70 percent of the current generation of young adults.

Thus a very high percentage of people in the United States cohabit outside of marriage. It is now normative behavior. Wendy Manning has estimated that "the percentage of women ages 19–44 who have ever cohabited has increased by 82 percent over the past twenty-three years."[5] For those aged thirty to thirty-four in 2009–2010, she has shown that 73 percent of women had already cohabited with someone. If you combine such numbers with the fact that, as Susan Brown has shown, there is a steady increase in cohabitation among older adults (after the death of a spouse or divorce),[6] it is easy to imagine that the number of people who will eventually cohabit outside of marriage could reach 80 percent or more.

Cohabitation has greatly increased in large measure because, while people are delaying marriage to ever greater ages, they are not delaying sex, living together, or childbearing. In fact, on the latter point, Manning noted in her recent address to the Population Association of America that almost all of the increase in nonmarital births in the United States since 1980 has taken place in the context of cohabiting unions.

Cohabiting with more than one partner outside of marriage has also gone steadily higher.[7] The NCHS report does not demonstrate the trend, but the data reported do show that 44 percent of the currently cohabiting group and 20 percent of the neither cohabiting nor married group has already lived with *two or more* partners. Ever higher levels of serial cohabitation mean that more people are on one of the pathways strongly associated with risks for family instability or divorce.[8] Prior research has shown that serial cohabitation is strongly associated with economic disadvantage among unmarried couples,[9] lower odds of marriage, and increased odds of poor marital outcomes, but serial cohabitation is growing rapidly among different population groups.[10]

5. W. D. Manning, *Trends in Cohabitation: Over Twenty Years of Change, 1987–2010* (FP-13–12), National Center for Family & Marriage Research (2013), http://ncfmr.bgsu. edu/pdf/family_profiles/file130944.pdf.

6. Susan L. Brown, Jennifer Roebuck Bulanda, and Gary R. Lee, "Transitions Into and Out of Cohabitation in Later Life," *Journal of Marriage and Family* 74, no. 4 (2012): 774–93.

7. This trend is noted in the NCHS report, but the report itself does not present data on that trend. The authors cite earlier studies on the increase in serial cohabitation: Jessica A. Cohen and Wendy D. Manning, "The Relationship Context of Premarital Serial Cohabitation," *Social Science Research* 39, no. 5 (2010): 766—76; Daniel T. Lichter, Richard N. Turner, and Sharon Sassler, "National Estimates of the Rise in Serial Cohabitation," *Social Science Research* 39, no. 5 (2010): 754–65.

8. Lichter, Turner, and Sassler, "National Estimates," 754–65.

9. Lichter, Turner, and Sassler, "National Estimates," 754–65; Daniel T. Lichter and Zhenchao Qian, "Serial Cohabitation and the Marital Life Course," *Journal of Marriage and Family* 70, no. 4 (2008): 861–78.

10. Lichter, Turner, and Sassler, "National Estimates," 754–65.

Increasing rates of cohabitation as well as serial cohabitation might be of no special consequence except for the point noted above, that many births now occur in cohabiting unions. Some percentage of these couples has a long-term commitment similar to marriage, but on average cohabiting parents are much more likely than married parents to break up,[11] resulting in increasing odds of family instability for children. Much of this risk is due to selection, a subject we will come to below.

OTHER CHARACTERISTICS OF THESE GROUPS

Other findings from the NCHS report are consistent with the way that basic family patterns have increasingly diverged around cultural, educational, and economic lines. For example:

1. 47.9 percent of cohabiting women had household incomes less than 150 percent of the federal poverty line compared to 25.6 percent of married women.
2. 36.1 percent cohabiting men had incomes less than 150 percent of the federal poverty line compared to 21.2 percent of married men.
3. 25.2 percent cohabiting women had incomes over 300 percent of the federal poverty line compared to 48.1 percent of marrieds.
4. 32.4 percent of cohabiting men had incomes over 300 percent of the federal poverty line compared to 52.4 percent of marrieds.

This is one of the more striking examples of the fact that a lot of cohabiting women and men tend to be poor compared to married women and men. The data on education follow the same pattern, of course. Married people had the most education followed by those who are not married or cohabiting, with cohabiting people reporting lower levels of education than the other two groups. For example:

1. 25.3 percent of cohabiting women had a bachelor's degree compared to 43 percent of married women.
2. 16.2 percent of cohabiting men had a bachelor's degree compared to 36.5 percent of married men.

While the education levels of many of the cohabiters in this sample will go higher over time, the findings from many studies show that cohabitation (particularly with cohabiting relationships not leading directly to marriage) is

---

11. "Only one out of three children born to cohabiting parents remains in a stable family through age twelve, in contrast to nearly three out of four children born to married parents" (Wendy D. Manning, "Cohabitation and Child Wellbeing," *The Future of Children* 25, no. 2 (2015): 51–66; see also Sara McLanahan and Audrey N. Beck, "Parental Relationships in Fragile Families," *The Future of Children* 20, no. 2 (2010): 17–37.

associated with being more disadvantaged, on average.[12] The data are consistent with the story of a class divide around marriage and cohabitation.[13]

ATTITUDES AND EXPERIENCES

This NCHS report also presents differences in the three groups based on attitudes and experiences about unmarried sex, cohabitation, and having children outside of marriage. Not surprisingly, both of the nonmarried groups are less traditional in their views than those who are married.

While there are clear differences, large majorities of every group believe that having and raising children without being married is fine; this is endorsed by the greatest number of cohabiters. Of course, that finding would have been quite different decades ago. Marrieds are the most disapproving of cohabitation outside of marriage, but even most of the married group agreed that it is all right to do so.

Majorities of every group also believe that living together before marriage may help prevent divorce. This is of particular interest to us given our research related to this question.[14] The percentage believing this was highest for those currently cohabiting.

This notion has had wide acceptance since at least the mid 1990s, when three-fifths of high school students believed that "it is usually a good idea for a couple to live together before getting married in order to find out whether they really get along."[15] There is virtually no evidence in support of this belief. However, it is fair to note that there used be a lot clearer evidence to the contrary.

Regardless, we believe that there is considerable evidence that some patterns of living together before marriage are associated with increased risks for less success-ful marriages. We do think experiences and choices matter for future outcomes. This assertion is mildly controversial among those who study cohabitation. To be sure, there is a mountain of evidence for selection in both who cohabits and who

---

12. It is important to note that this type of data also cannot distinguish between cohabiters who will transition into marriage with their current (or a future) cohabiting partner and those who will not.

13. See, e.g., Pamela J. Smock and Fiona Rose Greenland, "Diversity in Pathways to Parent-hood: Patterns, Implications, and Emerging Research Directions," *Journal of Marriage and Family* 72, no. 3 (2010): 576–93.

14. For more on theory and research on this subject, see the following: Scott M. Stanley, "Citations for Tests of the Inertia Hypothesis about the Timing of Cohabitation and Marital Outcomes," *Sliding vs Deciding: Scott Stanley's Blog*, March 26, 2018, http://slid-ingvsdeciding.blogspot.com/2018/03/citations-for-tests-of-inertia_26.html; and Scott M. Stanley and Galena K. Rhoades, "A Summary of Our Work on Cohabitation," July 2018, https://app.box.com/s/ugfa85i6lly8hp76qey7. These sources include summaries and links to many (non-gated) papers.

15. Arland Thornton and Linda Young-DeMarco, "Four Decades of Trends in Attitudes toward Family Issues in the United States: The 1960s through the 1990s," *Journal of Marriage and Family* 63, no. 4 (2001): 1009–37.

will cohabit in the riskier ways. What this means is that people who are already at greater risk for worse outcomes in relationships because of things like family background, disadvantage, or individual vulnerabilities are also more likely to do any of the following: cohabit and not marry, cohabit before having clear, mutual plans to marry, or cohabit with a number of different partners over time. There is plenty of evidence of other patterns in the NCHS report related to cohabiters being more select for various relationship risks. Consider the following findings.

RELATIONSHIP RISKS ASSOCIATED WITH COHABITATION

Cohabiters were more likely (74 percent) than those currently married (56 percent) to have had sexual intercourse before the age of eighteen. Cohabiting women were also more likely to report ever having an unintended birth (43.5 percent) compared to married women (23.9 percent). These types of patterns are associated with lifelong risk factors already present in the lives of many people. Of course, you could argue that such differences also reflect choices people make that have potentially causal, life-altering consequences. Such debates are endless, but we do not doubt a huge role for selection in all of this. And yet, we believe there often are causal elements affecting life outcomes related to the experience of cohabitation.

First, it has been shown that cumulative cohabiting experience changes peoples' beliefs about marriage.[16] While that research is older, the theory behind the research is compelling. Much research shows we learn from experiences, and experiences change our beliefs. We believe that the increase in cohabitation, serial cohabitation, and premarital cohabitation has led to consistent downward trends in belief that marriage is special.

Second, cohabitation makes it harder to break up, net of everything else. Because of the inertia of living together, some people get stuck longer than they otherwise would in relationships they might have left, or left sooner.[17] In fact we believe some people marry someone they would otherwise have left because cohabitation made it too hard to move on. Inertia can be the greatest problem for couples who had not decided beforehand on their future, such as by already having mutual plans to marry (e.g., engagement) or, of course, by first marrying. While the increased risk can be modest, the prediction is consistently supported with at least seven reports using six different samples, showing that those who start cohabiting before deciding to marry report lower average marital quality and are more likely to divorce.[18] This added risk is compounded by the fact that

---

16. William G. Axinn and Jennifer S. Barber, "Living Arrangements and Family Formation Attitudes in Early Adulthood," *Journal of Marriage and Family* 59, no. 3 (August 1997): 595–611.

17. Scott M. Stanley, Galena K. Rhoades, and Howard J. Markman, "Sliding versus Deciding: Inertia and the Premarital Cohabitation Effect," *Family Relations* 55, no. 4 (2006): 499–509.

18. In addition to the list of the body of studies on the marriage-plans timing effect (partial list following), a recent study shows that relationship quality is highest (on average) for

most couples slide into cohabiting rather than making a clear decision about what it means and what their futures may hold.[19]

Third, cohabitation is increasingly a context for childbearing. Since cohabiting parental unions are relatively unstable, the increasing number[20] of couples who break up[21] in such unions will mean more people entering future relationships with the challenge of children in tow.

Evidence of selection abounds, but so do reasons for believing that experiences[22] and personal choices[23] are relevant to life outcomes.

COMPLEXITY ABOUNDS

These ever-changing patterns in relationship and family development are complex, and they do not operate in the same way for all. For example, there

---

married and lowest for cohabiting couples without plans to marry, with marrieds who cohabited before marriage and cohabiters who currently had plans in between those two groups: Susan L. Brown, Wendy D. Manning, and Krista K. Payne, "Relationship Quality among Cohabiting Versus Married Couples," *Journal of Family Issues* 38, no. 12 (2017): 1730–53. (First appeared in advance online publication in 2015: https://doi.org/10.1177/0192513X15622236); examples of studies with the engagement-plans timing effect see Galena H. Kline et al., "Timing Is Everything: Pre-engagement Cohabitation and Increased Risk for Poor Marital Outcomes," *Journal of Family Psychology* 18, no. 2 (2004): 311–18.; Galena K. Rhoades, Scott M. Stanley, and Howard J. Markman, "The Pre-engagement Cohabitation Effect: A Replication and Extension of Previous Findings," *Journal of Family Psychology* 23, no. 1 (2009): 107–11; Scott M. Stanley et al., "The Timing of Cohabitation and Engagement: Impact on First and Second Marriages," *Journal of Marriage and Family* 72, no. 4 (2010): 906–18.

19. See Jo M. Lindsay, "An Ambiguous Commitment: Moving into a Cohabiting Relationship," *Journal of Family Studies* 6, no.1 (2000): 120–34; Wendy D. Manning and Pamela J. Smock, "Measuring and Modeling Cohabitation: New Perspectives from Qualitative Data," *Journal of Marriage and Family* 67, no. 4 (2005): 989–1002; Scott M. Stanley, Galena K. Rhoades, and Frank D. Fincham, "Understanding Romantic Relationships among Emerging Adults: The Significant Roles of Cohabitation and Ambiguity," in *Romantic Relationships in Emerging Adulthood*, ed. Frank D. Fincham and Ming Cui (Cambridge: Cambridge University Press, 2011), 234–51.

20. Scott M. Stanley, "Not Your Steppin Stone," *Sliding vs Deciding: Scott Stanley's Blog*, January 16, 2014, http://slidingvsdeciding.blogspot.com/2014/01/not-your-steppin-stone.html.

21. Scott M. Stanley, "Moving In and Moving On: Cohabitation is Less Likely Than Ever to Lead to Marriage," *Sliding vs Deciding: Scott Stanley's Blog*, July 25, 2014, http://slidingvsdeciding.blogspot.com/2014/07/moving-in-and-moving-on-cohabitation-is_25.html.

22. Scott M. Stanley and Galena K. Rhoades, "Practice May Not Make Perfect: Relationship Experience and Marital Success," *Institute for Family Studies Blog*, March 17, 2016, https://ifstudies.org/blog/practice-may-not-make-perfect-relationship-experience-and-marital-success.

23. Scott M. Stanley and Galena K. Rhoades, "Selection Effects and Personal Choice," *Institute for Family Studies Blog*, August 20, 2014, https://ifstudies.org/blog/selection-effects-and-personal-choice.

is research[24] suggesting that cohabiting experiences may lead to more positive attitudes about marriage among young African American adults. More broadly, as Sharon Sassler and Amanda Miller argue in *Cohabitation Nation*,[25] there are various social-class disparities that have an impact on things such as whether and how soon a person will move in with a partner. Some pathways will lead to different sets of outcomes for different people, and some people have more ability (economic and personal) to avoid paths that increase the odds of poor outcomes.[26] The extraordinary changes of the past four decades reflect how ordinary cohabitation has become. There is not a simple story here, only an ever-unfolding one of increasingly complex families.

PREMARITAL COHABITATION AND THE ODDS OF DIVORCE

One of the most perplexing findings in the history of the study of marriage is that living together beforehand is associated with greater, not lesser, odds of struggling in marriage. This association had been clear in study after study up to around 2007, and then a number of studies and social scientists declared that the association between living together before marriage and difficulties in marriage had disappeared. To be clear, we never thought the association had disappeared. While we believe the association got weaker, we have long believed that the understanding of it mostly became better understood. For example, we predicted and found—repeatedly, and in numerous samples— that an important part of the story had to do with whether a couple started living together before or after having come to a clear commitment to marry. Those who cohabited only after engagement (or marriage, of course) have an edge in odds for doing well in marriage compared to those who started living together before clarifying the big question about the future. We will explain that more below.

Among some scholars in family science, the belief had been settled that there simply is no risk for worse outcomes in marriage associated with living together beforehand. But that no-risk story just received a jolt. A new study published in the *Journal of Marriage and Family*[27] finds that the "premarital cohabitation effect" lives on, despite earlier claims to the contrary. The premarital

---

24. Scott M. Stanley, "How Cohabitation Shapes African Americans' Marriage Attitudes," *Institute for Family Studies Blog*, September 28, 2015, https://ifstudies.org/blog/how-cohabitation-shapes-young-african-americans-marriage-attitudes.

25. Sharon Sassler and Amanda Jayne Miller, *Cohabitation Nation: Gender, Class, and the Remaking of Relationships* (Oakland, CA: University of California Press, 2017).

26. For example, Sharon Sassler, Katherine Michelmore, and Zhenchao Qian, "Transitions from Sexual Relationships into Cohabitation and Beyond," *Demography* 55, no. 2 (2018): 511–34.

27. Michael Rosenfeld and Katharina Roesler, "Cohabitation Experience and Cohabitation's Association with Marital Dissolution," *Journal of Marriage and Family* 81, no. 1 (2019): 42–58.

cohabitation effect is what this is all about: the finding (over many studies, over decades of time) that those who live together prior to marriage are more likely, not less, to struggle in marriage.

The new study is by Michael Rosenfeld and Katharina Roesler. Their findings suggest that there remains an increased risk for divorce for those living together prior to marriage, and that prior studies suggesting the effect went away had a bias toward analyzing shorter- versus longer-term effects. They found that living together before marriage was associated with lower odds of divorce in the first year of marriage, but increased odds of divorce in all other years tested, and this finding held across decades of data.

NUMEROUS RECENT STUDIES REPORTED NO IMPACT OF PREMARITAL COHABITATION

A number of relatively recent studies suggested that the premarital cohabitation effect had gone away for those marrying in the past ten or fifteen years. Rosenfeld and Roesler pay particular attention to a report from the NCHS by Copen, Daniels, Vespa, and Mosher in 2012, which suggested there was no increased risk associated with premarital cohabitation, in the most recent (at the time) cohort of the National Survey of Family Growth (NSFG; 2006–2010).[28] The NSFG is a large, ongoing sampling of those living in the United States with regard to many aspects of family formation, cohabitation, and marriage. Other researchers, such as Wendy Manning and Jessica Cohen,[29] reached the same conclusion as the authors of the NCHS in 2012, incorporating data from as late as the 2006 to 2008 cohort of the NSFG.[30]

While all of these studies used the same large sampling effort, Rosenfeld and Roesler had longer-term data for the most recent cohort they studied (up to 2015). Contrary to these prior conclusions, they found that there remains a clear link between premarital cohabitation and increased odds of divorce regardless of the year or cohort studied. (In all these studies, the focus is on first marriages.)

Many experts believed that the cohabitation effect, well understood since the 1980s, would go away as living together became more the thing to do— that it would no longer be associated with negative outcomes in marriage. This hypothesis is based on the idea that the prior stigma among friends and family about living together before marriage was a cause of the increased risk. And

---

28. Casey E. Copen et al., "First Marriages in the United States: Data From the 2006–2010 National Survey of Family Growth," CDC National Health Statistics Reports, Number 49, March 22, 2012, https://www.cdc.gov/nchs/data/nhsr/nhsr049.pdf.

29. Wendy D. Manning and Jessica A. Cohen, "Premarital Cohabitation and Marital Dissolution: An Examination of Recent Marriages," *Journal of Marriage and Family* 74, no. 2 (2012): 377–87.

30. Why the new paper does not cite or address the findings by Manning and Cohen is mystifying. Theirs is the most recent major study directly addressing the question Rosenfeld and Roesler examine.

clearly, there is not much, if any, stigma now. The other reason for expecting the cohabitation effect to go away is a little more arcane, having to do with the fact that as it became common (at least 70 percent of couples live together before marriage now), those who chose to do so are no longer more select for being at greater risk than others.

Based on a different line of reasoning than the other studies suggesting no risk, another prominent study had also concluded that there was no longer an added risk for divorce associated with premarital cohabitation. However, in that study, Arielle Kuperberg[31] concluded the risk was more about moving in together at a young age (before the middle twenties) than moving in together before marriage per se. That's one among many potentially important nuances in this complex literature.[32]

PUMPING THE BRAKES ON THE CONCLUSIONS OF NO ADDED RISK

Cohabitation is the gift that keeps on giving to family science, providing generations of scholars with the opportunity to say, "Look here, wow, this is strange." And people remain interested. We have seen major stories on cohabitation break across the media for more than twenty years, because it's interesting. In fact, there was a 2018 story in *The Atlantic*[33] about this very thing, and it includes numerous quotes from Galena Rhoades, based on our work. We think this subject keeps getting lots of ink because the findings have tended to be so counterintuitive. Most people believe that living together before marriage should improve the odds of doing well in marriage. Yet whatever else is true, there is very scant evidence to support this belief in a positive effect.[34]

There is something to learn from the research that bears on what pathways may be wiser than others for the average person. Rosenfeld and Roesler's study is quite complex statistically, but their insight boils down to two things easily

---

31. Arielle Kuperberg, "Age at Coresidence, Premarital Cohabitation, and Marriage Dissolution: 1985–2009," *Journal of Marriage and Family* 76, no. 2 (2014): 352–69.

32. Stanley wrote about the Kuperberg study at that time, taking far more issue with the media stories about it than the actual study, suggesting there are many ways people could misconstrue to whom those, and other findings of differential risk, applied. Those articles are: Scott M. Stanley, "Time to 'Go Ahead and Shack Up'?," *Institute for Family Studies Blog*, March 20, 2014, https://ifstudies.org/blog/time-to-go-ahead-and-shack-up; and Stanley, "The Complex Risks Associated with Cohabitation," *Institute for Family Studies Blog*, April 3, 2014, https://ifstudies.org/blog/the-complex-risks-associated-with-cohabitation.

33. Ashley Fetters, "So Is Living Together before Marriage Linked to Divorce or What?," *The Atlantic*, October 24, 2018, https://www.theatlantic.com/family/archive/2018/10/premarital-cohabitation-divorce/573817/.

34. Scott M. Stanley, "The Mystery: Why Isn't Living Together Beforehand Associated with Improved Odds in Marriage?," *Sliding vs Deciding: Scott Stanley's Blog*, July 29, 2014, http://slidingvsdeciding.blogspot.com/2014/07/the-mystery-why-isnt-living-together.html.

explained. First, they believe studies which suggested that the premarital co-habitation effect has disappeared simply did not have outcomes for divorce far enough out for those who had married in the recent cohorts that they examined. Second, they show that premarital cohabitation is associated with a lower risk for divorce, but only very early in marriage (in the first year); in contrast, the finding flips, with premarital cohabitation being associated with higher risks for divorce in years after that first year. That's what earlier studies could not address.

In particular, Rosenfeld and Roesler suggest that those who live together before marriage have an advantage in the first year, because they are already used to all the changes that come with living together. Those who go straight into marriage without living together have a bigger immediate shock to negotiate after marriage and, as a result, have a short-term increased risk that's greater than those already living together. But that's the short term, and the risk remains long term.

THEORIES OF INCREASED RISK

There are three main theories for how living together before marriage could be causally associated with worse outcomes (on average) in marriage. Rosenfeld and Roesler address the first two but say nothing about the third.[35]

Selection

The selection theory is simply that there are many factors associated with who cohabits when, why, and with whom, and that those factors are also associated with how marriages will turn out, regardless of cohabiting experience. For example, it's well known that those who are more economically disadvantaged are more likely to do the following: live together outside of marriage; live together with more than one partner; have a child with a cohabiting partner prior to marrying; and struggle in marriage. Other factors are religiousness, traditionality, and family history (such as parental divorce). The selection explanation is that those who cohabit in riskier ways (e.g., before marriage, before engagement, with more than one partner) were already at greater risk. In the strongest view of selection, living together does not add to the risk at all, because it's all already baked in. There is a lot of evidence for selection playing an important role in this literature, and scholars in this area note this and address it in various ways.

The Experience of Cohabiting Changes Things

In an older line of research that was clever, but needs to be tested again with those marrying in more recent years, William Axinn and Jennifer Barber showed

---

35. This omission does not seem as striking to us as the omission of Manning and Cohen's paper, since their paper is already complex, and they are intent on addressing one moderator of the cohabitation effect: how long after marriage the effect is measured. They do not address at all the growing literature on moderators of the cohabitation effect. Still, inertia is one of the major theories of increased risk, and only selection itself has more publications addressing it.

that cohabiting changes attitudes about marriage and divorce, lowering esteem for marriage and increasing acceptance of divorce.[36] This is consistent with scores of studies in psychology showing that attitudes will cohere to behavior. In other words, people will bring beliefs around to fit their behavior. Earlier, Thornton, Axinn, and Hill showed that cohabiting led to people becoming less religious.[37] Rosenfeld and Roesler included a lot on the theory of experience, but mostly they used it to emphasize the short-term benefit of already experiencing living together when transitioning into marriage.

Inertia

We have argued since the early 2000s for another causal theory in this line of research. Drawing on theories of commitment, we suggested that what nearly everyone misses in understanding the risk associated with cohabitation is pretty simple: Moving in together makes it harder to break up, net of everything else. The added risk is due to how cohabitation substantially increases constraints to remain together prior to a dedication to a future together maturing between two partners. Two key papers on this perspective are footnoted.[38]

One primary prediction from the inertia hypothesis is that those who started living together only after being already committed to marriage (e.g., by engagement or actual marriage) should, on average, do better in marriage than those who may have prematurely made it harder to break up by living together before agreeing on marriage. The inertia hypothesis completely embraces selection, suggesting that relationships already at greater risk become harder to exit because of cohabitation. Various predictions from the inertia hypothesis have been supported in ten or more studies,[39] seven of which include tests of the prediction about pre-cohabitation level of commitment to marriage (a.k.a. plans for marriage prior to living together)—and this latter finding exists in at least six different samples across a range of outcomes.[40]

There is no particular reason to expect that the inertia risk will dissipate with increased acceptance of cohabitation, because the mechanism is about the timing of the development of aspects of commitment, not about societal views and personal attitudes. For living together to lower risk in marriage, the benefit of

---

36. Axinn and Barber, "Living Arrangements and Family Formation."
37. A. Thornton et al., "Reciprocal Effects of Religiosity, Cohabitation, and Marriage," *American Journal of Sociology* 98, no. 3 (1992), 628–51, https://doi.org/10.1086/230051.
38. Stanley, S. M., Rhoades, G.K., and Markman, H. J., "Sliding versus Deciding: Inertia and the Premarital Cohabitation Effect," *Family Relations* 55, no. 4 (2006): 499–509; and Stanley and Rhoades, "Summary."
39. Scott M. Stanley, "Citations for Tests of the Inertia Hypothesis about the Timing of Cohabitation and Marital Outcomes," *Sliding vs Deciding: Scott Stanley's Blog*, March 26, 2018, http://slidingvsdeciding.blogspot.com/2018/03/citations-for-tests-of-inertia_26.html.
40. We have found evidence for inertia whether or not someone has cohabited only with their mate, and in numerous samples of people marrying after 2000 and later.

learning something disqualifying about a partner has to exceed the costs of making it harder to break up that come with sharing a single address. Hence, inertia is another possibility, along with experience, that could explain the persistence of a cohabitation effect, such as that found by Rosenfeld and Roesler.[41]

Other Possibilities

Other factors that may be associated with differential outcomes include pacing;[42] age at the time of moving in together;[43] and having children before marriage.[44] All such theories suggest that the risks of living together before marriage are greater for some people than others. Rosenfeld and Roesler are not really addressing this issue. They did find, however, that the risks associated with premarital cohabitation were lower for African Americans. While that's a subject far beyond our focus here, it does not surprise us. For most groups, cohabitation is no particular indicator of higher commitment.[45] However, it may well signal higher levels of commitment among groups where marriage has declined a great deal, such as among African Americans.

Rosenfeld and Roesler also note that the risks of living together before marriage were even greater among those who had lived with more than just their mate prior to marriage. That finding is consistent with many other studies.[46]

THE EFFECT AND THE CONTROVERSY LIVES

Research on premarital cohabitation has long been mired in arguments about causality, with the dominant view being that what we describe about selection explains most, if not all, of the added risk, when found. However, many studies in the history of this field have controlled for all sorts of variables associated with selection and still found an additional risk. In fairness, it is not possible to control for all aspects of selection in such studies. Without randomly assigning people to walk different pathways before marriage, causality can never be proved. And we think it's going to be a long time before researchers are allowed to flip a

---

41. As an interesting side point on the subject of the inertia hypothesis, the commitment-to-marriage timing effect exists in the NSFG. It was mentioned in passing in a working paper leading up to the 2010 publication by Reinhold, and it is mentioned prominently in the abstract (and paper) in Manning and Cohen, "Premarital Cohabitation."

42. Sassler, Michelmore, and Qian, "Transitions," 511–34.

43. Kuperberg, "Age at Coresidence," 352–69.

44. Laura Tach and Sarah Halpern-Meekin, "How Does Premarital Cohabitation Affect Trajectories of Marital Quality?," *Journal of Marriage and Family* 71, no. 2 (2009): 298–317.

45. Scott M. Stanley, "Give Me a Sign: What Signals Commitment?," *Sliding vs Deciding: Scott Stanley's Blog*, July 5, 2017, https://slidingvsdeciding.blogspot.com/2017/07/give-me-sign-what-signals-commitment.html.

46. E.g., Jay Teachman, "Premarital Sex, Premarital Cohabitation, and the Risk of Subsequent Marital Dissolution among Women," *Journal of Marriage and Family* 65, no. 2. (2003): 444–55.

coin about who does what in their love lives so that we can study the phenomena better. Oh, how great that would be, though, for figuring things out. Since we have to live with studying what people end up doing on their own, arguments ensue. Besides, since when does evidence stop arguing anyway when people are passionate about their view on something? Rosenfeld and Roesler's new study breathed life into a finding many concluded was dead.

FOR DISCUSSION

1. What do you think accounts for the significant increase in cohabitation over the past three decades? What has contributed to the "sliding versus deciding" trend?

2. What is your response to the report that the percentage of people living together before tying the knot is now at an all-time high of more than 70 percent of couples, and will continue to increase in the future?

3. How do biblical teaching on relationships and the current research findings on relationships sync up? What is the significance of commitment in outcomes of stability and satisfaction in relationships from the viewpoint of both research and the Bible?

FOR FURTHER READING

Rosenfeld, Michael, and Katharina Roesler. "Cohabitation Experience and Co-habitation's Association with Marital Dissolution." *Journal of Marriage and Family* 81, no. 1 (2019): 42–58.

Stanley, Scott M., Galena K. Rhoades, and Frank D. Fincham. "Understanding Romantic Relationships among Emerging Adults: The Significant Roles of Cohabitation and Ambiguity." In *Romantic Relationships in Emerging Adulthood*, edited by Frank D. Fincham and Ming Cui, 234–51. Cambridge: Cambridge University Press 2011.

Stanley, Scott M., Galena K. Rhoades, and Howard J. Markman. "Sliding versus Deciding: Inertia and the Premarital Cohabitation Effect." *Family Relations* 55, no. 4 (2006): 499–509.

CHAPTER 15

DIVORCE AND REMARRIAGE: EVIDENCE FROM THE BIBLICAL TEXT

W. HALL HARRIS

INTRODUCTION

The topic of divorce and remarriage in the church today is difficult to talk about. It is extremely difficult because, first of all, there are New Testament passages that are not totally clear about what exactly is involved or permitted. Furthermore, there are some Old Testament texts that come into the discussion, and we have to take at least a preliminary look at those to get some understanding of where the New Testament is coming from. Part of what I'm going to do is simply to walk us through the key passages in the Bible related to divorce and remarriage. Then I will try to provide some insight into the New Testament perspective and what the interpretive options are. Following this examination of biblical texts, there is the need to explore more about current practices, that is, what goes on today. There are serious hermeneutical issues involved with addressing current approaches to divorce and remarriage. First, I think it is simplistic to insist that our practice exactly conforms to the New Testament practice when we are not absolutely sure what the New Testament practice is to begin with. Second, there's the question of whether the church down through the ages has the right, permission, or ability to modify some of the biblical teachings from the first century to respond to changes in culture and historical setting. The need for answering this second question may come as a surprise to some people, but I would simply observe that if we read the book of Acts closely, we see the apostle Paul making those kinds of adjustments to differing cultural situations (particularly among the gentiles, the primary target audience of his gospel proclamation) on numerous occasions. But the refinement that goes along with the second question will have to wait. First, we have to sift through the biblical evidence on divorce and remarriage, beginning with the Old Testament.

To illustrate the difficulties in making sense of the three Synoptic Gospels alone (Matthew, Mark, and Luke) on divorce, I begin with a quote from a British scholar, J. L. Houlden, who summarized the problems this way:

> There is a vital, common connection about the relations between the sexes underlying the positions we have outlined. It meant an enhanced position for women, which went quite beyond much Jewish practice. But by the time our writers were at work, there had come from it four quite distinct lines, or at any rate, context or argument. Paul is situational and eschatological; his question is, "What, in the light of the Lord's Word and the imminence of the end shall Christians do?" Mark is concerned with theology, God's fundamental will in the matter, and the nature of man. Matthew presents a rabbinic argument on the basis of Torah; his concern is chiefly practical. Luke wishes to encourage compassion. Assuming that there was a word from Jesus, which in some terms or other opposed divorce, we cannot tell what its context was. And already by the end of the first century, Christians had contextualized it in writing in four quite different ways. In practical terms, four distinct policies were available. How rough and ready, then, seems the tradition by which we live, which is to enforce upon Christians the Markan teaching in a Matthean spirit.[1]

Houlden's point is well taken. There is ample agreement among our sources (Matthew, Mark, Luke, and Paul—with Paul the earliest) to conclude that Jesus indeed addressed divorce, and in some sense, limited it or condemned it outright. But each of the sources has placed that teaching in its own context, for its own purposes, and so we cannot determine the original context in which Jesus himself spoke these pronouncements with any certainty.

These problems are not limited to the New Testament. Before examining Old Testament texts on the topic, we must consider another comment, this one by Robert Wall: "The biblical teaching on divorce is much debated for two reasons. First, while the relevant texts are not numerous, they provoke exegetical issues, which are complex and difficult. Second, since the church and synagogue look to Scripture for moral guidance and since divorce continues to be a pressing moral problem, the pastoral issues these texts envisage are important and urgent."[2]

---

1. J. L. Houlden, *Ethics and the New Testament* (London: T&T Clark, 1992), 80.
2. Robert W. Wall, "Divorce," in *The Anchor Bible Dictionary*, ed. David Noel Freedman (New York: Doubleday, 1992), 2:217.

CRUCIAL OLD TESTAMENT TEXTS

Deuteronomy 24:1–4

"If a man marries a woman and she does not please him because he has found something indecent in her, then he may draw up a divorce document, give it to her, and evict her from his house. When she has left him, she may go and become someone else's wife. If the second husband rejects her and then divorces her, gives her the papers, and evicts her from his house, or if the second husband who married her dies, her first husband who divorced her is not permitted to remarry her after she has become ritually impure, for that is offensive to the LORD. You must not bring guilt on the land that the LORD your God is giving you as an inheritance" (Deut. 24:1–4 NET). This text, along with Genesis 2:22–24 (the well-known "leave and cleave" passage, which was viewed as establishing marriage), formed the center of the great debate over divorce among the rabbis of the Second Temple period.[3] The debate concerned the grounds for a legitimate divorce, which we'll return to shortly. The text of Deuteronomy 24:1–4 (also recalled later in Jer. 3:1) assumes the presence of divorce in the culture of the time; it gives regulations under which a wife could legally be divorced by her husband. Note that no reciprocal right of divorce of the husband by the wife is envisioned here. The Jewish approach allowed the husband the right to divorce his wife, but did not extend the same privilege to the wife to divorce her husband.[4] We will see later that in gentile (non-Jewish) culture, there were reciprocal rights of divorce for husbands and wives. The point of Deuteronomy 24:4 is that the wife divorced by husband number one who then marries husband number two is never under any circumstances permitted to marry husband number one again, regardless of whether husband number two divorces her or dies. Presumably, though not explicitly stated in the text, the woman divorced by husband number two, or widowed by his death, is permitted to marry husband number three. She is merely forbidden from returning to husband number one. Also not stated is whether the process continues indefinitely. So, if this wife is divorced by husband number three, or widowed by his death, she cannot return to remarry either husband number one or number two, though this progression is not explicitly stated either. This "prohibition of return," however, does not apply at all to the question posed to Jesus in Matthew 22:28 and parallels. In this well-known incident, the wife has seven husbands, they die one after the other, and then Jesus is asked whose wife she will be in the resurrection, because all the husbands had her as wife. To this

---

3. The Second Temple period is also referred to as the intertestamental period, the period between the conclusion of the Old Testament and the beginning of the New, several hundred years BC.

4. Some attribute the lack of reciprocity to the patriarchal society of the time, but whatever the cause, it was still in effect in the Jewish culture of Judea in the first century AD.

Jesus replied in effect, "Wait a minute. You are wrong. They neither marry nor are given in marriage, but are like the angels in heaven, so that situation doesn't apply."[5] But the question originally asked of Jesus ("Whose wife will she be?") doesn't answer the question posed by Deuteronomy 24:4, because all previous husbands in the Matthew 22 example are presumed to have died, and thus the woman (while still alive) could not return to any of the previous ones who were dead. In any case, the point of the Deuteronomy 24 text is to prevent a woman from remarrying her former husband in the case where she has been married to other husbands in the intervening period. It says nothing about remarrying the former husband if she has not remarried someone else after being divorced from the first husband. Presumably, this would be permitted, because the reason given for the prohibition against remarrying the original husband is that the woman has been "ritually impure" by her marriage to the second husband (v. 4), and this would not be the case if the woman remained unmarried after the original divorce from her first husband.

This brings us to the great debate in the Second Temple period between two rabbinic schools led by the rabbis Shammai and Hillel, who lived at the end of the first century BC and the early part of the first century AD. Their views were well known in Jesus's day. The debate they had over Deuteronomy 24:1 revolved around the meaning of the phrase "something indecent"—literally, a "shameful thing" or a "repulsive thing," according to the Hebrew—which forms the cause for the man to divorce his wife. Rabbi Shammai's followers were the narrow and restrictive ones. They believed the phrase "indecent thing" had to refer to some sort of immoral or indecent sexual behavior (almost universally agreed to be related to adultery). Rabbi Hillel's disciples held a much broader interpretation that said that a man, if he found an "indecent thing" in his wife, could divorce her. The "indecent thing" could be inability to have children, failing to keep the ritual law of Judaism adequately, or even bad cooking—if she spoiled his meal. These positions are summarized in the Mishnah, the later collection of Jewish commentary on the Torah that is dated to around AD 175, and the even later Babylonian Talmud, which is dated to the end of the sixth century, circa AD 575.

The section on divorce is found in Gittin 9–10 in the Mishnah and Gittin 90a in the later Talmud. It takes the form of a dialogue between the rabbis, which is how the Mishnah typically works: "The House of Shammai say, 'A man should divorce his wife only because he has found grounds for it in unchastity since it is said, "Because he has found in her indecency in anything," (Deuteronomy 24).' And the House of Hillel say, 'Even if she spoiled his dish, since it is said, "Because he has found indecency in her in anything."' Rabbi Akiva says, 'Even if he found someone else prettier than she since it is said, Deuteronomy 24:1, "And it shall be if she find no favor in his eyes."'" It seems clear that Rabbi

---

5. My paraphrase of Matt. 22:29–30.

Akiva had broadened the meaning of "indecency" here even beyond that of the Hillelites!

It is important to note that the teaching of Jesus in the New Testament, particularly—with the exceptions given in Matthew 5:31–32 and Matthew 19:3–9—is best understood against the background of this rabbinic debate. Every technical commentary on Matthew since the mid nineteenth century has held that the debate between the schools of Shammai and Hillel is behind Jesus's debate with the Pharisees over divorce in Matthew 19, without exception. Such is really pretty much a closed case as far as New Testament scholarship is concerned.

Malachi 2:16

A reference in Malachi is the only other Old Testament passage to be considered, and that only briefly. It contains the famous "I hate divorce" line (literally in Hebrew, "I hate sending away," but it is generally understood that "sending away" here means "divorce"). This passage is often quoted as a proof text for the view that holds to no divorce for any reason whatsoever. However, in the context of Malachi 2, the reference is not universal, but refers to one Jewish person divorcing another Jewish person. Technically, it does not contradict the call of Ezra (Ezra 9–10) for Jewish men to divorce their heathen wives. Taking the context of Malachi 2 into consideration seems to make the statement a little less absolute.

CRUCIAL NEW TESTAMENT TEXTS

Direct Teaching from Jesus in the Gospels

Matthew 5:31–32

Jesus told his disciples, "It was said, 'Whoever divorces his wife must give her a legal document.' But I say to you that everyone who divorces his wife, except for immorality, makes her commit adultery, and whoever marries a divorced woman commits adultery" (Matt. 5:31–32 NET). The initial passage on divorce in Matthew is part of the Sermon on the Mount (Matt. 5–7); in fact, verse 31 with its "legal document" sounds very much like an allusion to Deuteronomy 24:1–4. The phrasing of the exception clause "except for immorality" appears to reflect pretty closely the Shammai phrase "indecency in anything," where "anything" translates the Hebrew דָּבָר, "word, thing, matter," exactly in parallel to the Greek text of Matthew 5:32, where the term is λόγος, "word, thing, matter." In other words, the lexical meaning of דָּבָר in Hebrew and λόγος in Greek overlap here. So in effect the two passages are talking about the same thing. The similarity of the wording between Jesus's phrase here and the phrase used by the school of Shammai suggests that Jesus is following Shammai's interpretation of Deuteronomy 24:1 by limiting the only legitimate cause for divorce to some type of sexual immorality. On the other hand, it is somewhat surprising that in Matthew's gospel Jesus uses the Greek word πορνεία for "immorality" instead of the more specific term μοιχεία, which refers to adultery. Πορνεία has a much broader meaning in both the New Testament and the Greco-Roman culture of the time; the most common meaning is "sexual immorality in general" (cf. Acts 15:20; Eph. 5:3; Col. 3:5). In effect, this broadens the reasons for legitimate divorce beyond "technical adultery" to other more general instances of sexual immorality. Also note that according to Matthew 5:32 the husband incurs culpability as well, indicated by phrases such as "makes her commit adultery" and "whoever marries a divorced woman commits adultery."

Matthew 19:3–9

The reference to divorce in Matthew 19 is part of a controversy dialogue with Jesus's opponents the Pharisees:

> Then some Pharisees came to him in order to test him. They asked, "Is it lawful to divorce a wife for any cause?" He answered, "Have you not read that from the beginning the Creator made them male and female, and said, 'For this reason a man will leave his father and mother and will be united with his wife, and the two will become one flesh'? So they are no longer two, but one flesh. Therefore, what God has joined together, let no one separate." They said to him, "Why then did Moses command us to give a certificate of dismissal and to divorce her?" Jesus said to them, "Moses permitted you to divorce your wives because of your hard hearts, but from the beginning it was not this way. Now I say to you that whoever divorces his wife, except for immorality, and marries another commits adultery." (Matt. 19:3–9 NET)

The mention of the "any cause" divorce by the Pharisees (v. 3) almost certainly alludes to the "anything" divorce of the school of Hillel discussed earlier. The purpose of the Pharisees was "to test him," that is, to force Jesus to declare himself on the side of the school of Shammai or the school of Hillel in the divorce debate of Second Temple Judaism. In his reply, Jesus quoted Genesis 2:24 in relation to marriage and underscored the permanence of the marriage bond as ordained by God. Apparently puzzled by how Jesus's statement fits with the "divorce document" required by Deuteronomy 24:1, the Pharisees saw Jesus as contradicting Moses. So they asked, "Why then did Moses command us to give a certificate of dismissal and to divorce her?"

Jesus resolved the contradiction by correcting the Pharisees. He changed "Why then did Moses *command* us" to "Moses *permitted* you to divorce your wives because of your hard hearts." Then Jesus continued, "*But from the beginning it was not this way.*" His qualification is usually understood to refer to the original plan of God for permanent, lifelong marriage relationships.

Mark 10:1–12

Just when it appeared that Jesus had successfully resolved the problem in Matthew by pointing out that the Pharisees were misquoting Moses, that fine distinction is overturned in Mark 10:2. That text says, "Then some Pharisees came, and to test him they asked, 'Is it lawful for a man to divorce his wife?' He answered them, 'What did Moses command you?' They said, 'Moses permitted a man to write a certificate of dismissal and to divorce her.'"

Here Jesus said "command," and the Pharisees said "permit." Following this, verses 6–8 are essentially the same as Matthew 19:5–6, with Jesus quoting Genesis 2 again. Then Mark 10:9 says, "Therefore what God has joined together, let no one separate." This was mentioned earlier in Matthew 19:6. Mark continues with a private clarification by Jesus to his disciples: "In the house once again, the disciples asked him about this. So he told them, 'Whoever divorces his wife and marries another commits adultery against her. And if she divorces her husband and marries another, she commits adultery'" (vv. 10–12 NET). Here, Jesus did extend the teaching to cover a woman divorcing her husband, something not addressed in Deuteronomy 24 or in Matthew 19, or, as we'll see, in Luke 16:18. But the qualification "except for immorality" that Matthew included is not found in Mark or Luke. The reason for that omission is debated: (1) A popular suggestion has Mark and Luke omitting that qualification because they're both intended for gentile audiences (a point Mark appears to support by looking at divorce from both the husband's and wife's point of view, since wives had an equal right of divorce under Greco-Roman law). (2) Others have noted that for gentile audiences a precise and somewhat obscure rabbinic debate such as Matthew describes would have had little meaning. (3) Still others see Matthew adding the extra qualifications for the sake of his readers, who are assumed to be mainly Jewish and for whom the Shammai and Hillel debate may lie so far in the past they may not be thinking about it. (4) The qualification only applies to the betrothal period in Jewish marriages, which would not apply to the broader Greco-Roman society, since they didn't have betrothal periods. These are the major explanations given for the inclusion of the "exception clause" in Matthew and its omission in Mark and Luke. While each view has had supporters, there is no clear and compelling evidence from context or historical background to promote one explanation over the others.

Luke 16:18

Luke's gospel has only a single verse addressing the issue: "Everyone who divorces his wife and marries someone else commits adultery, and the one who marries a woman divorced from her husband commits adultery" (Luke 16:18 NET). This is by far the briefest account of all: no qualifications, no exceptions. It is similar to the private summary statement of Jesus to his disciples in Mark 10:10–12. Divorce is apparently permitted to the husband, presumably within the guidelines of Deuteronomy 24—though this Old Testament passage is neither mentioned nor alluded to—but remarriage to another woman is not permitted. Furthermore, the man who marries a divorced woman commits adultery. So again, there is male culpability.

To summarize evidence from all the Synoptic accounts, Jesus clearly states that remarriage constitutes adultery. This is specified in a variety of ways: (1) husband number one who institutes the divorce (Matt. 19:9; Luke 16:18); (2) the wife who divorces her husband and remarries another (Mark 10:12); (3) husband number two of a divorced woman (Matt. 5:32; Luke 16:18); (4) in addition, Matthew 5:32 says that husband number one who divorces his wife, except for immorality, causes her to commit adultery. Although there are differing details, including how to understand and apply the "exception clause" for unfaithfulness to the marriage, it seems generally clear that Jesus opposed divorce in general, and especially the for-any-cause (broader) view of divorce held by the school of Hillel.

Teaching from Paul in His Letters

1 Corinthians 7:10–16
When we turn to Paul's writings, things become more complicated, because Paul introduces situations confronted by his gentile converts and not considered by Jesus, thus forcing Paul to render "apostolic" judgments on these new cases. We have to deal with the so-called Pauline privilege: optional divorce for unbelievers married to believers, and what to do in the case of abandonment of a believing spouse by an unbeliever. In 1 Corinthians 7:10–16, Paul states, "To the married I give this command—not I, but the Lord—a wife should not divorce a husband (but if she does, let her remain unmarried, or be reconciled to her husband), and a husband should not divorce his wife. To the rest I say—I, not the Lord—" (here Paul is distinguishing between what the Lord taught and what Paul himself is saying), "if a brother has a wife who is not a believer and she is happy to live with him, he should not divorce her. And if a woman has a husband who is not a believer and he is happy to live with her, she should not divorce him. For the unbelieving husband is sanctified because of the wife, and the unbelieving wife because of her husband. Otherwise your children are unclean, but now they are holy" (NET). The problem of the status of children in so-called mixed marriages between believers and unbelievers is difficult—indeed, the problem of divorce in general in families where children are present is extremely complex, although that topic is beyond the scope of our present discussion. Paul then continues, "But if the unbeliever wants a divorce, let it take place. In these circumstances the brother or sister is not bound. God has called you in peace. For how do you know, wife, whether you will bring your husband to salvation? Or how do you know, husband, whether you will bring your wife to salvation?" (vv. 15–16 NET). Paul's comment in 1 Corinthians 7:10, "not I, but the Lord," appears to be an allusion to

Jesus's teaching, as recorded in the Synoptic Gospels, concerning divorce. If so, Paul's words are closest to those recorded in Mark 10:12 (see above), since Mark is the only one of the Synoptic Gospels to mention the possibility of a wife divorcing a husband. This would, of course, be very relevant in Paul's churches, which were primarily gentile—not Jewish—churches. Under Greco-Roman law there was reciprocal right of divorce for men and women. Paul presents two options for the woman: (1) remain unmarried; (2) be reconciled to the original husband. It is often pointed out that the Greek verb frequently translated "separate" can be found in legal documents with the meaning "divorce," and under Greco-Roman law there was no distinction between separation and divorce anyway. Anyone who separated from a spouse with a view to ending the marriage was considered fully divorced—no written document or court appearance was necessary under that law. This historical background is important, because it would imply that the two people are fully divorced, not just separated (in a modern technical sense).

Paul's statement in verses 12–13, "To the rest I say—I, not the Lord—if a brother has a wife who is not a believer and she is happy to live with him . . . if a woman has a husband who is not a believer and he is happy to live with her," can be viewed as an extension of Jesus's command mentioned by Paul in verse 10. It can be construed as a concession to the fact that all might not obey the Lord's teaching. In that case, if one went ahead and divorced anyway, the only option would be to remain single or be reconciled to the original spouse. If Matthew's tradition with its exception clause could be shown to be behind Paul's words to the Corinthians, it might be possible to argue that Paul is only commenting here on divorce for reason of adultery, and again, the only options would be to remain single or be reconciled to the original spouse. However, an allusion by Paul specifically to Matthew's teaching does not appear likely to most New Testament scholars, because (1) Matthew's teaching never looks at divorce from the woman's perspective as Paul does here in verses 10 and 13; and (2) the Markan version of Jesus's teaching, which is closer to Paul in terms of mentioning women, does not mention any exceptions for immorality. Many popular interpretations hold that after mentioning divorce between believers (the situation the Lord dealt with in vv. 10–11), Paul moved on in verse 12 to a second situation, the question of mixed marriages between believers and unbelievers. However, as David Instone-Brewer points out, "Although the latter section speaks about mixed marriages, there is nothing in the first section to indicate that it applied only to nonmixed marriages."[6] In this section Paul commands believers to stay married and the question of whether a divorce occurs is left up to the unbelieving spouse, since presumably the unbeliever would not be expected to obey (or even to care about) the Lord's teaching to believers. In such a case, if the unbelieving spouse chooses to separate (which would amount to full divorce

---

6. David Instone-Brewer, *Divorce and Remarriage in the Bible: The Social and Literary Context* (Grand Rapids: Eerdmans, 2002), 200.

under Greco-Roman law) the believer who is abandoned by the unbeliever is said to be "not bound" (v. 15). Whether this frees the abandoned believer to enter into another new marriage is highly disputed. Instone-Brewer argues that the only interpretation that makes sense is "free to remarry."[7] It would be meaningless to declare the person "free to remain divorced," because there's nothing one could do to reverse the divorce (other than pestering one's former partner to return to the marriage).

1 Corinthians 7:25–28

This last passage is one of the more difficult texts because it talks about "virgins," yet the identification of the virgins is ambiguous. "With regard to the question about people who have never married [Greek: virgins]," Paul says, "I have no command from the Lord" (1 Cor. 7:25). It is fair to assume this refers to virgins (unmarried, presumably never having had sexual relations), but are they men? Are they women? Are they daughters? Are they fiancées? There are all kinds of questions to be addressed, but before we look at these, let's look closely at the text itself: "With regard to the question about people who have never married, I have no command from the Lord, but I give my opinion as one shown mercy by the Lord to be trustworthy." (Paul is saying, in effect, "I have a pretty good track record, therefore trust me on this.") "Because of the impending crisis" (which Paul leaves undefined) "I think it best for you to remain as you are." (What does "as you are" refer to?) "The one bound to a wife should not seek divorce. The one released from a wife should not seek marriage. But if you marry, you have not sinned. And if a virgin marries, she has not sinned. But those who marry will face difficult circumstances, and I am trying to spare you such problems" (vv. 25–28 NET). Paul appears to be addressing males who are in some way responsible for female virgins, advising against marriage because of the "impending crisis" (persecution?). Major interpretative approaches are: (1) the passage concerns an unmarried man whom Paul is advising not to marry his "virgin," that is, his fiancée (NRSV, NIV, NLT, ESV); (2), the passage concerns a father whom Paul is advising not to marry off his unmarried virgin daughter (NASB and NASBU); (3) the passage concerns an ascetic (or sex-free) marriage, and Paul is advising the couple not to go back on that vow and start having normal sexual relations, even though they are already married. The last option has little to support it this early in the history of the church. This is important because later there is evidence for such a practice, and some interpreters try to apply it here, but it seems to run counter to Paul's teaching about sexual relations within marriage back in 1 Corinthians 7:3–5, where Christians are to abstain from sexual relations only for a limited time (for prayer), and then resume normal sexual relations as a guard against temptation.

The second option (the father-daughter view), while traditional, is based on the distinction between textual variants in verses 26 and 28, a distinction that is present in classical Greek, but does not appear to be maintained in

---

7. Instone-Brewer, *Divorce*, 202.

Koine Greek, which is the Greek the New Testament was written in. This leaves the first option (fiancé-fiancée) as the most likely, and the one represented by the majority of recent English translations (see above). However, since we are only considering divorce and remarriage, we don't need to solve these issues about who the virgin is. Only 1 Corinthians 7:27 need concern us here: "The one bound to a wife should not seek divorce. The one released from a wife should not seek marriage."

In verse 27 Paul first addressed those who are married. Some interpreters insist "the one bound to a wife" does not refer here to an existing marriage, but a betrothal (alluding back to the concept of Jewish betrothal). This would cast the section in a predominantly Jewish, rather than Greco-Roman, context. Given what we know about Paul and the church at Corinth, this seems extremely unlikely to most interpreters. The predominant cultural background in Corinth is not Jewish, but gentile. However, if Paul is addressing existing marriages here, "should not seek divorce" would have to mean "don't seek to get out of the existing marriage." The following line, "the one released [Greek: free] from a wife" is not problematic as long as it applies only to those who are "free" through the death of a spouse, or "free" in the sense that they've never been married before. In these cases, verse 28 grants permission for them to marry without sin. But if "released from a wife" includes those "free" through divorce or abandonment by the spouse, then Paul also seems to be granting permission to remarry without sin. There are a lot of assumptions here, and it is difficult to build a dogmatic case for one interpretation or the other based on 1 Corinthians 7:28.

CONCLUSIONS

If one thing has emerged from our examination of biblical teaching on divorce and remarriage, it's that the evidence is fairly complicated—especially the evidence from the Synoptic Gospels and how that fits with the apostle Paul's teachings. But we need to step back and say that, in general, divorce is nowhere presented in a particularly favorable light, and in particular (however one goes about reconciling differences between Matthew, Mark, and Luke), Jesus does not appear to support the "for any cause" divorce advocated by the school of Hillel. Paul, due to differing situations occurring in his predominantly gentile churches, expands on Jesus's teaching (as recorded in the Synoptic Gospels) to cover additional situations, such as a case in which an unbeliever abandons a Christian spouse, or a couple (probably engaged to be married) contemplates whether to go through with the marriage. Paul seems to acknowledge the necessity of arriving at additional approaches to address different cultural and societal situations among his own predominantly gentile churches. So it seems reasonable to conclude that, to some extent, doing the same remains the prerogative of the church today. This in turn suggests a trajectory, rather than a fixed point—when it comes to the shaping of Jesus's original teaching—to fit new cultural and social situations.

The most important takeaway from a ministry perspective is the need for compassion, understanding, and grace, along with elements of wisdom and flexibility. There will be situations in the pastor's study or in the counselor's office that do not fall clearly into the categories outlined in the biblical passages we have examined: What about physical abuse on the part of one of the marriage partners? What about emotional abuse? What about emotional abandonment as opposed to physical abandonment? When such situations occur, and they inevitably will, the pastor, leader, or counselor will have to rely on wisdom, experience, prayer, and the guidance of the Holy Spirit to extend God's redemptive and restorative love to those involved.

FOR DISCUSSION

1. When we look at the differences between Matthew, Mark, and Luke in how Jesus's teaching on divorce is presented, what can we say about how the evangelists appear to have contextualized the sayings and related them to the evangelists' own themes and purposes in writing?

2. Can we extend this contextualization back to the passages in the Old Testament, where—between the passages establishing marriage as a divinely ordained institution in Genesis 2 and the "allowance" made by Moses for a certificate of divorce in Deuteronomy 24:1—a new situation has arisen in which divorce is not to be eradicated completely but limited?

3. Why does Paul need to address situations (1 Cor. 7) that Jesus did not mention in his teachings as presented in the Synoptic Gospels? Does the church have the authority to continue to address new cultural and social situations today?

FOR FURTHER READING

House, H. Wayne, ed. *Divorce and Remarriage: Four Christian Views.* Downers Grove, IL: InterVarsity Press, 1990.

Instone-Brewer, David. *Divorce and Remarriage in the Bible: The Social and Literary Context.* Grand Rapids: Eerdmans, 2002.

———. *Divorce and Remarriage in the Church: Biblical Solutions for Pastoral Realities.* Downers Grove, IL: InterVarsity Press, 2003.

CHAPTER 16

DIVORCE: A RESEARCH-BASED PERSPECTIVE

C. GARY BARNES

This week a couple came to my office seeking pre-engagement counseling. She is thirty-three years old, and he is thirty-eight. She has never married. He was married five years ago and divorced two years ago; he also has a three-year-old son. She grew up in an intact family in a conservative Christian home as the youngest of three children. Her father has been a pastor all her life, and she professed having an active faith that has been her guide throughout her life. His parents divorced when he was four years old, and he grew up with no faith background. Following his divorce, he embraced a personal faith in Christ and has made his faith central to his present and future life decisions.

They met in church and have dated for one year. They now want to get engaged, but they do not have the support of her family. They came to a Christian marriage counselor to determine what to do. What would you tell them if you were their Christian marriage counselor?

There is much to offer this couple from the revealed truths of Scripture regarding a Christian marriage. There is also much to offer this couple from God's general revelation. This chapter will move from looking at the revealed truths of God to exploring the discovered truths in research regarding relationships, marriage, and divorce. Three different areas of research will be examined to better understand relationships in the premarital, marital, and divorced stages. The first research area is that of descriptive statistics, based on survey research. The second area is predictive research, based on longitudinal, empirical studies of repeated direct observations. The third area of research will focus on outcome studies, based on random assignments with treatment groups and control groups. Research-based applications will be drawn for the premarital, marital, and divorce stages of relationships.

DESCRIPTIVE STATISTICS

Top Ten Myths of Divorce

Research providing descriptive statistics can be very helpful in correcting myths about marriage and divorce. The National Marriage Project, led by two highly respected sociological researchers—David Popenoe and Barbara Dafoe Whitehead—has identified the top ten myths of divorce along with the corresponding truths from research.[1]

Myth number one: Because people learn from their bad experiences, second marriages tend to be more successful than first marriages.

Some people do learn from their earlier marriages, and there are a number of second marriages that are wonderful, successful marriages. Yet the truth about the overall average is that second marriages have higher divorce rates than first marriages. Third marriages have higher divorce rates than second marriages. And fourth marriages have higher divorce rates than third marriages. Negative interactive patterns that erode away the good things in a relationship tend to follow people from one failed marriage into the next.[2]

Myth number two: Living together before marriage is a good way to reduce the chances of eventually divorcing.

One of the most perplexing findings in the history of the study of marriage is that living together beforehand is associated with greater, not lesser, odds of struggling in marriage. This association had been clear in study after study up to around 2007. A number of studies and social scientists since then have declared that the association between living together before marriage and difficulties in marriage had disappeared. Yet based on longer-term outcome studies published in 2019, Michael Rosenfeld and Katharina Roesler clarified that those who live together before engagement have an advantage in the first year, because they are already used to all the changes that come with living together. Those who go straight into marriage without living together have a bigger immediate shock to negotiate after marriage and, as a result, have a short-term increased risk that's greater than those already living together. Some studies after 2007 were short-term studies and were therefore limited to making short-term predictions. But

---

1. David Popenoe, "The Top Ten Myths of Divorce," National Marriage Project, 2002, https://www.catholiceducation.org/en/controversy/marriage/the-top-ten-myths-of-divorce.html.

2. Joshua R. Goldstein, "The Leveling of Divorce in the United States," *Demography* 36, no. 3 (1999): 409–14; Andrew J. Cherlin, *Marriage, Divorce, Remarriage* (Cambridge, MA: Harvard University Press, 1992).

the more recent and longer-term-outcome study demonstrates that long-term risk remains, and living together before engagement is associated with greater, not lesser, odds of struggling in marriage.[3]

Myth number three: Divorce may cause problems for many of the children affected by it, but by and large these problems are not long-lasting and the children recover relatively quickly.

Children of divorce have been studied in both small, qualitative studies and large, long-term, empirical studies. The evidence indicates that, overall, children experience immediate and long-term problems both personally and interpersonally as a result of divorce. Judith Wallerstein has spent more than twenty years following children of divorce, and her book *The Unexpected Legacy of Divorce* is a great follow-up study.[4]

Myth number four: Having a child together will help a couple improve their marital satisfaction and prevent a divorce.

Many studies have shown that one of the most stressful times in a marriage is after the first child is born. Couples who have a child together have a slightly decreased risk of divorce compared to couples without children, but the decreased risk is far less than it used to be when parents with marital problems were more likely to stay together for the so-called sake of the children. John and Julie Gottman developed a research-based program to help young couples weather this adjustment of having a third person in the relationship.[5]

Myth number five: Following divorce, the woman's standard of living plummets by 73 percent while that of the man's improves by 42 percent.

It is true that there is a significant gap in the standard of living between men and women following divorce. And it is also true that men have a more favorable outcome compared to women. But it is not true that the difference is as extreme

---

3. Michael Rosenfeld and Katharina Roesler, "Cohabitation Experience and Cohabitation's Association with Marital Dissolution," *Journal of Marriage and Family* 81, no. 1 (2019): 42–58; Scott M. Stanley and Galena K. Rhoades, "A Summary of Our Work on Cohabitation," July 2018, https://app.box.com/s/ugfa85i6lly8hp76qey7.

4. Judith Wallerstein, Julia Lewis, and Sandra Blakeslee, *The Unexpected Legacy of Divorce* (New York: Hyperion, 2000); Andrew J. Cherlin, P. Lindsay Chase-Landsdale, Christine McRae, "Effects of Parental Divorce on Mental Health throughout the Life Course," *American Sociological Review* 63, no. 2 (1998): 239–49; Paul Amato and Alan Booth, *A Generation at Risk: Growing Up in an Era of Family Upheaval* (Cambridge, MA: Harvard University Press, 1997).

5. John Gottman and Julie Gottman, *And Baby Makes Three* (New York: Three Rivers Press, 2007), 5; Tim Heaton, "Marital Stability throughout the Child-Rearing Years," *Demography* 27, no. 1 (1990): 55–63; Linda Waite and Lee Lillard, "Children and Marital Disruption," *American Journal of Sociology* 96, no. 4 (1991): 930–53; Carolyn Cowan and Philip Cowan, *When Partners Become Parents: The Big Life Change for Couples* (New York: Basic Books, 1992).

as the above numbers suggest. Initial calculations were faulty. After the data was correctly examined, it was determined that the woman's loss was 27 percent, while the man's gain was 10 percent.[6]

Myth number six: When parents don't get along, children are better off if their parents divorce than if they stay together.

It is true that children remaining in the presence of high-conflict marriages have worse outcomes than children of divorce. However, high-conflict marriages represent a minority of couples seeking divorce. In most cases, going through a divorce also has negative effects on children. Therefore, in most cases, absent high conflict, going through a divorce is harder on children than living in a family with marital dissatisfaction. So the key predictive factor for outcomes of children of divorce is the degree of high conflict between their parents. Of course, the best outcome for children is living with parents who work out their differences, dissatisfactions, and problems without high conflict.[7]

Myth number seven: Children who grow up in a home broken by divorce tend to have as much success in their own marriages as those from intact homes.

Marriages of children from intact families have a much lower rate of divorce than marriages of children with parental divorce. Modeling by parents is very influential for outcomes in children's future relationships. This is particularly true in terms of commitment, communication, and conflict resolution. The sense of commitment to a lifelong marriage has been undermined by divorcing parents. Also, much of what gets modeled and learned from divorcing parents is unhealthy communication and conflict resolution. Humans are not born knowing how to do healthy communication and conflict resolution, and without models we're even more prone to adopt unhealthy attempts.[8]

Myth number eight: Following divorce, the children involved are better off in stepfamilies than in single-parent families.

The correct answer here is that it depends. There is no clear winner. Both stepfamilies and single-parent families have distinct sets of problems and

---

6. Leonore Weitzman, "The Economics of Divorce: Social and Economic Consequences of Property, Alimony, and Child Support Awards," *UCLA Law Review* 28 (August, 1981): 1251; Richard Peterson, "A Re-evaluation of the Economic Consequences of Divorce," *American Sociological Review* 61, no. 3 (June 1996): 528–36; Pamela J. Smock, "The Economic Costs of Marital Disruption for Young Women over the Past Two Decades," *Demography* 30, no. 3 (August 1993): 353–71.

7. Amato and Booth, *A Generation at Risk.*

8. Paul Amato, "What Children Learn from Divorce," Population Reference Bureau, January 2001, https://www.prb.org/whatchildrenlearnfromdivorce/; Nicholas Wolfinger, "Beyond the Intergenerational Transmission of Divorce," *Journal of Family Issues* 21, no. 8 (2000): 1061–86.

challenges. Single-parent families have less support and resources. Stepfamilies have more challenges interpersonally with stepparents and stepsiblings. The top argument starter for first marriages is money, whereas the top argument starter for second marriages is children. Ron Deal has studied this extensively and is a useful resource for stepfamilies.[9]

Myth number nine: Being very unhappy at certain points in a marriage is a good sign that the marriage will eventually end in divorce. So, therefore, why prolong your unhappiness? You might as well just end it soon, shorten the suffering, and then move on with life.

A study conducted by a team of leading family scholars headed by University of Chicago sociologist Linda Waite found no evidence that unhappily married adults who divorced were typically any happier than unhappily married people who stayed married. Research using a large, national sample identified a large subgroup who were very unhappy in their marriage. A portion of this group decided not to divorce and the others decided to divorce. Most of the couples who decided to divorce reported five years later that they did not have better outcomes overall in life. The study also found that 86 percent of people who were unhappy in their marriage but yet stayed with the marriage reported five years later that they were happier. In fact, three-fifths of the formerly unhappy married couples rated their marriage as either very happy or quite happy.[10]

---

9. Ron Deal, *The Smart Step-Family: Seven Steps to a Healthy Family* (Bloomington, MN: Bethany House, 2002); Sara McLanahan and Gary Sandefur, *Growing Up with a Single Parent* (Cambridge, MA: Harvard University Press, 1994); Alan Booth and Judy Dunn, eds., *Stepfamilies: Who Benefits? Who Does Not?* (Hillsdale, NJ: Lawrence Erlbaum, 1994).

10. Linda Waite et al., "Does Divorce Make People Happy? Findings from a Study of Unhappy Marriages," Smart Marriages, July 11, 2002, http://smartmarriages.com/does.divorce.html:

> The research team used data collected by the National Survey of Family and Households, a nationally representative survey that extensively measures personal and marital happiness. Out of 5,232 married adults interviewed in the late 1980s, 645 reported being unhappily married. Five years later, these same adults were interviewed again. Some had divorced or separated and some had stayed married.
>
> The study found that on average unhappily married adults who divorced were no happier than unhappily married adults who stayed married when rated on any of 12 separate measures of psychological well-being. Divorce did not typically reduce symptoms of depression, raise self-esteem, or increase a sense of mastery. This was true even after controlling for race, age, gender, and income. Even unhappy spouses who had divorced and remarried were no happier on average than those who stayed married. "Staying married is not just for the children's sake. Some divorce is necessary, but results like these suggest the benefits of divorce have been oversold," says Linda J. Waite.

Myth number ten: It's usually men who initiate divorce.

One-third of all divorces are initiated by men. A likely explanation would be that divorce laws in most states favor women if they initiate. This is particularly the case regarding child custody. Statistics also establish that husbands are bigger offenders than wives regarding problems with drinking, drug abuse, and infidelity.[11]

Marital Outcome Groups

Descriptive statistics have also provided a basis for categorizing relationships before marriage, during marriage, and after divorcing by identifying levels of satisfaction and stability. With such an approach, researchers have identified three basic outcome groups: (1) those who split up because of low satisfaction; (2) those who stay together but with low satisfaction; and (3) those who stay together with overall satisfaction. Generally speaking, young couples marrying for the first time still face roughly a 40–50 percent chance of divorce over the full span of their relationship.[12] There's also a high number of those who don't divorce that are stable but overall are unhappy. Over the full span of their relationship, this group is in the 20–30 percent range. The people who stay together and on the overall average are glad they're staying together represent about the remaining 20–30 percent over the full span of their relationship.[13] The emergence of these three groups can be seen early in a three-year follow-up study of premarital couples getting married. After three years, 28 percent of the couples were in the separated or divorced group, 32 percent of the couples were in the married but dissatisfied group, and 40 percent of the couples were in the married and satisfied group.[14]

There are many subgroups within those three groups, but these basic three groups are easily identified and studied. It becomes useful to identify more clearly what differentiates one group from the other two and to determine whether predictable variables exist at the beginning of the relationship. It is especially significant to establish whether predictable variables are changeable and whether that actually makes a difference in relationship outcomes.

PREDICTION RESEARCH

Prediction research is extremely significant for understanding what differentiates the three basic outcome groups: (1) those who split up because of low satisfaction;

---

11. Margaret Brinig and Douglas Allen, "These Boots Are Made for Walking: Why Most Divorce Filers Are Women," *American Law and Economics Review* 2, no. 1 (2000): 126–69.

12. Scott M. Stanley, "What Really Is the Divorce Rate?," PREP-Prevention and Relationship Enhancement Program, August 3, 2007, https://www.prepinc.com/docs/content/articles/What_is_Divorce_Rate_8-3-2007.pdf.

13. David Popenoe and Barbara Dafoe Whitehead, *The State of Our Unions 2010* (Piscataway, NJ: National Marriage Project, Rutgers University, 2010).

14. Blaine Fowers, Kelly Montel, and David H. Olson, "Predicting Marital Success for Premarital Couple Types Based on Prepare," *Journal of Marital and Family Therapy* 22, no.1 (1996): 103–19.

(2) those who stay together but with overall low satisfaction; and (3) those who stay together with overall satisfaction. Scott Stanley used a puppy metaphor for marriage for understanding the basic findings from prediction research. He asks, "Have you ever gone puppy shopping with a child? What's the inevitable outcome? You either come home with a puppy, or you don't come home with the child. And why is that? Because there's just something about puppies, right?" He goes on to explain that there's this initial attraction and attachment to the front end of the puppy. What's the number-one reason that pet stores have puppies returned? It's not because the front end of the puppy changed. It's because people weren't able to deal with the back end of the puppy. Now how is that a good metaphor for marriage? Every marriage comes with a back end. The back end of a relationship is dealing with the inevitable differences, problems, and conflicts that all relationships experience. There's no such thing as a marriage with just a front end. When we are not able to manage the back end of the marriage, we erode away our initial attraction and attachment to the front end of the marriage. We don't just fall out of love the way we fall out of trees. Research tells us that we erode away all of the positive things that we initially start off with by one negative-interaction exchange after another. The relationship dies by a cumulative effect of negative interactional choices. This can be demonstrated as early as three years after the marriage.[15]

Predictive research has identified two different categories of predictive variables for outcomes of satisfaction and stability: unchangeable variables and changeable variables.[16] Examples of some of the unchangeable or the very difficult factors to change are as follows: some personality factors, parental divorce, cohabitation history, previous divorce, religious dissimilarity, young age at marriage, and economic status. Examples of some of the changeable factors are as follows: interaction danger signs or automatic natural ways of interacting under the influence of negative emotions; communication and conflict-resolution skills; and use of aggression, attitudes, and commitment in motivation.

Even though both the unchangeable and changeable variables have value, a key finding from the prediction research is that the changeable variables have greater significance than the unchangeable variables. John Gottman has said that the most important discovery to come from his research is that not only can he predict divorce, but more importantly he can identify specifically what couples need to change to strengthen their relationships. Couples can actually change the outcome of their relationships by changing the negative behaviors that predict divorce to more positive behaviors that predict success.[17]

---

15. Fowers, Montel, and Olson, "Predicting Marital Success."
16. Howard J. Markman, Scott M. Stanley, and Susan Blumberg, *Fighting for Your Marriage: PREP Program* (San Francisco: Jossey-Bass, 2010), 17.
17. John Gottman, "Research FAQ," The Gottman Institute: A Research Based Approach to Relationships, https://www.gottman.com/about/research/faq/.

Close examination of the stable and satisfied group demonstrates that some of the couples in that group have as many or more of the unchangeable variables as the other two groups (not staying together or stable but not satisfied). Therefore, a good summary of prediction research for marital outcomes is that it is not so much your history or your current differences or circumstances as it is how you handle these factors interpersonally.

Predictive research has also identified that within the realm of interpersonal choice-making there are two domains: relationship enrichment and relationship management.[18] Relationship-enrichment choices may include such things as fun, friendship, companionship, commitment, and intimacy (including physical, emotional, and spiritual intimacy). Relationship-management choices include such things as communication, conflict resolution, problem solving, expectations, affect regulation, and forgiveness. Although both of these domains—relationships enrichment and relationship management—are important in marital outcomes, the relationship-management choices have far greater predictability. A key discriminating finding of the stable and satisfied couples is that they are more intentional and effective at making *both* relationship-enrichment choices and relational-management choices.[19]

Gottman's research has also provided a scientific understanding of what differentiates outcome groups in marriage and how to transform marriages.[20] One of the many predictors of particular importance involves the interactional choices that he identifies as "bids" and "turns."[21] A "bid" is something we may or may not be aware of. It could be a verbal or a nonverbal message that is given as an "invitation" that will help evaluate or judge the nature of the present emotional connection in the relationship. A "turn" is the resulting response. There are three turns. Someone can turn toward, turn away, or turn against. In the course of a day, any couple could have hundreds of these "bids" and "turns" going on. After following couples for six years, Gottman looked at people who were in the happily married category, and he tallied all of their bids and turns and demonstrated that there's a cumulative effect.

Picture three file folders, and at the end of the day one such folder is bigger than the other two. At the end of the week, at the end of a month, at the end of a

---

18. C. Gary Barnes and Scott M. Stanley, "Christian PREP: The Prevention and Relationship Enhancement Program," in *Evidence-Based Practices for Christian Counseling and Psychotherapy*, ed. Everett L. Worthington Jr. et al., Christian Association for Psychological Studies Books (Downers Grove, IL: IVP Academic, 2013), 176.

19. Markman, Stanley, and Blumberg, *Fighting for Your Marriage*, 30.

20. John Gottman, *Why Marriages Succeed or Fail: And How You Can Make Yours Last* (New York: Simon & Schuster, 1994); John Gottman, *The Marriage Clinic: A Scientifically Based Marital Therapy* (New York: Norton, 1999); John Gottman and Nan Silver, *The Seven Principles for Making Marriage Work* (New York: Three Rivers Press, 1999); John Gottman and Julie Gottman, *Ten Lessons to Transform Your Marriage* (New York: Three Rivers Press, 2006).

21. Gottman and Gottman, *Ten Lessons*, 236.

year, and at the end of a decade, you have these cumulative file folders. Gottman identified that at the end of six years, the happily married couples had 86 percent of turning toward compared to the combined 14 percent of turning away or turning against. If you look at those who divorced, 67 percent of their turns were turning away from or turning against. Another way of describing this is that it's just the mathematics of interpersonal exchanges. You can't be turning away from one another or turning against one another and be in the happily married group. Those things just don't add up for positive relationship outcomes.[22]

OUTCOME RESEARCH

Outcome research naturally follows prediction research. Marital-outcome research addresses these key questions: Is it possible that you could actually help people change the changeable variables? and, Would this result in a sustainable change in marital-outcome groups? In order to determine this, researchers create methodology that is actually measuring this through the random assignment of couples to control groups and treatment groups. And after examining the results in long-term follow-up studies, there are two key categories that are the big difference makers. One would be called "raising the protection." This is making sure the good stuff stays good in the relationship. The other has to do with "lowering the risk." All couples, just like the puppies, have a back end, and it has to be dealt with. This is about dealing with the inevitable differences, problems, and conflicts in constructive ways.[23]

HOW A MARRIAGE DIES: ONE COMMON PATH

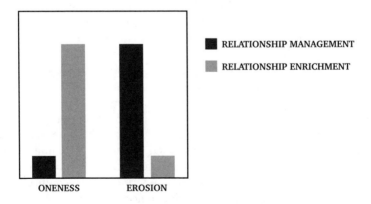

■ RELATIONSHIP MANAGEMENT

▨ RELATIONSHIP ENRICHMENT

ONENESS   EROSION

Figure 5. Choosing Us

---

22. Gottman and Gottman, *Ten Lessons*, 236.
23. Barnes and Stanley, "Christian PREP," 176.

A conceptual schema that summarizes the prediction and outcome research and emphasizes the significance of interactional choices may be visualized in figure 5.[24] Individuals can make choices that either protect or deepen oneness in their marriages or weaken it. The high light-shaded bar in the figure represents choices that protect or deepen connection, and thereby foster oneness. Such choices create the impact of love in each other. It is insufficient to intend that the other person feel loved, and it is not even sufficient to make efforts for the other person to feel loved. The key is whether a partner is actually creating the impact of love in the other. When each person is creating the impact of love in the other, the relationship is enriched and is protected.

Too often, in most marriages partners don't elect the "choose us" option, such as making the time to sit and talk with one's mate. Instead, whether actively or passively, they choose pathways that undermine "us" or erode oneness—amounting to choosing erosion. For example, all couples struggle with discordant desires to one degree or another, and in response some people choose avoidance ("turning away") while others choose or lose control to destructive conflicts ("turning against").

Patterns of how couples handle these inevitable differences, problems, and conflicts are associated with relationship outcomes. In the language of Gottman, this pattern should involve choices to "turn toward" rather than choices of "turning away" or "turning against."[25] The degree to which such negative patterns are destiny for couples has likely been overstated in our field for some time. Nevertheless, there is much evidence that communication danger signs as taught in the Prevention and Relationship Enhancement Program (PREP; see below)[26] (e.g., withdrawal, escalation, negative interpretation, and invalidation) or the four horsemen as taught in Gottman[27] (i.e., criticism, defensiveness, contempt, and stonewalling) do real damage to a couple's ability to preserve strong, happy marriages. Such negative patterns are common, normal, and yet potentially destructive.

The next intentional step in the process of change is to adopt the attitude that even though these danger signs occur naturally and automatically, they can be diminished by strategies taught: for example, (1) making more benign interpretations of the partner's behavior in the first place; (2) limiting the negative impact of escalation by learning how to use strategies such as time-out; and (3) ameliorating damage, when done, through individual steps of humility (apologies, for instance) and dyadic commitment to a continual process of forgiveness. Finally, actions taught and practiced (communication skills, conflict management strategies such as time-out) can be chosen not only to prevent damage but

---

24. Barnes and Stanley, "Christian PREP," 176.
25. Gottman and Gottman, *Ten Lessons*, 236.
26. Markman, Stanley, and Blumberg, *Fighting for Your Marriage*, 37–63.
27. Gottman and Silver, *Seven Principles*, 27–34.

also to allow safe, effective, and constructive strategies for understanding issues and managing problems. When these things happen and the goal of mutual understanding is accomplished, the dark shaded bar in figure 5 is low and the risk interaction in the relationship is low.[28]

Most, but not all, relationships begin with a "oneness profile" of "high light-shaded bar" and "low dark-shaded bar" interaction choices. Couples who are not experiencing oneness are not experiencing relationship satisfaction and are therefore not likely to say to each other, "Let's spend the rest of our lives together." After starting out in marriage with a oneness profile, though perhaps limited in depth, many couples then slide to the "erosion profile," get dissatisfied, distressed, and even end up divorcing. We expect that a smaller number of couples go through that slide over time but do not divorce, becoming stably distressed. The remaining couples, which is surely a minority of all those who get married, are characterized by an overall average experience of stability *and* satisfaction, maintaining the oneness profile in some degree. It is not that these couples never experience the erosion profile. It's just that when they do, eventually both partners make the reversible choices for recapturing the oneness profile.[29]

The Gottman and PREP interventions represent research-based models designed to either help couples prevent what is a common slide in marriage from the oneness profile to the erosion profile or to help couples who may already have a higher-risk profile learn how to more consistently choose attitudes and behaviors that promote oneness. Either way, the practical goal is to help couples learn and implement strategies that will keep the light-shaded bar high (relationship enhancement) and the dark-shaded bar low (relationship management).

Researchers have conducted many outcome studies in the past three decades based on the new findings from prediction research. The validity of outcome-studies reporting on stability and satisfaction for marriages depends on the research design and methodology. It is not the purpose of this chapter to teach research design and methodology, but it is important to note that not all studies are created equal. Some fundamental factors are nonoptional, such as random assignment. There are other improvement factors, such as direct observation rather than only self-reporting. A key distinguishing factor is the length of time allowed for the post-follow-up measurement. Much research is limited to the comparisons immediately after an intervention, and this is not adequate research if we wish to know the sustainability of change in marital satisfaction and stability.

Studies have been conducted to compare the outcomes of satisfaction and stability in couples in a variety of groups. A possible three-group comparison would be (1) a control group that receives nothing; (2) a group that receives an intervention that is not research-based (often a religious-based group); and (3) a group that receives an intervention that is research-based.

---

28. Barnes and Stanley, "Christian PREP," 176.
29. Barnes and Stanley, "Christian PREP," 176.

When one compares the control group to the non-research-based treatment group immediately after the intervention, a positive change is reported by couples with the non-research-based treatment. There is also a positive change in the research-based group compared to the control group. Initially, there is typically no significant difference in the amount of change between the non-research-based group and research-based group.

When you go five years out and compare, you get a whole different outcome. Five years after the intervention, there is no significant difference between the non-research-based group and the control group that got nothing. Five years after the treatments, there is a significant difference between the research-based group and the control group, and also between the research-based group and the non-research-based group. What is it that distinguishes the research-based treatment group from the non-research-based treatment group? In the non-research-based group, two things most commonly occur: *information* and *inspiration*. When you give good information and good inspiration, immediately after your intervention or your training, people tend to like it and evaluate it positively. The thing that's different with the research-based group is the addition of *implementation*. A distinction about effective research-based models is that they actually walk couples through a process of skills acquisition. It's not just demonstrating skills, it's being sure that the couples actually acquire the skills. This is a significant predictor in marital-outcome research that makes a difference in couples' satisfaction and stability levels.[30]

---

30. Ryan G. Carlson et al., "Influence of Relationship Education on Relationship Satisfaction for Low-Income Couples," *Journal of Counseling and Development* 92, no.4 (2014): 418–27; Ryan G. Carlson, Andrew P. Daire, and Haiyan Bai, "Examining Relationship Satisfaction and Individual Distress for Low-to-Moderate Income Couples in Relationship Education," *Family Journal* 22, no. 3 (2014): 282–91; Ryan G. Carlson et al., "The Effectiveness of Couple and Individual Relationship Education: Distress as a Moderator," *Family Process* 56, no. 1 (2017): 91–104; Kurt Hahlweg et al., "Prevention of Marital Distress: Results of a German Prospective Longitudinal Study," *Journal of Family Psychology* 12 (1998): 543–56; W. Kim Halford, Matthew R. Sanders, and Brett C. Behrens, "Can Skills Training Prevent Relationship Problems in At-Risk Couples? Four-Year Effects of a Behavioral Relationship Education Program," *Journal of Family Psychology* 15, no. 4 (2001): 750–68; Andrea Kaiser et al., "The Efficacy of a Compact Psychoeducational Group Training Program for Married Couples," *Journal of Consulting and Clinical Psychology* 66, no. 5 (1998): 753–60; Jean-Philippe Laurenceau et al., "Community-Based Prevention of Marital Dysfunction: Multilevel Modeling of a Randomized Effectiveness Study," *Journal of Consulting and Clinical Psychology* 72 (2004): 933–43; Howard J. Markman et al., "The Prevention of Marital Distress: A Longitudinal Investigation," *Journal of Consulting and Clinical Psychology* 56, no. 2 (1988): 210–17; Howard J. Markman et al., "Preventing Marital Distress through Communication and Conflict Management Training: A Four and Five Year Follow-Up," *Journal of Consulting and Clinical Psychology* 61, no. 1 (1993): 70–77; Howard J. Markman et al., "A Randomized Clinical Trial of the Effectiveness of Premarital Intervention: Moderators of Divorce Outcomes," *Journal of Family Psychology* 27, no. 1 (2013): 165–72; Ronald D. Rogge et al., "Is Skills Training Necessary for the Primary Prevention of Marital Distress

Striking examples of marital-outcome studies were conducted by PREP[31] with five-year post-follow-up measurements. PREP designed a psycho-educational intervention in a twelve-hour training curriculum program. They had various delivery systems. Some systems were one night a week for two hours for six weeks. In one of the most extensive, long-term studies on PREP, couples who took the program before marriage had less negative interaction, more positive interaction, lower rates of relationship aggression, lower combined rates of breakup or divorce, and higher levels of relationship satisfaction up to five years following the training. The breakup rate was 12 percent for couples who got the PREP training compared with 36 percent in the people who were in the control group. This means that there was one-third of the breakup rate based on a twelve-hour workshop training program measured five years later.[32] A replication study was conducted with the PREP program in Germany. After five years, the breakup rate in that particular sample was 3 percent compared with 16 percent in the comparison group without the research-based program.[33]

CONCLUSIONS

This chapter has examined psychological research on marital outcomes. The conceptual schema identified in "Choosing Us" (figure 5) summarizes the significance of interactional choices for outcomes of stability and satisfaction in marriages.[34] Individuals can make choices that either protect and deepen oneness in their marriages or erode it. Considered over the long term, a couple's presence in the stable and satisfied group does not mean the couple never slides to the erosion choices. Everybody slides there for some amount of time. But the stable and satisfied couples do something different from the divorced couples

and Dissolution? A Three-Year Experimental Study of Three Interventions," *Journal of Consulting and Clinical Psychology* 81, no. 6 (2013): 949–61; Elizabeth A. Schilling et al., "Altering the Course of Marriage: The Effect of PREP Communication Skills Acquisition on Couples' Risk of Becoming Maritally Distressed," *Journal of Family Psychology* 17, no. 1 (2003): 41–53; Scott M. Stanley et al., "Decreasing Divorce in Army Couples: Results from a Randomized Clinical Trial of PREP for Strong Bonds," *Journal of Couple and Relationship Therapy* 9, no. 2 (2010): 149–60; Scott M. Stanley et al., "A Randomized Controlled Trial of Relationship Education in the U.S. Army: Two-Year Outcomes," *Family Relations* 63, no. 4 (2014): 482–95; Brigit Van Widenfelt et al., "The Prevention of Relationship Distress for Couples at Risk: A Controlled Evaluation with Nine-Month and Two-Year Follow-Ups," *Family Relations* 45, no. 2 (1996): 156–65.

31. PREP is the "Prevention and Relationship Enhancement Program" directed by Howard Markman and Scott Stanley. Based on more than twenty years of research, PREP teaches marital/premarital couples essential skills: how to communicate effectively, work as a team, solve problems, manage conflict, and preserve and enhance love, commitment, and friendship.

32. Markman et al., "Prevention of Marital Distress," 210–17; Markman et al., "Preventing Marital Distress through Communication," 70–77.

33. Hahlweg et al., "Prevention of Marital Distress," 543–56.

34. Barnes and Stanley, "Christian PREP," 176.

and from the stable but dissatisfied couples. The divorcing couples slide to the erosion profile and become dissatisfied, and their solution is, "Let's leave each other." In contrast, when the stable but dissatisfied couples slide to the erosion profile, they get dissatisfied and say, "We're going to stay together no matter what." However, they stay together with negative interactional choices, and they continue to erode away all of their satisfaction. Now, the stable and satisfied couples also slide to the erosion profile for some amount of time, but they distinctively say, "We're dissatisfied with this relationship experience, but we are not going to leave each other, *and* we are not going to continue with the erosion profile. Let's divorce the erosion profile from our relationship." The empirical data has established the solid finding that even couples who have been in the erosion profile for long periods of time can reverse their interaction patterns to the oneness profile. This occurs only when *both* people make choices to go back to positive relationship-enrichment and positive relationship-management choices. The sad truth, however, is that one person cannot do the work for two people.

A theological foundation of redemption and reconciliation can provide a basis for *information* and *inspiration* for marriages. Psychological research provides an empirical basis for *implementation* for outcomes of stability *and* satisfaction in marriage. Revealed and discovered truths together can motivate us, inspire us, and empower us for *self* to get out of the way of *us* as we rightly establish, grow, and protect the three identities of "you," "me," and "us" in a healthy expression of oneness that is not based in sameness.

FOR DISCUSSION

1. What are the myths of divorce that you may have held before learning about the truths research revealed? How can knowing the truth change your personal beliefs or choices or how you relate to others?

2. How does the predictive research influence your choices to pursue a relationship outcome of stability and satisfaction? How would it influence your choices if you were in a relationship of stability and dissatisfaction?

3. How does the outcome research influence your choices in assisting others seeking your help to have a relationship of stability and satisfaction? How would it influence your choices if another couple was struggling and considering divorce but wanted your opinion on what they should do? According to research, who should be encouraged not to divorce? (a) all couples; (b) some couples; (c) most couples.

FOR FURTHER READING

Barnes, C. Gary, and Scott M. Stanley. "Christian PREP: The Prevention and Relationship Enhancement Program." In *Evidence-Based Practices for Christian Counseling and Psychotherapy*, edited by Everett L. Worthington Jr., Eric L. Johnson, Joshua N. Hook, and Jamie D. Aten, 166–88. Christian Association for Psychological Studies Books. Downers Grove, IL: IVP Academic, 2013.

Gottman, John, and Nan Silver. *The Seven Principles for Making Marriage Work.* New York: Three Rivers Press, 1999.

Markman, Howard J., Scott M. Stanley, and Susan Blumberg. *Fighting for Your Marriage: PREP Program.* San Francisco: Jossey-Bass, 2010.

CHAPTER 17

FORCED SEXUALITY: RAPE

JOY PEDROW SKARKA

On day three of my freshman year of college, I was raped. I had said no countless times. Yet when I tell my story, people blame me. They ask questions such as, "Why did you go to his apartment?" "How could you have let this happen?" "What were you wearing?" and "Were you drinking?" Such questions blame the victim. In fact for years, I blamed myself, and the lies implied by these questions blanketed my mind and body with shame. These questions and others like them perpetuate rape culture—a context in which prevailing social attitudes have the effect of normalizing or trivializing sexual assault and abuse—suggesting that rape is the victim's fault. And sadly, millions share a story similar to mine.

THE STATISTICS

Every ninety-eight seconds an American is sexually assaulted.[1] One in five women experience sexual assault during college.[2] Each year, 321,500 victims age twelve or older experience rape and sexual assault in the United States.[3]

Sexual assault affects an enormous number of victims, yet most of the perpetrators walk away. Out of 1,000 rapes, 995 perpetrators will not go to jail.[4] Consequently, many women do not report rape crimes to the police. In fact, only

---

1. Department of Justice, "National Crime Victimization Survey, 2012–2016," Bureau of Justice Statistics, 2017.
2. Christopher Krebs et al., *Campus Climate Survey Validation Study Final Technical Report*, Bureau of Justice Statistics Research and Development Series (Research Triangle Park, NC: RTI International, 2016).
3. Department of Justice, "National Crime Victimization Survey."
4. Department of Justice, "National Crime Victimization Survey."

230 out of every 1,000 sexual assaults are reported.[5] That means about three out of four rapes go undocumented, causing rape statistics to be grossly underestimated.

Rape is a crime, and sadly, crime is an immense part of the culture in which we live. Failure to recognize rape culture and the associated manipulation of power leads survivors to continue entering into abusive relationships, possibly becoming abusers themselves, and thus immortalizing the statistics.[6] Christian ethics demand that followers of Christ learn how to challenge rape culture to protect both current and potential victims.

KEY TERMS

Rape is a form of sexual assault, though not all sexual assault is rape. The FBI defines rape as "penetration, no matter how slight, of the vagina or anus with any body part or object, or oral penetration by a sex organ of another person, without the consent of the victim."[7] Legally, rape is sexual penetration without consent.

Culture involves a development or improvement of the mind by education or training along with the behaviors and beliefs characteristic of a particular social, ethnic, or age group.[8] Notice two words in this definition: "education" and "training"; these two words applied negatively create learned responses that perpetuate rape culture.

Rape culture is a term that describes the normalization and frequency of sexual assault, violence, and victimization. Rape culture makes excuses or minimizes the behavior of predators (e.g., he was drunk or young, so he should be forgiven), and emphasizes the victim's behavior as inviting assault (e.g., she was wearing skimpy clothes and "asking for it"). Rape culture is a systemic phenomenon; it protects abusers and silences victims—a system of oppression. Coined by second-wave feminists—some of whom were Christians—in the 1970s, rape culture describes the relationship between rape, popular culture, sexual violence, and the media.

In a rape culture, people silence and blame victims, while predators' lives remain unchanged. Rape culture is not a "woman" issue; rape culture is a "human" issue. The issue will not change until men join together with women to fight against the injustice. Statistically, most rapists are male, and most victims are female.[9] Therefore, this chapter will focus on rape victims

---

5. Department of Justice, "National Crime Victimization Survey."
6. Jacob Denhollander and Rachael Denhollander, "Justice: The Foundation of a Christian Approach to Abuse" (paper presented at the 70th Annual Meeting of the Evangelical Theological Society, Denver, Colorado, November 13, 2018).
7. RAINN, "Sexual Assault," https://www.rainn.org/articles/sexual-assault.
8. Sandra Glahn, "Part 1: Rape Culture 101," *Aspire2* (blog), April 2, 2018, http://aspire2.com/2013/12/part-1-of-18-rape-culture-101/.
9. Department of Justice, "Sexual Assault of Young Children as Reported to Law Enforcement," Bureau of Justice Statistics, 2000. A separate CDC study found that, in the United States, 1 in 71 men had been raped or suffered an attempt within their lifetime. The same study found that approximately 1 in 21, or 4.8 percent, of men in a survey had been made to penetrate someone else, usually an intimate partner or

as female, but we must remember that men can be raped, and women can be rapists.

Rape affects every society in the world and is often used as a weapon. Rape is used in wars, as women in war zones are easy targets for sexual violence. In deeply patriarchal societies, rape often leads to death or exile of the victim. Sadly, in such societies, after a woman is raped, her community classifies her as "ruined goods." Some families send women away from the home, while others kill their female family members to redeem the family name, a practice known as "honor killing."

Every person affected by rape experiences some sort of trauma that can range from nightmares to panic attacks. The experience of rape can completely change a woman's personality, causing her to lack confidence and live with a loss mentality.[10] Other effects of sexual trauma include a sense of powerlessness, loss of control, helplessness, emotional numbness, disturbed sleep, flashbacks, isolation, extreme emotions, extreme shame, self-loathing, and disgust.[11] All of these symptoms can lead to long-term anxiety and depression.

In America during 2017 and 2018, a phenomenon that became known as the #MeToo movement went viral, resulting in public figures facing consequences for sexual assault and harassment. The movement created an unprecedented cultural acknowledgment about sexual assault, as millions came forward to share their stories and start a conversation, using the MeToo hashtag. Because of this movement, rape culture took center stage and resulted in many people learning about the systemic history of rape culture and gendered power imbalances. In this chapter, we will learn what we need to know about rape culture, how Christians have both consciously and inadvertently contributed to it, how we can prevent rape, and how we can help victims.

WHAT WE NEED TO KNOW

Myth: Rape Happens Mostly in Dark Alleys

Abusers include acquaintances, friends, spouses, dates, or family members. In fact, most victims know their perpetrators. Seven out of ten rapes, a full 70 percent, are committed by someone the victim knows.[12] Rape happens on first dates, in long-term dating relationships, and in marriages. Even if the person had consenting sex with the abuser in the past, rape is still rape. It happens on college campuses,

---

acquaintance: Michele C. Black et al., "The National Intimate Partner and Sexual Violence Survey (NISVS): 2010 Summary Report," National Center for Injury Prevention and Control, Centers for Disease Control and Prevention, 2011, 1–2, https://www.cdc.gov/violenceprevention/pdf/nisvs_report2010-a.pdf.

10. Elaine Storkey, *Scars across Humanity: Understanding and Overcoming Violence against Women* (Downers Grove, IL:IVP Academic, 2018), 125.

11. Storkey, *Scars across Humanity*, 126–27.

12. Department of Justice, "National Crime Victimization Survey."

apartments, behind dumpsters, at restaurants, on buses, in bars, in jail cells, even in the victim's own home—rape happens absolutely everywhere.

What Is Consent?

Where does consent end, and where does sexual assault begin? Some people believe that "no means no" and "yes means yes"; however, consent is more complicated than that. For example, the person could say yes at first and then say no soon after. The abuser could have power or authority over the victim, and the victim could feel trapped in the situation—such as a physician, pastor, or therapist with a patient or congregant. If the victim is under legal age, intoxicated by alcohol or drugs, passed out, asleep, powerless, too frightened to protest, or pressured—the perpetrator lacks consent to proceed, and the law would classify the situation as sexual assault. Other examples of "no" besides a woman audibly saying "no" include the following: avoiding eye contact, turning away her face, avoiding reciprocating touch, nervousness, anger, or sadness. When people fail to believe the above examples are situations where the victim has not given consent, rape myths continue, and rape culture is perpetuated. Often in such cases, women blame themselves for the rape, and men live without consequences.

Others, especially college boys, argue that when a woman says no, she really means yes. But empirical research fails to support this claim.[13] Many convince themselves and others that forcefulness is a normal part of seduction or the experience was a "miscommunication," not rape. Especially in colleges, alcohol is often used as a justification for men's sexual behaviors and women's consent. A man can argue that he was so intoxicated that he misperceived the woman's degree of sexual interest. A common rape myth says that if a woman drank alcohol, she asked for it. Interestingly, the Barna Group conducted research on the incidence of "miscommunication," and they found that Americans were actually in agreement about what constituted sexual harassment, and that they were quick to include *most* unwanted sexual behavior, no matter how seemingly benign.[14]

A Sense of Entitlement

In rape culture, the more power a man has, the more he can get away with sexual assault and avoid punishment. Powerful people tend to live in a cloud of entitlement. Rich men especially can sexually assault a woman, get a slap on the wrist and a fine, and walk away, bullying women into silence. Forfeiting what amounts to them as loose change costs these men nothing, especially when compared to the pain suffered by the victims.

---

13.   Charlene L. Muehlenhard et al., "The Complexities of Sexual Consent among College Students: A Conceptual and Empirical Review," *Journal of Sex Research* 53, no. 4 (2016): 457–87.

14.   Barna Group, "The Behaviors Most Americans Count as Sexual Harassment," November 28, 2017, https://www.barna.com/research/behaviors-americans-count-as-harassment/.

Entitlement takes place in Hollywood, politics, business, and religion, where men use their power to gain get-out-of-jail-free cards. For example, one pastor received applause because he publicly confessed that he sexually assaulted a teen twenty years earlier while serving as a youth pastor and now was apologizing for his actions, even though he had not made restitution with his victim.[15] Years earlier this pastor had asked his victim, who publicly told her story, to perform oral sex, and she complied. In an interview, she said, "Compliance is not consent."[16] As a young girl, she trusted her youth pastor, and he used his position and power to take advantage of her.

Why Don't Victims Report?

The list of reasons why women do not report is long: Fear. Stigma. Rejection. The length of court cases. The continuation of trauma. The two-hour rape kit, which can feel like getting raped all over again. The responses from family and friends: "You'll embarrass your family"; "You'll lose your job"; "They'll never believe you." In a justice system that is slanted in favor of the perpetrator, victims think twice before reporting. Many choose not to report to protect the rest of their household from the abuser. If he stays out of jail, and statistics suggest he will, he could come back for revenge against any member of the household. Some victims cannot report because of their immigration status; the fear of deportation causes crimes to go unreported—especially when those crimes are sexual in nature.[17] Our world is an unsafe place for victims to report crimes.

Other women who do come forward get blamed for "crying rape." People argue that maybe after consenting to sex, a woman regrets it and now cries rape. The statistics demonstrate that such a scenario happens only rarely. Only 2–8 percent of reported rapes turn out to be false.[18] What should a woman do—report and not be believed and risk putting herself or her loved ones in danger? Or suffer in silence? What happens when a victim does come forward and shares her story? She gets mocked and receives death threats, yet people argue, "Why didn't she come forward sooner?" Such responses maintain the cycle of rape culture.

The victim also gets blamed for failing to remember details. Yet it's important to understand that traumatic experiences have an impact on the brain. In moments of high stress or fear, such as during sexual assault, the prefrontal

---

15. Jules Woodson, "I Was Assaulted. He Was Applauded," *New York Times*, March 9, 2018, https://www.nytimes.com/video/opinion/100000005724879/i-was-assaulted-he-was-applauded.html.

16. Abby Perry, "Compliance Is Not Consent," *Fathom Mag*, May 1, 2018, https://www.fathommag.com/stories/compliance-is-not-consent.

17. Jennifer Medina, "Too Scared to Report Sexual Abuse. The Fear: Deportation," *New York Times*, April 30, 2017, https://www.nytimes.com/2017/04/30/us/immigrants-deportation-sexual-abuse.html.

18. Kirby Dick and Amy Ziering, *The Hunting Ground: The Inside Story of Sexual Assault on American College Campuses*, ed. Constance Matthiessen (New York: Hot Books, 2016).

cortex is impaired and sometimes even shuts down.[19] Consequently, often victims remember only fragments. One cannot reasonably expect a victim to recall, detail for detail, her rape, especially if years have passed and she has spent those years trying to forget the painful details.

HOW HAVE WE MADE IT WORSE?

Rape Myths

Rape myths are "attitudes and beliefs that are generally false but are widely and persistently held, and that serve to deny and justify male sexual aggression against women."[20] Some examples of rape myths include the following: "If a woman is raped when drunk, she is somewhat responsible." "A woman who goes to the home of a man on the first date is implying that she wants to have sex." "She asked for it." "If the rapist doesn't have a weapon, you really can't call it rape." And "Rape is unlikely to happen in a woman's own neighborhood."[21] Acceptance of such rape myths prevents sexual assault victims from receiving justice. Research suggests that eliminating such rape myths is key to ending sexual violence.[22] Yet the excuses cited above, and those like them, are cultural narratives of rape that dominate not only in the media but also in churches. Sometimes in stressing abstinence, ministers fail to help congregants understand how consent works. And sometimes in stressing how to reduce risk of danger, we communicate that victims bring crimes on themselves.

Victim-Blaming and Slut-Shaming

Questioning a victim is a very common response when someone first hears about a rape. People ask questions like: "Were you drinking?" or "Did you lead him on?" Yet people don't ask such questions of the rapist. In a rape culture, victims lack a presumption of innocence. And as mentioned, such questioning of the victim is equivalent to blaming the victim. It communicates a condoning of the rapist's aggressive behaviors based on the victim's clothing choices because the victim "asked for it." And when people blame the victims, victims also blame themselves. When victims experience abuse, they often

19. James Hopper and David Lisak, "Why Rape and Trauma Survivors Have Fragmented and Incomplete Memories," *Time*, December 9, 2014, http://time.com/3625414/rape-trauma-brain-memory/.

20. Kimberly A. Lonsway and Louise F. Fitzgerald, "Rape Myths: In Review," *Psychology of Women Quarterly* 18, no. 2 (1994): 133–64, https://doi.org/10.1111/j.1471-6402.1994.tb00448.x.

21. Michael D. Barnett, Taylor M. Hale, and Kylie B. Sligar, "Masculinity, Femininity, Sexual Dysfunctional Beliefs, and Rape Myth Acceptance among Heterosexual College Men and Women," *Sexuality and Culture* 21, no. 3 (2017): 741–53.

22. Gerd Bohner, Frank Seiber, and Jürgen Schmelcher, "Social Norms and the Likelihood of Raping: Perceived Rape Myth Acceptance of Others Affects Men's Rape Proclivity," *Personality and Social Psychology Bulletin* 32, no. 3 (March 2006): 286–97.

believe that something about them makes them abuse-worthy—that they are bad or unworthy of love.

Slut-shaming, a type of victim-blaming, focuses on the outer appearance of the victim. Usually with a woman, slut-shaming focuses on clothing, makeup, and physical characteristics. Questions such as, "What was she wearing?" or "Did she have on excess makeup?" are forms of slut-shaming. Curvy women have said after experiencing sexual assault that they want breast-reduction surgery because they want to remove the "reason" they were raped. Instead of teaching women to love their bodies, we teach women that their bodies caused their abuse. We must remember that even if a woman was wearing a short skirt or has a past of sleeping around, this is never an excuse for someone to assault or rape her. In fact, if a woman is naked, that is still not an excuse for someone to rape her. Women are not responsible for a man's actions. By blaming the women's appearance, we lower the responsibility of men. Indeed, slut-shaming falls short of God's design for men and the Spirit's enabling power. Slut-shaming says, "Men have no control. They just can't help themselves."

"Locker Room Talk"

Rape-culture language is normalized in everyday life. And powerful people often write off such language as "locker room talk," arguing that the kind of offensive, "macho" language used to objectify women is acceptable in all situations in which only men are present. One study created a local "rape culture index" consisting of language patterns that fall into four broad categories: blaming victims, empathizing with perpetrators, implying victim consent, and questioning victim credibility. Researchers then analyzed over 300,000 articles on rape from 279 mostly local US newspapers between 2000 and 2013.[23] The research revealed that "where local coverage is consistent with rape culture, that language correlates with real-world behavior."[24] In other words, the more the media used or reported rape-culture language, the more sexually violent behaviors went unchecked in the cities where such reporting happened.

We "Cover Up" Abuse

When victims share their stories, many organizations—especially those seeking to protect the reputation of Christ—choose not to go to the police and report, keeping the issues in-house. When a rape or sexual-abuse claim first becomes public, organizational leaders often first think, "How can we protect our institution?" For example, college rape victims who do report their abuse at their universities rarely see their abusers expelled. When victims report rape to their

---

23. Matthew A. Baum et al., "The Way Kavanaugh's Supporters Are Talking about Sexual Assault Allegations Can Be Dangerous, Our New Study Finds," *Washington Post*, September 27, 2018, https://www.washingtonpost.com/news/monkey-cage/wp/2018/09/27/the-way-kavanaughs-supporters-are-talking-about-sexual-assault-allegations-can-be-dangerous-our-new-study-finds/?utm_term=.5106a684a41d.

24. Baum et al., "Kavanaugh's Supporters."

campuses, many faculties and institutions try to cover them up, fail to report them to authorities, or ignore them completely.

In 2017, the media reported that college football players gang-raped a woman as part of a "bonding experience" for new recruits. The university was served with their seventh Title IX lawsuit, a federal civil rights law against sex-based discrimination, which included as many as eight football players drugging a student and taking turns raping her.[25] Another investigation found that seventeen women reported sexual assault or domestic violence carried out by nineteen players, including at least four gang rapes.[26] When these sexual assaults were brought to the attention of the football department, the staff used its own internal disciplinary system that treated the players in a special way and kept all allegations in-house.[27]

The language used around such situations also often perpetuates rape culture. People talking to the media or writing editorials described the men as "young, promising students and athletes." It was said that their "one mistake" could affect their future "promising careers," and it was tragic that these students with good grades have to register as sex offenders and will experience remorse for the rest of their lives. Yet what about the victims? They will suffer for the rest of their lives because of the abuse their rapists put them through.

If we are called to do justice, love mercy, and walk humbly with our God (Micah 6:8), and if we are to speak for those who cannot speak for themselves (Prov. 31:8–9), Christians must stand on the front lines demanding that criminals take responsibility for their actions. Sadly, too often believers call only for victims to forgive, according to Rachael Denhollander, the first woman to publicly accuse former USA Gymnastics doctor Larry Nassar of sexual abuse. Following her, more than 250 women came forward, resulting in a 175-year sentence for the former doctor. Denhollander, now an attorney who is outspoken about her Christian faith, has publicly noted, "Justice is not in opposition to forgiveness. Rather, justice is the foundation for forgiveness."[28]

Pornography
Pornography consumption is linked with sexual aggression. In 2017, the world's largest porn website reached 28.5 billion visitors, which averages 81 million people

---

25. Phillip Ericksen, "Baylor Hit with 7th Title IX Lawsuit, Plaintiff Alleges Gang Rape by Football Players," *Waco Tribune-Herald*, May 17, 2017, https://www.wacotrib.com/news/crime/baylor-hit-with-th-title-ix-lawsuit-plaintiff-alleges-gang/article_1b391c59-1722-5532-9c3b-058b07850249.html.

26. Tom Dart, "Baylor Football Players Raped Women as 'Bonding Experience,' Lawsuit Alleges," *The Guardian*, May 17, 2017, https://www.theguardian.com/us-news/2017/may/17/baylor-university-lawsuit-rape-allegations.

27. Dart, "Baylor Football Players."

28. Simone C. Chu, "First Nassar Accuser Denhollander Talks Justice, Forgiveness at Harvard," *Harvard Crimson*, April 6, 2018, https://www.thecrimson.com/article/2018/4/6/denhollander-talk/.

per day.[29] Research shows that men and women who blame rape victims are more likely to use pornography.[30] One study demonstrates the association between frequent pornography use and sexually aggressive behaviors.[31] True, violent sexual crimes existed before pornography; pornography is thus not the main problem. But it does perpetuate a culture in which sexual crimes are minimized.

Some argue that porn prevents abuse by allowing for a "safer" option for people to let out aggressive sexual energy. Instead of raping someone, it is reasoned, a person can watch porn. Yet in actuality, the more people watch porn, the more likely it is that they will desire to act out what they see in real life.[32] Porn changes the brain, rewiring it and creating new neurological pathways, even to the point of changing perceived reality.[33] The brain is the body's most intricate organ—wired to repeat what it sees and hears.

John D. Foubert, a professor in an endowed position at Oklahoma State University and a leading expert on sexual violence, has stated, "That ingredient responsible for giving young men the permission-giving beliefs that make rape so much more likely and telling young women they should like it is today's high-speed Internet pornography. Pornography provides a recipe for rape that has rewritten the sexual script for the millennial generation and is currently rewiring the brains of the generation to follow."[34] Foubert points out that in porn, 88 percent of the scenes include verbal or physical aggression, usually against women, and the women are shown either enjoying it or bypassing an objection to it.[35] For example, one common porn scene includes multiple men ejaculating on a woman's face and she "likes" it. Pornography perpetuates rape culture by teaching boys and girls false messages.

Another problem: children are now watching pornography at younger and younger ages, even as young as four and five years old.[36] So porn becomes a

---

29. Pornhub, "2017 Year in Review," January 9, 2018, https://www.pornhub.com/insights/2017-year-in-review.

30. John D. Foubert and Ana J. Bridges, "What Is the Attraction? Pornography Use Motives in Relation to Bystander Intervention," *Journal of Interpersonal Violence* 32 (2017): 3071–89.

31. Neil M. Malamuth, Tamara Addison, and Mary Koss, "Pornography and Sexual Aggression: Are There Reliable Effects and Can We Understand Them?," *Annual Review of Sex Research* 11, no. 1 (2000): 26–91.

32. Jochen Peter and Patti M. Valkenburg, "Processes Underlying the Effects of Adolescents' Use of Sexually Explicit Internet Material: The Role of Perceived Realism," *Journal of Research in Crime and Delinquency* 37, no. 3 (April 7, 2010): 375–99, https://doi.org/10.1177/0093650210362464.

33. Fight the New Drug, "How Porn Changes the Brain," Fight the New Drug, June 26, 2018, https://fightthenewdrug.org/how-porn-changes-the-brain/.

34. John D. Foubert, "Public Health Harms of Pornography: Brain, Erectile Dysfunction, and Sexual Violence," *Dignity: A Journal on Sexual Exploitation and Violence* 2, no. 3 (2017).

35. Foubert, "Public Health Harms."

36. Sarah Plake, "KSHB 41: Children Abusing Children: Children's Mercy Sees Dangerous Trend Involving Children and Porn." Children's Mercy (website), December 5, 2018,

child's sex education. A sexual-assault nurse examiner at a children's hospital said, "To sexually assault someone else, that's a learned behavior."[37] Our children are being trained at the age of four or five to be rapists. The nurses said that they had encountered young perpetrators, boys eleven to fourteen, who committed sexual crimes and confessed that they had previously watched pornography and acted out on someone else what they had seen.[38]

Gender Stereotypes

At a young age, children pick up on gender stereotypes. Football players invited into the classroom to give motivational talks say things like, "All my boys, stand up. We strong, right? We strong . . . boys aren't supposed to be soft-spoken. One day, you'll have a very, very deep voice . . . But the ladies— they're supposed to be silent, polite, gentle."[39] Girls are portrayed as *weak*. Boys are portrayed as *strong*. And when we define masculinity as power, authority, assertiveness, or lack of emotions, and we define femininity as submissive, passive, delicate, and weak, we endorse rape culture. Never mind that the woman was given dominion alongside man (Gen. 1:28). Or that Esther embodies courage (Esther 4:16). Or that gentleness is a fruit of the Spirit (Gal. 5:23), not a "female" quality. Yet unbiblical gender stereotypes are passed off as men "just being men."

In our churches we often inadvertently sexualize women. "Modesty talks" often characterize women as sexual tempters and men as sexual animals. Women become defined by their bodies, and men become defined by their brains. From a young age we teach girls to cover, not because their bodies are wonderful gifts, but in order to avoid "tempting" the boys. Instead of teaching love for one's brothers accompanied by teaching boys that self-control is a fruit of the Spirit (v. 23), we communicate that the girl's body is the problem. The responsibility falls on the girls to protect themselves against wild sexual men and to avoid rape. Girls are even held responsible for what boys *think*.

Blinded by Racism

Faces of Black men—those are the rapists we see on TV.[40] Yet statistically,

     https://news.childrensmercy.org/kshb-41-children-abusing-children-childrens-mercy-sees-dangerous-trend-involving-children-and-pornography/.

37. Plake, "Children Abusing Children."

38. Plake, "Children Abusing Children."

39. Alanna Vagianos, "NFL Player to Elementary School Class: Girls Are 'Supposed to Be Silent,'" *Huffington Post*, February 23, 2017, https://www.huffingtonpost.com/entry/jameis-winston-accused-of-rape-to-elementary-class-girls-are-supposed-to-be-silent_us_58af20a2e4b0a8a9b78012e6.

40. Kassia E. Kulaszewicz, "Racism and the Media: A Textual Analysis" (MSW clinical research paper, St. Catherine University School of Social Work, May 2015), https://sophia.stkate.edu/cgi/viewcontent.cgi?article=1478&context=msw_papers.

such images are unwarranted. When looking at the perpetrators of rape, 57 percent are White, and 27 percent are Black.[41]

And the injustice does not stop with imagery. When arrested for sexual assault, White men receive minor punishments when compared to members of underrepresented groups. For example, a White college student was arrested for sexually assaulting an unconscious woman behind a dumpster and sentenced to six months of jail time—a comparatively short sentence for this type of crime. After three months in jail, he was released for "automatically applied credits" for good behavior prior to sentencing.[42] His jailers patted him on the back for good behavior while his victim was left to spend a lifetime overcoming the violence committed against her. Often prosecutors give leniency to first-time offenders to avoid "hurting their future." In the above-mentioned case, the student's father asked the judge to go easy on his son's punishment. In a character-witness letter, he described his son's sexual assault as "20 minutes of action."[43] Would a Black man have the same experience when accused of the same crime?

Tarana Burke, the originator of the #MeToo hashtag, states in an article, "Ending sexual violence will require every voice from every corner of the world, and it will require those whose voices are most often heard to find ways to amplify those voices that often go unheard."[44] When we discuss rape culture, we need to listen to the marginalized voices. In fact, women of color are more vulnerable to sexual harassment than White women, while also less likely to be believed if they do report harassment, assault, or rape.[45]

HOW CAN WE PREVENT RAPE?

Almost every woman has a story in which she has experienced some form of sexual assault, abuse, or harassment. Rape culture is so pervasive that it can feel unconquerable; however, there are ethical steps we can take to fight against it.

41. Department of Justice, "Female Victims of Sexual Violence, 1994–2010," Bureau of Justice Statistics, 2013.

42. Alanna Vagianos, "Remember Brock Turner? From 3 Months Ago? He'll Leave Jail on Friday," *Huffington Post*, March 20, 2017, https://www.huffingtonpost.com/entry/remember-brock-turner-from-3-months-ago-hell-leave-jail-on-friday_us_57c58c81e4b0cdfc5ac9256b.

43. Vagianos, "Brock Turner."

44. Tarana Burke, "#MeToo Was Started for Black and Brown Women and Girls. They're Still Being Ignored," *Washington Post*, November 9, 2017, https://www.washingtonpost.com/news/post-nation/wp/2017/11/09/the-waitress-who-works-in-the-diner-needs-to-know-that-the-issue-of-sexual-harassment-is-about-her-too/?utm_term=.ef070863a937.

45. Katherine Giscombe, "Sexual Harassment and Women of Color," *Catalyst* (blog), February 13, 2018, https://www.catalyst.org/blog/catalyzing/sexual-harassment-and-women-color.

Educate Yourself and Others

As part of "doing justice" in an unjust world, we must seek to advocate for victims. Our world will continue to perpetuate rape culture unless we challenge its precepts and help people understand what causes it and how they can prevent it. Rape culture needs to be confronted at the dinner table, from the pulpit, in youth-group curricula, in school curricula, as part of police-training programs, in public awareness literature, in legislation, in art, in counseling, during sentencing—all of these can contribute to changing rape culture.[46]

Speak Up

Address sexual violence. If you see rape culture in action, speak out against it. Talk about race, privilege, and power in public and private settings. God calls his people to defend, protect, and rescue the weak and powerless. If you see someone being harassed or attacked, step in—without putting your own safety in jeopardy—and ask how you can help them. If you need to intervene but cannot safely do so, call the police. Next time you hear a person ask a question that perpetuates victim-blaming or slut-shaming or a rape myth, kindly intervene.

Educate Young People

Train young men to respect women rather than promoting the "boys will be boys" message. Show neighborhood guys, youth-group guys, and your own sons how to properly respect women and girls and teach them about boundaries. Explain to your daughters that *everyone* should respect their bodies. When young people go to school, educate them about rape. If you are a husband, love your wife sacrificially (see Eph. 5:25) and grant her honor (1 Pet. 3:7) as an example to your children and others of how to treat another or be treated.

Delay Giving Children Cell Phones, and Encourage Others to Do the Same

Once a child has a phone, he or she has immediate access to pornography, which can lead to trauma, addiction, and perpetuating rape culture. A child who has been watching porn since he or she was four years old has been training the brain and body for sexual perversion and learning to take pleasure in it. Once kids have phones, keep up to date on all the options for controlling use, including internet filters and blockers.

Develop and Teach a Theology of Women

What messages do we preach on women in the Bible? Does our theology and teaching blame victims and wrongly sexualize women? While many women in the Bible have historically been treated as vixens (e.g., Eve, Bathsheba, the

---

46. Storkey, *Scars across Humanity*, 133.

woman of Samaria), Jesus elevated and dignified women.[47] We must look to Jesus as our example of how to treat women. Paul praised women as ministry partners (see Rom. 16). Like him, we must model healthy male-female relationships, changing the way society, including the church, views gender and sexuality. We must teach a biblical view of sexuality for single and married people. Jesus refused to treat women as inferior to men or objectify them. His followers must do likewise.

Raise Up Women Leaders

Women were historically involved in early church leadership, yet especially since the third century, they have often been left out of spaces where they are needed.[48] In many churches, women lack opportunities to use their voices. Yet God designed male and female for partnership (Gen. 1:26). So a healthy church will invite women into the upper levels of leadership. Encourage women to sit in on meetings and to share their opinions and insights. Challenge women to serve on committees and teams. Incorporate them in counseling teams. Invest in and train up young women with leadership potential. Model how men, instead of avoiding women, can have familial friendships with women.

Create a Game Plan and Tell the Church

Every church needs a plan for when a victim comes forward and shares an abuse story. What are the first steps to help the victim? With whom will the victim share his or her story? When do you involve authorities, investigations, and elders? If the victim is a woman, should she have to face an all-male elder board? And if so, who will advocate for her? To whom will you report the crime? Share your arrangements publicly with the church leadership and members.

HOW CAN WE HELP VICTIMS?

What is the ethical thing to do if someone comes to you and says she was raped?

Respond in Love

When someone shares an abuse story with you, respond with love, empathy, and concern. Assume a posture of belief. Empathize with the victims and say, "I'm so sorry that happened to you. How are you feeling? What can I do to help you begin healing?" Know the best resources in your area to help victims find healing. For example, have a list of recommended counselors, support groups, and doctors available.

---

47. Sandra Glahn, ed., *Vindicating the Vixens: Revisiting Sexualized, Vilified, and Marginalized Women of the Bible* (Grand Rapids: Kregel Academic, 2017).

48. Robert L. Saucy, and Judith K. TenElshof, eds., *Women and Men in Ministry: A Complementary Perspective* (Chicago: Moody Press, 2001), 179–81.

Seek Justice

In many sexual-assault situations, we tend to emphasize forgiving the perpetrator instead of seeking help for the victim; churches tend to protect priests and pastors instead of advocate for victims. Often justice is completely missing from the equation. As mentioned, both forgiveness and justice are biblical concepts that need addressing in abusive situations. Jacob and Rachael Denhollander write, "When forgiveness is seen as the opposite of justice, despair ensues. In this way, forgiveness becomes another means of abuse—shutting the victim out, denying the rightness of their cry for justice, and heaping further shame."[49] We cannot simply focus on forgiveness. God is both a forgiving God and a just God. When survivors of abuse doubt whether God cares about the evil that was done to them, the Denhollanders say to point to the cross. Encourage victims to see where God incarnate suffered, and say, "This is how much it matters."[50] Help victims look to the cross to see how much God cares about seeking justice.

Believe the Victim

Research consistently shows that 92–98 percent of sexual-assault accusers tell the truth, yet we fail to believe victims because we have a misplaced trust in powerful men and institutions.[51] Statistics tell us that we worry more about someone enduring false accusations than we do about victims being disbelieved, despite the evidence. We more often believe the high-profile person over the less powerful person. Women fear coming forward because, historically, their stories have been discounted. If they finally do come forward, they are not believed. And such a reaction causes other victims to stay quiet; thus the cycle continues, silencing women. Research has shown that one of the greatest ways to help a victim recover from rape is to have their pain and experience validated.[52] Have a posture of believing the victim and affirming that the experience was a crime, and emphasize that coming forward and sharing their story matters.

Report It

In certain situations, such as in a context of foster-parenting or if a minor is involved, if someone does something illegal (e.g., rape, child porn), you have an obligation to report it to the police. To report it, you must understand what constitutes abuse and harassment. Learn the laws and when you are required to report. Reporting abuse will not harm the name of Jesus or the gospel. In reality, excusing rapists and silencing victims actually shames the gospel. Jesus never would have silenced or shamed anyone, especially when he often called out the

---

49. Denhollander and Denhollander, "Justice."
50. Denhollander and Denhollander, "Justice."
51. Dick and Ziering, *Hunting Ground*.
52. Sarah E. Ullman, "Social Reactions, Coping Strategies, and Self-Blame Attributions in Adjustment to Sexual Assault," *Psychology of Women Quarterly* 20, no. 4 (1996): 524.

Pharisees and lifted up the marginalized, abused, and hurting. The apostle Paul exhorted the Ephesians to do the opposite of covering sin: "Have nothing to do with the fruitless deeds of darkness, but rather expose them" (Eph. 5:11 NIV).

Churches should be safe environments where men and women can come for hope, help, and healing. The body of Christ should be where healthy brother-sister relationships are modeled. Creating safety and opportunity for victims is an integral part of ministry, a form of standing with the powerless. Yet for many the church does not feel like a safe place. So believers must create cultures of men and women in friendship, community, and collaboration. Leaders need to look for ways to create opportunities for women to have a voice. Men in power need to ask: Where in the church are women's voices lacking? Where can men better partner with women? Where can we better model mutual respect rather than segregation and fear? And how can we create systems of accountability where the powerful cannot prey on those with less power?

CONCLUSION

Today my traumatic experience is part of my ministry. Through a lot of work and the help of men and women committed to living biblically, I have found hope and healing and redemption. The same can be true for those with whom you have influence.

The process of responding to rape and rape culture in ethical ways requires changes in our thinking, changes in our relationships, changes in our teaching, and changes in our institutions. In this essay we have looked at false messages that lead people to minimize sins against victims. We have considered how to model healthy relationships, expose sin, and promote healing. An ethical leader will combine compassion and courage to step into the trauma, shepherd people well, and model healthy relationships of men and women in partnership. With these dynamics in place, we can help the church and her people be less enabling of evil and instead be sources of righteousness and consolation.

FOR DISCUSSION

1. Where in the church are women's voices lacking?

2. Where can men better partner with women?

3. How can we create systems of accountability where the powerful cannot prey on those with less power?

FOR FURTHER READING

Allender, Dan B. *Healing the Wounded Heart: The Heartache of Sexual Abuse and the Hope of Transformation.* Grand Rapids: Baker Books, 2016.

DeMuth, Mary. *We Too: How the Church Can Respond Redemptively to the Sexual Abuse Crisis.* Eugene, OR: Harvest House, 2019.

Gay, Roxane. *Not That Bad: Dispatches from Rape Culture.* New York: Harper-Collins, 2018.

Holcomb, Justin S., and Lindsey A. Holcomb. *Rid of My Disgrace: Hope and Healing for Victims of Sexual Assault.* Wheaton, IL: Crossway, 2011.

Storkey, Elaine. *Scars across Humanity: Understanding and Overcoming Violence against Women.* Downers Grove, IL: IVP Academic, 2018.

CHAPTER 18

PORNOGRAPHY, PROSTITUTION, AND POLYAMORY

JAMES K. CHILDERSTON AND DEBBY WADE

God's blueprint for sexual health contributes to human flourishing. And that blueprint includes a positive and respectful approach to sexuality and sexual relationships. Yet many see the blueprint as limiting, ignoring it as they build their own structures on a fractured foundation. In this chapter we will look at some specific ways they do so—through pornography, prostitution, and polyamory—in addition to pointing readers to moral absolutes, which serve as the foundation for sexual flourishing.

PORNOGRAPHY

The Relational Challenges of Porn Engagement

Human beings are a unique blend of mind (mental, emotional, psychological creatures), body (physical, biological, biochemical, genetic, and reproductive creatures), and spirit (spiritual and relational creatures). The mind, body, and spirit affect one another and are inextricably linked in how they influence human behavior. Consider depression, for example. When a person becomes depressed, the etiology can be certain thoughts; it could be due to physiological problems; or it may be rooted in spiritual issues. Left untreated, depression saturates mind, body, and spirit, and only in addressing each of these areas does one find transformational healing. Similarly, we can think of sexual challenges as strictly physical and focus primarily on the body when considering treatment. But that would do a disservice to the person because such an approach fails to consider the intricacy of human sexuality. Engaging with pornography has an impact on the mind, body, and spirit, each in unique and substantial ways.

For the purposes of this discussion, we'll define pornography as the portrayal of sexual subject matter for the purpose of sexual arousal. The porn industry makes a lot of money. According to Alex Helmy, founder and publisher of an adult-entertainment trade publication, the industry made more than $6 billion in 2018. But, he said, "Revenue estimates for the porn industry vary widely. Some believe the industry does not even make $6 billion a year, while others say it makes $10 billion, $15 billion, or even $97 billion. Because most porn firms are privately held, it's impossible to get a completely accurate estimate."[1] The *New York Times* reporter responsible for covering the porn industry places that number at $1 billion. But whatever the number, it's in the billions, not millions.[2] And that represents a lot of users.

Long gone are the days when curious individuals had to go to the store to buy a *Penthouse* or *Playboy*. These days, a new porn video is produced about every thirty-nine minutes,[3] and it's likely made available for free. Twenty percent of men and 13 percent of women access pornography while at work, accounting for a staggering $16.9 billion annual productivity loss to companies.[4]

Pornography is no small problem. And it's certainly not confined to one age group or demographic. Analyzing how younger generations interact with and access porn, however, provides insight into our future. Roxanne Stone says, "There appears to be a momentous generational shift underway in how pornography is perceived morally speaking within our culture. This shift is particularly notable when it comes to personal choice regarding pornography use, but these attitudes and preferences toward porn among the younger generations need to consider the broader social and cultural context that American young people inhabit. For one, they're coming of age in a culture that is giving preference to personal experience and personal morality."[5]

In 2016, the Barna Group published extensive research on human attitudes and behaviors surrounding porn.[6] Barna triangulated data related to viewing

1. Ross Benes, "Porn Could Have a Bigger Economic Influence on the US than Netflix," Yahoo Finance, June 20, 2018, https://finance.yahoo.com/news/porn-could-bigger-economic-influence-121524565.html.

2. Katie Van Syckle, "What It's Like to Report about the Porn Industry," *New York Times*, March 26, 2018, https://www.nytimes.com/2018/03/26/insider/reporting-the-porn-industry.html.

3. Strange but True, "How Big Is the Porn Industry?" Medium, February 19, 2017, https://medium.com/@Strange_bt_True/how-big-is-the-porn-industry-fbc1ac78091b.

4. Webroot, "Internet Pornography by the Numbers: A Significant Threat to Society," https://www.webroot.com/us/en/resources/tips-articles/internet-pornography-by-the-numbers.

5. Roxanne Stone, "Teens and Young Adults Use Porn More than Anyone Else," Barna, January 28, 2016, https://www.barna.com/research/teens-young-adults-use-porn-more-than-anyone-else/.

6. Stone, "Teens and Young Adults."

porn and a person's intention to view porn. Their researchers found that young adults between the ages of eighteen and twenty-four are the most likely to encounter porn on a regular basis. More than seven in ten (71 percent) said they encounter porn at least once or twice a month. Only three in ten said they never or rarely ran into pornographic content. In contrast, between 50 and 60 percent of teens and older millennials ages twenty-five to thirty, and 58 percent of Gen Xers reported encountering porn at least once or twice a month.

Young adults ages eighteen to twenty-four reported seeking out porn at least once or twice a month. They did so more than those in any other generational group, due in part to widespread availability, access, and inherent sexual curiosity at this developmental stage.

In addition to viewing habits, researchers also analyzed attitudes. Teens, young adults, and adults aged twenty-five and older rated a series of action statements according to a five-point scale. Results revealed that barely half (54 percent) of adults consider viewing porn to be wrong. In terms of ethics, porn ranked seventh on a list of eleven actions, behind overeating, which ranked fourth. Teens considered not recycling to be more immoral than any of the actions related to porn use. The nonchalance of teens and young adults is also revealed by how often they talk about, or share, porn with friends. Barna research found that one-third of eighteen- to twenty-four-year-olds and one in six teens talk about or share porn with friends very often or occasionally. The level of casual acceptance of porn makes sense, given that half of young adults and one-third of teens report that all or most of their friends regularly view porn. From this we can conclude that viewing porn is perceived as normal within these age groups.

Given the widespread use and acceptance of pornography, why should we as humans, Christians, and counselors care? Because God's beautiful and good design calls us to a much higher good than objectification and self-gratification. In her book *Alone Together: Why We Expect More from Technology and Less from Each Other*, Sherry Turkle wisely observes, "A love relationship involves coming to savor the surprises of the rough patches of looking at the world from another's point of view, shaped by history, biology, trauma, and joy. Computers and robots do not have these experiences to share. We look at mass media and worry about our culture being intellectually 'dumbed down.' [David Levy's book] *Love and Sex* seems to celebrate an emotional dumbing down, a willful turning away from the complexities of human partnerships—the inauthentic as a new aesthetic."[7] Technology will continue to advance and further transform how humans relate to one another, shaping global opinions on sex and love. And as our digital lives evolve, the impact on our brains of what we view and how we view it remains to be fully seen. But we know God made us for so much more.

---

7. Sherry Turkle, *Alone Together: Why We Expect More from Technology and Less from Each Other* (New York: Basic Books, 2011), 268. See David Levy, *Love and Sex with Robots: The Evolution of Human-Robot Relationships* (New York: HarperCollins, 2009).

Since the mind, body, and spirit affect one another and are inextricably linked in how they influence human behavior, we cannot think of sexual challenges as strictly physical. However, we must examine closely the physical and biological to better understand its impact on the intricacies of whole-person human sexuality.

The Neuroscience of Porn Addiction

Why does porn prove time and again to be so significantly influential on the brain (and the male brain especially)? William Struthers, author of *Wired for Intimacy*, introduces an apt metaphor. He says that pornographic content is like a high definition (HD) signal, and the male brain is a perfectly built and tuned HD receiver, wired to be on alert. The depiction of nudity and sexual acts have a hypnotic, transfixing effect, much like an HD television. When men fixate on porn, the repeated and extended exposure creates neural pathways. Over time, a habit forms. From a neurological perspective, humans don't unlearn habits. Once a neural pathway is formed, it stays in the brain until a new and different pathway replaces it.[8]

According to Struthers, 50 percent of human brain activity is dedicated to the reception and interpretation of visual stimuli. Sexual stimulation, in particular, causes the male limbic system, the amygdala, and other brain-stem structures in charge of emotion to fire at the same time. Meanwhile, the prefrontal cortex checks out, leaving the judgment area vacant. When one engages with porn, the nucleus accumbens—the pleasure center of the brain—is flooded with dopamine, which activates the same receptors as opioids do. The result: engaging with porn can become incredibly addictive.

How does porn addiction become hardwired into the male brain? As men arouse themselves and masturbate to porn, they establish a complex, multi-system neurological habit that involves the visual system (looking), the motor system (masturbation), the sensory system (genital stimulation), and the neurological aftermath of orgasm (euphoria from addictive dopamine in the nucleus accumbens and increased activity in the amygdala). Because of the intricacy of reactions generated by the act of engaging with porn, the cycle of this addiction, like so many, can prove extremely difficult to break.

Research on the female brain and porn is late to the lab, as Beverly Whipple—the scientist known for "discovering" the G-Spot—has noted. Women were not even included in such research until after 1993. "Most of the research that was conducted in terms of human sexual responses was conducted in men and findings were extrapolated to women," she said. "We found out that that doesn't work because women are different from men."[9]

---

8. William M. Struthers, *Wired for Intimacy: How Pornography Hijacks the Male Brain* (Downers Grove, IL: InterVarsity Press, 2010).
9. Beverly Whipple, "Big Think Interview with Beverly Whipple," Big Think, November 2, 2009, https://bigthink.com/videos/big-think-interview-with-beverly-whipple.

Nevertheless, we do know this: porn is not just a "guy thing." The same 2015 Barna study referenced earlier revealed that teens and young women were significantly more likely to seek out porn than women over twenty-five—a statistic similar to rates for men. More than half of women twenty-five and under reported seeking out porn, and one-third sought it out at least monthly. In contrast, among teen and young adult men, 81 percent seek it out at times and 67 percent do so at least monthly.[10]

Patrick Carnes, author of *Facing the Shadow: Starting Sexual and Relationship Recovery*, proposes that anything affordable, accessible, and anonymous holds the potential for addiction. Porn checks all those boxes. And an addiction to porn skews intimacy and obscures relationships. In fact, the more one looks at and engages with porn, the more real relationships can begin to feel laborious and even extraneous. The human ability to connect diminishes with lack of practice, and the more an individual addicted to porn detaches from the real world, the more difficult it becomes to engage effectively once more.[11]

Prostitution and Pornography

Adjacent to pornography is prostitution; a striking relationship exists between them. In a study that compared men who buy sex with those who don't buy sex, researchers found that sex buyers masturbated to pornography more often than those who did not buy sex. The sex buyers also imitated pornography with partners more often, and had more often received their sex education from pornography than the non-sex buyers. Over time, as a result of their prostitution and pornography use, sex buyers reported that their sexual preferences changed to mimic what they viewed in pornography.[12]

Catharine MacKinnon, who has interviewed many people in the business of pornography, states, "To distinguish pornography from prostitution . . . is to deny the obvious: when you make pornography of a woman, you make a prostitute out of her. In the immortal words of one trick, 'Yes, the woman in pornography is a prostitute. They're prostituting right before the cameras. They're getting money from a film company rather than individuals.' [To distinguish porn from prostitution] is also to deny the plain fact that pornographers

10. David Kinnaman, "The Porn Phenomenon" Barna, February 5, 2016, https://www.barna.com/the-porn-phenomenon/.

11. Bethesda Workshops, "Definition of Sexual Addiction," https://www.bethesdaworkshops.org/sexual-addiction/. See also Patrick Carnes, *Facing the Shadow: Starting Sexual and Relationship Recovery*, 2nd ed. (Carefree, AZ: Gentle Path Press, 2008).

12. Melissa Farley et al., "Comparing Sex Buyers with Men Who Don't Buy Sex: 'You Can Have a Good Time with the Servitude' vs. 'You're Supporting a System of Degradation'" (report at Psychologists for Social Responsibility Annual Meeting, Boston, 2011), http://www.prostitutionresearch.com/pdfs/Farleyetal2011ComparingSexBuyers.pdf.

are pimps, third-party sex profiteers, buying and selling human beings to johns, who are consuming them as and for sex."[13]

PROSTITUTION

A Global Issue

Prostitution is the business or practice of engaging in sexual relations in exchange for payment, sometimes described as commercial sex, or euphemistically referred to as the "world's oldest profession." Estimates from *Prostitution: Prices and Statistics of the Global Sex Trade* place the annual revenue generated by prostitution worldwide to be more than $186 billion.[14]

According to *Business Insider*, there are more than 42 million prostitutes living in the world. An estimated 1 million prostitutes live in the United States, even though it's legal only in Nevada.[15]

In 1949, the United Nations General Assembly adopted a convention stating that prostitution and the accompanying evil of the traffic of persons for the purpose of prostitution are incompatible with the dignity and worth of a human person. The United Nations required all signing parties to punish pimps and brothel owners, and they required operators to abolish all special treatment or registration of prostitutes.[16] As of December 2013, eighty-two states were party to the convention including France, Spain, Italy, and Denmark. It was not ratified by another ninety-seven member nations, including Germany, the Netherlands, New Zealand, Greece, Turkey, and, interestingly, the United States. One of the main reasons the convention has not been ratified by many countries is because it applies both to voluntary and involuntary prostitution.

By the Numbers

Melissa Farley, a research and clinical psychologist, is the executive director of Prostitution Research and Education. In her research she has found that about 2 percent of prostitutes work for a lot of money for a short period of time and then get out or are financially taken care of by one man. However, 38 percent of prostitutes are in dire need of money and become prostitutes as a result of

13. Catharine A. MacKinnon, "Pornography as Trafficking," *Michigan Journal of International Law* 26, no. 4 (2005), http://www.prostitutionresearch.com/MacKinnon%20Pornography%20as%20Trafficking.pdf.

14. *Prostitution: Prices and Statistics of the Global Sex Trade* (n.p.: Havocscope, 2015), http://www.prostitutionresearch.com/pdfs/Farleyetal2011ComparingSexBuyers.pdf.

15. Gus Lubin, "There Are 42 Million Prostitutes in the World, and Here's Where They Live," *Business Insider*, January 17, 2012, https://www.businessinsider.com/there-are-42-million-prostitutes-in-the-world-and-heres-where-they-live-2012-1.

16. United Nations Human Rights Office of the High Commissioner, "Convention for the Suppression of the Traffic in Persons and of the Exploitation of the Prostitution of Others," December 2, 1949, https://www.ohchr.org/EN/ProfessionalInterest/Pages/TrafficInPersons.aspx.

childhood abuse or incest. Sixty percent of prostitutes are the poorest people in the prostitution industry. Prostitutes typically have enormously restricted life choices, and many female prostitutes have been physically coerced into the profession.[17]

Farley also notes the following statistics highlighting the violent nature of prostitution:

1. 95 percent of those in prostitution have experienced sexual harassment that would be legally actionable in another job setting.
2. 65–95 percent of those in prostitution were sexually assaulted as children.
3. 70–95 percent were physically assaulted while engaging in prostitution.
4. 60–75 percent were raped while engaging in prostitution.
5. 75 percent of those in prostitution have been homeless at some point in their lives.
6. 85–95 percent of those in prostitution want to escape it, but have no other options for survival.
7. 68 percent of 854 people in strip club prostitution, massage prostitution, and street prostitution in nine countries met criteria for posttraumatic stress disorder (PTSD).
8. 80–90 percent of those in prostitution experience verbal abuse and social contempt which adversely affect them.[18]

An Ethical Dilemma

It's generally accepted by secular ethicists that when coercion is involved (e.g., through trafficking, slavery, threat, or desperation) prostitution is immoral and harmful. But when individuals freely choose to become prostitutes, the question of whether prostitution is harmful becomes more nuanced. The secular premise is that casual sex is permissible. Thus those selling their bodies of their own will and freedom aren't in the wrong. Additionally, some secular ethicists argue that almost all jobs involve someone benefiting from another's efforts, so what's the difference if it's prostitution? In other words: Is exploitation acceptable if it's within a certain range?

Philosopher and ethicist Scott Anderson argues that prostitution should be considered a violation of one's sexual autonomy. Further, there are consequences

---

17. Melissa Farley, Prostitution Research and Education Website, 2008, prostitutionresearch.com. How many people are being trafficked as prostitutes? According to prostitutionresearch.com, "It is our suggestion that in the absence of any estimates with any good scientific basis, that scholars, writers and advocates stop using the unsubstantiated estimates and simply indicate that the true incidence is currently unknown." http://www.prostitutionresearch.com/Juvenile_ProstitutionFactsheet2008.pdf.
18. Melissa Farley, "Prostitution Is Sexual Violence," Psychiatric Times, October 1, 2004, http://www.psychiatrictimes.com/sexual-offenses/content/article/10168/48311.

inherent in treating sex like any other commercial service. In fact, if such consequences make us feel uncomfortable, Anderson points out, then that must mean there is something unique and special about sexuality that warrants segregating sexual activity from commercial activity.[19]

Eighteenth-century philosopher Immanuel Kant argued that prostitution violates the duty to oneself:

- "A man who fails in his duty to himself loses worth absolutely."
- "If you fail in your duty to yourself, then you cannot do your duty towards others" both in terms of goodwill and justice.
- "If a man for gain or profit submits to all indignities and makes himself the plaything of another, he casts away the worth of his manhood . . . to let one's person out on hire and to surrender it to another for the satisfaction of his sexual desire in return for money is the depth of infamy."
- "It is absurd that a reasonable being, an end for the sake of which all else is means, should use himself as a means. It is true that a person can serve as a means for others, but only in a way whereby he does not cease to be a person and an end."
- "Sexual love makes the person an Object of appetite; as soon as that appetite has been stilled, the person is cast aside as one casts away a lemon which has been sucked dry."[20]

So, from the Kantian view, prostitution fails to fulfill the duties to oneself, it fails the duties to others, and it also fails the universal and means-to-end test.

To Legalize or Not to Legalize?

Pro-legalization proponents argue that women do not, in fact, sell *themselves* but instead sell a service. Secular ethicist Lars Ericsson writes that people who view prostitution negatively are prevented from seeing otherwise due to their own "cultural blindness and sexual taboos."[21] Therefore, he argues, the extrinsic source of the harm suffered by prostitutes lies in how prostitutes are socially and legally treated. He believes the violence, harm, and stigma associated with prostitution can be eliminated if legalized. For prostitution to become a profession of only moderate risk requires a shift in the social and legal treatment of prostitutes.[22]

---

19. Scott Anderson, "Prostitution and Sexual Autonomy: Making Sense of the Prohibition of Prostitution," *Ethics* 112, no. 4 (July 2002): 748–80.
20. Immanuel Kant, *Lectures on Ethics*, trans. Louis Infield (Indianapolis: Hackett, 1980), 163.
21. Lars O. Ericsson, "Charges against Prostitution: An Attempt at a Philosophical Assessment," *Ethics* 90, no. 3 (April 1980): 353.
22. Ericsson, "Charges against Prostitution," 335–66.

However, the legalization of prostitution could force unwelcome pressure on society's sexual attitudes. For example, imagine if prostitution were legal and large companies chose to get involved, offering sexual services marketed aggressively to the public consumer, cultivating brand loyalty and establishing niche markets for underserved sexual needs. Imagine if we had companies on the stock market selling sex—how might that change our global landscape and societal values?[23]

Dispelling Myths Surrounding the Legalization of Prostitution

To further emphasize the difficulty in legitimizing prostitution as a legal entity, let alone as an ethically acceptable behavior, Farley and others have addressed myths associated with the legalizing of prostitution:[24]

Myth 1: Legalizing prostitution gets rid of its criminal elements.

Fact: Legalizing prostitution *benefits* pimps and traffickers. It also benefits johns. Some people believe that legalizing prostitution would offer dignity and professionalism to women in prostitution. But legitimizing prostitution through legalization does not change the actual experience of sex work, nor does it dignify prostituted women who still experience a range of harms, even in legal prostitution.

Myth 2: Men need sex; therefore, prostitution must exist. Prostitution is a natural form of human sexuality.

Fact: Buying women and children in prostitution is less about sexual gratification than power gratification. Most men who use women in prostitution have other sexual partners. In fact, 85 percent of johns in the United States have regular sexual partners; 60 percent of them are married.

Myth 3: Prostitution is sexual liberation.

Fact: Prostitution is sexual exploitation. One of the long-term effects of prostitution is the destruction of an individual's sexuality.

Myth 4: Prostitution is a choice. It's better to choose to make lots of money as a prostitute than to work at a minimum-wage job.

Fact: Prostitution represents primarily the lack of choice among the most vulnerable. Most women in prostitution suffer from poverty, and their entry into the industry happens as a result of their desperate need for

---

23. Anderson, "Prostitution and Sexual Autonomy," 748–780.
24. Melissa Farley, "Myths and Facts about Trafficking for Legal and Illegal Prostitution," Prostitution Research, March 2009, http://www.prostitutionresearch.com/pdfs/Myths%20&%20Facts%20Legal%20&%20Illegal%20Prostitution%203-09.pdf.

money. Yet almost no one gets out of poverty through prostitution. In addition to poverty, a prior history of childhood physical and/or sexual abuse is common among prostituted women.[25]

A five-country study found that 92 percent of women, men, and transgendered people in prostitution wanted immediate help to escape it. In the United States, 81 percent of the women in Nevada's legal brothels urgently want to escape prostitution.

Myth 5:   Prostitution is a victimless crime.
Fact: Legal prostitution does not protect women in prostitution from harm. One study from the United Kingdom found that 63 percent of women in prostitution had experienced violence. Women who have worked in prostitution exhibit the same incidence of traumatic brain injury as has been documented in torture survivors. These traumatic brain injuries are a result of being beaten, hit, kicked in the head, strangled, or having their head slammed into objects.[26]

Myth 6:   Most prostitution does not involve pimps.
Fact: Health-service providers, shelter staff, survivors of prostitution, and law-enforcement sources estimate that 65–85 percent of all prostitution is pimp-dominated.

Myth 7:   Legalizing prostitution would protect sexually exploited children. When prostitution is legal, licensed brothel owners do not hire minors or trafficked women.
Fact: Legal prostitution increases the sexual assaults of children in prostitution. The Amsterdam-based organization ChildRight estimates that the number of children in prostitution increased by more than 300 percent between 1996 (four thousand children) and 2001 (fifteen thousand children).[27]

---

25.   Catharine A. MacKinnon, "Trafficking, Prostitution, and Inequality," *Harvard Civil Rights–Civil Liberties Law Review* 46 (2011): 271, http://www.prostitutionresearch.com/pdfs/MacKinnon%20(2011)%20Trafficking%20Prostitution%20and%20Inequality.pdf.

26.   Uwe Jacobs and Vincent Iacopino, "Torture and Its Consequences: A Challenge to Clinical Neuropsychology," *Professional Psychology: Research and Practice* 32, no. 5 (2001): 458–64.

27.   Janice G. Raymond, "Ten Reasons for Not Legalizing Prostitution and a Legal Response to the Demand for Prostitution," *Journal of Trauma Practice* 2, nos. 3–4 (2003): 315–32; Melissa Farley, ed., *Prostitution, Trafficking and Traumatic Stress* (Binghamton, NY: Haworth, 2004).

Myth 8:   Social stigma is the most harmful aspect of prostitution.

Fact: The worst thing about prostitution is not social stigma. It is rape, strangulation, beatings, toxic verbal abuse, and other violence from johns and pimps.

Myth 9:   If you try to abolish prostitution, it will go underground.

Fact: There is no evidence to support that extortionate attitude.

Myth 10:   Prostitution is a deterrent to sex crimes.

Fact: Research indicates that prostitution is associated with increased rates of rape and other sexual violence. Evidence from Nevada and Australia, where prostitution is legal, indicates that legal prostitution fosters a "prostitution culture" that affects all women and children. Nevada's women are raped at rates twice that of New York and one-fourth higher than the US average.

Myth 11:   Pornography and stripping are not prostitution.

Fact: Pornography, stripping, exotic dancing, and lap dancing are almost always associated with prostitution. Pornography actresses have much in common with others in prostitution such as their poverty, history of sexual abuse, and drug addictions. One hundred percent of women at a strip club in one study said they had been propositioned as prostitutes by strip-club patrons.

Myth 12:   Legalization of prostitution is an entirely separate issue from human trafficking.

Fact: Prostitution is the destination point for trafficking. Legalization of prostitution promotes sex trafficking. Since 1999, there have been reports that at least 80 percent of women in Dutch legal prostitution had been trafficked. By 2009, the Dutch government closed approximately two out of three legal brothels in Amsterdam because of the inability to control traffickers and other organized crime. By the mid 1990s, 75 percent of women in legal German prostitution were from countries other than Germany, with most being trafficked from Eastern Europe.

Myth 13:   Even if it's not perfect, legalizing prostitution would at least make prostitution a little bit better.

Fact: Legalization of prostitution increases illegal prostitution. It does not improve the lives of women in prostitution. A truly progressive law promotes women's equality, not women's prostitution. A model example is a 1999 Swedish law, which describes prostitution as a human-rights violation against women. Understanding the massive social and legal power difference in the prostitution transaction, Sweden arrests johns but not the women in prostitution. Trafficking and prostitution have plummeted in Sweden since the law was introduced.

Myth 14: Legalized prostitution would control the sex industry.
Fact: Legalization/decriminalization of prostitution expands the sex industry. Over the past decade in the Netherlands, as pimping was legalized and brothels decriminalized in the year 2000, the sex industry increased by 25 percent.

Myth 15: Legal prostitution brings tremendous tax benefits to cash-strapped regions. Nevada's rural counties reap economic benefits from legal prostitution.
Fact: Regions with legal prostitution experience adverse economic effects. By the time licensing, policing, and other state-paid tasks are performed, most counties with legal brothels barely break even.

Myth 16: If you oppose legal prostitution, you're a moralistic, judgmental, prudish person who is pushing your value system on people who think differently from you.
Fact: While people are entitled to their moral and religious beliefs, much opposition to the institution of prostitution is based on evidence of the harms of prostitution documented by researchers, health-service providers, and law enforcement.

It has been said that prostitution is the world's oldest profession. But it would be more accurate to say that prostitution is the world's oldest oppression. Those called to "do justice" (Micah 6:8) do well to "speak out for those who cannot speak for themselves" (Prov. 31:8)—which includes those caught in the web of selling access to their bodies for profit.

POLYAMORY

The Basics

Polyamory—from the Greek πολύ, meaning "many, several," and the Latin *amor* or "love"—is the practice of or desire for intimate relationships involving more than two people, with the knowledge and consent of everyone involved. Polyamory has been described as consensual, ethical, and responsible nonmonogamy.[28] People

---

28. See Elisabeth Sheff, *When Someone You Love Is Polyamorous: Understanding Poly People and Relationships* (Portland: Thorntree, 2016). Also Preston Sprinkle and Branson Parler, "Polyamory: Pastors' Next Sexual Frontier," *Christianity Today*, Fall 2019, September 25, 2019, https://preview.tinyurl.com/CT-polyamory.

who identify as polyamorous typically reject the view that sexual and relational exclusivity are necessary for deep, committed, long-term loving relationships.

It is difficult to accurately assess the number of polyamorous relationships because they are not included in census data, and many are "closeted" and unwilling to publicly declare their relationship. Kelly Cookson, an independent academic, summarized his findings this way: "It appears that sexually non-monogamous couples in the United States number in the millions. Estimates based on actually trying sexual non-monogamy are around 1.2 to 2.4 million. An estimate based solely on the agreement to allow satellite lovers is around 9.8 million. These millions include poly couples, swinging couples, gay male couples, and other sexually non-monogamous couples."[29] In practice, polyamorous relationships are highly varied and individualized, depending on those participating.

Although society as a whole generally disapproves of polyamorous relationships, the acceptance of alternative lifestyles has been increasing. According to a 2015 Gallup poll, 16 percent of Americans viewed the concept of a married person having more than one partner as "acceptable." This, compared to a 7 percent acceptability rating in 2001, showed a 9 percent increase over those fourteen years.[30]

Polyamory Values

Polyamorists subscribe to a notion of "ethical nonmonogamy" that, as they describe it, values integrity, honesty, kindness, decency, and belief in the truth, justice, honor, respect, compassion, and working together to make life better. The values of polyamory emphasize fidelity and loyalty. But those in polyamorous lifestyles define "fidelity" not as sexual exclusivity, but rather as faithfulness *to the promises and agreements within the relationship*. These relationships stress open communication and negotiations, ensuring that all involved consent to the terms of the relationship. In a polyamorous relationship, it's imperative that the partners be accepted into each other's lives fully, rather than merely being tolerated. For some polyamorous groups, the primary relationship is the marital relationship. Anything that has a negative impact on that relationship could mean elimination of the other partners.

Most polyamorous relationships practice equality—meaning that there are not different rules based on whether one is male or female. Some adhere to male- or female-specific boundaries until all parties become comfortable with the new dynamic. For example, a wife might agree to refrain from engaging sexually

29. Elisabeth Sheff, "How Many Polyamorists Are There in the U.S.?," *Psychology Today*, May 2014, https://www.psychologytoday.com/us/blog/the-polyamorists-next-door/201405/how-many-polyamorists-are-there-in-the-us.

30. Frank Newport, "Americans Continue to Shift Left on Key Moral Issues," Gallup Social and Policy Issues, May 2015, https://news.gallup.com/poll/183413/americans-continue-shift-left-key-moral-issues.aspx.

with another man at her husband's request but may still be allowed to have romantic and sexual relationships with women. Interestingly, a primary goal for polyamorous relationships is to achieve what's referred to as "compersion," or the opposite of jealousy, a sense of joy in witnessing a lover or partner love another.

Why Choose a Polyamorous Lifestyle?

The reasons individuals choose polyamory are many and varied. Some come to the polyamorous lifestyle hoping that it will allow them to avoid dealing with problematic personal or relational issues. As with any lifestyle change, polyamory can shake things up and stave off the monotony of a long-term relationship. But more often, one partner reluctantly agrees to polyamory to win the affections of the other, secretly hoping that this unwelcome twist will magically vanish once they recommit to one another and to this new life.[31]

Some individuals use polyamory to consciously or unconsciously create a situation in which they can heal childhood wounds or replicate a large extended family. Still others believe in the benefits of rearing children in a stable, nurturing environment with several other responsible adults to help. For some people, polyamory provides a mask for their addiction to sex or drama, while others may use it as a vehicle for rebellion or as a weapon against a controlling partner.

The "Benefits" of Polyamory

Advocates of polyamory see strength in numbers. When conflicts arise, multiple adults can step in to problem-solve, deliberate, mediate, and/or listen, offering more emotional support and often a more stable home environment. Polyamorous relationships bring together an extended "family" with a wide range of experiences, skills, resources, and perspectives. These families can share the burden of chores and childrearing while greatly reducing the per capita cost of living, thus improving financial security. Additionally, polyamory can offer relief from the unspoken expectation that one must meet all of the partner's primary needs, both physical and emotional.[32]

Certainly there are also downsides to polyamory, as one might expect. Elisabeth Sheff noted five specific problem areas. (1) Romantic relationships are complex and can be highly emotional, and that intensity can be multiplied by the number of people involved. (2) There can be frequent partner turnover—the larger a poly groups get, research indicates, the more often they experience a change in membership. (3) Consent negotiated under duress can destroy [or "will damage"] a polyamorous relationship. (4) Polys can experience legal problems,

---

31. Deborah Anapol, "Why Do People Choose Polyamory?," *Psychology Today*, August 2010, https://www.psychologytoday.com/us/blog/love-without-limits/201008/why-do-people-choose-polyamory.

32. Cherie L. Ve Ard and Franklin Veaux, "Polyamory 101," More than Two: Franklin Veaux's Polyamory Site, 2003, https://www.morethantwo.com/poly101.pdf.

and sexual minorities have traditionally fared poorly in court. Finally, (5) kids complain that they have had difficulty getting away with anything because there were too many adults paying attention.[33]

It is interesting to hear the perspective from a "former" polyamorist. Robert Masters is a Canadian therapist who previously headed an intentional community that utilized many radical measures to help people "awaken to their divinity," including nonmonogamy. But Masters changed his views. He now believes that

> if we were to put monogamy up against polyamory, with regard to depth, awakening potential, and capacity for real intimacy, which would come out on top? Monogamy, by a landslide, so long as we're talking about mature monogamy, as opposed to conventional (or growth-stunting and passion-dulling) monogamy, referred to from now on as immature monogamy. Immature monogamy is, especially in men, frequently infected with promiscuous desire and fantasy, however much that might be repressed or camouflaged with upstanding virtues. Airbrush this, infuse it with talk of integrity and unconditional love and jealousy-transcending ethics, consider bringing in another partner or two, and you're closer than near to polyamorous or multiple-partnering territory.[34]

Masters came to his appreciation for monogamy relatively late in life, after years of multiple-partner relating. While he does not emphasize stability as a criterion for preferring monogamy, it does appear that stability is part of the appeal for him. Instead, Masters uses the language of attachment, and he critiques multipartner relating as a way to avoid attachment.

Polyamory in the Law

The Unitarian Universalists of Polyamory Awareness (UUPA), founded in 2001, engage in ongoing education and advocacy for greater understanding and acceptance of polyamory within the Unitarian Universalist Association (UUA).[35] At the 2014 General Assembly, two UUPA members moved to include the categories of family and relationship structures in the UUA's nondiscrimination rules, with the intention that polyamory would become a protected state.[36]

Having multiple nonmarital partners, even if married to one, is illegal in most United States jurisdictions. At most, having multiple partners constitutes

---

33. Elisabeth Sheff, "Five Disadvantages of Polyamory," *Psychology Today*, September 2015, https://www.psychologytoday.com/us/blog/the-polyamorists-next-door/201509/five-disadvantages-polyamory.

34. Anapol, "Why Do People Choose Polyamory?"

35. Unitarian Universalists for Polyamory Awareness website, http://www.uupa.org.

36. Unitarian Universalist Association Bylaws and Rules, rule 2, section C-2.3.: Non-discrimination.

grounds for divorce if one spouse is nonconsenting or feels that this destabilizes the marriage. More recently, some states have reviewed their laws criminalizing consensual sexual activity in the wake of the Supreme Court's ruling in *Lawrence v. Texas*, which struck down the sodomy law in Texas.[37] Social conservatives hold that the reading of Justice Kennedy's opinion in *Lawrence*, which concludes that states may not constitutionally burden any private, consensual, sexual activity between adults, could bring laws against fornication, adultery, and even incest into question.

Is Polyamory Immoral?

When we consider the intricacies of morality and ethics, it's useful to consider that morals tend to be absolute and are usually grounded in religious tenets, whereas ethics are more situational and emphasize conduct, especially in the postmodern, relativistic world in which we live. Rather than an external set of rules that define good and bad behavior, ethics has come to be interpreted sometimes as an internal sense of what is right and wrong depending on how an action fits with internalized values and affects other people.

If morality is conceived as adherence to a specific version of religious tenets, then polyamory is definitely immoral. Nevertheless, advocates of this lifestyle—many of whom claim to be religious—maintain that polyamory should be seen as amoral in the sense that it rejects the morality that depends on sexual exclusivity. Defending such a viewpoint, Sheff, in her *Psychology Today* article "(Im)morality and Polyamory" raises this point: "The polyamorous obsession with honesty and self-responsibility encourages a highly ethical (at least ideally) relationship style. Of course, poly people lie and cheat too, they are mere mortals after all. But with their concern for truth and care for others' wellbeing, polys have a built-in ethical system to help them decide what is right."[38]

Applying a Biblical Ethic

Polyamory has long been common in secular dating relationships. But recently, the concept has transformed into "open marriages." Yet polyamory is absolutely incompatible with what the New Testament says about marital love; Scripture clearly and consistently declares that marriage is the context for sexual intimacy, and marital love is to be pure, faithful, and committed.

Sexual intimacy is moral only within marriage (Eph. 5:3; Col. 3:5; 1 Thess. 4:3). The apostle Paul wrote to the church at Galatia, "The wrong things the sinful self does are clear: being sexually unfaithful, not being pure, taking part in sexual sins" (Gal. 5:19 NCV). And if we allow for absolutes, we do not get to redefine what the Bible says is sin. Polyamory, pornography, and prostitution reveal the absence of moral absolutes. And in the words of the late pastor/

---

37. Lawrence v. Texas, 539 U.S 558 (2003).
38. Sheff, "Five Disadvantages of Polyamory."

philosopher Francis Schaeffer, "If there's no absolute moral standard, then one cannot say in a final sense that anything is right or wrong. . . . There must be an absolute if there are to be morals, and there must be an absolute if there are to be real values."[39] Otherwise, we just have conflicting opinions. Certainly we can see such to be the case as we read the rationales for pornography, prostitution, and polyamory. As was true in the time of the judges, "All the people did whatever seemed right in their own eyes" (Judg. 21:25 NCV).

CONCLUSION

Through the complicated challenges presented to us as Christians by the prevalence of pornography, prostitution, and polyamory, it's clear that without God's Word and its guidance toward true intimacy coupled with restrictions against moral corruption, society will undoubtedly fall deeper into the abyss of sexual deviation. Paul wrote to the Corinthians that the ruler of this world "has blinded the minds of those who do not believe. They cannot see the light of the Good News—the Good News about the glory of Christ, who is exactly like God" (2 Cor. 4:4 NCV). Moral integrity is the glue that holds relationships, if not all of civilization, together. With it we have light, good news, glory. Without it, we can have no well-functioning, law-abiding, or productive and progressive society. Without it, who might we become?

---

39. Francis Schaeffer, *How Then Should We Live?: The Rise and Decline of Western Thought and Culture* (New York: Fleming H. Revell, 1976), 3.

FOR DISCUSSION

1. If most adolescents currently appear to be receiving their sexual education from viewing pornography, what are the implications for relational and sexual intimacy as these youth become adults?

2. Pro-legalization proponents for prostitution argue that women do not in fact sell themselves but, instead, sell a service. The notion is that a prostitute is no different from a professional consultant who charges a fee for his or her efforts. How does selling sexual services differ from selling other types of services?

3. Polyamory advocates argue that their relationships value honesty, responsibility, and fidelity, which distinguishes them from "swingers," and that they have a built-in ethical system to help them decide what is right. Aside from utilizing a biblically based moral argument, how would you argue against such a mindset?

FOR FURTHER READING

Carnes, Patrick. *Facing the Shadow: Starting Sexual and Relationship Recovery.* 2nd ed. Carefree, AZ: Gentle Path Press, 2008.

Farley, Melissa, ed. *Prostitution, Trafficking, and Traumatic Stress.* Binghamton, NY: Haworth, 2004.

Struthers, William M. *Wired for Intimacy: How Pornography Hijacks the Male Brain.* Downers Grove, IL: InterVarsity Press, 2010.

CHAPTER 19

SEXUAL ORIENTATION AND IDENTITY

MARK A. YARHOUSE

Sexual identity refers to the labels people use to describe themselves, often with reference to their sexual preferences. Labels such as *gay, straight,* and *bi* or *bisexual* are common sexual-identity labels. Sexual-identity labels are often predicated on sexual orientation and are at times referred to as *sexual orientation identity*. In other words, when a woman describes herself as a lesbian, she is using a sexual-identity label or sexual-orientation label that presumes a homosexual orientation in which she experiences a strong, stable, and enduring attraction to the same sex.

In this chapter I want to cover three recommendations for engaging the topics of sexual orientation and identity. They are: (1) have humility regarding some of the most frequently asked questions about sexual orientation and identity; (2) engage the topic with "convicted civility"; and (3) remember that Christians navigating sexual-identity concerns are "our people," if you will.

Let's begin with the first recommendation. What may be helpful for understanding sexual orientation and identity is to address some of the most frequently asked questions that come up around these topics.

HUMILITY REGARDING FREQUENTLY ASKED QUESTIONS

Two of the most frequently asked questions have to do with causation and change. The questions are, What causes homosexual orientation, and essentially, can it be changed? Let's start with etiology or causation. Unfortunately, the whole discussion about causation, which is interesting, has been hijacked by the culture wars, which makes it nearly impossible to have a meaningful discussion about research here. The debate is usually framed as nature versus nurture, and you have people on both sides of a political and cultural debate who want to advance one or the other.

Proponents who say that nature is the cause of a homosexual orientation also often view it as an immutable characteristic, such as eye color or hair color. We know that, from other surveys, if people believe that there is a biological basis for sexual orientation and that sexual orientation is immutable, they vote differently in politics. They have different attitudes. And that is an interesting line of argument in part because of how interest in public policy or political ends has not always made understanding the research a priority.

There's interesting research about this from the early 1990s; that hypothesis has been forcefully advanced. But then you have people in the culture war who respond to that by saying, "It can't possibly be nature. It's got to be nurture." Or worse, they still just say, "It's willful disobedience. You're just choosing this." So I'm going to say up front that that's not it. I don't think people are making the choice to experience same-sex attraction. But could it be nurture?

Unfortunately, it's hard to look at "nurture" in a very serious way with research because of the culture wars. But that doesn't stop some within the church and others from entering into this debate in a very polarizing way—saying it's one or the other. And I think that's a mistake. I don't think it's one or the other. It's not nature or nurture. The answer to causation is probably better framed as nature *and* nurture. The influences on sexual orientation probably come from multiple sources and vary from person to person to some extent and are probably weighted differently for different people. So the way that I tend to organize the answer is this: You could look at research on biological antecedents, childhood experience, environmental influences, and adult decisions—which, again are not decisions about experiencing same-sex attraction, but decisions about behavior and identity. You could indeed look at these four areas, but I look at it more this way: If I want to get from Dallas to the East Coast of the United States, I know that there are many ways for me to get to the East Coast. It's the principle of equifinality. There are multiple ways to the same endpoint. But also, look at it this way: There are multiple ways to be at the East Coast, right? You can be in New England. You can be in Florida. You can be in Virginia Beach. So there is probably not one cause or even one causal pathway for sexual orientation. There are likely multiple ways to get there that are probably weighted differently for different people. The influences could come from both nature and nurture.

There are also multiple ways to *be* there, to be gay or homosexual or same-sex attracted. There are differences between male experiences and female experiences. There are differences among males and differences among females. It's that diverse. So to speak of "the gay community" or to say that "all homosexuals are like this" is really a mistake. It doesn't do justice to the complexity. And this discussion is only about causation.

In conservative Christian communities, there tend to be two favorite theories for causation: (1) childhood sexual abuse and (2) parent-child relationships. But we have to be careful with these theories. The research does suggest that there are higher rates of childhood sexual abuse in the background of adults who are gay or lesbian. In other words, if asked as adults, a higher percentage of sexual abuse makes people homosexual. But most people who've experienced childhood sexual abuse develop a heterosexual orientation. So if it were the causal pathway, it wouldn't play out that way. I'm sure abuse complicates sexuality and sexual identity for people, though. Sexual abuse raises questions that might be part of a larger discussion, but when you reduce it to such abuse, you're not doing justice to the complexity of the issue.

The other theory of causation that is preferred among Christians implicates parent-child relationships. This theory does much damage to people, to families. And I want to encourage us to think through this a little bit. I don't think we have good evidence that the cause of homosexuality is parent-child relationships that are somehow faulty in a way that creates homosexuality. Many gay and lesbian adults do not report difficulties in parent-child relationships, although some do; and many heterosexuals report faulty parent-child relationships that complicate their lives in other ways. Sure, parent-child relationships could have a contributing influence, but we have no real evidence that such is the causal pathway for homosexuality. Nevertheless, there are whole schools of therapy built on the premise that "I know what caused your homosexuality, and if you were just honest about the relationship you had with your parents, you too would know." When that gets imported into the church, look at what happens to pastoral care.

So, a young person who is sixteen shares with his parents, "Mom and Dad, I'm gay." Then the parents try to look for resources, and they're told, "You caused your child to be gay." Well, we don't know that. I don't believe that such is the case. I don't think we understand what causes the development of a homosexual orientation, but now blame has been placed on parents looking for resources. And most parents are willing to take a bullet for their son or daughter. They will sacrifice themselves. And placing fault on parenting gives them an explanatory framework for causation that provides them with meaning, even if it is untrue. They think, "Well, this is what caused it. It must have been me." And then clinicians often capitalize on such thinking by suggesting to the young person, "And if we could help you with that area, you can now become straight."

Such an approach says two things. One is, "We know what caused it. I'm laying this template on top of your experience. I know what caused you to be this way." The second is, "And if I help re-parent you, you'll now become straight." The latter offers a promise that I'm not sure we can deliver on. So there are two problems with that approach.

I want to encourage humility about what we know and what we don't know. Let's look, then, at the other most frequently asked question that has to do with change, particularly now as we see how causation and change can often be related to one another.

I conducted a study with a friend and colleague, Stan Jones, at Wheaton College. It was a seven-year longitudinal study of whether people who are Christians who experience homosexuality can change through involvement in Christian ministry. At year three, we published it in a book called *Ex-Gays*; and then in year seven, we published our findings in the *Journal of Sex and Marital Therapy*. So it's been peer reviewed. It's been published in two venues. And nobody committed to participating in the culture wars liked our study.

Remember that there are two groups—one on either side of the culture wars who want to take science to advance an argument. The one group says, "This is an immutable characteristic," and they cannot allow for data to show any movement along the continuum. Consequently, they did not like the study because we did show movement along the continuum.

The other group says, "Anybody who tries hard enough or has enough faith can experience dramatic change, 180-degree change, categorical change from gay to straight," and our data didn't show that either. Our data, I would say, showed that for some people, there was movement along a continuum. That movement was stronger when it was moving away from homosexuality rather than moving toward heterosexuality.

So then you raise the question pastorally: Where does that leave somebody? What does it mean to have less same-sex attractions, but not more attraction to the opposite sex?

Many of the people whom we studied did change their behavior. Also, many changed their identity from "gay" to "no label" or "gay" to "bisexual." We saw some behavioral changes. Some people did experience meaningful changes in their attractions. But most did not experience as much change as they had hoped for going into the ministry. And it was a very sobering experience.

So what does the church communicate in this area? On the one side, you could have cynical pessimism that says same-sex attraction is an absolutely immutable characteristic. People holding this view would insist that those who say otherwise are selling snake oil, and it's intrinsically harmful even to try to change. But you could also have, on the other side, an arrogant optimism that says, "Anyone can experience categorical change if he or she tries hard enough or has enough faith. Those who say otherwise promote the gay agenda, and there's no risk in attempting change."

My own view is somewhere in between. I would call it one of realistic biblical hope. First of all, I think there is a kind of natural fluidity for some people, more likely with females than males—it's been documented—but not for all. Most people don't have this kind of natural fluidity. Instead, they feel a kind of enduring attraction to members of the same sex or the opposite sex, and there's some debate about whether it's possible to have that enduring attraction to both sexes.

Research suggests that some people may experience meaningful change, but it's going to likely occur along a continuum and not be categorical. Now then, when you have someone in a church who gives a testimony of categorical change—that person is now married, has children—I'm not trying to take away from that testimony. Nevertheless, we have to be cautious to avoid creating that person's experience as the expectation or the standard for the next person. The reason one does research is to say, "How likely is that testimony for the next person going into a ministry or going into therapy?"

Also, as a church, I think it could be helpful to offer other testimonies. What about hearing from those who give a testimony of God's faithfulness to them with other outcomes? These people testify that the attractions didn't change, but they're living in a way that's faithful before God in light of that reality, in light of an enduring condition in their life; but God's being faithful there. I think that could be a testimony that we haven't heard as much of but would be compelling anyway.

Pastorally, that means that when we're counseling or engaging in this area and working with someone who has same-sex attraction, the real goal is to place the emphasis not just on dealing with the behavior. Rather, we must have people think about who they are in terms that go beyond their same-sex sexuality—looking to a broader sense of identity and what their sexuality means to them in light of their faith.

I'm much more comfortable working with someone on fostering their re-lationship with Christ. So let's say they experience same-sex attraction, they've prayed that it would go away, they've maybe been in ministry or therapy. Maybe they have been trying for years. I've known many people who could share that story. Can we ask, "Have you ever explored the possibility of not having to change your orientation, but to capitalize on the thing that you did see move when you sought God in prayer, which was your relationship with Christ?"

Unless we adopt such an approach, I grow concerned that a person's self-worth becomes measured by heterosexuality, a sense of, "Do I belong in the church? Does God love me? Does my shame go away? Well, it does if I'm straight. If I have the capacity to marry and have children." Is that the message the church wants to send, or do we want to emphasize knowing Christ, growing in relationship there and seeing what happens? This approach may not result in a move. Or a move may happen due to natural fluidity. I don't know. But what I think God does promise us is that he will be faithful to bring about sanctification in our lives. I'm more confident putting that forward than putting forward heterosexuality.

ENGAGE THE TOPIC WITH "CONVICTED CIVILITY"

Let's turn now to a second recommendation. Let me encourage you to engage this topic with convicted civility. The phrase *convicted civility* comes from Richard Mouw. It's this idea that there are far too many Christians with strong convictions, but you would not want them to represent you to the broader culture, because they're just not nice people. They're not people who really represent God's love to the larger culture and the larger world.

But then you have other Christians who are so strong on civility that you don't know what they believe in. Maybe they're strong on convictions, but they could use a little help in toning down their civility.

What would it look like to live with convicted civility in relationships, to be genuine in relationships with people with whom we disagree? I've dialogued at the American Psychological Association with gay psychologists. I've dialogued at my campus with gay psychologists and others about this issue. And my dialogues are not debates. That's not the approach I take. I dialogue, and I listen, and I think that has been good for me. It's been humbling.

Several years ago I was presenting research on whether people changed through their involvement in Christian ministries. I was reporting on the findings at my own university. A young man who identified himself as an activist—I'm not using that label out of turn—put up a YouTube video calling all of his LGBTQ friends to come and sit in the front row, and just "stare down this son of a gun." (He used other language.) But it was an interesting video to watch because it was like a call to arms—"We are gonna tear this guy up."

What does "convicted civility" do in such moments? I know there are people who would say, "Don't even let them on campus. Have security meet them at the entrance and tell them, 'This is our campus.'" That option was on the table, actually. I talked with a wise friend about this, and the decision was, "Let's call him. Let's just call him and invite him. He's coming anyway, right?" And so, I called him, and I said, "Look, why don't you come be our guest on campus? Let me meet you. Let's talk about this."

They did exactly what they said they were going to do. They sat in the first three rows and just stared daggers at me and my co-presenter. But we made our presentation and stayed with them for a long time afterward. We talked with them. We heard their stories. I've been out for coffee with the one person a few times.

With another, I went out for coffee several times. He said, "Mark, by the way people talked about you, I thought you'd have horns on your head, smoke coming out of your nostrils. You're not quite what I expected you to be." He put up a video shortly after that and explained, "It wasn't quite what I thought it was going to be. I didn't agree with everything this guy said, but it was more complicated, and there were some interesting points made." Sadly, he was eviscerated by others who felt he should have used that opportunity to capitalize on tearing me apart. The contrast between what he experienced within his own community and what he experienced on campus was striking and confusing for him.

The other person I met for coffee simply became a friend. He gave me permission to share this story. He was raised in the church, and he was really struck by the affection people had toward him in that encounter. He ended up recommitting his life, saying, "I want to explore faith again." And he's on that journey. His is not a typical encounter for me, but it is typical to reach out. It is typical for me to dialogue with people, to listen, and to not use language and categories that I know will offend people; I try to be thoughtful about that.

I think it's important for us to rise above the culture war whenever we can, to treat people respectfully. I try to talk dispassionately about the research, to recognize that I could be wrong about the things that I have studied, and there are things that I try to really be humble about. There are things that I do hold convictions about, though, and I know people push me on that. But I think that it's better to start a dialogue out of this place of convicted civility.

One of the elements of this conversation—convicted civility and culture wars—is the tendency in our language in the church to create an "us and them" environment. We can prepare ourselves to some degree by always assuming that in the audience there will be gay, lesbian, and bisexual people—people navigating this terrain. I assume such to be the case. And I'm surprised sometimes by how churches seem to interact as though there are no gay people in the church; they're all "out there." In doing so, so we risk coming together to talk about gay people as if they're the problem.

Imagine a fourteen-year-old—thirteen-year-old, twelve-year-old—who finds himself or herself experiencing same-sex attraction. They're raised in the church, and they're sitting in the pew listening to how we talk about this topic. How would a fifteen-year-old even process statements such as "homosexuality is a sin"—without really separating out what we're talking about there—or "This is an abomination," or "Gays are ruining this country"? So how does a young teen even process what is meant in light of their same-sex sexuality? They can't distinguish all the nuances that we may mean when we say such things. What they hear is, "I'm an abomination." I'm more amazed when a young person stays with the church than when a young person leaves the church and says, "I've got a better offer someplace else"; because, fundamentally, you have to look at the overall narrative that comes out of the local church and the overall narrative that comes out from the local gay community. The latter communicates, "We can answer questions for you about identity and community, about who you are, and of what community you're a part." The local church has an opportunity to answer those questions, but we fail on almost every turn to answer fundamental questions about identity and community because we use language that reflects the culture war. We talk about "us" versus "them," and most who are in our pews who are navigating this issue will see themselves as a "them" and leave. Can we blame them?

CHRISTIANS NAVIGATING THESE ISSUES ARE "OUR PEOPLE"
My third recommendation requires a little context. When I started my career, I was sitting in on a session at the American Psychological Association where two gay psychologists were talking about Christians who were leaving the gay community to go to Christian ministries that these experts believed were hurting them. And this is the phrase that just stunned me. The psychologist said, "We are failing our people," by which he meant "We're failing to meet the spiritual and religious needs of people in the gay community, so they're leaving for these

ministries that are hurting them." I had never thought that a gay psychologist would think he had more in common with these gay Christians by virtue of being gay than I did by virtue of being a Christian. I always assumed I had more in common with them by virtue of being a Christian.

I was struck later that day thinking about how I had never heard a pastor from the pulpit refer to Christians who navigate this issue as *our people* and that maybe we were failing *our people*. And I decided that my approach moving forward would be to see people who are Christians who are navigating these issues as *our people*.

Young people are navigating religious and sexual identity, and that's often felt as a conflict growing up by the way that it's talked about in their peer group or the way it's talked about in their church. But they feel this storm cloud, this conflict between their sexual identity and their religious identity. Now, developmentally, they're asking this question: "Who am I?" The developmental psychologist Erik Erickson explains that it is a normal development question in adolescence to ask, "Who am I?" and to try on different identities, different ways of being who you are, and you're looking for something stable at home, at church, in your peer group. It's a normal question that's made only more complicated with same-sex sexuality. And then you have, on the one hand, the gay community saying, "We can tell you who you are. Your same-sex attractions signal a naturally occurring distinction between types of people. Gay, straight, bisexual—you're a gay person. These attractions are at the core of who you are. They're central to your identity. Your behavior is not something to be evaluated whether it's right or wrong; it's an expression of who you are. And now we can talk about self-actualization of your sexual identity." I call that a gay script. I use "script" as simply a cultural expectation for how we behave and relate to one another. And I think that's a very compelling script for a teenager in the church today.

Now I contrast that with the local faith community. I don't think we have ever thought about what script is being offered to a young person who's navigating such terrain. I've come to conclude that the primary script that comes from the local faith community is a shame-based script that essentially says, "There's something defective in you," and the person feels responsible for it. It's not guilt, like, "I've done something and I regret it," or "I wish I'd done this, but I didn't do it, and I feel bad about that." Shame is more pernicious and more fundamental; it says, "There's something fundamentally flawed about me, and if you knew this about me, you would reject me." It usually involves self-rejection: "I reject myself because of shame, and I know you would reject me too if you knew this about me." So everything goes underground.

I think the way the local faith community interacts with this topic probably conveys a script that tends to shame. And then you have this young person saying, "Who am I in light of this?" I think it's a no-brainer. If we just did a mental exercise and said, "If I was fifteen and found myself with same-sex attractions, which script would I be more drawn to?" I think most of us, if we're honest, would say, "I'd be drawn to a gay script that answers fundamental questions about identity and community, that is, Who am I, and of what community am I a part?" In the local faith community, we may want to say, "You're one of us," but I don't think we communicate that. At nearly every turn we push people away. I think that's going to be a great challenge for the church in the next generation.

The first time I presented the gay script to a group of Christian leaders, one astute observer asked, "So what's the alternative script?" The problem was that I hadn't really begun to study alternative scripts. And I realized it can't come from me—it can't come primarily from a straight guy who's married and has three children. It seems that an alternative script or scripts must come from the community of Christians who are navigating this issue, who themselves say no to a gay script. It has to come from them, or in any case it must take their experiences into account.

What is a script that would be compelling? Keep in mind that the script received from many local faith communities has been shame or has been tied to an ex-gay narrative, meaning a script of change to heterosexuality. Our expectation has often been, "You are welcome in our church, but you've got to be straight with the capacity to have children."

And many of our churches function this way. Much of our programing goes toward couples and families. We don't tend to minister well to singles—and that adds another layer to this issue, because if we don't minister well and love and have a place of prominence for being single in the church, then we're saying to the person who navigates these issues, "You've got to become straight, with the capacity to marry and have children, to really be in the upper tier of what it means to be in the body of Christ." Is that the message we want to send people?

I left that meeting saying, "I'm going to conduct research with people who don't adhere to a gay script, and I'm going to hear from them what they do, and I'll present that to the Christian community." So I did that.

In one line of research I compared Christians who embraced a gay identity and Christians who did not identify as gay despite their enduring same-sex attractions. From the latter group, for example, came an alternative script; what they did was to form their identity around the person and work of Christ. Now I'm not saying that the former group never did that. I'm just saying the latter group said, "My same-sex attractions signal not a categorical distinction among types of people, but one of many human experiences that are just 'not the way it's supposed to be,'" to borrow language from Neal Plantinga. By this it is meant that we live in a fallen world, and the attractions reflect that. They were saying essentially, "My attractions are a part of my reality. They're part of my experience, but they're not central to my identity, so I say no to that. I acknowledge that they're a part of my experience, but I don't form my identity around them, and I form my identity around other aspects of personhood that are more salient for me."

Some elements of another identity were tied to being a man or a woman, not in being heterosexual or homosexual. Others discussed key roles like, "I'm a husband" or a "wife." "I'm a father." "I'm a son." These communicated a role-related identity. Others discussed, as I mentioned, their identity in Christ.

People formed all kinds of identities, but they tended to be positive identities, not ex-gay, not, "I'm not something negative." Rather, they seemed to be wanting to say, "I'm something positive," something more life-giving than a shame-based narrative. So, again, that was just one script. I wasn't trying to set up a contrast that it's *either* a gay script or an in-Christ script. This is just one of potentially dozens of possible other scripts (e.g., a celibate gay Christian script).

What may be helpful to do as a church is create an atmosphere in which such scripts can be developed, discussed, articulated, and lived out so that we have people who share a testimony of God's faithfulness as they walk out these other scripts. But their narrative is not necessarily that ex-gay narrative of heterosexuality; it's something else. We could potentially have dozens of other possible scripts, and I think young people would do well to see those possibilities, because when they don't see them, they don't see a future for themselves.

FOR DISCUSSION

1. Why do you suppose people are drawn to different theories of causation of a homosexual orientation?

2. Is there a testimony to be found in a person's experience of enduring same-sex sexuality? If so, what might that be? If not, why not?

3. Why might it be valuable to listen to the different identities and associated scripts of people navigating same-sex sexuality and faith?

FOR FURTHER READING

Yarhouse, Mark A. *Homosexuality and the Christian: A Guide for Parents, Pastors, and Friends.* Minneapolis: Bethany House, 2010.

———. *Understanding Sexual Identity: A Resource for Youth Ministry.* Grand Rapids: Zondervan, 2013.

Yarhouse, Mark A., and Erica S. N. Tan. *Sexuality and Sex Therapy: A Comprehensive Christian Appraisal.* Downers Grove, IL: IVP Academic, 2014.

C H A P T E R   2 0

SAME-SEX ATTRACTION: WASHED AND WAITING

WESLEY HILL

The former archbishop of Canterbury Rowan Williams wrote, "The Christian community lives in the exchange, not simply of charisms . . . but of stories, of memories. My particular past is there in the church as a resource for my relations with my brothers and sisters, not to be poured out repeatedly and promiscuously, but as a hinterland of vision and truth and acceptance, out of which I can begin to live in honesty."[1] Our stories are a resource that we offer up to the church. They belong to us. They are a part of the story of our life with God. But we don't hold them to ourselves; we offer them to one another for conversation. And ultimately we offer them up to the larger story of what God is doing in Christ in the church. So with that in mind I will tell you a bit of my story, and then tell you how I've come to understand it in light of the bigger story that I find in the gospel.

I grew up in a Christian family in Arkansas. I was raised in a Southern Baptist church. And my earliest childhood memories are of hearing my parents describe stories from the Bible. We were a family that lived by the Arch Books. They were colorful, rhyming, Bible storybooks. That was my introduction to the world of Scripture. My parents still have pictures that I drew of David and Goliath and other characters from these Arch Books. And as many children do in that kind of world, I came to my parents at the age of five or six and asked if I could invite Jesus to be my personal Lord and Savior. I had an experience of

---

1. Rowan Williams, *Resurrection: Interpreting the Easter Gospel* (London: Darton, Longman and Todd, 2002), 44.

consciously submitting my story and my life to Christ at that point. And I grew up in an environment that nurtured me in that.

My parents were and are deeply loving people. I was raised among Christians who loved me well. The church in which I grew up was far from perfect, but it was a welcoming church. I felt at home there. And as I grew, I became more of a church nerd. I enjoyed Sunday school. I was very committed to youth group. And at the suggestion of my youth pastor, I began to memorize large portions of Scripture. I went on camping trips with my friends from the youth group, and I was involved in Bible studies and church camps. It was a deeply Christian upbringing. And I was open about the fact that I wanted to learn more about the faith. I wanted to learn to pray. I was asking questions. I wasn't holding it to myself. I was wanting to be in dialogue with my fellow Christians about the Christian story and the Christian life.

But what I wasn't telling anyone, and what I couldn't imagine telling anyone, is that from about the age of twelve or so I was beginning to experience same-sex attractions. As far as I knew, in the small, sheltered town in Arkansas in which I grew up, there were no other gay people. And somehow or other I had absorbed the idea that this was something I ought not to talk about. This was something that was shameful. It was something I should not be experiencing. Something had gone wrong; there had been a glitch that had happened somewhere in my development that had caused this. And so I kept it a secret.

I was very close with my parents, very close with my siblings, very close with my youth pastor and my Christian friends from church. But I decided at an early age, as a young teenager, that this was something I could not be open about. It would be beyond the realm of conversation. And so I just assumed, "I'll go away. I'll go to a Christian college, and something will click. Something will change. A shift will happen. I'll meet the right girl, this will dramatically shift, and no one will ever have to know about this." As a teenager, I had the thought that maybe I would take this secret to my grave.

When I got to college, my attraction to the Christian faith and my commitment to Jesus had grown stronger. Yet, if anything, my same-sex attraction, my same-sex orientation, my homosexual orientation had also grown stronger; it had grown more central to my identity. And I came into college wondering how to reconcile my Christianity and my attractions. Up to that point, my strategy had been to turn a blind eye to them, hoping that they would go away. When I was in high school, I read a well-known Christian book that said, "If you're someone worrying you will turn out to be gay, I can assure you, you don't need worry about it, because it happens to so few people, statistically." I closed the book and thought, "This is totally discouraging."

By the time I reached my junior year, I still lacked the courage or the safety to talk about this. At that time, I had lunch with a friend with whom I was close, and she described something that I had not known about her: her experience with clinical depression. As she spoke, I felt saddened that I hadn't known this about my friend, that she hadn't been able to confide this. And she said, "You know, Wes, I think for a long time I was ashamed of dealing with this, and I just hoped that it would go away. I hoped that with enough ignoring and enough papering over of the wounds, it would disappear." Then she added, "What I finally came to realize is that ignoring is not the path to redeeming." She had begun to see a therapist.

I left that lunch feeling that that phrase "ignoring is not the path to redeeming," was somehow meant for me. I had been attempting to deal with my own sexual orientation by turning a blind eye to it, and if I wanted to flourish—as I said I did—if I wanted to go on in my life in Christ, and deepen it, and become a richer, fuller, human person, then ignoring my sexuality and attempting to cope with it was not the way forward.

So I determined something had to change. I was especially close to one of my philosophy professors. In his class students were made aware that this was someone who had been through deep waters. This was someone who could move from talking about Plato to talking about his own bouts with depression. And I thought, "This would be someone, if I ever did feel that I needed to talk about my sexuality with someone, this would be that sort of person." And so I made an appointment to talk with him. I wrote one of those vague emails that allows an "out"—the kind you write in such a way that if you decide to back out of the appointment, you'll still have an excuse. You don't mention what it will be about.

As I walked to the appointment a week later, I was telling myself, "I still have time to turn back to my apartment. He will never know what I was going to ask about."

But I kept the appointment. I showed up to his office. And it took me awhile to get the words out. But I said, "You know I think that I have a homosexual orientation, and I don't know what that means for my future. I don't know what that means for my life of faith. And I'm asking for your help."

The first gift he gave me was the gift of not being surprised. Francis Schaeffer has a great line in which he says, "Christians should never have the reaction designated by the term 'shocked.'"[2] I love that line, because we inhabit a story that's capacious enough to handle whatever life throws at us. We inhabit a story that is full enough and deep enough and true enough to undergird us when we feel as though things have become shaky. And that was the first gift he gave me that day.

But he assured me that whatever other conversations we would have—and he told me he wanted to have more—"need to be based on your assurance that God loves you, that God is for you in Christ. And whatever confusion you want to bring to the surface, whatever pain you want to talk about, whatever shame you want to explore, is already able to be dealt with by the gospel that you profess, by the story that you're a part of." And that was another great gift.

And so began a process for me of coming out. I came out to pastors and friends at church. I later came out to peers and friends who were close to my own

---

2. Francis Schaeffer, *No Little People* (Wheaton, IL: Crossway, 1974), 49.

age. And it was a one-by-one process. It wasn't until I wrote my book *Washed and Waiting* that I spoke to groups. My coming out was in what a therapist has called "circles of appropriate transparency." I wasn't talking to the church youth group. I wasn't talking to the Bible study all at once. I was finding those safe people, those trustworthy people with whom I could entrust my story.

But the question that became urgent to me was, What larger story does the story I just told fit into? How do I make sense of my own personal story in light of some larger reality? There's that wonderful line from the philosopher Alasdair MacIntyre in *After Virtue* in which he says, "I can only answer the question 'What am I to do?' if I can answer the prior question 'Of what story or stories do I find myself a part?'"

I can only begin to explore what my vocation in the world might be—what I might be called to do, how I might be called to steward my sexuality—if I first back up and ask the larger question about what vision I am accepting as true. And so that became my question. Of course, there are many scripts, there are many stories, there are many narratives on offer in the church today. And this is part of the pain of being a Christian at our historical moment. We're finding that our denominations are splitting apart, our churches are fighting about what the biblical story is that someone like me is called to inhabit.

So I began to explore that for the first time in my life. And of course I encountered quickly the story that would say, "Your own homosexuality, your being gay, is something that can fit into a before-and-after narrative." I can remember sitting in a Wheaton College chapel service, and a speaker told about a life of promiscuity—having had many, many same-sex partners. He explained this story in some detail as both a life of alienation from God and a life of alienation from himself. And his story concluded with him putting a slide up on the projector of himself and his wife and their children. Students rose to their feet and gave this speaker a standing ovation. And it was a profoundly alienating moment for me, because it was a story with a very clear before and after. I wondered, "Is that the story that I belong to? Is that the narrative I'm called to inhabit?" So I began to explore that. I read books about that. There's a whole literature around "reparative therapy." Reparative therapy suggests there is a causal narrative about why some turn out to be gay or lesbian. And with enough repair of that deficit in same-sex love that such a person experienced as a child, it is said, he or she can actually leave behind same-sex attraction.

One of the things that I found frustrating as I began to explore explanation that was that I was expected to explain my past in a way that felt untrue. I met with several therapists and counselors who wanted to explore with me whether my own homosexuality could be owing to a deficit in father love and/or to a deficit in same-sex peer love during my formative childhood years. And as I explored these things, I felt they were out of step with my own story. I'd had a father who loved me. I felt affirmed by my father. I felt that my father was proud of me. I felt that I was intimately close with same-sex peers growing up.

This narrative of a deficit and repair was something artificially superimposed on the details of my life, and it didn't illuminate my life in the way that I might have hoped it would. So I explored other narratives. And, of course, the other narrative that I quickly became aware of is the narrative that would say, "This is how God created me. This—when I look inside and find these deep-seated, seemingly irreversible attractions for members of my own sex—this is the good creation of God, and I'm meant to celebrate this. I'm meant to live into this, to welcome it, and to seek to channel it and steward it in a way that would be holy and sanctified by sanctifying it in a same-sex marriage." And so I began to explore that option.

But I came to find that narrative unpersuasive. I couldn't make sense of the fact that we were talking not about a theology of creation, but a theology of fall and redemption eclipsed in a certain way by the theology of creation. If I found myself entertaining and exploring the idea that my same-sex attractions were simply the good gift of God in my life, meant to be affirmed, meant to be welcomed by me, meant to be channeled and sanctified, I found that I was not doing justice in my own mind and heart to the other acts of the story—the biblical story.

If we put that narrative in summary form, according to classic Christian theology, it is a four-act story. (1) It involves creation: the good creation of God, blessed and hallowed on the seventh day. (2) But it also involves a story of creation having gone wrong, a story of creation marred and deformed by sin and death. (3) The third act is redemption. And redemption in the New Testament is not so much the replacing of an originally good creation with something else. It is rather the taking up of what has been marred by sin and death, and the redeeming of it, the reclaiming of it for God's kingdom. (4) And then finally act four is the restoration, which is the crowning of the redemption that was begun in the life, death, and resurrection of Jesus.

What I found, to my surprise, is that when I went to the Gospels and I heard Jesus announcing the new wine of the kingdom, I was totally prepared for him to say, "And the old wineskins of marriage as you knew it in the original creation have now been set aside because God is doing a new thing in the gospel. There's a new kingdom power at work, and the old has been set aside, and the new has come." Yet that isn't the way I found Jesus speaking.

I came, for instance, to Matthew 19. This is, of course, the passage where Jesus is asked about marriage, and he's asked about divorce: "Some Pharisees came to him, and to test him, they asked, 'Is it lawful for a man to divorce his wife for any cause?'" (Matt. 19:3 NRSV). And here I thought was the golden opportunity for Jesus to outline the new kingdom principles of marriage, to set aside the old, and to bring in the new. Yet here is how he replies: "Have you not read that the one who made them at the beginning made them male and female, and said, 'For this reason a man shall leave his father and mother and be joined to his wife, and the two shall become one flesh? So they are no longer two, but one flesh. Therefore, what God has joined together, let no one separate'" (vv. 4–6 NRSV).

As I explored that, I concluded, "This is a theology not so much of creation replaced, but of a theology of creation reclaimed. The originally good and hallowed creation of male and female—different and yet complementary—is here taken up and healed in the work of the kingdom." And I found that perspective confirmed as I went on to the epistles. In Ephesians, Paul goes back to the same text, Genesis 2, and quotes the portion about male and female becoming one flesh. And then he says that this union, this reunion of male and female—estranged in the fall, but now brought together in marriage—is itself a sign and a parable and a pointer to an even greater reality, which is the union of Christ and the church.

And from there I began to see that this is how to make sense of the celibate vocation as well. Celibacy can also be a sign and an anticipation of that great eschatological marriage of Christ and the church. Because celibate people say—as Jesus affirms in Matthew 22—that they, with their bodies, are pointing toward the future. They are pointing forward to a time when, as British ethicist Oliver O'Donovan puts it, "the fidelity of love which marriage makes possible will be extended beyond the limits of marriage" to the whole community.[3] A celibate person lives already in anticipation of that, witnessing together with male and female who are married, to the future restoration of God's kingdom.

And so that's the story I found myself embracing. It has not been an easy story. But that is the story I have found myself seeking to take as authoritative for my own narrative.

And so my question became, How, then, is someone like me—who identifies as gay, who identifies as a Christian, who wants to remain in the church—supposed to flourish within that story? How am I supposed to live a celibate life in a parish that often seems more interested in having marriage retreats or family retreats than it is in welcoming single people into its life? How do I practice what a friend has called "parish celibacy," where I accept this celibate vocation as a call from God, and yet I seek to make it not primarily or simply about a renunciation, a saying no, a being abstinent? How do I make it a life of flourishing love, pouring out love for others, pouring out love to God, receiving love from others in the fellowship of the church?

My journey eventually led me to write *Washed and Waiting*. The title is my shorthand way of describing how I've come to understand my life as a celibate, gay Christian in the body of Christ. Those two words, "washed" and "waiting," come from two places in the apostle Paul's epistles. The first is from 1 Corinthians 6:9–11. It is one of those places in Paul where he is giving a kind of before-and-after narrative. It's not a clean and simple one, but it is one with a dramatic break. He's describing to the Corinthians who they formerly were when they were still pagans. He tells them they have been grafted into the family of God, but they formerly were something else. And he describes many of the identifying markers of their old life, concluding

---

3. Oliver O'Donovan, *Resurrection and Moral Order: An Outline for Evangelical Ethics*, 2nd ed. (Grand Rapids: Eerdmans, 1994), 70.

with, "But you were washed, you were sanctified, you were justified in the name of our Lord Jesus Christ and in the Spirit of our God" (1 Cor. 6:11 NRSV). Most New Testament scholars think that the image of "washed" is a reference to their baptism. That was the demarcating moment when they said no to their old life. As they were submerged in the waters of baptism, the event symbolized and enacted death to their old life in Adam. As they rose up from the waters and were clothed in white, it symbolized and enacted the new life in Christ. That's the image Paul leaves them with: "Whatever you formerly oriented your life around, whatever story you took as authoritative, has been left behind in the baptismal waters. And as you emerge into the new life of Christ, you are oriented to a new love. You're given a new name. You're stamped with a new identity. You inhabit, now, a new narrative."

That, for me, was foundational. Whatever questions I have about my vocation, whatever questions I have about where I belong in the church, I now answer, "I belong to the story of the baptized. I belong to the story of the washed."

All my coordinates now differ from what they formerly were. I take my cues now from this larger story. And I know my belovedness. Those words "justified" and "sanctified" speak of God's determination to take us to himself, not leave us alienated, not leave us far off without hope, as Paul writes in Ephesians. But they are to take us to himself, and to give us his own name, and to cleanse us and renew us and remake us.

The second word of my title, "waiting," comes from Romans 8. The apostle Paul in verses 18–25 is painting a rather dispiriting portrait of the Christian life. But for me it is a word of liberation. Paul describes the Christian life in those verses in terms of groaning. He uses this image of labor pains. And he says, in effect, that such groaning not only is true of individual Christians, but it's true of creation at large. All of the world, including the earth, is, as it were, groaning in labor pains, waiting for the renewal of all things. And that's where we all—gay or straight, married or celibate—live out our days. We are practicing the virtue of hope, because we don't yet see everything God has ultimately promised, which is the renewal of the world on a cosmic scale.

For me this was liberating, because it meant that I could be honest about my own feelings of incompleteness. I could be honest about my own state of being a pilgrim, the *status viatoris*, being on the way. I could be honest about that, because I knew from that word "waiting" that it was the normal Christian experience for all believers. New Testament scholar Richard B. Hayes says this in his commentary on those verses,

Anyone who does not recognize [that verse that says we are groaning as we wait eagerly for the redemption of our bodies] as a description of authentic Christian existence has never struggled seriously with the imperatives of the gospel, which challenge and frustrate our "natural" impulses in countless ways.[4]

---

4. Richard B. Hays, *The Moral Vision of the New Testament: Community, Cross, New Cre-*

The normal Christian experience is to be groaning, to be yearning, to be straining forward to what we don't yet see, and to be waiting for it with endurance.

I find myself inhabiting a story of what we might call waiting or enduring with a vocation to love. Although somewhat outdated—I don't accept all the language used—there's a quote along these lines that's come to mean a lot to me. It's is from C. S. Lewis and comes from a correspondence he had with a young man named Sheldon Vanauken. Vanauken was a graduate student at Oxford in the 1950s, and he was a new Christian. With his wife he started a Bible study for students. They found that many gay and lesbian people started attending, and the Vanaukens didn't know how to respond. They were receiving questions about what the Christian faith has to say to people who identify as homosexual. So they wrote to Lewis. And Lewis wrote back. He drew in the story from John 9 of the man born blind. Lewis said, "Our speculations on the cause of homosexuality are not what matters, and we must be content with ignorance." The disciples were not told why (in terms of efficient cause) the man was born blind: only the final cause, that the works of God should be manifest in him. This suggests, said Lewis, "that in homosexuality . . . those works [of God] can be made manifest," and then he added, "every disability [whatever it may be for any of us] conceals a vocation, if only we can find it, which will turn the necessity to glorious gain."[5]

Everything in our lives that we come to see as an evidence that creation is not the way it's supposed to be—which is how I understand my own homosexuality—is evidence that we live east of Eden. The fact that I am experiencing this unchosen, same-sex attraction is, for me in my understanding of the Christian story and of Scripture, evidence that things are not the way they're supposed to be. But Lewis says we can't end there. Every disability, whatever it may be, conceals a vocation. It contains a calling to pour our life out in love for others and to receive love from others. And that's the way I've begun to understand my story—as one who has been washed in baptism, as one who is waiting for the redemption of the body, as one who places his hope in that. My calling in the meantime as I practice parish celibacy, as I seek to live faithfully and in a way that is flourishing in the church, is a calling to pour out love, a calling to give and receive love.

I've come to embrace Lewis's words here that, ultimately, this thorn in the flesh—as I think of it—leads to a positive calling. It's given me a vocation. And I interpret that as a call to friendship, a call to deep, same-sex love in the church, a call to community, a call to hospitality. And I join St. Paul in saying that in all these things I groan, waiting eagerly for the redemption of the body and adoption as sons.

---

ation; *A Contemporary Introduction to New Testament Ethics* (San Francisco: HarperSan-Francisco, 1996), 402.

5. C. S. Lewis as quoted in Sheldon Vanauken, *A Severe Mercy* (San Francisco: HarperSan-Francisco, 2009), 146–48.

FOR DISCUSSION

1. Do you find the description "celibate gay Christian" helpful? Why or why not?

2. How is the content in this essay applicable to and useful for individuals struggling with any temptation?

3. How is the content in this essay applicable to and useful for individuals struggling with any "thorn in the flesh"?

FOR FURTHER READING

Hill, Wesley. *Spiritual Friendship: Finding Love in the Church as a Celibate Gay Christian.* Grand Rapids: Brazos, 2015.

———. *Washed and Waiting: Reflections on Christian Faithfulness and Homosexuality.* Grand Rapids: Zondervan, 2010.

Yarhouse, Mark A. *Homosexuality and the Christian: A Guide for Parents, Pastors, and Friends.* Minneapolis: Bethany House, 2010.

CHAPTER 21

GENDER DYSPHORIA

MARK A. YARHOUSE AND JULIA A. SADUSKY

GENDER DYSPHORIA

G ender dysphoria is the experience of distress associated with lack of congruence between a person's gender identity and biological sex. The classic example might be captured in the experience of being "a woman trapped in the body of a man." The current diagnostic nomenclature extends this discussion from a cross-gender identity concern to the experience of distress when there is lack of congruence, which could include nonbinary gender identities as well, such as genderfluid, genderqueer, bigender, and so on.

In our previous work, *Understanding Gender Dysphoria*,[1] we discussed how gender dysphoria resides along a continuum of severity, and only a subset of individuals will meet criteria for the formal diagnosis of gender dysphoria. Also, only a subset of these individuals appear to pursue medical interventions, which we define as either taking cross-sex hormones or undergoing one of many surgeries associated with sex reassignment (or gender affirmation).

Mental-health fields and popular culture today are moving toward an emphasis on transitioning. What we have found to be true is captured in the words of a transgender Christian who described her understanding of the landscape: "Transitioning is the main secular response; healing through counseling is the main Christian response. Dealing with it daily is the reality for most of us."[2]

---

1. This chapter is adapted from a series of posts that first appeared on the website In All Things (https://inallthings.org/), adapted here with permission from the publisher. Mark A. Yarhouse, *Understanding Gender Dysphoria: Navigating Transgender Issues in a Changing Culture*, Christian Association for Psychological Studies Books. (Downers Grove, IL: IVP Academic, 2015).
2. Mark A. Yarhouse and Dara Houp, "Transgender Christians: Gender Identity, Family

We agree with the transgender Christian that, not only is there a cultural emphasis on transitioning, but there is also a Christian emphasis on healing. That is, many Christians hold out an expectation that the person who suffers from gender dysphoria should simply pursue "healing" to restore their gender identity so it is congruent with their biological sex. Yet psychological or emotional healing often does not occur; the gender dysphoria typically remains and is painful for the person living in that reality. What we would like to do in this chapter is explore further the reality of living with an enduring condition like this: that is, dealing with gender dysphoria daily.

Most of what we see in the realm of "coping" with an enduring condition of gender dysphoria is the use of adaptive coping strategies, such as deep breathing, progressive muscle relaxation, and so on. When these are insufficient, people often turn to gender-symbolic coping strategies, such as how they wear their hair, the clothing they choose, the use of preferred names and pronouns, and so on. Still others use low-dose or clinical-dose cross-sex hormones or consider sex-reassignment surgery. These coping strategies can be thought of as residing along a continuum from least invasive to most invasive. The World Professional Association for Transgender Health organizes interventions as reversible, partially reversible, and irreversible. These are all "on the table" in the sense that such interventions are readily available to people who meet criteria for gender dysphoria. And our understanding of treatment options might shift as we learn more both about the etiology of gender dysphoria and about outcomes of various treatment approaches over time.

Now, what are some distinctly Christian contributions to the discussion of adaptive coping? Some of these involve integrating religious elements into existing coping strategies. For example, the person who adapts a meditation practice by meditating on a scene from the Bible is integrating Christian elements into a widely practiced relaxation approach. Something similar happens when people incorporate spiritual words into breathing exercises, so that, in deep breathing, they whisper "amen" or "peace" to themselves as they exhale.

Without detracting from these adaptive coping strategies, it should be noted that people with more severe gender dysphoria often find that such strategies, while somewhat helpful, do not relieve gender dysphoria. In some cases, then, the failure of the adaptive coping strategies above may lead them to consider other coping or management strategies.

So, if even the integration of Christian elements into adaptive coping doesn't work for a dysphoric individual, *what else* does Christianity potentially bring to the discussion of coping? We turn now to a discussion of the unique gifts God offers those within the Christian faith to support themselves and others in the midst of navigating these troubled waters in daily life.

Relationships, and Religious Faith," in *Transgender Youth: Perceptions, Media Influences, and Social Challenges*, ed. Sheyma Vaughn (New York: Nova Science Publishers, 2016), 59.

CARRYING THE CROSS OF GENDER DYSPHORIA

One thing we have seen as a successful method of coping for gender dysphoria is offering oneself in service to others. This may seem counterintuitive at first. Isn't it draining to invest in other people, especially in the very moments when a person is struggling immensely? But one biological female who uses she/her pronouns and describes herself as transgender shared otherwise on what works for her: "Helping other people—focusing on the problems of others. I was created to love God and love people. God made me generous and empathic and that's what matters."[3] This is not as surprising a conclusion as it might seem, at least not when taken in light of the many scriptural references to receiving much in giving of one's self (Prov. 11:25; Matt. 10:8; Luke 6:38; 2 Cor. 9:11; Gal. 5:13). In fact, we are told that the greatest among us will be servants to others (Matt. 23:11), and that the mission of Jesus was "to serve, and to give his life as a ransom for many" (Matt. 20:27–28; Mark 10:45). Thus the transgender person's generosity with her time and talents is a beautiful response to Christ's call to follow his example. In the midst of her own struggle, she can offer a powerful witness of Christlike love and humility in serving.

Perhaps the greatest contribution from Christianity has to do with our experience of enduring hardship. A discussion of hardship and pain in the life of a Christian is often Christ-centered, as it entails uniting with Jesus in his suffering. Certainly, it is true that Christ invites each person to follow him through concrete acts of charity and service. After all, the ultimate expression of Christ's love for us, the greatest expression of love and the most radical act, was his suffering and death (John 15:13). His suffering, once for all, won our salvation. But still Christ commanded that we pick up the daily cross and follow him (Matt. 16:24–26). In Paul's words, the task for us is to identify with his suffering.

But why? Why would a loving God command the embracing of a cross? If he loved us, wouldn't he carry the burden *for* us? What is the value of his carrying it *with* us?

Because he knew what we do not always remember: Death is the door to resurrection. Encountering our weakness is the path to experiencing grace beyond human comprehension. It seems that we would be much less aware of our need for God if we were not brought face-to-face with crosses that are too heavy for one person to carry alone. Grace makes possible what certainly is, apart from grace, impossible. If we are hyperaware of our weakness, our lack, and our inability to cope, precisely there is the place where our childlike need for a Savior is discovered. Jesus, perhaps, is able to unite more fully to us in those moments, and to work more fully within us when we come to him as children, desperately in need of him.

Uniting suffering to Christ involves a conscious choice to embrace the cross and share it with him. We can fight the cross, drop the cross, look away from the cross, compare it to that of others, but it will still be there. How are we to

---

3. Yarhouse and Houp, "Transgender Christians," 58.

respond to the cross? Surely God knows our desire to distance ourselves from it. Why then does he call us to "come"? Again, he knows that which we easily forget. Embracing the cross is a prerequisite to Christian joy. Whether it be minor inconveniences, temporary pain, chronic illness, or death itself, the freedom that is promised to the Christian is discovered in a willful assent to the pain of the present moment. Rather than fighting it, which brings its own challenges, accepting the cross is liberating. And in this freedom, we can face the cross that we fear most, and enter into joy beyond all telling.

Every person longs for joy, and the early Christians wrote less about pleasure than they did about joy, according to Servais Pinckaers's book *Morality: The Catholic View*. We are fully alive when we are most joyful. This reality reveals the supreme human calling to endless joy: that is, eternal life. But joy, properly understood, is associated with enduring hardship. Joy is tied to pain that is endured, and, as a result, joy itself is enduring: "Joy is lasting, like the excellence, the virtues, that engender it. Sense pleasure is individual, like sensation itself. It decreases when the good that causes it is divided up and shared more widely; it ceases altogether when the good is absent. Joy is communicable; it grows by being shared and repays sacrifices freely embraced. Joy belongs to the purity and generosity of love."[4]

Too often, we long to find life for ourselves, but we find ourselves less drawn to the way by which this life and this joy comes—by risking or even losing life for Christ's sake (Matt. 16:24–26). We are much more comfortable praying for healing than for the grace to suffer well. And perhaps as a result of our constant exposure to hedonic goals of the avoidance of pain and the pursuit of pleasure, we easily forget that the Christian faith stands in opposition to an easy life, even going so far as to say that Jesus on the cross embodies an absolute rejection of the notion. His embracing of his cross with absolute consent of his will reveals an altogether different goal for the Christian, and a potential pathway when faced with enduring conditions.

Christian history demonstrates rich examples of embracing suffering. Many Christians before us have walked this path, and we stand on ground soaked with the blood of martyrs who were witnesses of the fruit of this embrace of suffering. In suffering, though, they did not lose sight of Christian hope. Their hope was the root of their joy. Theirs was not a grim-faced suffering, or a begrudging acceptance. At the same time, the saints certainly were not superficial or naively optimistic. Rather, their hope was a grace itself, sufficient for their present difficulty. It was a hope that did not disappoint, we are told.

Still, how can we be sure, lest we find ourselves expecting good things to come and left wanting? We only have to look back to the reason for our hope. Hope certainly did not disappoint the first Christians when they found an

---

4. Servais Pinckaers, *Morality: The Catholic View*, trans. Michael Sherwin (South Bend, IN: St. Augustine's Press, 2003), 78.

empty tomb and came to know that our Lord had risen, just as he had said (Matt. 28:6). Hope did not disappoint when the Holy Spirit descended in the upper room, soon after Jesus had promised he would send the Advocate. Hope did not disappoint when thousands were converted and baptized in the name of the Father, the Son, and the Holy Spirit, just as he had told them.

Certainly Christ loves us now with as much love as he loved his other disciples. He will give hope in our own dark nights and raise us into newness of life, just as he said. This brings us back to the reminder that it is in suffering well that the beauty of life in Christ is made manifest. We rejoice in our suffering precisely because it is through our hardships (and handling of those hardships) that God is glorified. This joy is not exhibited primarily through a smiling face. Sometimes it is through tears and open hands that might feel empty. Suffering in these moments, especially, is an act of worship, in which believers unite their suffering to Christ.

Gender dysphoria is painful and real. The question is, Is it possible to validate the reality and depth of the suffering and invite one another to pursue Christian joy in and through this particular hardship? Or will our doing so only ever lead to trivializing another's pain? Can we discuss sanctification without moving the entire discussion of gender dysphoria into the realm of morality or moral categories of sin? With our transgender family, friends, and neighbors, we as Christians have not always done so well. This could be because we have been less vocal in calling one another to be sanctified through suffering, while shouting down those we have labeled "uniquely sinful." (Perhaps the phrase "uniquely wounded" is more appropriate in these cases.) Thus we have missed the opportunity to recognize the real place for exploring what sanctification could look like in the lives of transgender Christians, and all other Christians.

That such a perspective is counterintuitive to the American Christian makes it difficult to apply it to gender dysphoria. This is a countercultural move that requires a more substantive shift in perspective. This shift would necessarily include a discussion of gender dysphoria, but wouldn't focus on it exclusively while at the same time maintaining hedonic presuppositions for others of maximizing pleasure and avoiding pain.

Only if we agree that we all are in need of embracing suffering fully, of being sanctified through our crosses, can we begin to find unity, rather than division, when we discuss gender dysphoria. Before any discussion, we must first acknowledge that we struggle to love well when another is suffering. Too often, we have abandoned one another to carry these painful crosses in isolation, masking our departure by quoting Scripture verses as we walk out the door. Next, we must resist the urge to avoid our own pain and the pain of others. In Christian communities, we have gotten quite good at praying for miraculous healing, but there is also much to be gained in praying for the grace to suffer well, even praying for *the desire* to want to suffer for love of God and love of one another.

It is certainly natural and good to ask for healing, to beg Jesus to give us reprieve from the weight of the cross. And sometimes Jesus does give reprieve through miraculous healing, whether it be physical or psychological, or the timely support of another person. Sometimes we have to think to ask, *What is our response when the cross is not lifted?* Can healing take the form of spiritual healing as we receive the grace of God in the presence of our real and enduring psychological and emotional distress?

These questions are ones we will discuss further in the next section.

SHARING THE BURDEN OF GENDER DYSPHORIA

A Christian couple came to us for a gender-dysphoria consultation, desperately seeking answers about how to manage gender dysphoria. The wife, who had experienced gender dysphoria since childhood, shared that for years she had asked God for healing. She wanted to know how other Christians have navigated this experience in light of their faith. We discussed the potential value of the couple meeting with their pastor and trusted members of their faith community for support as they live with and make decisions about how to cope with the distress of this experience. The wife looked back at us, looked at her husband, and replied, "We tried that. When we went to our faith community and asked for guidance, our pastor told us to pick up our cross and follow Jesus. We don't even know what that means, and aren't sure our pastor knows what that means. Either way, that response didn't help. We haven't found support. That's why we are here." This answer gave us pause. As we explored it further, the wife told us that she is actually longing to learn the meaning of Christ's call to each of us to carry our cross. But the comment from her pastor was experienced more as a pat answer to a difficult circumstance than a genuine desire to support her and her spouse. Similar to telling a grieving person, "Stop crying, your loved one is with God," this response, albeit true, did not honor the pain of the moment, or offer a model for what healing would look like. Such a response is typically more about reducing the discomfort of the pastor or the faith community rather than entering into the moment and the pain. In other words, the response seemed to say, "I know you are called to suffer, but I am not prepared to help you do it." If we only quote Romans 5:3–5, and this is the end of the conversation, the person suffering is left to suffer alone.

Sometimes the typical response has been, "I can't imagine dealing with that" or "What a tragedy." This is followed by prayer for healing, asking God to take away the pain through radical lifting of the cross. We have two thoughts about this. First, most Christians we know who suffer from gender dysphoria *have* been in prayer and *have* asked God for healing. They can continue to ask, of course. But a second thought is this: We may be missing something important when we only ever respond with a prayer of deliverance. Let's keep in mind that God's plan does not always include healing on this side of eternity—particularly not if we are focused only on physical or emotional healing (rather than spiritual healing or a journey toward greater spiritual growth). Further, because *the cross is the way to resurrection*, the ultimate Christian healing, it seems inadequate to think of the cross as something bad, or only ever to be prayed away. The cross, perhaps, is an opportunity. But for what?

In the case of the person with gender dysphoria, they may have been told, like the man born blind in John's gospel, that it was their own brokenness, or the brokenness of their parents, that brought on this cross. We recall the words of Jesus in response: "Neither this man nor his parents sinned," said Jesus, "but this happened so that the works of God might be displayed in him" (John 9:3).

Imagine meeting with this woman and her husband. What should your Christian ministry be?

First, we could listen to them. We could start by saying, "As you've shared with me about your pain, it feels as though I am meeting you at about chapter 7 or 8 of your life, but I haven't had the opportunity to hear about chapters 1 through 6, and I'd like to." Then listen. Ask questions. Resist the urge to oversimplify what they have been facing all these years.

Second, we could ask what strategies they have used to respond to their pain. "I can't begin to fully appreciate how difficult this has been for you. I am imagining that you have probably—perhaps through trial and error—tried different ways of responding to what has been really painful. Can you say more about what you've tried over the years?"

Third, we could honor the strategies the person has used, even as we set aside our own initial reactions about whether we think each strategy was the best idea.

Fourth, we could discuss how their Christian walk has been affected by facing such enduring hardship. "I can't imagine what this has been like for you. I'm wondering to what extent your faith has been a resource to you, or if that might be a tender subject. Maybe facing such pain has had an impact on you in profound ways, including your faith."

What you might have in the back of your mind is whether such hardships could lead to God's work being made manifest in a person's life, but you would not start there. There are no shortcuts. You have to enter in and abide and walk with the person. You have to display true empathy before you explore the pastoral question: *In what ways might the works of God be displayed in you?*

In other words, we are suggesting, and at this time only suggesting, that the steps needed to explore this possibility will take time and an understanding of how enduring hardship can lead to a lasting joy and point to an eternal, transcendent reality. You would have to keep in the forefront of your mind: *This does not soften the pain, but it may transform its meaning.*

We can turn to St. Mother Teresa of Calcutta for another model of this alternative understanding of suffering.

"One day," Teresa writes, "I met a lady who was dying of cancer in a most terrible condition. And I told her, I say, 'You know, this terrible pain is only the kiss of Jesus—a sign that you have come so close to Jesus on the cross that he can kiss you.' And she joined her hands together and said, 'Mother Teresa, please tell Jesus to stop kissing me.'"

Mother Teresa did not pray away the cancer in that moment, although we all can be certain she believed in the healing power of Christ, and likely witnessed it throughout her work. But, in the moment, she responded by highlighting the present moment as a kiss from the Lover to the Beloved. She was gentle in her reminder, seeing the terrible pain of the woman. She did not look away from the pain, or trivialize it, but spoke life into it. She proclaimed the light of truth into the darkness of the shadow of death, calling attention to the fact that the cross is a kiss from Jesus, a love letter from the Father to his daughter. Most importantly, Mother Teresa remained with the dying woman, hearing her pain, and receiving her understandable desire that the cup of suffering be taken away.

Also, it should be noted that Mother Teresa was able to say such things out of a posture of integrity. In other words, her life of sacrifice on behalf of orphans in Calcutta gave her remarkable credibility that most pastors and Christians would not have in a discussion with someone suffering from gender dysphoria. *Never underestimate the value of living your life by the very principles you suggest others consider relying on in response to enduring hardship.*

To wish that one's cross was different is not a flaw. In fact, Jesus in Gethsemane asked that the cup of suffering be taken from him, and then he submitted to the Father's will regarding it all, and we want to convey that there is no sin or shame to be found in such a request. Indeed, our desires for healing, for restoration, for relief from the cross are a reminder that we are not made for this fallen world we find ourselves in. Things are not as they should be. We are made for Christian joy. But we must remember, in the moments where we beg for the cup of suffering to be given to someone else, that the joy we seek is the fruit of suffering. It is in the painful experience of delivering the child that new life is brought forth. Every aspect of our human experience points to this reality. But suffering, whether in the delivery room, the nursing home, or on the streets of Calcutta, is not meant to be carried alone. If no one is there to bear witness, how can we see the glory of God manifest in the suffering?

This is where the rubber meets the road. All of us are called to share the burdens of this life, whether the burden is financial, emotional, spiritual, or psychological. When it comes to gender dysphoria, carrying the burden within Christian communities is long overdue. We may be missing a unique revelation of God's glory, manifest in the suffering of our fellow Christians. It is not so much for us to "diagnose" the source of the burden as it is for us to learn to help carry it.

CONTINUING TO SEEK ANSWERS FOR GENDER DYSPHORIA

Imagine for a moment the size and weight of the cross of Christ. Bulky, awkward, and heavy, for sure. Jesus learned obedience in carrying it (Heb. 5:8), but not before he fell three times beneath its weight. Simon of Cyrene, too, had to learn to bear its weight, to shift the weight, through trial and error, so that they could eventually make it to Golgotha. For the person with gender dysphoria, much like Christ himself, no how-to manual on carrying the cross is provided. Only grace will be sufficient here. Yet this is good news. Jesus promised that his grace is sufficient for us, and he certainly knew some would experience gender dysphoria when he made that promise. This means there is sufficient grace for the person with gender dysphoria, and grace offered to others who are willing to learn to bear the weight with them.

Does this mean that the Christian should forgo other interventions or management strategies in response to gender dysphoria? We are not taking that position at this time. Instead, we are inviting the Christian to spend more time in the questions of whether meaning and lasting joy can be found through enduring hardship, even though we cannot ask these questions as they might of themselves. We are not in their shoes. We do not ourselves suffer as they suffer; besides, gender dysphoria varies in severity from person to person and can vary in strength and severity in the same person over time. We also know of others who have suffered with severe, life-threatening gender dysphoria such that more urgent management strategies were also on the table.

We also want to ask whether insights into etiology will shape pastoral care. We do not know what causes gender dysphoria, but there are some interesting brain-scan studies that appear to support a neurodevelopmental theory in which the brain of a person with gender dysphoria may include both male-typical and female-typical brain characteristics.[5] When thinking of this theory, we call to mind the reality of those with physical intersex conditions, in which one is born with ambiguous genitalia (due to shared male-female sexual characteristics) that makes it difficult to determine the child's biological sex. Subsequently, there has been a practice of medical consultation and possible surgical intervention to "assign" a sex to the child. Some have suggested that, if the current line of brain research were to find additional support, we may be entertaining the idea of something closer to an intersex condition of the brain. If so (and we are not claiming that this is where the research is just yet), in what ways would this have implications for counseling and pastoral care and the morality of particular interventions? Or would it?

A final point: Many people we meet with have wondered whether their experience of gender dysphoria precludes them from a life in Christ. In their angst,

---

5. See Antonio Guillamon, Carme Junque, and Esther Gomez-Gil, "A Review of the Status of Brain Structure Research in Transsexualism," *Archives of Sexual Behavior* 45, no. 7 (October 2016): 1615–48.

they may ask, "Why does God love me less than others? How am I a beloved child of God when this is my life?" These are weighty questions, shared by many in moments when we feel forsaken by God. In journeying with one another through these difficult moments, we can be reminded, once again, to ask Christ our questions and to listen for his answers. He is no foreigner to suffering, and to the human feeling of being forsaken by his Father. But Jesus knew he was the Son of God. His entire ministry was dedicated to revealing this profound truth. "Son though he was, he learned obedience from what he suffered" (Heb. 5:8 NIV). He was the Son of God *and* he suffered. He remembered this. Maybe the best thing is to be reminded of this too.

We are beloved children of God, drawn close to the cross so we can be kissed by Jesus. This kiss may be bitter at times, but this kiss is sanctifying. Sanctification brings glorification and ultimately endless joy. We remember that, "if we are children, then we are heirs: heirs of God and co-heirs with Christ—if indeed we suffer with Him, so that we may also be glorified with Him" (Rom. 8:17 BSB). The first door we enter—suffering—leads to our final home, eternity.

Suffering makes it hard to remember eternity. In the midst of suffering, the glorification we are made for feels inaccessible. As Christians, we grieve our suffering, but not as those who have no hope (1 Thess. 4:13). We maintain our hope that the Lover will return for his Beloved, and will make all things new (Rev. 21:5). In suffering, we might feel broken, weak, and anything but lovable. So, gentle reminders that we are beloved may help. Many people with gender dysphoria are never told that they, too, are beloved. Who will remind them when pain makes them forget this fundamental truth and the source of their dignity? If anywhere, that's where you come in.

FOR DISCUSSION

1. What does healing mean to you? Does it help to distinguish among physical, psychological, and spiritual healing? If so, why? If not, why not?

2. Are there any management strategies (for gender dysphoria) that concern you? If so, why? If not, why not?

3. Would your faith community have a different response to gender-identity concerns if there were more research suggesting something like an intersex condition of the brain? If so, why? If not, why not?

FOR FURTHER READING

Yarhouse, Mark A., and Erica S. N. Tan. *Sexuality and Sex Therapy: A Comprehensive Christian Appraisal.* Downers Grove, IL: IVP Academic, 2014.

Yarhouse, Mark A., and Julia Sadusky. *Approaching Gender Dysphoria.* Cambridge, MA: Grove, 2018.

———. "A Christian View of Sex Reassignment Surgery and Hormone Therapy." Center for Faith, Sexuality and Gender, 2017. https://www.centerforfaith.com/resources?field_product_category_tid=1.

CHAPTER 22

HOW TO MAKE ETHICAL DECISIONS

DARRELL L. BOCK

We live in a messy world. And in many ways, it is becoming messier. As polarization has grown and in some places hostility to Christianity has become more intense, Christians need more than ever to make good ethical decisions. Such decisions always have two components—a content component and a relational one. The content part of ethical decisions involves reflecting true and authentic living; values as we deal with others.

In this chapter I want to consider not only how we make ethical decisions for ourselves and our communities but also how we serve one another as accountable friends, encouraging one another to love and good deeds by how we respond to challenges. So I will focus on more than merely how we make ethical decisions for ourselves, as important as that is. I will also address how the leader encourages others in his or her sphere of influence to engage faithfully and ethically with God, that is, "to live obediently before your God" (Micah 6:8).[1] We live as a community in the church, and encouraging each other to be our spiritual best is part of authentic community.

In a world crushed by the fall, being our spiritual best often means dealing with tensions that fall in the gray, as opposed to clear black-and-white decisions. I once heard the late theologian Haddon Robinson say, "The Bible often operates in black and white, but people often find themselves living in the gray." A fallen world can do that to people. Our world often can leave us facing competing biblical values bumping into each other and calling for balance. I will start out considering this dilemma and then move to how to analyze the confusing signals such dilemmas often present to us. Then we will turn to how relationally

---

1. All Scripture quotations in this chapter are from the NET Bible.

to step into such challenges, especially when the ethical call argues for a change in the way we live.

TYPES OF PROBLEMS

There are basically three types of ethical problems in terms of relational orientation. And when exploring these, we must consider both how we see the issue and how we communicate it to a person or community whose view(s) may differ or in which an array of opinions exists.

The first type of ethical problem involves situations where the present viewpoints in the conversation and core filters used to read the situation are so distinct that there is little common ground. In our current environment, abortion (pro-choice versus pro-life) and same-sex marriage fall in this category. So, for example, the earlier that sacred life is seen as created and tied to the work of God, the more likely one is to be pro-life. And taking such a position draws a line between how people approach the issue. Where one sees an issue of freedom of choice distinct from questions of the nature of the life within, a response to ethical choices will differ from that of one who sees a child as a creation of God bearing the divine image from fertilization or shortly thereafter. In another example, the belief that marriage is between a man and a woman as ordained by God versus marriage simply being a choice between independent human beings also produces a huge dividing line. Both the subjects of abortion and of same-sex marriage have caused enormous contemporary debate. The existence of very distinct starting points is the cause.

Yet even as we possess core differences, we are still faced with the question of how to have ethical conversations and discuss such ethical decisions with each other. In other words, the relational dimension never leaves us as we make ethical choices. Those choices are also important because they set a course for how our society functions and the values about life they reflect. Those in the helping professions need to consider how to guide people to think through the levels involved in such choices, reaching into the values they represent, not merely treating them as rules to be followed.

The second type of problem is where there is general agreement about what life calls for in a given area, but there is more debate about how to get there. Perhaps the clearest illustration of this category is the topic of racial reconciliation. Most people recognize that the goal of reconciliation is a worthy one, but most also wrestle with how to get there. Is the best way a form of identity advocacy in which each group looks at the issue from its own set of concerns? Or is the best way to listen and try empathetically to move outside of our own race or ethnicity to find a way forward? Or is the better way forward a combination of these two approaches, recognizing some value in each? The kind of problem in which most agree on the goal is less common, but it has the advantage of people sharing some common ground coming into the conversation.

The third area seems to be by far the most common one. In this scenario biblical values lie in tension with each other. And such tensions need discussion about how to balance competing elements. The tensions result from life in a fallen world, a world of gray or of lives out of whack. Numerous public issues reside here. Immigration is a classic example. How does one honor the law of a country so as to provide safety and stability and yet also operate with appropriate compassion and an awareness of the full array of circumstances that lead people to the need to emigrate? How do we avoid the kind of generalizing that denies an ear to genuine refugees and those seeking relief from violence? How open should we be to others' need for the opportunity to pursue a new life like the one many of us get to live? How do we read the moral responsibility we share in the nonapplication of our laws over decades in which enforcement was not pursued and entry into an underground form was encouraged and supported by cultural acceptance?

In this third situation, health care might serve as another example. Is life so precious that basic care should be provided? What kind of a system is just, when providing such care may not be socially affordable? How does one balance such contrasting goals?

It is important to begin here because life often deals us a mixed hand. Knowing what kind of decision one faces and what elements are in play helps to make for more careful decision-making. Having an awareness of these tensions within an issue and how to treat them is important. It will protect us from a tendency to cherry-pick issues in which only one biblical value is put forward while others are ignored or minimized.

Yet even in cases in which a biblical directive is clear, the way we handle the more delicate relational dimension also is an essential part of good ethics. So both content and tone in engagement and in ethical decision-making are important. First we consider content, then the relational side of the equation.

ASSESSING THE SITUATION THROUGH THE TEXT

When seeking to make ethical decisions, there are two dimensions relating to the biblical text to keep in view for believers: what the biblical parameters are on the topic and how to apply them relationally. One without the other can mean being right about content and yet applying the truth in a way that fails to reflect the way God calls us to relate to others. One can fail at the level of content or at the relational level. And both failures are significant.

The issue of content gets into the issue of interpretation. Content is affected at two levels as we read the Scripture. First there is the way one's culture can frame an issue as good or bad. This is a *cultural level* of reading. And this level needs assessment. Sometimes a shift in culture can change the way, the manner, and the care with which the text is read.

Consider, for example, the topic of same-sex marriage. The cultural reading of the "right or wrong" of same-sex marriage has changed significantly in the past few decades. Right after I finished my PhD in Aberdeen in the early 1980s, a fellow Aberdeen grad took a pastorate in California. His first major pastoral problem involved an elder in his church who had pursued a sex-change operation (nearly unheard of at the time). The pastor's wife wrote to my wife, Sally, and me asking if we had covered such a scenario in seminary or discussed it, because it was not covered where he had gone to school. Sally and I responded saying that sex-change as related to Christian ethics had not come up in the seminary program, nor had we really discussed it. The pastor and his wife, as well as Sally and I, were working from square one, not in terms of what Scripture said, but about how to handle a sex change as a pastoral issue in the congregation.

Given the larger cultural framework, however, that pastor was really not in that much of a dilemma, because the cultural consensus was that getting a sex change was disqualifying of a church leader. Needless to say, today that cultural view has shifted. Today such scenarios are becoming more common with a variety of views being defended that were once considered unacceptable.

So what was once virtually a given is no longer necessarily the case now. Nothing in the cultural shift changes what the pastor would do in response; but what a leader in such a scenario would face today includes the possibility of a different reaction to the decision. Consequently, *how* the decision gets implemented needs more thought.

Another example is how the change in American law has affected the discussion about same-sex marriage. I note this *not* to say the church needs to change its views on sexuality, but simply to note that the dynamics of such a pastoral-community decision became more complicated culturally and thus relationally with a legal sanction for something many in the church reject and the Bible questions. The difference that came with the passage of a law that redefined marriage also means that at one time what could almost be assumed (marriage = man + woman) is no longer the case. And because assumptions have changed, the church has to give more time than it did in the past to explaining its ethical views. More pushback in response to ethical decisions may result from such a cultural change, or at least an awareness that there may be more difference of opinion than existed previously. The topic of "difference of opinion" moves us into the issue of interpretation.

Sometimes we mistake our reading of a biblical text as the only way that text can be read. But we must justify our interpretations by careful textual work and an awareness of other readings. We also need to reflect on the level of certainty we have about our own understanding of what the text says. One of the aspects of careful decision-making, even about interpretations, is to be aware of how confident we are of the views we hold. Some interpretations of Scripture are clearer than others. So it helps to consider a scale of certainty the Bible interpreter has about the way the text is read. With my students I use this spectrum:

1. I am virtually positive of this reading.
2. I'm aware of a difference, but I'm fairly confident I'm right, though you might have it correct.

3. If we get to heaven and I find out you are right, I will not be surprised.
4. Let's both be honest: We might as well flip a coin, because neither of us can be sure.

Where we fall in our assessment of a given text will have an impact on the passion and certainty we give to specific readings and even the priority we give to the various factors involved in making ethical decisions. The kind of interpretative awareness described above is important, because none of us is omniscient. And the fact that an interpretation can be wrong is a reason to pursue such a decision in community. There is some protection in having many eyes engage the text together to help each other detect blind spots.

So we have to engage the text honestly and fully with an awareness of how others read it and why. Teaching pastors have a special responsibility in this regard because of their role in instruction and the fact that they have often received some training in Bible interpretation. As good interpreters, we must become acquainted with how others read the text and honestly engage with their reasons. The views we hold should be held with a commitment to be able to make a good case for why we affirm what we do and with an awareness of the judgments involved in taking that position.

Such research and self-awareness takes work, but it is a function of responsible pastoral commitments to view the teaching role with this kind of integrity. It is important to have a shared awareness of the kind of problem we are dealing with: (1) a clear, single-level conflict of views; (2) a searching for the right way to solve a shared commitment; or (3) values operating in tension. Recognizing where we are in the type of problem we are facing helps us assess more carefully what we are dealing with in facing a particular decision. Such assessment is necessary in setting up satisfactory, faithful engagement at a relational level as well as in helping us make good, biblically rooted decisions.

We have to start with the text, but the way we deal with any challenges relationally is just as important. An honest awareness of views and an ability to weigh priorities carefully make for a mind-set that is better prepared relationally to engage often controversial areas with sensitivity.

In addition, possessing a sense of how strongly we hold a view, what judgments are involved in getting there, or how clear the priorities are also has an effect on how the decision is made or how strongly to engage with another who is thinking differently. In other words, even our content reflections have layers we need to be aware of as we engage with others or face a choice about what to do. So if I am less certain about a decision, if I recognize there are judgments being made, and/or if I see the spectrum of options in weighing tensions, such situations differ from those in which content is clear and I'm unequivocal about what the text is saying. Ethical decisions are not just made but weighed.

CONSIDERING THE RELATIONAL DIMENSION

In some ways the trickiest part of ethical decisions is relational. Because even after we recognize what God calls on people to do, actually getting any of us to acknowledge a need for change can be hard.

Four concerns drive ethical decisions: (1) the content; (2) the weighing of that content; (3) the person/people being engaged; (4) and the impact on the community. Being ethical can involve making tough decisions in which these concerns are in conflict or, at least, in severe tension. That is why we often speak of ethical dilemmas as we make decisions in a fallen world. Such deliberations often come with challenges to a person's previous choice or way of life, affecting personal and community well-being. God is in the business of shaping us to be like him, and often that means changing from how we have lived. A core ethical decision involves being willing to let God change us when we see our choices fall short. The minister is often used by God as a catalyst to make another person aware of such a need and to urge a community to see this need as well. In the challenge to an ethical life and community well-being, the relational dimension becomes crucial.

Two characteristics of this relational dimension are fundamental: humility and listening well. These two may seem counterintuitive, for usually the key concern is to get the decision right or convince another of a decision that needs to be made. Yet there is a way to get the content right and miss relationally. Consider the apostle Paul's exhortation to the church in Galatia:

> Brothers and sisters, if a person is discovered in some sin, you who are spiritual restore such a person in a spirit of gentleness. Pay close attention to yourselves, so that you are not tempted too. Carry one another's burdens, and in this way you will fulfill the law of Christ. For if anyone thinks he is something when he is nothing, he deceives himself. Let each one examine his own work. Then he can take pride in himself and not compare himself with someone else. For each one will carry his own load. (Gal. 6:1–5)

It is too easy to give advice and not actually apply it in humility to oneself. Paul's instruction to the Galatians reminds us that even in challenge and confrontation, we are to be careful not to be proud or think we are immune, for such an attitude breeds insensitivity.

There is a self-assessment and a humility in ethical decision-making that also echoes the call to have the same attitude that was in Christ with a desire to serve and give (Phil. 2:5–11). Such self-assessment recognizes the possibility of our own failures, even as we urge change in others. Confrontation comes best when it is accompanied by a humility in the one issuing the challenge. This relational commitment is a reflection of a deep love for truth *and* the well-being of the person you are dealing with.

Actually our experience with the gospel starts here. We all fall short and are in need of what God has done through Christ. When I discuss issues tied to same-sex marriage, I take a close look at Romans 1:18–32, which is probably the passage most people know about the topic. The observation is made that Paul is pretty direct and harsh about same-sex sexual relationships. That is certainly correct. Although many minimize the text and say it is only about certain kinds of same-sex abuse, the Jewish background regarding the idea of same-sex relationships makes this view unlikely from Paul's lips. Leviticus 20:13 is very direct in saying same-sex relations are wrong. And Paul uses same-sex relations as the example that demonstrates creation gone awry: "Just as they did not see fit to acknowledge God, God gave them over to a depraved mind, to do what should not be done" (Rom. 1:28).

Yet there is something else not to miss in the chapter. Paul introduces a vice list. It reads, "They are filled with every kind of unrighteousness, wickedness, covetousness, malice. They are rife with envy, murder, strife, deceit, hostility. They are gossips, slanderers, haters of God, insolent, arrogant, boastful, contrivers of all sorts of evil, disobedient to parents, senseless, covenant-breakers, heartless, ruthless" (vv. 29–31). The punch line comes next: "Although they fully know God's righteous decree that those who practice *such things* deserve to die" (v. 32). Now the key term here, "such things," is plural, so Paul is not just challenging readers with one sin, but with anything in the vice list. Something catches each of us out and puts us in need of God. Paul is not highlighting one area alone, but the array of sin, any one of which makes every reader/hearer a transgressor. There is no hierarchy of sin here. Paul is building to a point he finally makes in Romans 3: "For all have sinned and fall short of the glory of God" (v. 23).

The awareness of our sin should create in us humility as we consider how we challenge people with the gospel and face ethical decision-making relationally, especially when we are challenging someone else's choice. So humility is important. It is ideas like this that set up the exhortation cited from Galatians 6 to engage others ethically but to do so with humility.

In addition to having a heart of humility, we must also listen. Part of what one hopes to do relationally is to connect with people so they will engage and be open to God's working in their ethical choices. That takes caring about people, encouraging them to a place of being open to respond. An ethical challenge can bring defensiveness. Bad ethical choices emerge from both a flawed theology and a flawed psychology a person bears. These flaws often come out of self-interest, but sometimes they stem from a mistaken view of freedom or of self-protection through previous harm done in a fallen world.

Listening for what is driving a person is important, not because unethical choices should be affirmed in counseling, but to bring to the surface what needs attention and where misdirection may be coming from as decisions are made. I call this getting a spiritual GPS on a person. It involves listening for how a person puts together life and its choices. Such listening also seeks to pay attention to why a person makes those choices. To listen well, we need to put our "heresy meter" on mute for a time, not because truth does not matter, but because our initial goal is to understand where another person is coming from and what drives them to respond as they do.

Such listening also communicates care, because it shows we wish to understand people and their stories. Such listening connects us to the person and allows us to gain insight about the situation and motivation for why a person acts as he or she does. In many ways, this is step one in relating, to listen well. As James 1:19 says, we should be "quick to listen, slow to speak, and slow to anger." The groundwork laid by good listening sets up the opportunity to engage in relational ethical reflection. It is after this initial step of listening that we begin to apply and discuss what had been muted earlier. So ethical reflection follows good listening instead of being immediately applied.

Just because I have the right to do something does not mean it is good for me to do it (1 Cor. 6:12). Where an ethical challenge needs to be addressed, the person needs to know we care in order to hear any critique that is coming in the conversation. It is in moving too quickly that the application of a call to be ethical often fails. In the pursuit of making or insisting on the right choice, the minister can fail to communicate the care that can motivate a desire to pursue change. Good listening for what may be going on with the person may help build the bridges of communicating care. Such care can open up the conversation for the recipient to consider new ways of living. This brings us to the issue of how conversations work, especially when the topic involves disagreement or give rise to difficult conversations.

HAVING DIFFICULT CONVERSATIONS

Those who study conversations tell us that verbal discourse operates at three levels. These levels are especially important to understand in the context of difficult conversations. All hard or deep exchanges are actually triphonic conversations.[2]

The first level is the one we tend to focus on, *the topic at hand.* This level includes both the topic of discussion (such as abortion, immigration, or marriage) and our contribution to the topic. The focus of this level is, as Jack Webb's character on the old TV show *Dragnet* said, "Just the facts, ma'am." We communicate what we see and why, frequently with a goal of persuading. Establishing assertions, garnering our evidence, and making the case happen at this level. Yet when we set up a discussion only in this way, the path is set for a debate versus a conversation. That said, often there is a case to be made, and the rationale undergirding the position taken is crucial. But so are the relational elements of what is going on, along with what underlies the positions we take. Tone matters. And it is at the level of tone that triphonics steps in. That is, knowledge of the three levels reminds us there are other things going on in our conversations in addition to the topic and

---

2. A book discussing this topic effectively is *Difficult Conversations: How to Discuss What Matters Most,* the work of professional mediators Douglas Stone, Bruce Patton, and Sheila Heen (New York: Penguin, 2010).

the facts being pursued. Sometimes those other two levels drive the conversation, an important point to understand in the midst of communication.

The second level of triphonics is *a combination of emotions, perceptions, and judgments* at work as we speak. At this second level, conversations can get murky because people will look at the same scenario and read it differently. So at play is a strange brew of emotions and perspectives that actually work as filters in what we see and how we arrange the "facts." Sometimes we promote emotions, perceptions, and judgments to level one (facts) when they don't belong there. Conversely, though, we may bypass or dismiss them as irrelevant when these emotions, perceptions, and judgments can be central to how a person is reacting.

The level-two mix of emotional drivers and differing perceptions requires that we advocate for and listen to the conversation partner in order to discern why differences exist. A core goal in good conversations is understanding these differences and why they are there. Such understanding differs from the assessment of who is right or wrong or what mix of right or wrong is going on. Yet often we confuse these two distinct categories and jump to assessing *before* understanding each other. Such a premature leap often creates misunderstanding in what is happening, preventing the conversation from progressing.

For example, when my wife communicates that I could help her more or that I'm falling short of caring well for her, my instinct is to get defensive: defend myself (emotional level) and perceive her as accusing me of being a poor husband (identity level). But instead, my response ought to be to probe why she feels the way she does and find out what I can do better to be of help. Do I understand where she is coming from so we can have a profitable conversation about the concerns she has raised? Being aware of our own and others' emotions, perceptions, and judgments helps us in these difficult conversations. Unfortunately, often we seek to mind-read our conversation partner at these levels ("you are just angry with me so much of the time"), while ignoring what is going on within us at the same level ("I feel threatened, so I react to protect myself"). That emotive leap can short-circuit a good conversation by casting blame—often for reasons other than the topic at hand—while ignoring what may be going on within us. This emotive leap is especially problematic, because we humans make poor prophets. So one should hesitate to attribute motives to another, thereby deflecting the conversation in the process. Being open to "owning our own junk" means seeking to hear what is being said to us and to engage in a real exchange of ideas. Disagreement may still exist, but the actual causes of disagreement will become more clear.

The third level of triphonics concerns *how our identity and self-understanding are affected* by what we are discussing. The deepest and trickiest level, this third one is almost always in play in important conversations. What is at stake for me in this conversation? How am I seen as a result? How does what is going on affect my soul? Am I looking bad or good in this? Such thoughts are often not shared, and yet they can direct how we respond and why. When we block conversation, we often short-circuit a discussion that actually has some potential for our own learning. Often we remain unaware of this dynamic because we are too busy simply reacting with our defensive shields up.

Think about what happens as we engage, especially on difficult topics. If you are like me, you simultaneously listen and formulate responses in reaction to what you hear. And often the response you're formulating is in defense of your position. But a key element missing in this mode of conversation is curiosity and actual engagement with the other person about what drives him or her to express themselves the way they are.

So three voices—triphonics—are in play in us at different levels; and without some awareness and self-discipline, these voices can drown out our ability to hear and connect to the other person in the conversation. As a result, we fail to make a real effort to understand our conversational partner before engaging in any problem-solving about the topic.

So what can help us? First, when discussions become difficult, we choose to become more curious as to why the person thinks differently from how we do without trying to be a mind-reading prophet. Second, we avoid charges based on assumptions about motives or questioning of integrity. This includes letting the other speak and taking his or her initial responses as sincere. We avoid a blame game that might include venting or dismissive labeling of the other's response. Third, by paying attention to the three levels within our own conversational perspective *that might be getting in the way*, we also seek to understand where the other person is coming from and why. This is "owning our own junk." Fourth, we are curious and ask questions *not to defeat the other person but to move toward mutual understanding* about why we disagree or where the differences and tension points lie. Fifth, we seek to understand before assessing. There will be time for assessment later, once everyone can agree on what the issues really are. Sixth, we paraphrase in the difficult moments in a way that causes our conversation partner to conclude, "Yep, you understand me." We can also ask others to paraphrase what they have heard us say.

What does paying attention to triphonics and to the other person accomplish in a conversation? Doing so communicates respect for the other and allows the potential for a better exchange. Paying attention to triphonics establishes connection because the real reasons for differences surface in ways both participants can recognize. It may also open up new avenues or a recalibration of the topic in positive directions.

When I discuss this recalibration, there is one key question I always get: What if I try this but others are not there? What if they just want to duke it out in debate? What do I do then? The best approach is to try and reframe the conversation in a direction that pushes toward the curiosity door. As you ask questions, invite them to ask you about something you have said. Invite them to paraphrase or offer to paraphrase what they have said. In other words, redirect the conversation in a way that walks through the listening door searching to be curious. If the other pushes toward debate or to assess and make judgments before you have understood each other, ask to defer that question until you both *mutually* agree you understand each other's position. Promise you will get to that stage of conversation, but only after you are agreed about the playing field you are both on and why. Having this kind of a conversation takes discipline, but it can also pay rich dividends if both conversation partners can get there. Honor the sequence of understanding each other first, and then assess what to do about it.

When people see we care about and understand them, they tend to open up more to us and are in better positions to hear what we have to say. Reaching an understanding first can also open us up to learn and grow by hearing things we need to hear as well. In short, such communication leads to better decisions at a relational level, even where content disagreement exists. Having achieved some level of mutual understanding and agreement about the topic and the nature of the disagreement(s), assessment can follow much more effectively.

ASSESSMENT AND MAKING JUDGMENTS

In the end, ethical decisions for believing communities should be rooted in the teaching of Scripture, inspired to guide us in all matters of faith and practice. Such decisions should be made with an awareness of what Scripture teaches, having sorted through the ways in which the truth is read and the judgments concerning why a particular reading is preferred. Rooting faith and practice in Scripture is not a matter of simply working through a given text or two, but reading the whole of Scripture for how the topic gets handled. This is because in the whole of Scripture one can get a variety of angles from which a topic may be addressed. Texts are not automatically universal, but may be contextually defined. So how broadly a given text applies has to be a part of such a process.

An example of this kind of contextual work can be seen in 1 Corinthians 8–10, where Paul handles how meat offered to idols is handled in four different situations: (1) if meat is offered at the pagan temple, don't eat it, (2) if food is bought at the marketplace, one is free to eat the meat and not ask questions about its previous use, (3) if meat is served in a home, one is free to eat it, unless (4) someone notes it has been part of the pagan sacrifice. Then it is to be bypassed. This text shows how context can affect how broadly to interpret a text. So such questions must be pursued. Still in the end, the combination of what the text teaches along with examining its scope gives direction to what the Scripture teaches and how far the application extends.

There are still relational and community elements regarding how one explains and handles the results of an ethical decision. Such elements become more complex when one holds that Scripture takes a stand counter to that of the larger culture. Introducing a practice that differs from what is acceptable within the larger culture means teaching and explaining clearly the textual basis for the stand coupled with a call to follow the textual direction.

Implementation should also be done with some awareness of the interpretive judgments involved in cases where there is community disagreement, as well as with sensitivity to the impact on those affected by such a decision. In cases in which one is balancing tensions, as is often the case with complex decisions, how one has prioritized those tensions also will need careful reflection and articulation. Difficult decisions often demand high pastoral and community care as well as effective communication as a part of carrying them out. One has to step in relationally to wisely execute a difficult decision. Simply issuing a decree rarely works out well. Often it is especially at this point that both content and tone matter most.

CONCLUSION

The process of making ethical decisions is multidimensional. We have traced several aspects and levels tied to this process in the midst of seeking to love people well and serving a community faithfully. Prayer and humility should undergird the entire process. What is called for is a combination of seeking to do right and caring for people in the process. Sometimes doing so is especially challenging.

Both content and tone matter equally. To miss on either side can turn a potentially good decision into a poor one. But a servant of others will wed concern for truth to compassion and courage to step into controversial places, carefully sorting through this process of making biblically rooted, ethical decisions with relational awareness.

FOR DISCUSSION

1. Name the three levels of any conversation and discuss how they affect your own difficult conversations.

2. Taking the various levels of weighing decisions, what would you place in the A, B, C, and D categories?

3. What is a challenging ethical decision you face now, and how would you go about resolving it?

FOR FURTHER READING

Guinness, Os. *The Global Public Square*. Downers Grove, IL: InterVarsity Press, 2013.

Rae, Scott B., Robert P. George, and Melissa Moschella. *Doing the Right Thing: Making Moral Choices in a World Full of Options*. Grand Rapids: Zondervan, 2013.

Stone, Douglas, Bruce Patton, and Sheila Heen. *Difficult Conversations: How to Discuss What Matters Most*. New York: Penguin, 2010.

CHAPTER 23

PERSONAL AND INTERPERSONAL SEXUAL ETHICS

C. GARY BARNES

Because God gives us sexuality, we are to be stewards, stewards of this dimension of our existence. We are to employ our sexuality to fulfill God's intention. What is God's intention? Namely, as sexual creatures we actualize the divine design. We reflect the nature of God, and thereby bring glory to the creator.
—Stanley Grenz

In the quotation above, Stanley Grenz is trying to help us understand what it means to be stewards of our sexuality so that we may better reflect the nature of God and thereby glorify God.[1] We cannot think of ourselves as not being sexual beings. We are sexual beings. And as sexual beings, we must demonstrate a good personal sexual ethic and also a good interpersonal sexual ethic to more fully glorify God.

Personal and interpersonal sexual ethics may be driven by two different psychologies. There is the motivating psychology of the cosmos and there is also the redeeming psychology of Christ.[2] Someone might say, "I'm not so sure those two words, *psychology* and *Christ*, should go together." If someone is having

---

1. Stanley J. Grenz, *Sexual Ethics: An Evangelical Perspective* (Louisville: Westminster John Knox, 1990), 52.
2. C. Gary Barnes, "Sexuality, Diversity, Religiosity and Ethics" (paper presented at Christian Association for Psychological Studies, National Annual Conference, Chicago, Illinois, March 30, 2017).

that conflict, he or she might be using the wrong point of reference—and it is probably modern psychology—from the past one hundred years. If you go back to New Testament teaching, particularly the Greek word ψυχή, you find another point of reference. What's the best translation of that word? It is commonly translated as "soul." Then the word *psychology* is understood to be the study of the soul. It has a meaning of the *whole person*, the *self*. And so the best translation words for ψυχή in the New Testament would be either "person" or "self."[3] The ψυχή is the totality of the person.

The fuller understanding of the soul is the material and the immaterial dimensions of the self. David Benner says that the soul is "the meeting point of the psychological and the spiritual."[4] This of course includes the sexual dimension of our being. We're not just talking about the Freudian idea of psychology here. And this is exactly what Christ came to redeem, the whole person. He didn't come to redeem only our spirits. He came to redeem the whole person, including our sexual dimension. Now, that's an important thing to consider in terms of the implications for both a personal and interpersonal sexual ethic.

PERSONAL SEXUAL ETHIC

The diagram "The Slippery Slope of Sacred Sexuality" (see figure 6)[5] demonstrates the difficulty of elevating our personal experience of sexuality to its designed theological significance. We tend to slide in one of two different directions. We tend to demonize sex, or we tend to deify sex. As sexual beings, we cannot demonize sex and thus take away from the greatness of sex. We also cannot deify sex and in so doing attempt to meet nonsexual needs sexually. Particular church and cultural time periods have served as influential factors that push in one or the other direction. We also have individual differences. Because of who you are as a person, your family of origin, and your life experience outside of your family, you are going to lean in a particular direction on the slippery slope to either demonize or deify sex. The direction you lean may differ from your overall current slice of church or cultural influence, but it's going to be the way you lean. It's important that you have an awareness of your tendency, and that you are not on autopilot with the slippery slope. To develop a personal sexual ethic, you must intentionally work with yourself and with God and his revelation to elevate sexuality back to its theological significance.

---

3. Donald Guthrie, *New Testament Theology* (Downers Grove, IL: InterVarsity Press, 1981), 64.
4. David Benner, *Care of Souls: Revisioning Christian Nurture and Counsel* (Grand Rapids: Baker, 1998), 13.
5. C. Gary Barnes, "Sacred Sexuality: Foundations and Motivations for a Sexual Ethic" (lecture presented at Dallas Theological Seminary, Dallas, Texas, May 2018).

The Slippery Slope of Sacred Sexuality

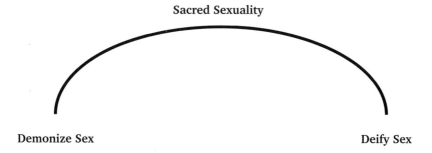

Figure 6. The Slippery Slope of Sacred Sexuality

Many have identified the four big chapters or four stages of redemptive history in the Bible as creation, fall, redemption, and glorification. And rather than simply looking at separate verses about sexuality, it is more useful to take a broader view of how the Bible as a whole informs and guides a personal ethic of sexuality.[6] As a basic guideline, two significant theological anchor points from each chapter of redemptive history can be identified for elevating a personal sexual ethic.

Creation

In the creation account, we uniquely see what life was like before the negative effects of the fall. In the original design we see that (1) sex is glorious and (2) sex is greater than the individual.[7] It's not meant to be an individual thing or an individual experience. The big idea behind seeing sexuality before the fall is to be able to see the potential, the capacity of God's design. God's gift of sex was designed to elevate and point us to something outside of time and space. Human experience of sex is grounded in time and space, but God's gift of sex was designed to point us beyond to truths far more significant.

God's idea of sex as seen in Genesis 1 and 2 is to help us have an experiential object lesson that drives home the truth of *oneness that is not based in sameness.*[8] Such oneness that is not based on sameness is the truth experienced

---

6. Mark A. Yarhouse, *Homosexuality and the Christian: A Guide for Parents, Pastors, and Friends* (Minneapolis: Bethany House, 2010), 19.

7. C. Gary Barnes, "Christian Theology, Psychology, and Homosexuality: Foundations for Loving Your Neighbor" (paper presented at World Evangelization Conference, Annual Conference at Dallas Theological Seminary, Dallas, Texas, March 12, 2013).

8. C. Gary Barnes, "Marriage Strong: Academic Applications at Dallas Theological Seminary" (paper presented at The Boone Center for the Family, Pepperdine University, Malibu, California, October 17, 2015).

inclusively in social sexuality by singles.[9] This is also the truth experienced exclusively in erotic sexuality by a husband and wife in covenant relationship engaged in sexual union.[10] Most significantly, it is the truth about the Trinity. In the Trinity (three persons in one being) there is perichoresis, the *eternal exchange of love.*[11] The additional unfathomable truth is that as God's created beings, we have been invited to become participants in this eternal exchange of love. In the pre-fall state as created humans, we were created to know the oneness that is not based on sameness that is characterized by the Trinity. God designed us as sexual beings to experience this humanly in interpersonal relationships, and to experience this as humans in a relationship of love with the divine Trinity.

Fall

From Genesis 3 onward, we learn that, as a result of the fall, all creation has been tarnished. We have depravity with a capital *T*—as in total. And total depravity means that there's no part of us that is untouched by sin. Under this condition, sin disconnects all things that God designed to be connected, and disconnects all things from their deeper, true meaning and purpose. As a result of the fall, the two truths related to sex are: (1) sex is not dirty, and (2) sex is derailed.[12]

We don't lose the total significance of sex in the fall, but sex is negatively affected. Sex doesn't accomplish what it was going to accomplish in its full sense before the fall. We actually have a much greater difficulty elevating sacred sexuality. It is now much easier for sexuality to slide on the slippery slope into either demonization or deification.

By demonizing sexuality, we lose the elevation benefit. We miss the whole glorious contribution of God's design. Since the fall, we naturally think about sexuality in a way that further clouds God's idea of how it should have been elevated, therefore diminishing our understanding and experience of God.

By deifying sex, we take it to a function beyond what it was designed to do. By deifying sex, we make it an idol. It becomes the source of needs that it was not meant to be. When we deify sex we make it address nonsexual needs sexually. So sex is not dirty, but it does get derailed. It enhances the slippery-slope tendency to either demonize or deify it and blocks our understanding and experience of oneness not based on sameness.

---

9. Grenz, *Sexual Ethics*, 195.
10. Grenz, *Sexual Ethics*, 195.
11. Christopher West, *Theology of the Body for Beginners: A Basic Introduction to Pope John Paul II's Sexual Revolution*, rev. ed. (West Chester, PA: Ascension, 2009), 7.
12. Barnes, "Christian Theology."

Redemption

Christian theology teaches us that God in his mercy did not leave us in our sin. This is the good news of the gospel. God intervened through his son, Jesus Christ. This redemption actually has transforming power, and it has power over the ill effects of sin, totally. That includes the ill effects of sin on sex.

The two sexual truths of redemption, even this side of heaven, and also this side of the fall, are that (1) sex can be a celebration,[13] and (2) sex functions as a crucible.[14] In our personal efforts to elevate sex to an experience of sacred sexuality, we are also truthful about our fallenness at the same time. God is doing an ongoing, redemptive work in us. Therefore, the experience of sexuality as a redeemed person who is not yet fully redeemed is that it provides a crucible function for us. It becomes the container where things get cooked and purified. That happens through a lot of heat and pressure.

When we experience sex in the context of *inclusive social sexuality*, singles with singles and singles with married individuals, the personal sexual ethic is put to the test.[15] In the third chapter of redemption, we experience the already-but-not-yet truths of redemption. We have a capacity as men and women to deepen and enrich our experience of oneness not based on sameness as we also socially relate as sexual beings in holy ways. Our doing so becomes a celebration in our personal and social experiences, and doing so points us to eternal truths about God.[16] But since we are not yet fully redeemed, we also have a capacity to relate sexually in unholy ways.

The potential for relating sexually in unholy ways brings us to the experience of the crucible and the difficult and challenging process of being transformed. Choosing to live in the tension of relating as holy sexual beings, rather than relating as neutered beings to avoid being unholy, is the far greater calling of those redeemed in Christ.[17]

When we experience sex in the *exclusive covenantal marriage relationship*[18] that God had intended it to be, it involves two fallen people who are in a redemption process. As redeemed individuals yearning for oneness with God and with spouses, we are still broken and not yet fully sanctified. We are still prone to hide behind our fig leaves for a sense of self-protection. The crucible of sex serves as a catalyst in the personal transformation journey.

---

13. Douglas E. Rosenau et al., "A Celebration of Sex: A Model for Teaching Creative Marital Intimacy" (paper presented at CAPS-Christian Association for Psychological Studies, National Annual Conference, Indianapolis, Indiana, March 31, 2011).

14. C. Gary Barnes, "Transforming Marital Sexuality: Applications for Husbands and Wives as People in Christ" (lecture presented at Dallas Theological Seminary, Dallas, Texas, May, 2017).

15. Grenz, *Sexual Ethics*, 195.

16. Douglas E. Rosenau and Michael Todd Wilson, *Soul Virgins: Redefining Single Sexuality* (Grand Rapids: Baker Books, 2006), 133.

17. Barnes, "Transforming Marital Sexuality."

18. Grenz, *Sexual Ethics*, 195.

Oneness not based on sameness will not naturally and automatically happen. We will have many opportunities for bumping into each as we seek intimacy and try to connect without our fig leaves. Self-protection drives us back to those fig leaves as we attempt to move into the sexual relational crucible with one another. Someone said, "When it comes to sex, that's when yer most bare necked." And such "neckedness" means a lot more than only physical nakedness. The deeper we go with intimate vulnerability, the deeper our potential for deeper-level oneness and connection. Of course, that requires the deepest level of trust and safety. That is the whole crucible process. An outcome of oneness not based on sameness with full whole-person nakedness is all ultimately possible because of the redemptive work of God.

Glorification

Glorification is the last major act of redemptive history. In the culmination story God gives those in Christ a wedding-feast banquet. This culminates with Jesus returning as the rightful ruler over all things. The negative effects of the fall will at this time be fully redeemed. The two truths of the glorification chapter are that (1) sex is simply an earthly reminder, and (2) sex is a heavenly pointer.[19] God's revelation says that when we get to chapter 4, there will be no marriage in heaven. There will not be that covenantal relationship within which sex was designed to point us to something. The tool, the object lesson, the instrument, will no longer be needed. There will be something far, far greater that accomplishes our experience and understanding of oneness not based on sameness. At this time we will fully behold the glory of God directly.

The need for a personal sexual ethic is illustrated in figure 6, The Slippery Slope of Sacred Sexuality.[20] As mentioned, we tend to slide in one of two different directions. We tend to demonize sex, or we tend to deify sex. As sexual beings who are being redeemed in chapter 3 of biblical history, we cannot demonize sex and take away from its greatness; we also cannot deify sex and in so doing attempt to meet nonsexual needs sexually.

INTERPERSONAL SEXUAL ETHIC

Psychology of the Cosmos

What does the world do when it bumps into differences? How does the psychology of the cosmos guide and motivate us in an interpersonal sexual ethic? There are two typical responses. One typical worldly interpersonal sexual ethic is intolerance. Intolerance results in exclusion, which can occur in two common

---

19. C. Gary Barnes, "Sexual Identity and the Church" (paper presented at CAPS-Christian Association for Psychological Studies, National Annual Conference, Atlanta, Georgia, April 5, 2014).
20. Barnes, "Sacred Sexuality: Foundations and Motivations for a Sexual Ethic."

ways: *expulsion* and *subjugation*. Expulsion says, "Get away from me, or I'll get away from you." Subjugation says, "Oh, yeah. I'd really like to have a relationship with you. I would like to be connected with you. But if we are going to relate, I'll have the power. I'll live here. You live there. I do this. You only get to do this. And then we can be connected, and then we can relate."[21] Ultimately this interpersonal sexual ethic is a oneness that is based on sameness or submission.

The other common interpersonal sexual ethic of the world is tolerance. Many recent events in America have spurred on this option. On the surface, tolerance looks like an attractive alternative to ugly intolerance. It is becoming so popular that many would even say that tolerance is the only absolute we have left to us. An ethical paradox has evolved in our culture that the only moral absolute left is to insist that no one's morals are absolute. Practically speaking, this becomes a process of assimilation that says, "Oh, yeah. I would love to have a relationship with you, if you become like me in terms of my core beliefs."[22] Such a plea for tolerance and inclusiveness translates to a sneaky outcome of exclusion. This worldly alternative to intolerance is, practically speaking, an exclusive inclusivism.[23] Ultimately this interpersonal sexual ethic is a oneness that is based in sameness of "essential" beliefs.

Psychology of Christ

Let's contrast this with the psychology of Christ. Actually, Christ and the apostle Paul call us far beyond *in*tolerance, but they also call us far beyond tolerance. Tolerance is not the solution to intolerance. The Christian interpersonal sexual ethic calls us to something much, much greater. It calls us to what pastor Tim Keller describes as receptive grace.[24] It could also be understood as connecting grace.[25] How does this psychology of Christ differ from the psychology of the cosmos? It's not like the old intolerance that says, "I have the truth and you don't, and we can't relate until you have my truth." Sadly, such has been a dominant message of the church to the unbelieving community. But it's also not the new detached tolerance. What does detached tolerance say? It says, "No one has the truth, so therefore we can be together without the problem of excluding truth."[26] Can you see how, if you don't believe that, and if you believe you have truth, you get excluded, because you believe you have truth? This becomes exclusive inclusiveness.[27]

The psychology of Christ guides and motivates us with connecting grace. There is an interesting play on words here. The Christian interpersonal sexual

21. Timothy Keller, "Receptive Grace" (sermon presented at Redeemer Presbyterian Church, New York, February 10, 2002).
22. Keller, "Receptive Grace."
23. Barnes, "Sexuality, Diversity."
24. Keller, "Receptive Grace."
25. Barnes, "Sexuality, Diversity."
26. Keller, "Receptive Grace."
27. Barnes, "Sexuality, Diversity."

ethic connects grace and truth. I have truth that has grace, and I have grace that has truth. I don't have grace without truth. I don't have truth without grace. I'm connecting grace and truth. When I'm connecting grace and truth, what happens? That becomes true connection, interpersonally, with another person. Jesus Christ was the full living embodiment and demonstration of a complete interpersonal social and sexual ethic, because he was full of grace *and* truth.

This psychology of Christ actually informs, guides, and motivates followers of Christ to live out an interpersonal sexual ethic that is distinct from the ethics of intolerance and tolerance characteristic of the psychology of the cosmos. Keller explains that "with receptive grace, you make an honest evaluation of a person's beliefs, values, or practices, and then you connect with that person in an honest, loving relationship without condescension."[28] That is the way of Jesus, full of grace *and* truth. Of course, he was the perfect model. He had the perfect balance. He never had grace without truth. He never had truth without grace. So that's a big challenge for us imperfect people. But that definitely is our model.

With compelling love, we go way beyond intolerance or tolerance when we are willing to actually change our life for that relationship. This is about an honest, authentic relationship. When we are committed to connecting grace and truth, we truthfully look at the ways we are different. We are being honest about those things, but we are not doing it in a condescending way; we are doing it in a connecting way. We are even making a connection when it comes at a personal inconvenience or cost to us. That is what Jesus did, and that is what he calls us to do.[29]

The psychology of Christ compels us, then, from a biblical perspective, to be a gospel person. The gospel person, as Keller explains, is a person who says, "I'm special because when I was deeply differing from him, Jesus Christ came and entered into my life in my reality, my weakness, my flesh. He didn't wait for me to believe or do right. I didn't have to first think like him or act like him before he received me. He radically adjusted his life for me to make space in it for me. I should do the same for others."[30]

Thus the gospel person has no basis for a moralistic condescension. Martin Luther said that we are *simul justis et peccator*—at once saint and sinner. Or as Keller says about the gospel, "I am more desperately wicked than I ever dared to imagine. And yet in Christ, I'm more deeply loved and accepted than I could ever dream."[31] That is the message of the gospel.

So, as a result of the connecting grace and truth of Christ, the gospel person has a new gospel freedom. Theirs is a whole-person freedom, not simply

---

28. Keller, "Receptive Grace."
29. Keller, "Receptive Grace."
30. Keller, "Receptive Grace."
31. Timothy Keller, "In Christ Jesus: How the Spirit Transforms Us" (sermon series presented at Redeemer Presbyterian Church, New York, November 19, 2006–January 7, 2007).

a spiritual freedom. The gospel is for the whole person, ψυχή. The person in Christ can truthfully say this: "I have a spiritual freedom in the sense that my destination, eternally, is changed. I have a spiritual freedom in the sense that sin no longer need have dominion over me, even while I'm on earth. But I have a psychological freedom as well, because I don't have to hide behind my fig leaves anymore. Because of the gospel, I can be honest with myself about my true state. I don't have to pretend to be somebody I'm not, to myself or to others."

We have not begun to scratch the surface of how the gospel gives us psychological freedom. This new and different identity in Christ frees us from all of the compulsive identities that we are driven to take on in order to get a sense of well-being about ourselves. The gospel gets to the heart of it all and frees us from our lack of a sense of well-being about personal significance and from our insecurity.

The psychology of Christ gives us a new interpersonal social and sexual ethic that changes how we relate and connect. A gospel person is freed from maladaptive coping strategies that leave us with no connections or with inauthentic or superficial connections. With the psychology of Christ, we should be on a campaign for new name tags in church. "Hello. My name is Gary. And it's worse than you think." Let's just get that up front. That's exactly the truth of the situation. I don't have to defend; I don't have to pretend. And if you falsely accuse me about something, I don't have to be defensive about that, because there's going to be something worse than that, that you don't even know about, so why waste time defending the lesser problem? That is psychological freedom sourced in the gospel.

The psychology of Christ also gives us the sociological freedom we need for an interpersonal ethic. If I'm really gripped by grace, I understand that there's nobody that is any more in need of God's grace than I am. This is really driven home to me each Sunday in our Anglican church. We have a form of worship that visually reinforces this truth. During Holy Communion, we all come forward to the altar. We all bend the knee and kneel with open hand and bowed head, and receive the bread and the wine. It's such a beautiful, visual picture, as we see many different types, colors, sizes, shapes, backgrounds, ages doing the very same thing. As gospel people, we are all in essence saying, "I've got nothing. I've got nothing. There is no one any more in need of God's grace than me." We're all saying that together as a form of gratitude and worship to God. That is sociological freedom. That is what the gospel will do for us. It takes away a higher-ground position that gets falsely supported by any difference that we stand on.

The psychology of Christ compels us with this ultimate example of connecting grace and truth in the cross of Christ. As Keller says, "On the cross, Christ was not tolerant. On the cross, we received our most critical evaluation. Christ had to die for us. That was the truth of it. But, we were so loved that he wanted to die for us. He chose to adjust his life for us, to connect us in grace."[32]

---

32. Keller, "Receptive Grace."

So the more that we are gripped by this connecting grace and truth, the more we'll show the world the way of compelling love. Compelling love gives us this ultimate example of connecting grace and truth in the cross of Christ. We could say the compelling love of Christ compels us with compelling love.[33]

CONCLUSION

God has revealed to us his story of sacred sexuality. In chapter 1 of the redemption story, God gives us a capacity for sacred sexuality so that we may more fully know him, reflect his nature, and bring glory to him. In chapter 2, as his creatures we turn from him and in our brokenness cannot meet his purposes for sacred sexuality, as we are prone to slide and either demonize or deify sexuality. In chapter 3, God intervenes with the gospel and redemptive purposes to restore an already-but-not-yet experience of sacred sexuality, also partially restoring his purposes with sacred sexuality. Finally, in chapter 4, sacred sexuality will no longer serve God's purpose, as that purpose will ultimately be met in our full gaze and experience of his glory.

Currently our personal sexual well-being and interpersonal sexual well-being greatly struggle to fulfill the divine design of sacred sexuality. Sexual experiences, interactions, and dialogue in our culture today have become difficult, distorted, divisive, and damaging. The interactions and dialogue can no longer be avoided, but they must be different. They must *not* be characterized by either intolerance or tolerance. It is so sad that many, in the name of Christ, have seriously damaged sexual minorities with intolerant, moralistic rejections. They've tried to move forward with the truth but without grace. As followers of Christ, we must go way beyond intolerance, but also way beyond tolerance. May we be characterized by the connecting grace and truth of Christ, as we adjust our lives for others at our own cost to make room for one another. So whether it is regarding singleness, or marriage, or sexual identity, or gender identity, or any other context for divisive sexual issues, as followers of Christ, as gospel people, may we be informed, guided, motivated, and characterized by the psychology of Christ and the compelling love of Christ.

"Accept one another, then, just as Christ accepted you, in order to bring praise to God" (Rom. 15:7 NIV).

---

33. Neale, Kurt and Barnes, Gary, producers. *Compelling Love and Sexual Identity*, documentary film, 2014, www.compellinglovefilm.com.

FOR DISCUSSION

1. How is your personal sexual ethic informed and assisted by the Slippery Slope of Sacred Sexuality in figure 6? What would you change to elevate "sacred sexuality" as an individual being redeemed?

2. Does your interpersonal sexual ethic tend toward a response of intolerance or tolerance? How would you develop a response to others with sexual differences and brokenness that would go beyond responses of intolerance or tolerance?

3. What do you consider the most challenging obstacle to actually experiencing and demonstrating oneness that is not based on sameness?

FOR FURTHER READING AND VIEWING

Neale, Kurt and Gary Barnes producers. *Compelling Love and Sexual Identity.* Documentary film, 2014. www.compellinglovefilm.com.

Miller, Bruce B. *Sexuality: Approaching Controversial Issues with Grace, Truth, and Hope.* McKinney, TX: Confia, 2015.

West, Christopher. *Theology of the Body for Beginners: A Basic Introduction to Pope John Paul II's Sexual Revolution.* Rev. ed. West Chester, PA: Ascension, 2009.

BIBLIOGRAPHY

Alföldy, Géza. *The Social History of Rome*. Translated by David Braund and Frank Pollock. Totowa, NJ: Barnes and Noble, 1985.

Allender, Dan B. *Healing the Wounded Heart: The Heartache of Sexual Abuse and the Hope of Transformation*. Grand Rapids: Baker Books, 2016.

Allender, Dan B., and Tremper Longman III. *God Loves Sex: An Honest Conversation about Sexual Desires and Holiness*. Grand Rapids: Baker Books, 2014.

Amato, Paul. "What Children Learn from Divorce." Population Reference Bureau, January 2001. https://www.prb.org/whatchildrenlearnfromdivorce/.

Amato, Paul, and Alan Booth. *A Generation at Risk: Growing Up in an Era of Family Upheaval*. Cambridge, MA: Harvard University Press, 1997.

American Academy of Medical Ethics. Position Statement on Abortion. https://www.ama-assn.org/delivering-care/ethics/abortion.

American Academy of Pediatrics. "Stages of Adolescence." 2017. https://www.healthychildren.org/English/ages-stages/teen/Pages/Stages-of-Adolescence.aspx.

American College of Obstetricians and Gynecologists (ACOG) Committee on Ethics. "Multifetal Pregnancy Reduction." ACOG committee opinion, 719, 2017.

American College of Obstetricians and Gynecologists (ACOG) Executive Board. "Some Ethical Considerations in Abortion." ACOG statement of policy, December 12, 1975.

American Medical Association. *Code of Ethics, Adopted 1847*. Philadelphia: T. K. and P. G. Collins, 1848.

Anapol, Deborah. "Why Do People Choose Polyamory?" *Psychology Today*, August 2010. https://www.psychologytoday.com/us/blog/love-without-limits/201008/why-do-people-choose-polyamory.

Anderson, Matthew Lee. *Earthen Vessels: Why Our Bodies Matter to Our Faith*. Bloomington, MN: Bethany House, 2011.

Anderson, Scott. "Prostitution and Sexual Autonomy: Making Sense of the Prohibition of Prostitution." *Ethics* 112, no. 4 (July 2002): 748–80.

Aristotle. *The History of Animals*. Translated by D'Arcy Wentworth Thompson. Adelaide, Australia: University of Adelaide, 2015.

———. *On the Generation of Animals*. Translated by Arthur Platt. Adelaide, Australia: University of Adelaide, 2015.

Augustine. *On Marriage and Concupiscence.* In *Nicene and Post-Nicene Fathers of the Christian Church*, series 1, vol. 5, *Anti-Pelagian Writings*, edited by Philip Schaff. Edinburgh: T&T Clark, 1902.

Axinn, William G., and Jennifer S. Barber. "Living Arrangements and Family Formation Attitudes in Early Adulthood." *Journal of Marriage and Family* 59, no. 3 (August 1997): 595–611.

Babylonian Talmud: Tractate Yebamoth. Translated by Israel W. Slotki. Edited by Isidore Epstein. http://halakhah.com/yebamoth.

Balch, David L., and Carolyn Osiek, eds. *Early Christian Families in Context: An Interdisciplinary Dialogue.* Religion, Marriage, and Family. Grand Rapids: Eerdmans, 2003.

Barclay, Robert Anderson. *The Law Givers: Leviticus and Deuteronomy.* New York: Abingdon, 1964.

Barna Group. "The Behaviors Most Americans Count as Sexual Harassment." November 28, 2017. https://www.barna.com/research/behaviors-americans-count-as-harassment/.

Barna Report and Josh McDowell Ministry. *The Porn Phenomenon: The Impact of Pornography in the Digital Age.* Ventura, CA: Barna Group and Josh McDowell Ministry (Cru), 2016.

Barnes, C. Gary. "Christian Theology, Psychology, and Homosexuality: Foundations for Loving Your Neighbor." Paper presented at World Evangelization Conference, Annual Conference at Dallas Theological Seminary, Dallas, Texas, March 12, 2013.

———. "Marriage Strong: Academic Applications at Dallas Theological Seminary." Paper presented at The Boone Center for the Family, Pepperdine University, Malibu, California, October 17, 2015.

———. "Sacred Sexuality: Foundations and Motivations for a Sexual Ethic." Lecture presented at Dallas Theological Seminary, Dallas, Texas, May, 2018.

———. "Sexual Identity and the Church." Paper presented at CAPS-Christian Association for Psychological Studies, National Annual Conference, Atlanta, Georgia, April 5, 2014.

———. "Sexuality, Diversity, Religiosity and Ethics." Paper presented at Christian Association for Psychological Studies, National Annual Conference, Chicago, Illinois, March 30, 2017.

———. "Transforming Marital Sexuality: Applications for Husbands and Wives as People in Christ." Lecture presented at Dallas Theological Seminary, Dallas, Texas, May, 2017.

Barnes, C. Gary, and Scott M. Stanley. "Christian PREP: The Prevention and Relationship Enhancement Program." In *Evidence-Based Practices for Christian Counseling and Psychotherapy*, edited by Everett L. Worthington Jr., Eric L. Johnson, Joshua N. Hook, and Jamie D. Aten, 166–88. Christian Association for Psychological Studies Books. Downers Grove, IL: IVP Academic, 2013.

Barnett, Michael D., Taylor M. Hale, and Kylie B. Sligar. "Masculinity, Femininity, Sexual Dysfunctional Beliefs, and Rape Myth Acceptance among Heterosexual College Men and Women." *Sexuality and Culture* 21, no. 3 (2017): 741–53.

Barrett, C. K. *The First Epistle to the Corinthians*. Black's New Testament Commentary. London: Black, 1968.

Bartchy, S. Scott, *ΜΑΛΛΟΝ ΧΡΗΣΑΙ: First-Century Slavery and 1 Corinthians 7:21*. Society of Biblical Literature Dissertation Series 11. Missoula, MT: Society of Biblical Literature, 1973.

Barth, Karl. *Church Dogmatics*. Translated by Geoffrey W. Bromiley. Edited by Geoffrey W. Bromiley and Thomas F. Torrance. 4 vols. Edinburgh: T&T Clark, 1956–1975.

Baugh, S. M. *Ephesians*. Evangelical Exegetical Commentary. Bellingham, WA: Lexham, 2016.

Baum, Matthew A., Dara Kay Cohen, Susanne Schwarz, and Yuri M. Zhukov. "The Way Kavanaugh's Supporters Are Talking about Sexual Assault Allegations Can Be Dangerous, Our New Study Finds." *Washington Post*. September 27, 2018. https://www.washingtonpost.com/news/monkey-cage/wp/2018/09/27/the-way-kavanaughs-supporters-are-talking-about-sexual-assault-allegations-can-be-dangerous-our-new-study-finds/.

Bayly, Joseph, "Saved, Single, and Second-Class." *Eternity*, March 1983, 23–26.

Beare, Francis W. *The Gospel according to Matthew*. San Francisco: Harper & Row, 1981.

Benedict XVI. *Deus Caritas Est*. Encyclical Letter. Vatican: Libreria Editrice Vaticana, 2006.

Benes, Ross. "Porn Could Have a Bigger Economic Influence on the US Than Netflix." Yahoo Finance, June 20, 2018. https://finance.yahoo.com/news/porn-could-bigger-economic-influence-121524565.html.

Benner, David. *Care of Souls: Revisioning Christian Nurture and Counsel*. Grand Rapids: Baker, 1998.

Best, Megan. *Fearfully and Wonderfully Made: Ethics and the Beginning of Human Life*. Kingsford, Australia: Matthias Media, 2012.

Bethesda Workshops. "Definition of Sexual Addiction." https://www.bethesda-workshops.org/sexual-addiction.

Black, Michele C., Kathleen C. Basile, Matthew J. Breiding, Sharon G. Smith, Mikel L. Walters, Melissa T. Merrick, Jieru Chen, and Mark R. Stevens. "The National Intimate Partner and Sexual Violence Survey (NISVS): 2010 Summary Report." National Center for Injury Prevention and Control, Centers for Disease Control and Prevention, 2011. https://www.cdc.gov/violenceprevention/pdf/nisvs_report2010-a.pdf.

Block, Daniel, "Old Testament Perspective on Marriage." Lecture given to Colloquium at The Southern Baptist Theological Seminary, October 2001.

Blomberg, Craig L. *1 Corinthians*. NIV Application Commentary. Grand Rapids: Zondervan, 1995.

———. *Matthew*. New American Commentary. Nashville: Broadman, 1992.

Bohner, Gerd, Frank Seiber, and Jürgen Schmelcher. "Social Norms and the Likelihood of Raping: Perceived Rape Myth Acceptance of Others Affects Men's Rape Proclivity." *Personality and Social Psychology Bulletin* 32, no. 3 (March 2006): 286–97.

Bonnard, Pierre. *L'Évangile selon Saint Matthieu*. 3rd ed. Commentaire du Nouveau Testament. Geneva: Labor et Fides, 1992.

Booth, Alan, and Judy Dunn, eds. *Stepfamilies: Who Benefits? Who Does Not?* Hillsdale, NJ: Lawrence Erlbaum, 1994.

Born Alive Infant Protection Act of 2001. Pub. L. No. 107–207. 116 Stat. 926 (2002). https://www.congress.gov/bill/107th-congress/house-bill/2175/text.

Bornkamm, Günther. "End-Expectation and Church in Matthew." In *Tradition and Interpretation in Matthew*, edited by Günther Bornkamm, Gerhard Barth, and Heinz Joachim Held, 15–51. New Testament Library. Philadelphia: Westminster, 1963.

———. *Paul*. Translated by D. M. G. Stalker. New York: Harper & Row, 1971.

Boswell, John. *Christianity, Social Tolerance, and Homosexuality: Gay People in Western Europe from the Beginning of the Christian Era to the Fourteenth Century*. Chicago: University of Chicago Press, 1980.

———. *The Marriage of Likeness: Same-Sex Unions in Pre-modern Europe*. London: Fontana, 1996.

Boyle, Robert J. "Paradigm Cases in Decision Making for Neonates." *NeoReviews* 5 (2004): 477–83.

Brenton, Charles Lee, trans. *The Septuagint*. 1884. http://qbible.com/brenton-septuagint/.

Brinig, Margaret, and Douglas. Allen. "These Boots Are Made for Walking: Why Most Divorce Filers Are Women." *American Law and Economics Review* 2, no. 1 (2000): 126–69.

Brisson, Luc. *Sexual Ambivalence: Androgyny and Hermaphroditism in Graeco-Roman Antiquity*. Translated by Janet Lloyd. Berkeley: University of California Press, 2002.

Brooten, Bernadette J. *Love between Women: Early Christian Responses to Female Homoeroticism*. Chicago Series on Sexuality, History, and Society. Chicago: University of Chicago Press, 1996.

Brown, Gabrielle. *The New Celibacy: A Journey to Love, Intimacy, and Good Health in a New Age*. Rev. ed. New York: McGraw-Hill, 1989.

Brown, Peter. *The Body and Society: Men, Women, and Sexual Renunciation in Early Christianity*. Rev. ed. New York: Columbia University Press, 2008.

Brown, Susan L., Jennifer Roebuck Bulanda, and Gary R. Lee. "Transitions Into and Out of Cohabitation in Later Life." *Journal of Marriage and Family* 74, no. 4 (2012): 774–93.

Brown, Susan L., Wendy D. Manning, and Krista K. Payne. "Relationship Quality among Cohabiting versus Married Couples." *Journal of Family Issues* 38, no. 12 (2017): 1730–53.

Buchanan, Jeff. "The New Sexual Identity Crisis." The Gospel Coalition, July 10, 2012. https://www.thegospelcoalition.org/article/the-new-sexual-identity-crisis-2.

Burke, Tarana. "#MeToo Was Started for Black and Brown Women and Girls. They're Still Being Ignored." *Washington Post*, November 9, 2017. https://www.washingtonpost.com/news/post-nation/wp/2017/11/09/the-waitress-who-works-in-the-diner-needs-to-know-that-the-issue-of-sexual-harassment-is-about-her-too/.

Caird, G. B. *New Testament Theology*. Edited by L. D. Hurst. Oxford: Clarendon, 1994.

Calabia, Alison. "Teens and Sex." *Psychology Today*, July 1, 2001. www.psychologytoday.com/us/articles/200107/teens-and-sex.

Calvin, John. *The First Epistle of Paul to the Corinthians*. Translated by John W. Fraser. Calvin's Commentaries. Edinburgh: Oliver and Boyd, 1960.

Cantalammessa, Raniero. *Virginity: A Positive Approach to Celibacy for the Sake of the Kingdom of Heaven*. Translated by Charles Serignat. New York: Alba, 1995. Kindle.

Cantarella, Eva. *Bisexuality in the Ancient World*. Translated by Cormac Ó. Cuilleanáin. 2nd ed. New Haven, CT: Yale University Press, 2002.

Carlson, Ryan G., Sejal M. Barden, Andrew P. Daire, and Jennifer Greene. "Influence of Relationship Education on Relationship Satisfaction for Low-Income Couples." *Journal of Counseling and Development* 92, no. 4 (2014): 418–27.

Carlson, Ryan G., Andrew P. Daire, and Haiyan Bai. "Examining Relationship Satisfaction and Individual Distress for Low-to-Moderate Income Couples in Relationship Education." *Family Journal* 22, no. 3 (2014): 282–91.

Carlson, Ryan G., Damon L. Rappleyea, Andrew P. Daire, Steven M. Harris, and Xiaofeng Liu. "The Effectiveness of Couple and Individual Relationship Education: Distress as a Moderator." *Family Process* 56, no. 1 (2017): 91–104.

Carnes, Patrick. *Facing the Shadow: Starting Sexual and Relationship Recovery*. 2nd ed. Carefree, AZ: Gentle Path Press, 2008.

Carr, David M. *The Erotic World: Sexuality, Spirituality, and the Bible*. Oxford: Oxford University Press, 2003.

Carson, D. A. "Matthew." In *The Expositor's Bible Commentary*, vol. 9, *Matthew and Mark*, edited by Tremper Longman III and David E. Garland, 23–670. Rev. ed. Grand Rapids: Zondervan, 2010.

Cartlidge, David R. "1 Corinthians 7 as a Foundation for a Christian Sex Ethic." *Journal of Religion* 55, no. 2 (1975): 220–34.

Cassuto, Umberto. *A Commentary on the Book of Genesis*. Translated by Israel Abrahams. 2 vols. Jerusalem: Magnes, 1961.

Catechism of the Catholic Church. 2nd ed. New York: Doubleday, 1995.

Catholic Answers. "Birth Control." August 10, 2004. http://www.catholic.com/tract/birth-control.

Catsanos, Ruby, Wendy Rogers, and Mianna Lotzz. "The Ethics of Uterus Transplantation." *Bioethics* 27, no. 2 (2013): 65–73.

Centers for Disease Control and Prevention. "Teenagers (15–17 Years of Age)." 2018 https://www.cdc.gov/ncbddd/childdevelopment/positiveparenting/adolescence2.html.

———. "Youth Risk Behavior Surveillance—United States 2015, 2016." Morbidity and Mortality Weekly Report, June 10, 2016. https://www.cdc.gov/healthyyouth/data/yrbs/pdf/2015/ss6506_updated.pdf.

Chapman, David W. "Marriage and Family in Second Temple Judaism." In *Marriage and Family in the Biblical World*, edited by Ken M. Campbell, 183–239. Downers Grove, IL: InterVarsity Press, 2003.

Charlesworth, James H., ed. *The Old Testament Pseudepigrapha*. Vol. 1, *Apocalyptic Literature and Testaments*. New York: Doubleday, 1983.

Cherlin, Andrew J. *Marriage, Divorce, Remarriage*. Cambridge, MA: Harvard University Press, 1992.

Cherlin, Andrew J., P. Lindsay Chase-Landsdale, Christine McRae. "Effects of Parental Divorce on Mental Health throughout the Life Course." *American Sociological Review* 63, no. 2 (1998): 239–49.

Chervenak, Frank A., and Laurence B. McCullough. "An Ethically Justified Practical Approach to Offering, Recommending, Performing, and Referring for Induced Abortion and Feticide." *American Journal of Obstetrics and Gynecology* 201 (2009): 560.e1–6.

Chicago Tribune. "AIDS Delegates Slam U.S. Policy." July 13, 2004. http://articles.chicagotribune.com/2004-07-13/news/0407140098_1_condoms-abstinence-until-marriage-international-aids-conference.

Christensen, Michael J., and Jeffery Wittung, eds. *Partakers of the Divine Nature: The History and Development of Deification in the Christian Traditions*. Grand Rapids: Baker Academic, 2007.

Christian Medical and Dental Associations. "Assisted Reproductive Technology Ethics." cmda.org.

———. "Beginning of Human Life Ethics Statement." https://www.cmda.org/library/doclib/the-beginning-of-human-life-concfert.pdf.

———. "Three-Parent Human Embryos Ethics." cmda.org.

———. "Use of Genetic Information and Technology Ethics Statement." cmda.org.

Chu, Simone C. "First Nassar Accuser Denhollander Talks Justice, Forgiveness at Harvard." *Harvard Crimson*, April 6, 2018. https://www.thecrimson.com/article/2018/4/6/denhollander-talk/.

Ciampa, Roy E., and Brian S. Rosner. *The First Letter to the Corinthians*. Pillar New Testament Commentary. Grand Rapids: Eerdmans, 2010.

Clapp, Rodney. *Families at the Crossroads: Beyond Traditional and Modern Options*. Downers Grove, IL: InterVarsity Press, 1993.

——. *Tortured Wonders: Christian Spirituality for People, Not Angels*. Grand Rapids: Brazos, 2004.

Clarke, John R. *Looking at Lovemaking: Constructions of Sexuality in Roman Art: 100 B.C.–A.D. 250*. Berkeley: University of California Press, 1998.

Cohen, I. Glenn, "Artificial Wombs and Abortion Rights." *Hastings Center Report* 47, no. 4 (2017): inside back cover. doi:10.1002/hast.730.

Cohen, Jessica A., and Wendy D. Manning. "The Relationship Context of Premarital Serial Cohabitation." *Social Science Research* 39, no. 5 (2010): 766–76.

Cohick, Lynn H. *Women in the World of the Earliest Christians: Illuminating Ancient Ways of Life*. Grand Rapids: Baker Academic, 2009.

Cole, Graham A. *He Who Gives Life: The Doctrine of the Holy Spirit*. Foundations of Evangelical Theology. Wheaton, IL: Crossway, 2007.

Collins, C. John. *Did Adam and Eve Really Exist? Who They Were and Why You Should Care*. Wheaton, IL: Crossway, 2011.

——. *Genesis 1–4: A Linguistic, Literary, and Theological Commentary*. Phillipsburg, NJ: P&R, 2006.

Collins, John J. "Sibylline Oracles." In *The Old Testament Pseudepigrapha*, vol. 1, *Apocalyptic Literature and Testaments*, edited by James H. Charlesworth, 317–472. New York: Doubleday, 1983.

Collins, Raymond F. *First Corinthians*. Sacra Pagina 7. Collegeville, MN: Liturgical Press, 1999.

Colman, Barry, ed. *Sex and the Single Christian: Candid Conversations*. Ventura, CA: Regal, 1985.

Colón, Christine A., and Bonnie E. Field. *Singled Out: Why Celibacy Must Be Reinvented in Today's Church*. Grand Rapids: Brazos, 2009.

Condren, Janson C. "Toward a Purge of the Battle of the Sexes and 'Return' for the Original Meaning of Genesis 3:16B." *Journal of the Evangelical Theological Society* 60, no. 2 (2017): 227–45.

Constantin, Daniel. "Esséniens et Eunuques (Matthieu 19:10–12)," *Revue de Qumran* 6 (1968): 353–90.

Conzelmann, Hans. *1 Corinthians*. Translated by James W. Leitch. Hermeneia. Philadelphia: Fortress, 1975.

Corbier, Mireille. "Divorce and Adoption as Roman Familial Strategies (Le divorce et l'adoption 'en plus')." In *Marriage, Divorce, and Children in Ancient Rome*, edited by Beryl Rawson, 47–78. Oxford: Oxford University Press, 1991.

Cortez, Marc. *Christological Anthropology: Ancient and Contemporary Approaches to Theological Anthropology*. Grand Rapids: Zondervan, 2016.

Cowan, Carolyn, and Philip Cowan. *When Partners Become Parents: The Big Life Change for Couples*. New York: Basic Books, 1992.

Cutrer, William, Sandra Glahn, and Michael Sytsma. *Sexual Intimacy in Marriage*. 4th ed. Grand Rapids: Kregel, 2020.

Cyranoski, David. "CRISPR Gene-Editing Tested in a Person for the First Time." *Nature* 539 (November 24, 2016): 479.

D'Ambra, Eve. "The Calculus of Venus: Nude Portraits of Roman Matrons." In *Sexuality in Ancient Art: Near East, Egypt, Greece, and Italy*, edited by Natalie Boymel Kampen, 219–32. Cambridge: Cambridge University Press, 1996.

D'Angelo, Mary R. "Sexuality in Jewish Writings from 200 BCE to 200 CE." In *Companion to Greek and Roman Sexualities*, edited by Thomas K. Hubbard, 534–48. Chichester, UK: Wiley-Blackwell, 2014.

Danker, Frederick W., Walter Bauer, William F. Arndt, and F. Wilbur Gingrich. *Greek-English Lexicon of the New Testament and Other Early Christian Literature*. 3rd ed. Chicago: University of Chicago Press, 2000.

Dart, Tom. "Baylor Football Players Raped Women as 'Bonding Experience,' Lawsuit Alleges." *The Guardian*, May 17, 2017. https://www.theguardian.com/us-news/2017/may/17/baylor-university-lawsuit-rape-allegations.

Davidson, Richard M. *Flame of Yahweh: Sexuality in the Old Testament*. Peabody, MA: Hendrickson, 2007.

Davies, W. D. *The Setting of the Sermon on the Mount*. Cambridge: Cambridge University Press, 1964.

Davies, W. D., and Dale C. Allison. *The Gospel according to Saint Matthew*. 3 vols. International Critical Commentary. Edinburgh: T&T Clark, 1988–1997.

Dawn, Marva J. *Sexual Character: Beyond Technique to Intimacy*. Grand Rapids: Eerdmans, 1993.

Deal, Ron. *The Smart Step-Family: Seven Steps to a Healthy Family*. Bloomington, MN: Bethany House, 2002.

DeMuth, Mary. *We Too: How the Church Can Respond Redemptively to the Sexual Abuse Crisis*. Eugene, OR: Harvest House, 2019.

Denhollander, Jacob, and Rachael Denhollander. "Justice: The Foundation of a Christian Approach to Abuse." Paper presented at the 70th Annual Meeting of the Evangelical Theological Society, Denver, Colorado, November 13, 2018. https://www.fathommag.com/stories/justice-the-foundation-of-a-christian-approach-to-abuse.

Department of Justice. "National Crime Victimization Survey, 2012–2016." Bureau of Justice Statistics, 2017.

Department of Justice. "Sexual Assault of Young Children as Reported to Law Enforcement." Bureau of Justice Statistics, 2000.

Dershowitz, Idan. "Revealing Nakedness and Concealing Homosexual Intercourse: Legal and Lexical Evolution in Leviticus 18." *Hebrew Bible and Ancient Israel* 6, no. 4 (2017): 510–26.

deSilva, David A. *Honor, Patronage, Kinship and Purity: Unlocking New Testament Culture*. Downers Grove, IL: InterVarsity Press, 2000.

Dibelius, Martin. *The Message of Jesus Christ: The Tradition of the Early Christian Communities*. Translated by Frederick C. Grant. New York: Scribner's Sons, 1939.

Dick, Kirby, and Amy Ziering. *The Hunting Ground: The Inside Story of Sexual Assault on American College Campuses*. Edited by Constance Matthiessen. New York: Hot Books, 2016.

Diedrich, Justin, Eleanor Drey, and Society of Family Planning. "Induction of Fetal Demise before Abortion: Clinical Guidelines.." *Contraception* 81, no. 6 (2010): 462–73.

Dixon, Suzanne. *The Roman Family*. Ancient Society and History. Baltimore: Johns Hopkins University Press, 1992.

Dodd, C. H. *New Testament Studies*. New York: Scribner's Sons, 1968.

Doe v. Bolton. 410 U.S. 179 (1973).

Dover, K. J. *Greek Homosexuality*. Cambridge, MA: Harvard University Press, 1978. Updated with a new postscript, 1989.

Downing, F. Gerald. "*A bas les aristos*: The Relevance of Higher Literature for the Understanding of the Earliest Christian Writing." *Novum Testamentum* 30 (1988): 212–30.

Duff, Raymond S., and A. G. M. Campbell. "Moral and Ethical Dilemmas in the Special-Care Nursery." *New England Journal of Medicine* 289 (1973): 890–94.

Dunn, James D. G. *Jesus and the Spirit*. London: SCM, 1975. Reprint, Grand Rapids: Eerdmans, 1997.

Ecker, Jeffrey L., Anjali Kaimal, Brian M. Mercer, Sean C. Blackwell, Raye Ann O. deRegnier, Ruth M. Farrell, William A. Grobman, Jamie L. Resnik, and Anthony C. Sciscione. "Periviable Birth." *Obstetrics and Gynecology* 130, no. 4 (2017): e187–99.

Edelstein, Ludwig. *Ancient Medicine*. Baltimore: Johns Hopkins University Press, 1967.

———. *The Hippocratic Oath: Text, Translation and Interpretation*. Baltimore: Johns Hopkins University Press, 1943.

Education.com. "Teenage Growth and Development: 15–17 Years." 2009. https://www.education.com/reference/article/teen-development-fifteen-seventeen-years (accessed August 14, 2018; article discontinued).

Edwards, Catharine. *The Politics of Immorality in Ancient Rome*. Cambridge: Cambridge University Press, 1993.

Engberg-Pedersen, Troels, ed. *Paul beyond the Judaism/Hellenism Divide*. Louisville: Westminster John Knox, 2001.

Enslin, Morton Scott. *The Ethics of Paul*. New York: Harper & Brothers, 1930.

Ericksen, Phillip. "Baylor Hit with 7th Title IX Lawsuit, Plaintiff Alleges Gang Rape by Football Players." *Waco Tribune-Herald*, May 17, 2017. https://www.wacotrib.com/news/crime/baylor-hit-with-th-title-ix-lawsuit-plaintiff-alleges-gang/article_1b391c59-1722-5532-9c3b-058b07850249.html.

Ericsson, Lars O. "Charges against Prostitution: An Attempt at a Philosophical Assessment." *Ethics* 90, no. 3 (April 1980): 335–66.

Esler, Philip F. "Social-Scientific Models in Biblical Interpretation." In *Ancient Israel: The Old Testament in Its Social Context*, edited by Philip F. Esler, 3–14. London: SCM, 2005.

Esler, Philip F., and Anselm C. Hagedorn. "Social-Scientific Analysis of the Old Testament: A Brief History and Overview." In *Ancient Israel: The Old Testament in Its Social Context*, edited by Philip F. Esler, 15–32. London: SCM, 2005.

Evdokimov, Paul. *The Sacrament of Love: The Nuptial Mystery in Light of the Orthodox Tradition*. Crestwood, NY: St. Vladimir's Seminary Press, 1985.

Fagan, Garrett G. *Bathing in Public in the Roman World*. Ann Arbor: University of Michigan Press, 1999.

Fantin, Joseph D. "Background Studies: Grounding the Text in Reality." In *Interpreting the New Testament Text: Introduction to the Art and Science of Exegesis*, edited by Darrell L. Bock and Buist M. Fanning, 167–96. Wheaton, IL: Crossway, 2006.

Farley, Melissa. "Myths and Facts about Trafficking for Legal and Illegal Prostitution." Prostitution Research, March 2009. http://www.prostitutionresearch.com/pdfs/Myths%20&%20Facts%20Legal%20&%20Illegal%20Prostitution%203-09.pdf.

————. "Prostitution Is Sexual Violence." *Psychiatric Times*, October 1, 2004. https://www.psychiatrictimes.com/sexual-offenses/prostitution-sexual-violence.

————, ed. *Prostitution, Trafficking, and Traumatic Stress*. Binghamton, NY: Haworth, 2004.

————. *Prostitution: Prices and Statistics of the Global Sex Trade*. n.p.: Havocscope, 2015. http://www.prostitutionresearch.com/pdfs/Farleyetal2011ComparingSexBuyers.pdf.

Farley, Melissa, Emily Schuckman, Jacqueline M. Golding, Kristen Houser, Laura Jarrett, Peter Qualliotine, and Michele Decker. "Comparing Sex Buyers with Men Who Don't Buy Sex: 'You Can Have a Good Time with the Servitude' vs. 'You're Supporting a System of Degradation.'" Report at Psychologists for Social Responsibility Annual Meeting, Boston, 2011. http://www.prostitutionresearch.com/pdfs/Farleyetal2011ComparingSexBuyers.pdf.

Farris, Joshua. "What's So Simple about Personal Identity?" *Philosophy Now*, April/May 2015. https://philosophynow.org/issues/107/Whats_So_Simple_About_Personal_Identity.

Fee, Gordon D. *The First Epistle to the Corinthians*. Rev. ed. New International Commentary on the New Testament. Grand Rapids: Eerdmans, 2014.

Fetters, Ashley. "So Is Living Together before Marriage Linked to Divorce or What?" *The Atlantic*, October 24, 2018. https://www.theatlantic.com/family/archive/2018/10/premarital-cohabitation-divorce/573817/.

Fight the New Drug. "How Porn Changes the Brain." June 26, 2018. https://fightthenewdrug.org/how-porn-changes-the-brain/.

Findlay, G. G. "St. Paul's First Epistle to the Corinthians." In *The Expositor's Greek Testament*, edited by W. Robertson Nicoll, 2:727–953. London: Hodder and Stoughton, 1897. Reprint, Grand Rapids: Eerdmans, 1983.

Fitzmyer, Joseph A. *First Corinthians*. Anchor Yale Bible 32. New Haven, CT: Yale University Press, 2008.

Foh, Susan T. *Women and the Word of God*. Phillipsburg, NJ: P&R, 1979.

———. "What Is the Woman's Desire?" *Westminster Theological Journal* 37 (1975): 376–83.

Foubert, John D. "Public Health Harms of Pornography: The Brain, Erectile Dysfunction, and Sexual Violence." *Dignity: A Journal on Sexual Exploitation and Violence* 2, no. 3 (2017).

Foubert, John D., and Ana J. Bridges. "What Is the Attraction? Pornography Use Motives in Relation to Bystander Intervention." *Journal of Interpersonal Violence* 32 (2017): 3071–89.

Foucault, Michel. *The History of Sexuality*. 3 vols. Reprint, New York: Vintage, 1978–1990.

Fowers, Blaine, Kelly Montel, and David H. Olson. "Predicting Marital Success for Premarital Couple Types Based on Prepare." *Journal of Marital and Family Therapy* 22, no.1 (1996): 103–19.

France, R. T. *The Gospel of Matthew*. New International Commentary on the New Testament. Grand Rapids: Eerdmans, 2007.

Friberg-Fernros, Henrik. "Clashes of Consensus: On the Problem of Both Justifying Abortion of Fetuses with Down Syndrome and Rejecting Infanticide." *Theoretical Medicine and Bioethics* 38, no. 3 (2017): 195–212.

Fuchs, Eric. *Sexual Desire and Love: Origins and History of the Christian Ethic of Sexuality and Marriage*. New York: Seabury, 1983.

Furnish, Victor Paul. *The Moral Teaching of Paul*. 3rd ed. Nashville: Abingdon, 2009.

Gacek, Christopher M. "Conceiving Pregnancy: U.S. Medical Dictionaries and Their Definitions of Conception and Pregnancy." *National Catholic Bioethics Quarterly* 9, no. 3 (2009): 543–57.

Gagnon, John H., and William Simon. *Sexual Conduct: The Social Sources of Human Sexuality*. 2nd ed. New Brunswick, NJ: AldineTransaction, 2005.

Galot, Jean. *Theology of the Priesthood*. Translated by Roger Balducelli. San Francisco: Ignatius, 1985.

Gardner, Jane F. *Family and Familia in Roman Law and Life*. Oxford: Clarendon, 1998.

Gardner, Paul. *1 Corinthians*. Exegetical Commentary on the New Testament. Grand Rapids: Zondervan, 2018.

Garland, David E. *1 Corinthians*. Baker Exegetical Commentary on the New Testament. Grand Rapids: Baker Academic, 2003.

Garnsey, Peter, and Richard P. Saller. *The Roman Empire: Economy, Society and Culture*. Berkeley: University of California Press, 1987.

Gay, Roxane. *Not That Bad: Dispatches from Rape Culture.* New York: Harper-Collins, 2018.

Geiger, Abigail, and Gretchen Livingston. "8 Facts about Love and Marriage in America." Pew Research Center, February 13, 2019. https://www.pewresearch.org/fact-tank/2019/02/13/8-facts-about-love-and-marriage/.

Gillham, Nicholas Wright. *A Life of Sir Francis Galton: From African Exploration to the Birth of Eugenics.* Oxford: Oxford University Press, 2001.

Giscombe, Katherine. "Sexual Harassment and Women of Color." *Catalyst* (blog), February 13, 2018. https://www.catalyst.org/blog/catalyzing/sexual-harassment-and-women-color.

Giubilini, Alberto, and Francesca Minerva. "After-Birth Abortion: Why Should the Baby Live?" *Journal of Medical Ethics* 39 (2013): 261–63.

Glahn, Sandra L. "The First-Century Ephesian Artemis: Ramifications of Her Identity." *Bibliotheca Sacra* 172, no. 688 (October–December 2015): 450–69.

———. "The Identity of Artemis in First-Century Ephesus." *Bibliotheca Sacra* 172, no. 687 (July–September 2015): 316–34.

———. "Manhood vs. Grandma?" bible.org, *Engage* (blog), April 3, 2012. https://blogs.bible.org/engage/sandra_glahn/manhood_vs_grandma.

———. "Part 1: Rape Culture 101." *Aspire2* (blog), April 2, 2018. http://aspire2.com/2013/12/part-1-of-18-rape-culture-101/.

———, ed. *Vindicating the Vixens: Revisiting Sexualized, Vilified, and Marginalized Women of the Bible.* Grand Rapids: Kregel Academic, 2017.

Glahn, Sandra L., and William R. Cutrer. *Control? A Couple's Guide to Contraception.* Plano, TX: Authenticity Book House, 2015.

———. *When Empty Arms Become a Heavy Burden: Encouragement for Couples Facing Infertility.* 2nd ed. Grand Rapids: Kregel, 2011.

Glancy, Jennifer A. *Slavery in Early Christianity.* Oxford: Oxford University Press, 2002. Reprint, Minneapolis: Fortress, 2006.

Glare, P. G. W., ed. *Oxford Latin Dictionary.* Oxford: Clarendon, 1982.

Glazebrook, Allison, and Kelly Olson. "Greek and Roman Marriage." In *A Companion to Greek and Roman Sexualities,* edited by Thomas K. Hubbard, 69–82. Chichester, UK: Wiley-Blackwell, 2014.

Gloyn, Liz. *The Ethics of the Family in Seneca.* Cambridge: Cambridge University Press, 2017.

Gnilka, Joachim. *Das Matthäusevangelium, II Teil.* Herders Theologischer Kommentar zum Neuen Testament. Freiburg: Herder, 1988.

Goguel, Maurice. *Jesus and the Origins of Christianity.* Translated by Olive Wyon. 2 vols. New York: Macmillan, 1933.

Goldstein, Joshua R. "The Leveling of Divorce in the United States." *Demography* 36, no. 3 (1999): 409–14.

Goldsworthy, Adrian. *Caesar: The Life of a Colossus.* 2006. Reprint, London: Phoenix, 2007.

Gottman, John. *The Marriage Clinic: A Scientifically Based Marital Therapy.* New York: Norton, 1999.

———. "Research FAQ." The Gottman Institute: A Research Based Approach to Relationships. https://www.gottman.com/about/research/faq/.

———. *Why Marriages Succeed or Fail: And How You Can Make Yours Last.* New York: Simon & Schuster, 1994.

Gottman, John, and Julie Gottman. *And Baby Makes Three.* New York: Three Rivers Press, 2007.

———. *Ten Lessons to Transform Your Marriage.* New York: Three Rivers Press, 2006.

Gottman, John, and Nan Silver. *The Seven Principles for Making Marriage Work.* New York: Three Rivers Press, 1999.

Grant, Jonathan. *Divine Sex: A Compelling Vision for Christian Relationships in a Hypersexualized Age.* Grand Rapids: Brazos, 2015.

Grant, Michael, and Antonia Mulas. *Eros in Pompeii: The Secret Rooms of the National Museum of Naples.* Milan: Arnoldo Mondadori, 1975. Reprint, n.p.: Bonanza Books, 1982.

Greeven, Heinrich. "Ehe nach dem Neuen Testament." *New Testament Studies* 15, no. 4 (1968–1969): 379.

Gregory of Nyssa. *On Virginity.* In *The Nicene and Post-Nicene Fathers,* series 2, vol. 5., edited by Philip Schaff. Reprint, Peabody, MA: Hendrickson, 1994.

Grenfell, Bernard P., Arthur S. Hunt, and J. Gilbart Smyly, eds. *The Tebtunis Papyri.* Part 1. London: Henry Frowde, 1902.

Grenz, Stanley J. *Sexual Ethics: An Evangelical Perspective.* 2nd ed. Louisville: Westminster John Knox, 1997.

———. *The Social God and the Relational Self: A Trinitarian Theology of the Imago Dei.* Louisville: Westminster John Knox, 2001.

Grenz, Stanley J., David Guretzki, and Cherith Fee Nordling. *Pocket Dictionary of Theological Terms.* Downers Grove, IL: InterVarsity Press, 1999.

Grobien, Gifford A. "From Taboo to Delight: The Body, Sex, and Love in View of Creation and Eschatology." In *Ethics of Sex: From Taboo to Delight,* edited by Gifford A. Grobien, 201–20. Saint Louis: Concordia, 2017.

Grubbs, Judith Evans. "Parent-Child Conflict in the Roman Family: The Evidence of the Code of Justinian." In *The Roman Family in the Empire: Rome, Italy, and Beyond,* edited by Michele George, 93–128. Oxford: Oxford University Press, 2005.

Grundmann, Walter. *Das Evangelium nach Matthäus.* 5th ed. Herders Theologischer Kommentar zum Neuen Testament. Berlin: Evangelische Verlagsanstalt, 1981.

Guillamon, Antonio, Carme Junque, and Esther Gomez-Gil. "A Review of the Status of Brain Structure Research in Transsexualism." *Archives of Sexual Behavior* 45, no. 7 (October 2016): 1615–48.

Guinness, Os. *The Global Public Square.* Downers Grove, IL: InterVarsity Press, 2013.

Gundry, Robert H. *Matthew: A Commentary on His Handbook for a Mixed Church under Persecution.* 2nd ed. Grand Rapids: Eerdmans, 1994.

Gunter, J. D. "Men as Providers." Council on Biblical Manhood and Womanhood, November 11, 2013. https://www.thespiritlife.net/about/69-holistic/holistic-publications/4350-men-as-providers-by-jd-gunter.

Guthrie, Donald. *New Testament Theology.* Downers Grove, IL: InterVarsity Press, 1981.

Hagner, Donald A. *Matthew.* 2 vols. Word Biblical Commentary 33. Dallas: Word, 1993–1995.

Hahlweg, Kurt, Howard J. Markman, Franz Thurmaier, Jochen Engl, and Volker Eckert. "Prevention of Marital Distress: Results of a German Prospective Longitudinal Study." *Journal of Family Psychology* 12 (1998): 543–56.

Haldane, J. B. S. *Daedalus; or, Science and the Future.* New York: Dutton, 1924.

Halford, W. Kim, Matthew R. Sanders, and Brett C. Behrens. "Can Skills Training Prevent Relationship Problems in At-Risk Couples? Four-Year Effects of a Behavioral Relationship Education Program." *Journal of Family Psychology* 15, no. 4 (2001): 750–68.

Hallett, Christopher H. *The Roman Nude: Heroic Portrait Statuary 200 BC–AD 300.* Oxford Studies in Ancient Culture and Representation. Oxford: Oxford University Press, 2005.

Hallett, Judith P., and Marilyn B. Skinner, eds. *Roman Sexualities.* Princeton, NJ: Princeton University Press, 1997.

Hamilton, Victor P. *The Book of Genesis Chapters 1–17.* New International Commentary on the Old Testament. Grand Rapids: Eerdmans, 1990.

Hammurabi. *The Code of Hammurabi, King of Babylon.* Translated by Robert Francis Harper. Clark, NJ: Lawbook Exchange, 2010.

Harré, Rom. Foreword to *Analysing Identity: Cross-Cultural, Societal and Clinical Contexts,* edited by Peter Weinreich and Wendy Saunderson, xvii–xxii. New York: Routledge, 2003.

Harrington, Daniel J. *The Gospel of Matthew.* Sacra Pagina. Collegeville, MN: Liturgical Press, 1991.

Harrison, Nonna Verna. *God's Many-Splendored Image: Theological Anthropology for Christian Formation.* Grand Rapids: Baker Academic, 2010.

Hauck, Friedrich. "Κοινός, etc." In *Theological Dictionary of the New Testament,* edited by Gerhard Kittel, translated by Geoffrey W. Bromiley, 3:798–810. Grand Rapids: Eerdmans, 1967.

Hauerwas, Stanley. *A Community of Character.* Notre Dame, IN: University of Notre Dame Press, 1981.

———. "On Bonhoeffer and John H. Yoder." Lecture, Theology Conference: Sermon on the Mount, Center for Applied Christian Ethics, Wheaton College, November 7, 2005. http://espace.wheaton.edu/cace/audio/05SOMhauerwas.mp3 (audio).

————. "Sex and Politics: Bertrand Russell and 'Human Sexuality.'" *Christian Century* April 19, 1978, 417–22.

Hays, Richard B. *First Corinthians*. Interpretation: A Bible Commentary for Teaching and Preaching. Louisville: John Knox Press, 1997.

————. *The Moral Vision of the New Testament: Community, Cross, New Creation; A Contemporary Introduction to New Testament Ethics*. San Francisco: HarperSanFrancisco, 1996.

————. "Relations Natural and Unnatural: A Response to John Boswell's Exegesis of Romans 1." *Journal of Religious Ethics* 14, no. 1 (1986): 184–215.

Healthlink BC. "Growth and Development, Ages 11–14." 2017. https://www.healthlinkbc.ca/health-topics/te7233.

Heaton, Tim. "Marital Stability throughout the Child-Rearing Years." *Demography* 27, no. 1 (1990): 55–63.

Hefling, Charles, ed. *Our Selves, Our Souls and Bodies: Sexuality and the Household of God*. Cambridge, MA: Cowley, 1996.

Heim, Erin M. *Adoption in Galatians and Romans: Contemporary Metaphor Theories and the Pauline* Huiothesia *Metaphors*. Biblical Interpretation Series. Leiden: Brill, 2017.

Hemez, Paul, and Wendy D. Manning. "Thirty Years of Change in Women's Premarital Cohabitation Experience." National Center for Marriage and Family Research, *Family Profiles* 5 (2017). https://www.bgsu.edu/ncfmr/resources/data/family-profiles/hemez-manning-30-yrs-change-women-premarital-cohab-fp-17-05.html.

Hersch, Karen K. *The Roman Wedding: Ritual and Meaning in Antiquity*. Cambridge: Cambridge University Press, 2010.

Hezser, Catherine. Review of *Jewish Marriage in Antiquity* by Michael L. Satlow. *Journal of Jewish Studies* 55, no. 1 (Spring 2004): 178–80.

Hill, David. *The Gospel of Matthew*. New Century Bible. Grand Rapids: Eerdmans, 1972.

Hill, Wesley. *Spiritual Friendship: Finding Love in the Church as a Celibate Gay Christian*. Grand Rapids: Brazos, 2015.

————. *Washed and Waiting: Reflections on Christian Faithfulness and Homosexuality*. Grand Rapids: Zondervan, 2010.

Holcomb, Justin S., and Lindsey A. Holcomb. *Rid of My Disgrace: Hope and Healing for Victims of Sexual Assault*. Wheaton, IL: Crossway, 2011.

Hollinger, Dennis P. *The Meaning of Sex: Christian Ethics and the Moral Life*. Grand Rapids: Baker Academic, 2009.

Holsteen, Nathan D. and Michael J. Svigel, eds. *Exploring Christian Theology*. 3 vols. Bloomington, MN: Bethany House, 2014–2105.

Holtz, Traugott. *Understanding Paul's Ethics*. Edited by Brian S. Rosner. Grand Rapids: Eerdmans, 1995.

Hopper, James, and David Lisak. "Why Rape and Trauma Survivors Have Fragmented and Incomplete Memories." *Time*, December 9, 2014. http://time.
com/3625414/rape-trauma-brain-memory/.

Horrell, J. Scott. "The Covenant of Singleness: The Bible and Church History."
Kindred Spirit, Spring/Summer 2015, 12.

Houlden, J. L. *Ethics and the New Testament*. London: T&T Clark, 1992.

House, H. Wayne, ed. *Divorce and Remarriage: Four Christian Views*. Downers
Grove, IL: InterVarsity Press, 1990.

Hsu, Albert. *Singles at the Crossroads: A Fresh Perspective on Christian Singleness*.
Downers Grove, IL: InterVarsity Press, 1997.

Hubbard, Thomas K., ed. *A Companion to Greek and Roman Sexualities*. Blackwell Companions to the Ancient World. Chichester, UK: Wiley-Blackwell,
2014.

Humanum. "The Humanum Series." Vimeo. Posted by Humanum, April 25,
2016. https://vimeo.com/ondemand/humanum.

Hunter College of Social Work. "Late Adolescence (18–21 Years Old)."
http://www.hunter.cuny.edu/socwork/nrcfcpp/pass/learning-circles/four/
Late%20Adolescence.pdf.

Hunter, David G., ed. *Marriage and Sexuality in Early Christianity*. Ad Fontes:
Early Christian Texts. Minneapolis: Fortress, 2018.

Hutchens, S. M. "Just Christians: On Homosexuality and Christian Identity."
Touchstone, July/August 2013, 3–4.

Hyun, Insoo, Amy Wilkerson, and Josephine Johnston. "Revisit the 14-Day
Rule." *Nature* 533 (May 12, 2016): 169–71.

Ingleheart, Jennifer, ed. *Ancient Rome and the Construction of Modern Homosexual Identities*. Classical Presences. Oxford: Oxford University Press, 2015.

———. "Introduction: Romosexuality: Rome, Homosexuality, and Reception."
In *Ancient Rome and the Construction of Modern Homosexual Identities*, edited by Jennifer Ingleheart, 1–35. Classical Presences. Oxford: Oxford University Press, 2015.

Instone-Brewer, David. *Divorce and Remarriage in the Church: Biblical Solutions
for Pastoral Realities*. Downers Grove, IL: InterVarsity Press, 2003.

Jacobs, Uwe, and Vincent Iacopino. "Torture and Its Consequences: A Challenge to Clinical Neuropsychology." *Professional Psychology: Research and
Practice* 32, no. 5 (2001): 458–64.

James, Carolyn Custis. *Half the Church: Recapturing God's Global Vision for
Women*. Grand Rapids: Zondervan, 2010.

———. *Malestrom: Manhood Swept into the Currents of a Changing World*.
Grand Rapids: Zondervan, 2015.

———. "Tamar: The Righteous Prostitute." In *Vindicating the Vixens: Revisiting
Sexualized, Vilified, and Marginalized Women of the Bible*, edited by Sandra
Glahn, 31–48. Grand Rapids: Kregel Academic, 2017.

Jennings, T. R., "God and Your Church: Preparing People to Meet Jesus." Come and Reason Ministries, 2015. http://www.comeandreason.com/index.php/en/media-center/column1/god-and-your-church-seminar/seven-levels-of-moral-decision-making.

Jensen, David H. *God, Desire, and a Theology of Human Sexuality*. Louisville: Westminster John Knox, 2013.

John Paul II. *The Gospel of Life: Evangelium Vitae*. Encyclical Letter. Culver City, CA: Pauline Books and Media, 1995.

———. *Letter to Families*. Rome: Libreria Editrice Vaticana, 1994.

———. *Man and Woman He Created Them: A Theology of the Body*. Translated by Michael Waldstein. Boston: Pauline Books and Media, 2006.

———. *On the Dignity and Vocation of Women: Mulieris Dignitatem*. Apostolic Letter. Culver City, CA: Pauline Books and Media, 1988.

———. *The Redemption of the Body and Sacramentality of Marriage (Theology of the Body*. Vatican: Libreria Editrice Vaticana, 2005.

———. *The Theology of the Body according to John Paul II: Human Love in the Divine Plan*. Boston: Pauline Books and Media, 1997.

Jones, David Albert. "Aquinas as an Advocate of Abortion? The Appeal to 'Delayed Animation' in Contemporary Christian Ethical Debates on the Human Embryo." *Studies in Christian Ethics* 26, no. 1 (2013): 97–124.

———. *The Soul of the Embryo: An Enquiry into the Status of the Human Embryo in the Christian Tradition*. London: Continuum, 2004.

Jones, Peter. *The God of Sex: How Spirituality Defines Your Sexuality*. Colorado Springs: Victor/Cook, 2006.

Jones, Stan, and Brenna Jones. *What's the Big Deal? Why God Cares about Sex*. Colorado Springs: NavPress, 2007.

Josephus. *Against Apion*. Translated by H. St. J. Thackeray. Loeb Classical Library 186. Cambridge, MA: Harvard University Press, 1926.

———. *Jewish Antiquities, Books 1–3*. Translated by H. St. J. Thackeray. Loeb Classical Library 232. Cambridge, MA: Harvard University Press, 1930.

Kaiser, Andrea, Kurt Hahlweg, Gabriele Fehm-Wolfsdorf, and Thomas Groth. "The Efficacy of a Compact Psychoeducational Group Training Program for Married Couples." *Journal of Consulting and Clinical Psychology* 66, no. 5 (1998): 753–60.

Kaiser, Walter, Peter H. Davids, F. F. Bruce, and Manfred T. Brauch. *Hard Sayings of the Bible*. Downers Grove, IL: InterVarsity Press, 1996.

Kamen, Deborah, and Sarah Levin-Richardson. "Lusty Ladies in the Roman Imaginary." In *Ancient Sex: New Essays*, edited by Ruby Blondell and Kirk Ormand, 231–52. Columbus: Ohio State University Press, 2015.

———. "Revisiting Roman Sexuality: Agency and Conceptualization of Penetrated Males." In *Sex in Antiquity: Exploring Gender and Sexuality in the Ancient World*, edited by Mark Masterson, Nancy Sorkin Rabinowitz, and James Robson, 449–60. New York: Routledge, 2015.

Kamitsuka, Margaret D. "Sexual Pleasure." In *The Oxford Handbook of Theology, Sexuality, and Gender,* edited by Adrian Thatcher, 505–22. Oxford: Oxford University Press, 2015.

Kant, Immanuel. *Lectures on Ethics.* Translated by Louis Infield. Indianapolis: Hackett, 1980.

Kautzsch, Emil, ed. *Gesenius' Hebrew Grammar.* Revised by A. E. Cowley. 2nd English ed. Oxford: Clarendon, 1910.

Keener, Craig S. *A Commentary on the Gospel of Matthew.* Grand Rapids: Eerdmans, 1999.

———. "Marriage." In *The Dictionary of New Testament Background,* edited by Craig A. Evans and Stanley E. Porter, 681–83. Downers Grove, IL: InterVarsity Press, 2000.

Keller, Timothy. "In Christ Jesus: How the Spirit Transforms Us." Sermon series presented at Redeemer Presbyterian Church, New York, November 19, 2006–January 7, 2007.

———. "Receptive Grace." Sermon presented at Redeemer Presbyterian Church, New York, February 10, 2002.

Kierkegaard, Søren. *Søren Kierkegaard's Journals and Papers, Volume 3: L–R.* Edited and translated by Howard V. Hong and Edna H. Hong. Bloomington: Indiana University Press, 1975.

———. *Training in Christianity and the Edifying Discourse Which "Accompanied" It.* Translated by Walter Lowrie. Princeton, NJ: Princeton University Press, 1941.

Kilner, John F. *Dignity and Destiny: Humanity in the Image of God.* Grand Rapids: Eerdmans, 2015.

King, Philip J., and Lawrence E. Stager. *Life in Biblical Israel.* Library of Ancient Israel. Louisville: Westminster John Knox, 2001.

Kinnaman, David, "The Porn Phenomenon." Barna, February 5, 2016. https://www.barna.com/the-porn-phenomenon/.

Kline, Galena H., Scott M. Stanley, Howard J. Markman, Antonio Olmos-Gallo, Michelle St. Peters, Sarah W. Whitton, and Lydia M. Prado. "Timing Is Everything: Pre-engagement Cohabitation and Increased Risk for Poor Marital Outcomes." *Journal of Family Psychology* 18, no. 2 (2004): 311–18.

Koehler, Ludwig, and Walter Baumgartner, eds. *The Hebrew and Aramaic Lexicon of the Old Testament.* Revised by Walter Baumgartner and Johann Jakob Stamm. Translated and edited under the supervision of Mervyn E. J. Richardson. Leiden: Brill, 2001.

Köstenberger, Andreas J. *God, Marriage, and Family: Rebuilding the Biblical Foundation.* 2nd ed. Wheaton, IL: Crossway, 2010.

Kraft, William. *Whole and Holy Sexuality: How to Find Human and Spiritual Integrity as a Sexual Person.* Eugene, OR: Wipf & Stock, 1998.

Krebs, Christopher, Christine Lindquist, Marcus Berzofsky, Bonnie Shook-Sa, Kimberly Peterson, Michael Planty, Lynn Langton, and Jessica Stroop.

Campus Climate Survey Validation Study Final Technical Report. Bureau of Justice Statistics Research and Development Series. Research Triangle Park, NC: RTI International, 2016.

Kreider, Glenn R. *God with Us: Exploring God's Interactions with His People throughout the Bible.* Phillipsburg, NJ: P&R, 2014.

Krueger, Paul, "Etiology or Obligation? Genesis 2:24 Reconsidered in the Light of Text Linguistics." In *Thinking towards New Horizons: Collected Communications of the XIXth Congress of the International Organization for the Study of the Old Testament, Ljubljana 2007*, edited by Matthias Augustin and Hermann Michael Niemann, 35–48. Beiträge zur Erforschung des Alten Testaments und des Antiken Judentums 55. New York: Peter Lang, 2008.

Kulaszewicz, Kassia E. "Racism and the Media: A Textual Analysis." MSW clinical research paper, St. Catherine University School of Social Work, May 2015. https://sophia.stkate.edu/cgi/viewcontent.cgi?article=1478&context=msw_papers.

Kunst, Christiane. *Römische Adoption: Zur Strategie einer Familienorganisation.* Frankfurter althistorische Beiträge. Hennef, Germany: Marthe Clauss, 2005.

Kuperberg, Arielle, "Age at Coresidence, Premarital Cohabitation, and Marriage Dissolution: 1985–2009." *Journal of Marriage and Family* 76, no. 2. (2014): 352–69.

Kvam, Kristen E., Linda S. Schearing, and Valarie H. Ziegler, eds. *Eve and Adam: Jewish, Christian, and Muslim Readings on Genesis and Gender.* Bloomington: Indiana University Press, 1999.

Laes, Christian. *Children in the Roman Empire: Outsiders Within.* Cambridge: Cambridge University Press, 2011.

———. "When Classicists Need to Speak Up: Antiquity and Present Day Pedophilia-Pederasty." In *Aeternitas Antiquitatis: Proceedings of the Symposium Held in Skopje, August 28 as Part of the 2009 Annual Conference of Euroclassica*, edited by Valerij Sofronievski, 30–59. Skopje, Macedonia: Association of Classical Philologists ANTIKA and Faculty of Philosophy in Skopje, 2010.

Lambert, W. G. "Celibacy in the World's Oldest Proverbs." *Bulletin of the American Schools of Oriental Research* 169 (1963): 63–64.

Laney, J. Carl. *The Divorce Myth.* Minneapolis: Bethany House, 1981.

Langlands, Rebecca. *Sexual Morality in Ancient Rome.* Cambridge: Cambridge University Press, 2006.

Larson, Jennifer, ed. *Greek and Roman Sexualities: A Sourcebook.* Bloomsbury Sources in Ancient History. London: Bloomsbury, 2012.

Laughery, Gregory J. "Paul: Anti-marriage? Anti-sex? Ascetic? A Dialogue with 1 Corinthians 7:1–40," *Evangelical Quarterly* 69 (1997): 109–28.

Laurenceau, Jean-Philippe, Scott M. Stanley, Antonio Olmos-Gallo, Brian R. W. Baucom, and Howard J. Markman. "Community-Based Prevention of Marital Dysfunction: Multilevel Modeling of a Randomized Effectiveness Study." *Journal of Consulting and Clinical Psychology* 72 (2004): 933–43.

Lawrence v. Texas. 539 U.S. 558 (2003).

Lawton, Robert B. "Genesis 2:24: Trite or Tragic?" *Journal of Biblical Literature* 105, no. 1 (1986): 97–98.

Lear, Andrew. "Ancient Pederasty: An Introduction." In *A Companion to Greek and Roman Sexualities*, edited by Thomas K. Hubbard, 102–27. Chichester, UK: Wiley-Blackwell, 2014.

Lear, Andrew, and Eva Cantarella. *Images of Ancient Greek Pederasty: Boys Were Their Gods*. New York: Routledge, 2008.

Lee-Barnewall, Michelle. *Neither Complementarian Nor Egalitarian: A Kingdom Corrective to the Evangelical Gender Debate*. Grand Rapids: Baker Academic, 2016.

Leick, Gwendolyn. *Sex and Eroticism in Mesopotamian Literature*. London: Routledge, 1994.

Leithart, Peter J. *Traces of the Trinity: Signs of God in Creation and Human Experience*. Grand Rapids: Brazos, 2015.

Lenski, R. C. H. *The Interpretation of Paul's First and Second Epistles to the Corinthians*. Minneapolis: Augsburg, 1937.

Levine, Étan. *Marital Relations in Ancient Judaism*. Beihefte zur Zeitschrift für Altorientalische und Biblische Rechtsgeschichte. Wiesbaden: Harrassowitz, 2009.

Levy, David. *Love and Sex with Robots: The Evolution of Human-Robot Relationships*. New York: HarperCollins, 2009.

Lewis, C. S. *Mere Christianity*. 1952. Reprint, San Francisco: HarperOne, 2013.

Lewis, Robert Brian. *Paul's "Spirit of Adoption" in Its Roman Imperial Context*. Library of New Testament Studies. London: T&T Clark, 2016.

Lichtenstein, Murray H. "Chiasm and Symmetry in Proverbs 31." *Catholic Biblical Quarterly* 44, no. 2 (1982): 202–11.

Lichter, Daniel T., and Zhenchao Qian. "Serial Cohabitation and the Marital Life Course." *Journal of Marriage and Family* 70, no. 4 (2008): 861–78.

Lichter, Daniel T., Richard N. Turner, and Sharon Sassler. "National Estimates of the Rise in Serial Cohabitation." *Social Science Research* 39, no. 5 (2010): 754–65.

Liddell, Henry George, Robert Scott, Henry Stuart Jones, and Roderick McKenzie. *A Greek-English Lexicon*. 9th ed. Oxford: Clarendon, 1940.

Lindsay, Hugh. *Adoption in the Roman World*. Cambridge: Cambridge University Press, 2009.

Lindsay, Jo M. "An Ambiguous Commitment: Moving into a Cohabiting Relationship." *Journal of Family Studies* 6, no.1 (2000): 120–34.

Lints, Richard, Michael S. Horton, and Mark R. Talbot, eds. *Personal Identity in Theological Perspective*. Grand Rapids: Eerdmans, 2006.

Livy. *History of Rome: Books 1–2*. Translated by B. O. Foster. Loeb Classical Library 114. Cambridge, MA: Harvard University Press, 1919.

Loader, William. *The Dead Sea Scrolls on Sexuality: Attitudes towards Sexuality in Sectarian and Related Literature at Qumran*. Attitudes towards Sexuality in Judaism and Christianity in the Hellenistic and Greco-Roman Era. Grand Rapids: Eerdmans, 2009.

——. *Enoch, Levi, and Jubilees on Sexuality: Attitudes towards Sexuality in the Early Enoch Literature, the Aramaic Levi Document, and the Book of Jubilees.* Attitudes towards Sexuality in Judaism and Christianity in the Hellenistic and Greco-Roman Era. Grand Rapids: Eerdmans, 2007.

——. *Making Sense of Sex: Attitudes towards Sexuality in Early Jewish and Christian Literature.* Grand Rapids: Eerdmans, 2013.

——. *The New Testament on Sexuality: Attitudes towards Sexuality in Judaism and Christianity in the Hellenistic and Greco-Roman Era.* Grand Rapids: Eerdmans, 2012.

——. *Philo, Josephus, and the Testaments on Sexuality: Attitudes towards Sexuality in the Writings of Philo and Josephus and in the Testaments of the Twelve Patriarchs.* Attitudes towards Sexuality in Judaism and Christianity in the Hellenistic and Greco-Roman Era. Grand Rapids: Eerdmans, 2011.

——. *The Pseudepigrapha on Sexuality: Attitudes towards Sexuality in Apocalypses, Testaments, Legends, Wisdom, and Related Literature.* Attitudes towards Sexuality in Judaism and Christianity in the Hellenistic and Greco-Roman Era. Grand Rapids: Eerdmans, 2011.

——. *Sexuality and the Jesus Tradition.* Grand Rapids: Eerdmans, 2005.

Lohmann, Raychelle Cassada. "Sexting Teens." *Psychology Today*, March 30, 2011. https://www.psychologytoday.com/us/blog/teen-angst/201103/sexting-teens.

Lonsway, Kimberly A., and Louise F. Fitzgerald. "Rape Myths: In Review." *Psychology of Women Quarterly* 18, no. 2 (1994): 133–64. https://doi.org/10.1111/j.1471-6402.1994.tb00448.x.

Lubin, Gus. "There Are 42 Million Prostitutes in the World, and Here's Where They Live." *Business Insider*, January 17, 2012. https://www.businessinsider.com/there-are-42-million-prostitutes-in-the-world-and-heres-where-they-live-2012-1.

Luther, Martin. *The Annotated Luther.* Vol. 5, *Christian Life in the World.* Edited by Hans J. Hillerbrand. Minneapolis: Fortress, 2017.

——. "The Estate of Marriage, 1522." In *Luther's Works*, vol. 45, *The Christian in Society II*, edited by Walther I. Brandt, 17–50. Philadelphia: Muhlenberg, 1962.

——. *Luther's Works.* Vol. 39, *Church and Ministry I.* Edited by Eric W. Gritsch and Ruth C. Gritsch. Philadelphia: Fortress, 1970.

Lutz, Cora E. "Musonius Rufus 'The Roman Socrates.'" *Yale Classical Studies* 10 (1947): 3–147.

Luz, Ulrich. *Matthew.* Translated by James E. Crouch. 3 vols. Hermeneia. Minneapolis: Fortress, 2001–2007.

Ma, Hong, Nuria Marti-Gutierrez, Sang-Wook Park, Jun Wu, Yeonmi Lee, Keiichiro Suzuki, Amy Koski et al. "Correction of a Pathogenic Gene Mutation in Human Embryos." *Nature* 548 (2017): 413–19. https://doi.org/10.1038/nature23305.

MacKinnon, Catharine A. "Pornography as Trafficking." *Michigan Journal of International Law* 26, no. 4 (2005). http://www.prostitutionresearch.com/MacKinnon%20Pornography%20as%20Trafficking.pdf.

———. "Trafficking, Prostitution, and Inequality." *Harvard Civil Rights–Civil Liberties Law Review* 46 (2011): 271–309. http://www.prostitutionresearch.com/pdfs/MacKinnon%20(2011)%20Trafficking%20Prostitution%20and%20Inequality.pdf.

Mahaney, C. J., with Carolyn Mahaney. *Sex, Romance, and the Glory of God: What Every Christian Husband Needs to Know.* Wheaton, IL: Crossway, 2004.

Mainwaring, Doug. "Your Marriage: You Have No Idea of the Good You Are Doing." *Public Discourse*, March 7, 2017. http://www.thepublicdiscourse.com/2017/03/18600/.

Malamuth, Neil M., Tamara Addison, and Mary Koss. "Pornography and Sexual Aggression: Are There Reliable Effects and Can We Understand Them?" *Annual Review of Sex Research* 11, no. 1 (2000): 26–91.

Malina, Bruce J. *The New Testament World: Insights from Cultural Anthropology.* 3rd ed. Louisville: Westminster John Knox, 2001.

Manning, Wendy D. "Cohabitation and Child Wellbeing." *The Future of Children* 25, no. 2 (2015): 51–66.

Manning, Wendy D., and Jessica A. Cohen. "Premarital Cohabitation and Marital Dissolution: An Examination of Recent Marriages." *Journal of Marriage and Family* 74, no. 2 (2012): 377–87.

Manning, Wendy D., and Pamela J. Smock. "Measuring and Modeling Cohabitation: New Perspectives from Qualitative Data." *Journal of Marriage and Family* 67, no. 4 (2005): 989–1002.

Markman, Howard J., Frank Floyd, Scott M. Stanley, and Ragnar Storaasli. "The Prevention of Marital Distress: A Longitudinal Investigation." *Journal of Consulting and Clinical Psychology* 56, no. 2 (1988): 210–17.

Markman, Howard J., Galena K. Rhoades, Scott M. Stanley, and Kristina M. Post. "A Randomized Clinical Trial of the Effectiveness of Premarital Intervention: Moderators of Divorce Outcomes." *Journal of Family Psychology*, 27, no. 1 (2013): 165–72.

Markman, Howard J., Mari Jo Renick, Frank Floyd, Scott M. Stanley, and Mari L. Clements. "Preventing Marital Distress through Communication and Conflict Management Training: A Four and Five Year Follow-Up." *Journal of Consulting and Clinical Psychology* 61, no. 1 (1993): 70–77.

Markman, Howard J., Scott M. Stanley, and Susan Blumberg. *Fighting for Your Marriage: PREP Program.* San Francisco: Jossey-Bass, 2010.

Martial. *Epigrams: Volume 1.* Translated by D. R. Shackleton Bailey. Loeb Classical Library 94. Cambridge, MA: Harvard University Press, 1993.

Marx, Alfred. "Les racines du célibat essénien." *Revue de Qumran* 7, no. 3 (1970): 323–42.

Masterson, Mark, Nancy Sorkin Rabinowitz, and James Robson, eds. *Sex in Antiquity: Exploring Gender and Sexuality in the Ancient World*. Rewriting Antiquity. New York: Routledge, 2015.

Matura, Thaddée. *Gospel Radicalism: The Hard Sayings of Jesus*. Translated by Maggi Despot and Paul Lachance. Maryknoll, NY: Orbis, 1984.

McCleese, Jessica, and Chelsi Creech. "Courageous Conversations: Discussing Biblically Based Sexuality with Your Teen." Fully Well (website), 2018. www.befullywell.com/birdsbeesbible (article discontinued).

McCreesh, Thomas. "Wisdom as Wife: Proverbs 31:10–31." *Revue biblique* 92, no. 1 (1985): 25–46.

McFarland, Ian A. *Difference and Identity: A Theological Anthropology*. Cleveland: Pilgrim, 2001.

———. *The Divine Image: Envisioning the Invisible God*. Minneapolis: Fortress, 2005.

McGrath, Alister E. *Christian Spirituality*. Malden, MA: Blackwell, 1999.

McLanahan, Sara, and Audrey N. Beck. "Parental Relationships in Fragile Families." *The Future of Children* 20, no. 2 (2010): 17–37.

McLanahan, Sara, and Gary Sandefur. *Growing Up with a Single Parent*. Cambridge, MA: Harvard University Press, 1994.

McMinn, Lisa Graham. *Sexuality and Holy Longing: Embracing Intimacy in a Broken World*. San Francisco: Jossey-Bass, 2004.

Medina, Jennifer. "Too Scared to Report Sexual Abuse. The Fear: Deportation." *New York Times*, April 30, 2017. https://www.nytimes.com/2017/04/30/us/immigrants-deportation-sexual-abuse.html.

Meggitt, Justin J. "Sources: Use, Abuse, Neglect; The Importance of Ancient Popular Culture." In *Christianity at Corinth: The Quest for the Pauline Churches*, edited by Edward Adams and David G. Horrell, 241–53. Louisville: Westminster John Knox, 2004.

Meier, John P. *A Marginal Jew*. Vol. 1, *Rethinking the Historical Jesus*. Anchor Yale Bible Reference Library. New Haven, CT: Yale University Press, 1991.

———. *Matthew*. New Testament Message 3. Wilmington, DE: Glazier, 1981.

Merrill, Eugene H. "Image of God." In *Dictionary of the Old Testament: Pentateuch*, edited by T. Desmond Alexander and David W. Baker, 441–45. Downers Grove, IL: InterVarsity Press, 2003.

Middleton, J. Richard. *The Liberating Image: The* Imago Dei *in Genesis 1*. Grand Rapids: Brazos, 2005.

Miles, Carrie A. *The Redemption of Love: Rescuing Marriage and Sexuality from the Economics of a Fallen World*. Grand Rapids: Brazos, 2006.

Miller, Bruce B. *Sexuality: Approaching Controversial Issues with Grace, Truth and Hope*. McKinney, TX: Confia, 2015.

Miner, Robert. *Thomas Aquinas on the Passions*. Cambridge: Cambridge University Press, 2009.

Mitchell, C. Ben. "Ectogenesis and the Future of Procreation." *Ethics and Medicine: An International Journal of Bioethics* 33, no. 3 (2017): 133–32.

Mohler, R. Albert, Jr. "The Mystery of Marriage, Part 2." Talk delivered at the New Attitude Conference, 2004. https://albertmohler.com/2004/08/01/the-mystery-of- marriage-part-2/ (audio).

Moore, Arthur L. *The Parousia in the New Testament.* Supplements to Novum Testamentum 13. Leiden: Brill, 1966.

Moore, George Foot. *Judaism in the First Centuries of the Christian Era: The Age of the Tannaim.* 3 vols. Cambridge, MA: Harvard University Press, 1927–1930.

Moore, Keith L., T. V. N. Persaud, and Mark G. Torchia. *The Developing Human: Clinically Oriented Embryology.* Philadelphia: Elsevier Saunders, 2013.

Morris, Leon. *The First Epistle of Paul to the Corinthians.* Rev. ed. Tyndale New Testament Commentary. Leicester, UK: Inter-Varsity Press, 1985.

———. *The Gospel according to Matthew.* Pillar New Testament Commentary. Grand Rapids: Eerdmans, 1992.

———. "Last Days." In *Evangelical Dictionary of Biblical Theology*, edited by Walter A. Elwell, 464–67. Grand Rapids: Baker, 1996.

Mounce, Robert H. *Letters of Paul to the Early Church: A Contemporary Translation.* Eugene, OR: Cascade, 2017.

Muehlenhard, Charlene L., Terry Humphreys, Kristen N. Jozkowski, and Zoe D. Peterson. "The Complexities of Sexual Consent among College Students: A Conceptual and Empirical Review." *Journal of Sex Research* 53, no. 4 (2016): 457–87.

Murphy-O'Connor, Jerome. *1 Corinthians.* New Testament Message 10. Collegeville, MN: Liturgical Press, 1979.

Murray, John. *Redemption Accomplished and Applied.* Grand Rapids: Eerdmans, 1955.

Myers, Nancy. "Cicero's (S) Trumpet: Roman Women and the Second Philippic." *Rhetoric Review* 22, no. 4 (2003), 337–52.

"Nakedness." In *Dictionary of Biblical Imagery*, edited by Leland Ryken, James C. Wilhoit, and Tremper Longman III, 581–82. Downers Grove, IL: Inter-Varsity Press, 1998.

Neale, Kurt, and Gary Barnes, producers. *Compelling Love and Sexual Identity.* Documentary film, 2014. www.compellinglovefilm.com.

Nelson, James B. *Embodiment: An Approach to Sexuality and Christian Theology.* Minneapolis: Augsburg, 1978.

Newport, Frank, "Americans Continue to Shift Left on Key Moral Issues." Gallup Social and Policy Issues, May 2015. https://news.gallup.com/poll/183413/americans-continue-shift-left-key-moral-issues.aspx.

Niederwimmer, Kurt. *Askese und Mysterium: Über Ehe, Ehescheidung, und Eheverzicht in den Anfängen des christlichen Glaubens.* Forschungen zur Religion und Literatur des Alten und Neuen Testaments 113. Göttingen: Vandenhoeck and Ruprecht, 1975.

Nissinen, Martti. *Homoeroticism in the Biblical World: A Historical Perspective.* Translated by Kirsi Stjerna. Minneapolis: Fortress, 1998.

Nolland, John. *The Gospel of Matthew.* New International Greek Testament Commentary. Grand Rapids: Eerdmans, 2005.

Nouwen, Henri J. M. *Clowning in Rome: Reflections on Solitude, Celibacy, Prayer, and Contemplation.* New York: Image, 1979.

Nugent, Colleen, and Jill Daugherty. "A Demographic, Attitudinal, and Behavioral Profile of Cohabiting Adults in the United States, 2011–2015." *National Health Statistics Reports* 111 (2018): 1–11.

Olson, Eric T. "Personal Identity." In *Stanford Encyclopedia of Philosophy.* Edited by Edward N. Zalta. Summer 2017 ed. https://plato.stanford.edu/archives/sum2017/entries/identity-personal/.

Ormand, Kirk. *Controlling Desires: Sexuality in Ancient Greece and Rome.* Praeger Series on the Ancient World. Westport, CT: Praeger, 2009.

Osborne, Grant R. *Matthew.* Zondervan Exegetical Commentary on the New Testament. Grand Rapids: Zondervan, 2010.

Osiek, Carolyn, and David L. Balch, eds. *Families in the New Testament World: Households and House Churches.* The Family, Religion, and Culture. Louisville: Westminster John Knox, 1997.

Ouellet, Marc Cardinal. *Divine Likeness: Toward a Trinitarian Anthropology of the Family.* Translated by Philip Milligan and Linda M. Cicone. Grand Rapids: Eerdmans, 2006.

Oxford Classical Dictionary. Edited by Simon Hornblower and Antony Spawforth. 4th ed. Oxford: Oxford University Press, 2012.

Parker, Holt N. "Love's Body Anatomized: The Ancient Erotic Handbooks and the Rhetoric of Sexuality." In *Pornography and Representation in Greece and Rome,* edited by Amy Richlin, 90–111. New York: Oxford University Press, 1992.

———. "The Teratogenic Grid." In *Roman Sexualities,* edited by Judith P. Hallett and Marilyn B. Skinner, 47–65. Princeton, NJ: Princeton University Press, 1997.

Partial-Birth Abortion Ban Act of 2003. Pub. L. No. 108–105. 117 Stat. 1201 (2003). https://www.congress.gov/bill/108th-congress/senate-bill/3/text.

Partridge, Emily, Marcus G. Davey, Matthew A. Hornick, Patrick E. McGovern, Ali Y. Mejaddam, Jesse D. Vrecenak, Carmen Mesas-Burgos, et al. "An Extra-Uterine System to Physiologically Support the Extreme Premature Lamb." *Nature Communications* 8 (2017). https://doi.org/10.1038/ncomms15112.

Pearcey, Nancy. *Total Truth: Liberating Christianity from Its Cultural Captivity.* Wheaton, IL: Crossway, 2004.

Penner, Clifford L., and Joyce J. Penner. *The Married Guy's Guide to Great Sex.* Colorado Springs: Focus on the Family Publishing, 2017.

Percival, Thomas. *Medical Ethics; or a Code of Institutes and Precepts, Adapted to the Professional Interests of Physicians and Surgeons.* Manchester: Russell, 1803.

Perry, Abby. "Compliance Is Not Consent." *Fathom*, May 1, 2018. https://www.fathommag.com/stories/compliance-is-not-consent.

Peter, Jochen, and Patti M. Valkenburg. "Processes Underlying the Effects of Adolescents' Use of Sexually Explicit Internet Material: The Role of Perceived Realism." *Journal of Research in Crime and Delinquency* 37, no. 3 (April 7, 2010): 375–99. https://doi.org/10.1177/0093650210362464.

Peters, Greg. "Spiritual Marriage in Early Christianity: 1 Cor 7:25–38 in Modern Exegesis and Earliest Church." *Trinity Journal* 23 (2002): 211–24.

Peterson, Richard. "A Re-evaluation of the Economic Consequences of Divorce." *American Sociological Review* 61, no. 3 (June 1996): 528–36.

Peterson, Robert A. *Salvation Applied by the Spirit: Union with Christ*. Wheaton, IL: Crossway, 2014.

Philo. *On Abraham. On Joseph. On Moses*. Translated by F. H. Colson. Loeb Classical Library 289. Cambridge, MA: Harvard University Press, 1935.

———. *On the Creation. Allegorical Interpretation of Genesis 2 and 3*. Translated by F. H. Colson and G. H. Whitaker. Loeb Classical Library 226. Cambridge, MA: Harvard University Press, 1929.

———. *On the Decalogue. On the Special Laws, Books 1–3*. Translated by F. H. Colson. Loeb Classical Library 320. Cambridge, MA: Harvard University Press, 1937.

Pierce, Ronald W., Rebecca Merrill Groothuis, and Gordon D. Fee, eds. *Discovering Biblical Equality: Complementarity without Hierarchy*. Downers Grove, IL: IVP Academic, 2005.

Pinckaers, Servais. *Morality: The Catholic View*. Translated by Michael Sherwin. South Bend, IN: St. Augustine's Press, 2003.

Pinto-Correia, Clara. *The Ovary of Eve: Egg and Sperm and Preformation*. Chicago: University of Chicago Press, 1998.

Piper, John. "Single in Christ: A Name Better Than Sons and Daughters." Sermon preached at Bethlehem Baptist Church, Minneapolis, MN, April 29, 2007. https://www.desiringgod.org/messages/single-in-christ-a-name-better-than-sons-and-daughters.

Piper, John and Wayne Grudem, eds. *Recovering Biblical Manhood and Womanhood: A Response to Evangelical Feminism*. Wheaton, IL: Crossway, 1991.

Plake, Sarah. "KSHB 41: Children Abusing Children: Children's Mercy Sees Dangerous Trend Involving Children and Porn." Children's Mercy (website), December 5, 2018. https://news.childrensmercy.org/kshb-41-children-abusing-children-childrens-mercy-sees-dangerous-trend-involving-children-and-pornography/.

Plantinga, Cornelius, Jr. *Not the Way It's Supposed to Be: A Breviary of Sin*. Grand Rapids: Eerdmans, 1995.

Pliny the Elder. *Natural History: Volume 9*. Translated by H. Rackham. Loeb Classical Library 394. Cambridge, MA: Harvard University Press, 1952.

Plutarch. "Advice to the Bride and Groom." Translated by Donald Russell. In *Plutarch's Advice to the Bride and Groom and A Consolation to His Wife: English Translations, Commentary, Interpretive Essays, and Bibliography*, edited by Sarah B. Pomeroy, 5–13. New York: Oxford University Press, 1999.

———. *Lives: Volume 2.* Translated by Bernadotte Perrin. Loeb Classical Library 87. Cambridge, MA: Harvard University Press, 1917.

Popenoe, David. "The Top Ten Myths of Divorce." National Marriage Project, 2002. https://www.catholiceducation.org/en/controversy/marriage/the-top-ten-myths-of-divorce.html.

Popenoe, David, and Barbara Dafoe Whitehead. *The State of Our Unions 2010.* Piscataway, NJ: National Marriage Project, Rutgers University, 2010.

Pornhub. "2017 Year in Review." January 9, 2018. https://www.pornhub.com/insights/2017-year-in-review.

Pride, Mary. *The Way Home: Beyond Feminism, Back to Reality.* Wheaton, IL: Crossway, 1985.

Pruss, Alexander R. *One Body: An Essay in Christian Sexual Ethics.* Notre Dame, IN: University of Notre Dame Press, 2013.

Psychology Today. "Spirituality." https://www.psychologytoday.com/basics/spirituality.

Rae, Scott B., and D. Joy Riley. *Outside the Womb: Moral Guidance for Assisted Reproduction.* Chicago: Moody Press, 2011.

Rae, Scott B., Robert P. George, and Melissa Moschella. *Doing the Right Thing: Making Moral Choices in a World Full of Options.* Grand Rapids: Zondervan, 2013.

RAINN. "Sexual Assault." https://www.rainn.org/articles/sexual-assault.

Ramsey, George W. "Is Name-Giving an Act of Domination in Genesis 2:23 and Elsewhere?" *Catholic Biblical Quarterly* 50, no. 1 (1988): 24–35.

Rawson, Beryl, ed. *A Companion to Families in the Greek and Roman Worlds.* Blackwell Companions to the Ancient World. Chichester, UK: Wiley-Blackwell, 2011.

———, ed. *Marriage, Divorce, and Children in Ancient Rome.* Oxford: Oxford University Press, 1991.

———. "The Roman Family." In *The Family in Ancient Rome*, edited by Beryl Rawson, 1–57. Ithaca, NY: Cornell University Press, 1986.

Raymond, Janice G. "Ten Reasons for Not Legalizing Prostitution and a Legal Response to the Demand for Prostitution." *Journal of Trauma Practice* 2, nos. 3–4 (2003): 315–32.

Rhoades, Galena K., Scott M. Stanley, and Howard J. Markman. "The Pre-engagement Cohabitation Effect: A Replication and Extension of Previous Findings." *Journal of Family Psychology* 23, no. 1 (2009): 107–11.

Rhoads, Steven E. *Taking Sex Differences Seriously.* San Francisco: Encounter, 2004.

Richlin, Amy. *The Garden of Priapus: Sexuality and Aggression in Roman Humor.* Rev. ed. New York: Oxford University Press, 1992.

————. "Not before Homosexuality: The Materiality of *Cinaedus* and the Roman Law against Love Between Men." *Journal of the History of Sexuality* 3, no. 4 (1993): 523–73.

————, ed. *Pornography and Representation in Greece and Rome.* New York: Oxford University Press, 1992.

————. "Reading Boy-Love and Child-Love in the Greco-Roman World." In *Sex in Antiquity: Exploring Gender and Sexuality in the Ancient World,* edited by Mark Masterson, Nancy Sorkin Rabinowitz, and James Robson, 352–73. New York: Routledge, 2015.

Riddle, John M. *Contraception and Abortion from the Ancient World to the Renaissance.* Cambridge, MA: Harvard University Press, 1994.

Riggio, Ronald E., "Women's Intuition: Myth or Reality?" *Psychology Today,* July 14, 2011. https://www.psychologytoday.com/us/blog/cutting-edge-leadership/201107/women-s-intuition-myth-or-reality.

Riley, D. Joy. "Applying Pressure to the 14-Day Rule." Christian Medical and Dental Associations, *The Point* (blog), June 15, 2017. https://cmda.org/applying-pressure-to-the-14-day-rule-2.

Roberts, Christopher C. *Creation and Covenant: The Significance of Sexual Difference in the Moral Theology of Marriage.* London: T&T Clark, 2007.

Roe v. Wade. 410 U.S. 113 (1973).

Rogers, Eugene F., Jr. *Sexuality and the Christian Body: Their Way into the Triune God.* Challenges in Contemporary Theology. Oxford: Blackwell, 1999.

Rogge, Ronald D., Rebecca J. Cobb, Erika Lawrence, Matthew D. Johnson, and Thomas N. Bradbury. "Is Skills Training Necessary for the Primary Prevention of Marital Distress and Dissolution? A Three-Year Experimental Study of Three Interventions." *Journal of Consulting and Clinical Psychology* 81, no. 6 (2013): 949–61.

Rooney, Andy. "Those Rotten Apples." *60 Minutes.* CBS, March 31, 2002. https://www.cbsnews.com/news/those-rotten-apples.

Rosen, Christine. *Preaching Eugenics: Religious Leaders and the American Eugenics Movement.* Oxford: Oxford University Press, 2004.

Rosenau, Douglas E. *A Celebration of Sex.* Rev. ed. Nashville: Thomas Nelson, 2002.

Rosenau, Douglas E., and Michael R. Sytsma. "A Theology of Sexual Intimacy: Insights into the Creator." *Journal of Psychology and Christianity* 23, no. 3 (2004): 261–70.

Rosenau, Douglas E., Lorraine Turbyfill, C. Gary Barnes, and Marilyn Harding. "A Celebration of Sex: A Model for Teaching Creative Marital Intimacy." Paper presented at CAPS-Christian Association for Psychological Studies, National Annual Conference, Indianapolis, IN, March 31, 2011.

Rosenau, Douglas E., and Michael Todd Wilson. *Soul Virgins: Redefining Single Sexuality.* Grand Rapids: Baker Books, 2006.

Rosenfeld, Michael, and Katharina Roesler. "Cohabitation Experience and Co-habitation's Association with Marital Dissolution." *Journal of Marriage and Family* 81, no. 1 (2019): 42–58.

Rosner, Brian. *Paul, Scripture and Ethics: A Study of 1 Corinthians 5–7.* Arbeiten zur Geschichte des antiken Judentums und des Urchristentums 22. Leiden: Brill, 1994.

Ryrie, Charles Caldwell. *Balancing the Christian Life.* Chicago: Moody Press, 1969.

Sabourin, Leopold. "The Positive Values of Consecrated Celibacy." *The Way Supplement* 10 (1970): 49–60.

Sassler, Sharon, Katherine Michelmore, and Zhenchao Qian. "Transitions from Sexual Relationships into Cohabitation and Beyond." *Demography* 55, no. 2 (2018): 511–34.

Sassler, Sharon, and Amanda Jayne Miller. *Cohabitation Nation: Gender, Class, and the Remaking of Relationships.* Oakland: University of California Press, 2017.

Satlow, Michael L. *Jewish Marriage in Antiquity.* Princeton, NJ: Princeton University Press, 2001.

Saucy, Robert L., and Judith K. TenElshof, eds. *Women and Men in Ministry: A Complementary Perspective.* Chicago: Moody Press, 2001.

Savulescu, Julian, and Guy Kahane. "The Moral Obligation to Create Children with the Best Chance of the Best Life." *Bioethics* 23, no. 5 (2009): 274–90.

Schaeffer, Francis. *No Little People.* Wheaton, IL: Crossway, 1974.

Scheler, Max. *Vom Umsturz der Werte: Der Abhandlungen und Aufsätze zweite durchgesehene Auflage: Volume 1.* Leipzig: Der Neue Geist, 1919.

Schillebeeckx, Edward. *Marriage: Human Reality and Saving Mystery.* Translated by N. D. Smith. New York: Sheed & Ward, 1965.

Schilling, Elizabeth A., Donald H. Baucom, Charles K. Burnett, Elizabeth Sandlin Allen, and Lynelle Ragland. "Altering the Course of Marriage: The Effect of PREP Communication Skills Acquisition on Couples' Risk of Becoming Maritally Distressed." *Journal of Family Psychology* 17, no. 1 (2003): 41–53.

Schlatter, Adolf. *Das Evangelium nach Matthäus.* In Erläuterungen zum Neuen Testament 1. Stuttgart: Calwer, 1961.

Schnackenburg, Rudolf. *The Gospel of Matthew.* Translated by Robert R. Barr. Grand Rapids: Eerdmans, 2002.

Schrage, Wolfgang. *The Ethics of the New Testament.* Translated by David E. Green. Philadelphia: Fortress, 1988.

———. *Kreuzestheologie und Ethik im Neuen Testament: Gesammelte Studien.* Forschungen zur Religion und Literatur des Alten und Neuen Testaments. Göttingen: Vandenhoeck and Ruprecht, 2004.

Schroeder, H. J., trans. *Canons and Decrees of the Council of Trent.* St. Louis: Herder, 1941. Reprint, Rockford, IL: Tan Books, 1978.

Schwartz, Debra A., and Ralph Rivas. "Humor." In *Encyclopedia of American Journalism,* edited by Stephen L. Vaughn, 216. New York: Routledge, 2008.

Schweizer, Eduard. *The Good News according to Matthew*. Translated by David E. Green. Atlanta: John Knox, 1975.

Scott, Joan. "Gender: A Useful Category of Historical Analysis." *American Historical Review* 91, no. 5 (December 1986): 1053–75.

Serva, Christine. "What Is Personal Identity? Definition, Philosophy and Development." Study.com. http://study.com/academy/lesson/what-is-personal-identity-definition-philosophy-development.html.

Sheff, Elisabeth. "Five Disadvantages of Polyamory." *Psychology Today*, September 2015. https://www.psychologytoday.com/us/blog/the-polyamorists-next-door/201509/five-disadvantages-polyamory.

———. "How Many Polyamorists Are There in the U.S.?" *Psychology Today*, May 2014. https://www.psychologytoday.com/us/blog/the-polyamorists-next-door/201405/how-many-polyamorists-are-there-in-the-us.

———. *When Someone You Love Is Polyamorous: Understanding Poly People and Relationships*. Portland: Thorntree, 2016.

Singer, Peter. *Practical Ethics*. Cambridge: Cambridge University Press, 2011.

Skinner, Marilyn B. *Sexuality in Greek and Roman Culture*. 2nd ed. London: Wiley-Blackwell, 2014.

Smedes, Lewis B. *Sex for Christians: The Limits and Liberties of Sexual Living*. 2nd ed. Grand Rapids: Eerdmans, 1994.

Smock, Pamela J. "The Economic Costs of Marital Disruption for Young Women over the Past Two Decades." *Demography* 30, no. 3 (August 1993): 353–71.

Smock, Pamela J., and Fiona Rose Greenland. "Diversity in Pathways to Parenthood: Patterns, Implications, and Emerging Research Directions." *Journal of Marriage and Family* 72, no. 3 (2010): 576–93.

Stanley, Scott M. "Citations for Tests of the Inertia Hypothesis about the Timing of Cohabitation and Marital Outcomes." *Sliding vs Deciding: Scott Stanley's Blog*, March 26, 2018. http://slidingvsdeciding.blogspot.com/2018/03/citations-for-tests-of-inertia_26.html.

———. "The Complex Risks Associated with Cohabitation." *Institute for Family Studies Blog*, April 3, 2014. https://ifstudies.org/blog/the-complex-risks-associated-with-cohabitation.

———. "Give Me a Sign: What Signals Commitment?" *Sliding vs Deciding: Scott Stanley's Blog*, July 5, 2017. https://slidingvsdeciding.blogspot.com/2017/07/give-me-sign-what-signals-commitment.html.

———. "How Cohabitation Shapes African Americans' Marriage Attitudes." *Institute for Family Studies Blog*, September 28, 2015. https://ifstudies.org/blog/how-cohabitation-shapes-young-african-americans-marriage-attitudes.

———. "Moving In and Moving On: Cohabitation is Less Likely Than Ever to Lead to Marriage." *Sliding vs Deciding: Scott Stanley's Blog*, July 25, 2014. http://slidingvsdeciding.blogspot.com/2014/07/moving-in-and-moving-on-cohabitation-is_25.html.

————. "The Mystery: Why Isn't Living Together Beforehand Associated with Improved Odds in Marriage?" *Sliding vs Deciding: Scott Stanley's Blog*, July 29, 2014. http://slidingvsdeciding.blogspot.com/2014/07/the-mystery-why-isnt-living-together.html.

————. "Not Your Steppin Stone." *Sliding vs Deciding: Scott Stanley's Blog*, January 16, 2014. http://slidingvsdeciding.blogspot.com/2014/01/not-your-steppin-stone.html.

————. "Time to 'Go Ahead and Shack Up'?" *Institute for Family Studies Blog*, March 20, 2014. https://ifstudies.org/blog/time-to-go-ahead-and-shack-up.

————. "What Really Is the Divorce Rate?" PREP-Prevention and Relationship Enhancement Program, August 3, 2007. https://www.prepinc.com/docs/content/articles/What_is_Divorce_Rate_8-3-2007.pdf.

Stanley, Scott M., Elizabeth S. Allen, Howard J. Markman, Galena . Rhoades, and Donella L. Prentice. "Decreasing Divorce in Army Couples: Results from a Randomized Clinical Trial of PREP for Strong Bonds." *Journal of Couple and Relationship Therapy* 9, no. 2 (2010): 149–60.

Stanley, Scott M., and Galena K. Rhoades. "Practice May Not Make Perfect: Relationship Experience and Marital Success." *Institute for Family Studies Blog*, March 17, 2016. https://ifstudies.org/blog/practice-may-not-make-perfect-relationship-experience-and-marital-success.

————. "Selection Effects and Personal Choice." *Institute for Family Studies Blog*, August 20, 2014. https://ifstudies.org/blog/selection-effects-and-personal-choice.

Stanley, Scott M., Galena K. Rhoades, Paul R. Amato, Howard J. Markman, and Christine A. Johnson. "The Timing of Cohabitation and Engagement: Impact on First and Second Marriages." *Journal of Marriage and Family* 72, no. 4 (2010): 906–18.

Stanley, Scott M., Galena K. Rhoades, and Frank D. Fincham. "Understanding Romantic Relationships among Emerging Adults: The Significant Roles of Cohabitation and Ambiguity." In *Romantic Relationships in Emerging Adulthood*, edited by Frank D. Fincham and Ming Cui, 234–51. Cambridge: Cambridge University Press, 2011.

Stanley, Scott M., Galena K. Rhoades, Benjamin A. Loew, Elizabeth S. Allen, Sarah Carter, Laura J. Osborne, Donella Prentice, and Howard J. Markman. "A Randomized Controlled Trial of Relationship Education in the U.S. Army: Two-year Outcomes." *Family Relations* 63, no. 4 (2014): 482–95.

Stanley, Scott M., Galena K. Rhoades, and Howard J. Markman. "Sliding versus Deciding: Inertia and the Premarital Cohabitation Effect." *Family Relations* 55, no. 4 (2006): 499–509.

Stauffer, Ethelbert. *Die Botschaft Jesu: Damals und Heute*. Dalp-Taschenbücher 333. Bern: Franke, 1959.

Stayton, William R. "A Theology of Sexual Pleasure in Sexuality: A Theological Conversation." *American Baptist Quarterly* 8, no. 2 (1989): 94–108.

Stein, Robert H. *The Method and Message of Jesus's Teachings*. Rev. ed. Louisville: Westminster John Knox, 1994.

Stewart, Janelle. "15–17-Year-Olds: Ages and Stages of Youth Development." State Adolescent Health Resource Center, Michigan State University Extension, 2013. https://www.canr.msu.edu/news/15_to_17_year_olds_ages_and_stages_of_youth_development.

Stone, Douglas, Bruce Patton, and Sheila Heen. *Difficult Conversations: How to Discuss What Matters Most*. New York: Penguin, 2010.

Stone, Ken. "Marriage and Sexual Relations in the World of the Hebrew Bible." In *The Oxford Handbook of Theology, Sexuality, and Gender*, edited by Adrian Thatcher, 174–80. Oxford: Oxford University Press, 2015.

Stone, Roxanne. "Teens and Young Adults Use Porn More than Anyone Else." Barna, January 28, 2016. https://www.barna.com/research/teens-young-adults-use-porn-more-than-anyone-else/.

Storkey, Elaine. *Origins of Difference: The Gender Debate Revisited*. Grand Rapids: Baker Academic, 2001.

———. *Scars across Humanity: Understanding and Overcoming Violence against Women*. Downers Grove, IL: IVP Academic, 2018.

Strange but True. "How Big Is the Porn Industry?" Medium. February 19, 2017. https://medium.com/@Strange_bt_True/how-big-is-the-porn-industry-fbc1ac78091b.

Stroll, Avrum. "Identity." In *The Encyclopedia of Philosophy*, edited by Paul Edwards, 4:121–24. New York: Macmillan and Free Press, 1967.

Struthers, William M. *Wired for Intimacy: How Pornography Hijacks the Male Brain*. Downers Grove, IL: InterVarsity Press, 2010.

Suetonius. *Lives of the Caesars*. 2 vols. Rev. ed. Translated by John C. Rolfe. Loeb Classical Library 31, 38. Cambridge, MA: Harvard University Press, 1997–1998.

Sutter Health Palo Alto Medical Foundation. "Parents and Teachers: Teen Growth and Development, Years 11–14." 2001. http://www.pamf.org/parenting-teens/health/growth-development/pre-growth.html (article discontinued).

Sytsma, Michael, and Debra L. Taylor. "Current Thinking in How to Help Couples and Individuals Struggling with Low Sexual Desire." *Marriage and Family Therapy: A Christian Journal* 5, no. 3 (2002): 311–20.

Tach, Laura, and Sarah Halpern-Meekin. "How Does Premarital Cohabitation Affect Trajectories of Marital Quality?" *Journal of Marriage and Family* 71, no. 2 (2009): 298–317.

Talbert, Charles H. *Matthew*. Paideia. Grand Rapids: Baker Academic, 2010.

Teachman, Jay. "Premarital Sex, Premarital Cohabitation, and the Risk of Subsequent Marital Dissolution among Women." *Journal of Marriage and Family* 65, no. 2. (2003): 444–55.

Teipel, K. "Understanding Adolescence: Seeing through a Developmental Lens." State Adolescent Health Resource Center, Konopka Institute, University of Minnesota. http://www.amchp.org/programsandtopics/AdolescentHealth/ projects/Documents/SAHRC%20AYADevelopment%20LateAdolescentY- oungAdulthood.pdf.

Tempkin, Owsei. *Soranus' Gynecology*. Baltimore: Johns Hopkins University Press, 1956.

Teresa of Calcutta. "Whatever You Did Unto One of the Least, You Did Unto Me." Address at the National Prayer Breakfast, February 3, 1994. https:// www.ewtn.com/library/issues/prbkmter.txt.

Thatcher, Adrian, ed. *The Oxford Handbook of Theology, Sexuality, and Gender*. Oxford: Oxford University Press, 2015.

Thiselton, Anthony C. *The First Epistle to the Corinthians*. New International Greek Testament Commentary. Grand Rapids: Eerdmans, 2000.

Thomas Aquinas. *Summa Theologiae*. Edited and translated by T. Gilby. 60 vols. London: Blackfriars, 1968.

Thomas, Gary. *Sacred Marriage*. Grand Rapids: Zondervan, 2000.

Thornton, Arland, and Linda Young-DeMarco. "Four Decades of Trends in Attitudes toward Family Issues in the United States: The 1960s through the 1990s." *Journal of Marriage and Family* 63, no. 4 (2001): 1009–37.

Thurian, Max. *Marriage and Celibacy*. Translated by Norma Emerton. London: SCM, 1959.

Tosato, Angelo. "On Genesis 2:24." *Catholic Biblical Quarterly* 52, no. 3 (1990): 389–409.

Treggiari, Susan. "Divorce Roman Style: How Easy and How Frequent Was It?" In *Marriage, Divorce, and Children in Ancient Rome*, edited by Beryl Rawson, 31–46. Oxford: Oxford University Press, 1991.

———. "Marriage and Family in Roman Society." In *Marriage and Family in the Biblical World*, edited by Ken M. Campbell, 132–82. Downers Grove, IL: InterVarsity Press, 2003.

———. *Roman Marriage: Iusti Coniuges from the Time of Cicero to the Time of Ulpian*. Oxford: Oxford University Press, 1991.

Trick, Bradley R. *Abrahamic Descent, Testamentary Adoption, and the Law in Galatians: Differentiating Abraham's Sons, Seed, and Children of Promise*. Supplements to Novum Testamentum. Leiden: Brill, 2016.

Trimm, Charlie. "Honor Your Parents: A Command for Adults." *Journal of the Evangelical Theological Society* 60, no. 2 (2017): 247–63.

Tripp, Paul David. *Sex in a Broken World: How Christ Redeems What Sin Distorts*. Wheaton, IL: Crossway, 2018.

Turkle, Sherry. *Alone Together: Why We Expect More from Technology and Less from Each Other*. New York: Basic Books, 2011.

Turner, David L. *Matthew*. Baker Exegetical Commentary on the New Testament. Grand Rapids: Baker Academic, 2008.

Ullman, Sarah E. "Social Reactions, Coping Strategies, and Self-Blame Attributions in Adjustment to Sexual Assault." *Psychology of Women Quarterly* 20, no. 4 (1996): 505–26.

United Nations Human Rights Office of the High Commissioner. "Convention for the Suppression of the Traffic in Persons and of the Exploitation of the Prostitution of Others." December 2, 1949. https://www.ohchr.org/EN/ProfessionalInterest/Pages/TrafficInPersons.aspx.

United States Census Bureau. "America's Families and Living Arrangements: 2016." https://www.census.gov/data/tables/2016/demo/families/cps-2016.html.

———. "By Decade." https://www.census.gov/programs-surveys/decennial-census/decade.2010.html.

———. "U.S. and World Population Clock." https://www.census.gov/popclock/.

University of Rochester Medical Center, Health Encyclopedia. "Understanding the Teen Brain." 2018. https://www.urmc.rochester.edu/encyclopedia/content.aspx?ContentTypeID=1&ContentID=3051.

Vagianos, Alanna. "NFL Player to Elementary School Class: Girls Are 'Supposed to Be Silent.'" *Huffington Post*, February 23, 2017. https://www.huffingtonpost.com/entry/jameis-winston-accused-of-rape-to-elementary-class-girls-are-supposed-to-be-silent_us_58af20a2e4b0a8a9b78012e6.

———. "Remember Brock Turner? From 3 Months Ago? He'll Leave Jail on Friday." *Huffington Post*, March 20, 2017. https://www.huffingtonpost.com/entry/remember-brock-turner-from-3-months-ago-hell-leave-jail-on-friday_us_57c58c81e4b0cdfc5ac9256b.

Van Syckle, Katie. "What It's Like to Report about the Porn Industry." *New York Times*, March 26, 2018. https://www.nytimes.com/2018/03/26/insider/reporting-the-porn-industry.html.

Van Widenfelt, Brigit, Clemens Hosman, Cas Schaap, and Cees van der Staak. "The Prevention of Relationship Distress for Couples at Risk: A Controlled Evaluation with Nine-Month and Two-Year Follow-Ups." *Family Relations* 45, no. 2 (1996): 156–65.

Vanauken, Sheldon. *A Severe Mercy*. San Francisco: HarperSanFrancisco, 2009.

Varro. *On the Latin Language: Volume 2*. Translated by Roland G. Kent. Loeb Classical Library 334. Cambridge, MA: Harvard University Press, 1938.

Ve Ard, Cherie L., and Franklin Veaux. "Polyamory 101." More than Two: Franklin Veaux's Polyamory Site, 2003. https://www.morethantwo.com/poly101.pdf.

Verhagen, Eduard, and Pieter J. J. Sauer. "The Groningen Protocol—Euthanasia in Severely Ill Newborns." *New England Journal of Medicine* 352 (2005): 959–62.

Vermes, Geza. *Jesus the Jew: A Historian's Reading of the Gospels*. Philadelphia: Fortress, 1981.

Villanueva, Sara. "Teens and Sex." *Psychology Today*, February 11, 2016. https://www.psychologytoday.com/blog/how-parent-teen/201602/teens-and-sex.

Waite, Linda, Don Browning, William J. Doherty, Maggie Gallagher, Ye Luo, and Scott M. Stanley. "Does Divorce Make People Happy? Findings from a Study of Unhappy Marriages." Smart Marriages, July 11, 2002. http://smartmarriages.com/does.divorce.html.

Waite, Linda, and Lillard, Lee. "Children and Marital Disruption." *American Journal of Sociology* 96, no. 4 (1991): 930–53.

Wall, Robert W. "Divorce." In *The Anchor Bible Dictionary*, edited by David Noel Freedman, 2:217–18. New York: Doubleday, 1992.

Wallerstein, Judith, Julia Lewis, and Sandra Blakeslee. *The Unexpected Legacy of Divorce*. New York: Hyperion, 2000.

Walters, Jonathan. "Invading the Roman Body: Manliness and Impenetrability in Roman Thought." In *Roman Sexualities*, edited by Judith P. Hallett and Marilyn B. Skinner, 29–43. Princeton, NJ: Princeton University Press, 1997.

Waltke, Bruce K. "The Role of the 'Valiant Wife' in the Marketplace." *Crux* 35, no. 3 (September 1999): 25–29.

Walton, John H. *Genesis*. NIV Application Commentary. Grand Rapids: Zondervan, 2001.

Ward, Roy Bowen. "Musonius and Paul on Marriage." *New Testament Studies* 36, no. 2 (1990): 281–89.

Webb, William J. *Slaves, Women and Homosexuals: Exploring the Hermeneutics of Cultural Analysis*. Downers Grove, IL: InterVarsity Press, 2001.

Webroot. "Internet Pornography by the Numbers: A Significant Threat to Society." https://www.webroot.com/us/en/resources/tips-articles/internet-pornography-by-the-numbers.

Weigel, George. *Witness to Hope: The Biography of Pope John Paul II*. New York: HarperCollins, 1999.

Weiss, Johannes. *The History of Primitive Christianity*. Translated by Frederick C. Grant. 2 vols. New York: Wilson-Erickson, 1937.

Weitzman, Leonore. "The Economics of Divorce: Social and Economic Consequences of Property, Alimony, and Child Support Awards." *UCLA Law Review* 28 (August 1981): 1181–1268.

Wenham, David. "Marriage and Singleness in Paul and Today." In *Readings in Christian Ethics*, vol. 2, *Issues and Applications*, edited by David K. Clark and Robert V. Rakestraw, 144–48. Grand Rapids: Baker, 1996.

Wenham, Gordon J. *Genesis 1–15*. Word Biblical Commentary. Waco, TX: Word, 1987.

West, Christopher. *Fill These Hearts: God, Sex, and the Universal Longing*. Cicero, NY: Image, 2013.

———. *Theology of the Body for Beginners: A Basic Introduction to Pope John Paul II's Sexual Revolution*. Rev. ed. West Chester, PA: Ascension, 2009.

West, Christopher, and Charles J. Chaput. *Good News about Sex and Marriage*. Rev. ed. Atlanta: Charis, 2004.

Wheeler, Benj. Ide. "The Origin of Grammatical Gender." *Journal of Germanic Philology* 2, no. 4 (1899): 528–45. https://www.jstor.org/stable/27699089.

Whipple, Beverly. "Big Think Interview with Beverly Whipple." Big Think, November 2, 2009. https://bigthink.com/videos/big-think-interview-with-beverly-whipple.

Whitmore, Alissa M. "Fascinating *Fascina*: Apotropaic Magic and How to Wear a Penis." In *What Shall I Say of Clothes? Theoretical and Methodological Approaches to the Study of Dress in Antiquity*, edited by Megan Cifarelli and Laura Gawlinski, 47–65. Boston: Archaeological Institute of America, 2017.

Williams, Craig A. *Roman Homosexuality*. 2nd ed. Oxford: Oxford University Press, 2010.

Williams, Margaret. "The Jewish Family in Judaea From Pompey to Hadrian— The Limits of Romanization." In *The Roman Family in the Empire: Rome, Italy, and Beyond*, edited by Michele George, 159–82. Oxford: Oxford University Press, 2005.

Williams, Rowan, *Resurrection: Interpreting the Easter Gospel*. London: Darton, Longman and Todd, 2002.

Winkler, John J. *The Constraints of Desire: The Anthropology of Sex and Gender in Ancient Greece*. New York: Routledge, 1990.

Winner, Lauren F. *Real Sex: The Naked Truth about Chasity*. Grand Rapids: Brazos, 2005.

Winston, George, and Dora Winston. *Recovering Biblical Ministry by Women: An Exegetical Response to Traditionalism and Feminism*. Longwood, FL: Xulon, 2003.

Winter, Bruce. *After Paul Left Corinth*. Grand Rapids: Eerdmans, 2001.

Witherington, Ben, III. *Jesus, Paul and the End of the World*. Downers Grove, IL: InterVarsity Press, 1992.

Wojtyła, Karol (Pope John Paul II). *Love and Responsibility*. San Francisco: Ignatius, 1993.

Wolff, Christian. "Humility and Self-Denial in Jesus's Life and Message and in the Apostolic Experience of Paul." In *Paul and Jesus: Collected Essays*, edited by A. J. M. Wedderburn. Journal for the Study of the New Testament Supplement Series 37. Sheffield: JSOT Press, 1989.

Wolfinger, Nicholas. "Beyond the Intergenerational Transmission of Divorce." *Journal of Family Issues* 21, no. 8 (2000): 1061–86.

Woodson, Jules. "I Was Assaulted. He Was Applauded." *New York Times*, March 9, 2018. https://www.nytimes.com/video/opinion/100000005724879/i-was-assaulted-he-was-applauded.html.

Yarhouse, Mark A. *Homosexuality and the Christian: A Guide for Parents, Pastors, and Friends*. Minneapolis: Bethany House, 2010.

————. *Understanding Gender Dysphoria: Navigating Transgender Issues in a Changing Culture.* Christian Association for Psychological Studies Books. Downers Grove, IL: IVP Academic, 2015.

————. *Understanding Sexual Identity: A Resource for Youth Ministry.* Grand Rapids: Zondervan, 2013.

Yarhouse, Mark A., and Dara Houp. "Transgender Christians: Gender Identity, Family Relationships, and Religious Faith." In *Transgender Youth: Perceptions, Media Influences, and Social Challenges,* edited by Sheyma Vaughn, 51–65. New York: Nova Science Publishers, 2016.

Yarhouse, Mark A., and Julia Sadusky. *Approaching Gender Dysphoria.* Cambridge, MA: Grove, 2018.

————. "A Christian View of Sex Reassignment Surgery and Hormone Therapy." Center for Faith, Sexuality and Gender, 2017. https://www.centerforfaith.com/resources?field_product_category_tid=1.

Yarhouse, Mark A., and Erica S. N. Tan. *Sexuality and Sex Therapy: A Comprehensive Christian Appraisal.* Downers Grove, IL: IVP Academic, 2014.

Yegül, Fikret. *Bathing in the Roman World.* Cambridge: Cambridge University Press, 2010.

Zahn, Theodor. *Das Evangelium des Matthäus.* 4th ed. Kommentar zum Neuen Testament. Leipzig: Deichert, 1922.